LITERATURE IN THE GREEK WORLD

Literature in the Greek World

Edited by Oliver Taplin

OXFORD
UNIVERSITY PRESS

OXFORD

UNIVERSITY PRESS

Great Clarendon Street, Oxford OX2 6DP

Oxford University Press is a department of the University of Oxford.
It furthers the University's objective of excellence in research, scholarship,
and education by publishing worldwide in

Oxford New York

Athens Auckland Bangkok Bogotá Buenos Aires Cape Town
Chennai Dar es Salaam Delhi Florence Hong Kong Istanbul Karachi
Kolkata Kuala Lumpur Madrid Melbourne Mexico City Mumbai Nairobi
Paris São Paulo Shanghai Singapore Taipei Tokyo Toronto Warsaw

with associated companies in Berlin Ibadan

Oxford is a registered trade mark of Oxford University Press
in the UK and in certain other countries

Published in the United States
by Oxford University Press Inc., New York

© Oxford University Press 2000

First published 2000

First issued as an Oxford University Press paperback 2001

British Library Cataloguing in Publication Data
Data available

Library of Congress Cataloging in Publication Data
Data available

ISBN 0-19-289303-3

1 3 5 7 9 10 8 6 4 2

Typeset by RefineCatch Limited, Bungay, Suffolk
Printed in Spain by Book Print S.L.

Contents

Preface

This is not just another collection of piecemeal essays: it is an attempt at an overview of a wide expanse of literature from a fresh perspective. The contributors have between them tried to survey all the major productions of ancient Greek literature (though inevitably some works are more fully covered than others). It is all the more remarkable that without exception they have been so prompt and responsive that the book has kept to its schedule—a rare feat! I wish to thank all for their good humour, flexibility, punctuality, and for their patience with my handwriting.

The relatively smooth and rapid progress of this book also owes much to the excellent team at Oxford University Press, especially George Miller, the editor who launched the project, and Shelley Cox, who skilfully piloted it over the waves to harbour. Ali Chivers has done sterling work on the production, especially on the division of the original single volume into two parts. I would also like to thank Ela Harrison, Mary Lale, and Mary Worthington for their efficient and intelligent work on various stages of the voyage. Many of the contributors are mutually indebted to each other for advice and help. One or other of us would also like to thank Ed Bispham, Jane Chaplin, Roger Crisp, Andrew Garrett, Mark Griffith, Edith Hall, Rachel Jacoff, Sandra Joshel, Bob Kaster, Tony Long, Kathleen McCarthy, Donald Mastronarde, Kathryn Morgan, Robin Osborne, Tony Woodman.

I have encouraged the contributors to quote liberally and try to give a taste of the literature they are discussing. All translations are by the author of the chapter in question, unless indicated otherwise. (Complete translations have been recommended in the section on Further Reading.)

The situation with the spelling of proper names is not so straightforward. Since this book deals with both Greeks and Romans and with their interactions, I have insisted that Greek names should be transcribed direct rather than into their more traditional Latin spelling. We have, however, kept the traditional spelling for names from both languages which are very familiar in their Englished form (such as Homer, Virgil, Athens, Rome, Oedipus (actually the Latin!), Hadrian etc, etc). The dividing line round this category is inevitably arbitrary (thus Ithake yet Attica, for example). Furthermore, when Greek names are being used in Roman or Latin contexts they are Latinized; when they are turned into adjectives they are Englished (eg callimachean, aeolic). This is an issue on which it is impossible to please everyone—indeed it is probably impossible to please anyone.

With the book as a whole we hope it will prove the reverse.

Oliver Taplin
Oxford
March 2001

List of illustrations

List of maps

Notes on contributors

OLIVER TAPLIN is Professor of Classical Languages and Literature at Oxford University, where he is a Tutorial Fellow at Magdalen College. He is also co-director (with Edith Hall) of the Archive of Performances of Greek and Roman Drama. His books include *Homeric Soundings* (Oxford, 1992) and *Comic Angels* (Oxford, 1993). He maintains the importance of reaching wider audiences, and has collaborated with various productions in radio, television, and the theatre.

CHRIS CAREY is part of the Liverpool diaspora. He studied at Jesus College, Cambridge and has taught at Cambridge, St Andrews, the University of Minnesota, Carleton College, and Royal Holloway, London, where he is Professor of Classics. His interests include Greek lyric poetry, drama, oratory and rhetoric, and law.

LESLIE KURKE is Professor of Classics and Comparative Literature at the University of California, Berkeley. She is the author of *The Traffic in Praise: Pindar and the Poetics of Social Economy* (Ithaca, NY, 1991) and *Coins, Bodies, Games, and Gold: The Politics of Meaning in Archaic Greece* (Princeton, 1999). With Carol Dougherty, she co-edited the volume *Cultural Poetics in Archaic Greece: Cult, Performance, Politics* (Oxford, 1998).

JANE LIGHTFOOT has been a Fellow of All Souls College, Oxford, since 1994, and is the author of *Parthenius of Nicaea* (Oxford, 1999). She is currently working on a study of Lucian's *On the Syrian Goddess*.

ANDREA WILSON NIGHTINGALE studied Classics at Stanford, Oxford, and Berkeley. She is presently an Associate Professor of Classics and Comparative Literature at Stanford University. Her publications include *Genres in Dialogue: Plato and the Construct of Philosophy* (Cambridge, 1996), and numerous articles on ancient Greek philosophy and literature. She is presently working on a book entitled *The Philosophic Gaze: Revisioning Wisdom in Fourth-Century Athens*.

PETER WILSON studied Classics in Australia and Cambridge and is now a Fellow of New College, Oxford. Previously he was a member of the Department of Classics and Ancient History of the University of Warwick. He has written on the Greek theatre, oratory, and music, and his first book is *The Athenian Institution of the 'Khoregia': The Chorus, the City and the Stage* (Cambridge, 2000).

Timeline of chapters

1 Homer and epic
2 Archaic poetry
3 Classical drama
4 Classical history
5 Wisdom literature
6 Athenian orators
7 Hellenistic literature
8 Later Greek literature

BCE: 750 650 550 450 350 250 150 50
CE: 50 150 250 350 450 550

Introduction

OLIVER TAPLIN

> The public is the manure round the roots of every artistic growth.
>
> (Cesare Pavese)

This book is for those who know a little and would like to know more about the literature which was written or composed in ancient Greek. It grows from a fundamental sense that this literature still has something significant to offer at the beginning of the third millennium—indeed, that some of the works still stand among the most worthwhile achievements of human creativity from any place or time. At the same time our access to them is not simple or direct. The approach taken here is at root historical: it looks, that is, at the literature within the world that first produced it. The focus, though—and this is what makes it distinctive from most previous overviews or surveys—is on the receivers of the literature, the public, readers, spectators, and audiences. The six contributors are various in their specializations and methodologies, but are united in the belief that it is valuable to ask who these works of literature were for. What did those people think they were getting from their literature; why did they give it their time and attention? For all our differences, we hold that our present appreciation of Greek literature can be informed and influenced by consideration of what it was originally appreciated for. The past, for all its alienness, can affect and change the present.

There is a kind of eternal triangle of elements or parties involved in any instance of literature: these are conventionally labelled Author, Reader, and Text. *Maker* may be a preferable word to 'author' because it comes without the controversial associations of, for example, 'authority' or 'intention'. Similarly *Receiver* has advantages over 'reader' since it includes audiences, spectators, and so forth. It is obvious, once you think about it, that literature does not necessarily have to be written down, and that it can be appreciated in other ways as well as being read; and this was actually far more the case in the ancient Greek world than it is in the modern era. As for the third element—the text, the words—this is clearly distinct from the other two, because, although it is conveyed through human-produced agency or technology (printed book, recitation, or whatever), it is not a sentient person. And by making the receivers our focus, it becomes obvious that there is bound to be a dynamic, an interaction, between the three elements rather than a static isolation of any one.

Claims for other parties might be made, and have been made, outside this triangle. The literature might be, for example, the creation of god or an oracle or a 'found poem'. But these are all, surely, subsidiary variations on the maker. Similarly with variant receivers such as god (again) or the universe or animals or an inanimate object. So peculiar exceptions who get wheeled out, like Orpheus, who performed for wild creatures, or Emily Dickinson, who kept her poems to herself, do not invalidate the basic claim that it takes an audience, receivers, to make literature. If Dickinson had never been discovered, her poems would not have become literature.

Most previous surveys and histories of literature have made either the authors or the texts their primary focus. It has been traditional to document the authors' biographies, the sequence of their mental lives, their interests, priorities, and beliefs, as revealed by external evidence, and as implied within their works. This kind of approach, which tends to put the fascination of creative genius in the spotlight, usually supposes that the lives of the authors somehow *explain* their literature. But is individual genius any more than a cipher as long as it is without surroundings, without circumstances of production, social context?

The approaches of some more recent literary theories, on the other hand, have tended to regard the texts as the only proper, or even possible, subject of attention. The texts have obligingly delivered meanings which 'anticipate' contemporary preoccupations with indeterminacy, the destabilization or fragmentation of conceptual monoliths, or the exposure of the operations of power through language. But these strategies should also leave room for approaches that treat the original production and communication of the texts as a valid subject for a kind of history. The fact that the history we can reconstruct is bound to be, to a greater or lesser extent, partial, speculative, and selective does not make it emptily arbitrary, merely or purely a construct. The first audiences of this literature did once live, and did once give their attention to the works.

In this interaction nearly all makers of literature want, and go out of their way to seek, an appreciative public: they desire attention and 'success'. There may be many ways of measuring that success; and it is not necessarily a matter of the numbers of the appreciative public. Artists often seek (or claim to seek, at least) the approval of only the select few—this is quite a common pose in the Greek world. Nor are celebrity or prosperity necessarily invariable criteria; and money is by no means the only possible reward. Sometimes success only comes posthumously, but makers prefer to have their appreciative public (and their rewards!) within their lifetimes. Correspondingly, a good proportion of those people who have the opportunity have been happy to give some of their time and resources to the benefits of literature, to become receivers, that is. The formative experience of listening to stories in childhood is undoubtedly very important here. Whatever the roots of the phenomenon, the public is generally on the look-out, perhaps surprisingly ready to be persuaded that paying attention to literature might be worth their time and trouble.

Throughout most of the history of most literatures the interaction between artist and public has, then, been by and large reciprocal, mutually beneficial. There has been a kind of *symbiosis*. The preferences and responses of the receivers have been assimilated by the makers, who have tried to meet them. And the makers, in their turn, have affected their audiences, have pleased them, and have led them to see things that were not already familiar and respectable. The maker looks to the public for attention and appreciation: the public expects some kind of benefit or gratification. Just what those hoped-for benefits were or are is elusive and shifting; and they are one of the major concerns of this book.

And yet, apparently in contradiction to this productive symbiosis, it is widely believed that most artists—or at least the great ones—suffer a flawed and difficult interaction with their contemporary public. Creative individuals are supposed to be alienated, ahead of their times, temperamental, tortured; and their potential public fails to recognize the genius in their midst. Audiences are characterized, on the other hand, as vulgar, fickle, conservative, complacent; they do not see what is good for them. This is one reason why so much emphasis has usually been put on makers and so little on receivers: the public is seen as irrelevant, and even obstructive, to genius. What is more this 'romantic' picture of the mismatch between the creative artist and the unappreciative public was familiar in the Greek world. The fascination with the creative misfit goes back as far as anything like literary history can be traced—though it must be pointed out that Greek and Roman literary biographies were far more overt than their modern counterparts in the invention of attractive fictions. From early days the poet was often seen as a lonely genius driven by creativity despite an unappreciative public: Euripides, and even the blind itinerant Homer, are archetypal examples. Behind this lurks a deep-seated desire for the prophet or genius to be a marginalized, tortured figure. Some great price must be paid for superhuman talent. Also, the later readers, who so love the stories of the unrecognized prodigy, can bask with hindsight in the complacent satisfaction of knowing better. We lavish on Mozart or Hopkins or Van Gogh the recognition that their contemporaries were too stupid to give. Yet how often has the creative maker really worked without *any* encouragement or appreciation, without any public? Take Euripides, who for the Greeks was the archetypal rejected and alienated genius. Year after year the Athenians welcomed him as a competitor in their highly selective tragedy competition; it is clear from the comic Aristophanes and other sources that he was the centre of much attention; he was already highly appreciated outside Athens in his own lifetime. The fact that he hardly ever won the first prize makes him more like the best-seller who does not win the Booker or the Nobel Prize than like a bohemian starving in a garret.

Hand in hand with this segregation of the individual genius from the mass of receivers goes a certain condescension and snobbishness—which can be seen already in Plato—towards the public of art, especially large popular bodies of receivers. This is another of the main reasons, I suspect, why they have been largely excluded from most accounts of literature. How could the crude people of that bygone age have appreciated the subtlety and complexity of the (our) literature? The artistry is too fine, the ambiguity too far-reaching, to be dragged down by mass appreciation. It needs the greater sophistication and insight and theoretical awareness of a later age (ours, of course) to see its true quality, to create meaning for it. There is often a taint of this superior self-promotion in recent academic writing.

It is bound to be true that we read very differently from the original receivers, but that does not necessarily mean that we read better. In fact, there is a disturbing presumptuousness about supposing that we can interpret and appreciate *better* than the audience that the literature was made for. The work was in a real sense made to their specifications—the carpenter built the house for them to live in. The literature came into existence in their world, in their language, society, and mental landscape. It might well be argued that, if we find any society in the past which has produced a particularly rich crop of creative achievements, then we should be asking what it was about the people of that time, the receivers and their symbiosis with their makers, that stimulated the productivity. We should be looking to them for ideas, not treating them with condescension.

Any work of literature that has stood the test of time has, by definition, been appreciated by many later receivers as well as the original public who had it fresh-minted from the maker. It has been the achievement of Reception Studies, especially in the last third of the twentieth century, to emphasize that all those many receptions are still of interest; and that many, if not all, of them contribute to our contemporary interpretation of the work. But the fact that a work of literature has survived across the centuries, and has been valued or devalued in various ways as time goes by, does not alter another fact: that it was once new, that before a certain time and context it did not exist, and that afterwards it did. Some theories have led to the claim that the genesis of the work in the symbiosis between maker and receivers is of no special interest (the term 'the originary fallacy' has been coined). But this volume takes the more historically minded view that the contextual genesis is bound to be particularly suggestive for our modern interpretation. To deny this is like digging up an artefact and having no curiosity about why anyone wanted to have that artefact in the first place.

So we believe that audiences and readers matter; that without them creative makers do not make. We do not believe that art is solely for art's sake: we believe that it is, and always has been, for people. And we do not believe that art is created in a vacuum, or in the isolated crucible of the unique mind. To have the potential to outlast its original public, it must have had an original public. Who were they? And what did they think that their literatures were for?

A sketch of the territory

Through this book we are talking of a span of time that extended for well over a thousand years, from roughly 750 BCE to even more roughly 500 CE. We are also talking about a geographical area greater than modern Europe, which spread, at one time or another, from Tunis to York to Budapest, from the Black Sea to the Dead Sea, from the Rhône to the Nile to the Euphrates. And the edges and limits of these times and places are quite indistinct; they are not neatly demarcated by frontiers and significant battles. It is often implied, and occasionally asserted, that the 'The Classical World' (or 'The Ancient World') has some special, stable unity: this is a myth.

On the other hand, we can, for the purposes of this volume, circumvent many difficult problems of military and administrative history, and of acculturation and ethnicity. The worlds in question are made up of the people who heard, watched, and read literature. What 'the Greek World' means here is, in effect, the primary receivers of Greek literature.

It seems best to 'plot' the people we are talking about against the two basic axes of Time and Place. Although there are other ways of 'locating' people historically, this will still make for the clearest introduction. The points that I plot against these axes will all have the making and receiving of literature primarily in mind; and they are, of course, highly summary and selective. What follows is, then, a kind of small-scale map of the literary lands that the rest of this book will be visiting in more detail.

Greece had enjoyed a materially and culturally advanced (and literate) era back in the second millennium BCE, the so-called Mycenean Age. But, while memories of this are reflected in myth and in Homer, no literature survived. There followed a time of severe economic and demographic depression (one of the so-called 'Dark Ages'). While there can be no doubt that during this some kinds of literature were performed, it is no coincidence that the earliest literature which was to be eventually preserved in writing comes from the following era of explosive development, cultural as well as economic and geographical.

Until about 750 the potential receivers of Greek poetry lived only in the southern parts of the Greek mainland , the islands of the Aegean Sea, and the coast of what is now western Turkey (Asia Minor). During the next two hundred years they spread to strings of newly founded communities all round the northern Aegean, the Black Sea, the coasts of Sicily and southern Italy, and even to scattered foundations in southern France and Spain and in North Africa. Generally these remained coastal settlements which interacted with the local non-Greek people but did not attempt to subdue them. The first material traces of Greek literature are lines of verse scratched on pottery dating from the second half of the 700s BCE, not long after the (re-) introduction of the alphabet into Greece (from the Semitic Phoenicians). A nice indicator of this spread of the Greek world is that one of the very earliest scraps of Greek verse has been found on a cup which was made in Rhodes but was buried in a grave on the island of Ischia in the bay of Naples (see illustration on p. 32).

But early Greek literature was performed not written; and performances of the poems of Homer and Hesiod (Ch. 1) in something like the forms in which we have them probably date from around 700. While some poetry had presumably been recorded in writing by 600, it was to be a long time yet before any literature was made exclusively to be read, or even to be read rather than to be heard. This protracted, and arguably never complete, transition must have somehow gone hand in hand with the rapid growth of significant *prose* literature in the 400s, continued in the 300s.

Throughout the 400 years or so that have conventionally been given the labels 'Archaic' and 'Classical'—say from the 730s to the 330s—each Greek *polis* (city-state) did its best to maintain an independent identity, even though this led to much terrible conflict between them. This independence extended to institutions, constitutions, religious cults, dialect, alphabet, coinage, measures, and even calendars. One might have expected this diversity, especially the differentiated dialects, to lead to highly localized and restricted literatures; but,

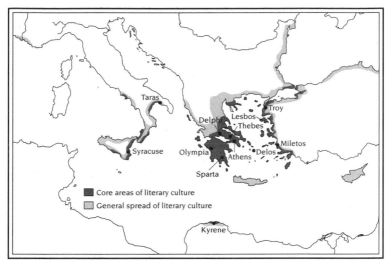

The world of Greek literature: 700–350 BCE

if anything, the opposite is the case. There subsisted a sense of shared Hellenic culture, which was reflected in the underlying language, social values, mythology, and religious practice, and which found symbolic expression in the great shared cult-centres and athletic festivals (above all those at Olympia and Delphi). This also found practical expression in the successful co-operative resistance to territorial threats launched by the Persian empire from the East, Phoenicians from North Africa, and Etruscans and others from central and northern Italy. In keeping with this sense of shared culture—and cutting across political and military lines—there was a fair amount of freedom of movement for those who were perceived as experts, reflecting an appreciation for achievements of culture, arts, and crafts, regardless of which polis had originally produced them.

So poets and word-craftsmen—just like architects, scientists, painters, musicians, and many others—enjoyed considerable inter-polis mobility. And so did their works. The Homeric epics, above all, were evidently performed from earliest days throughout the Greek world. Other early poets (Ch. 2) quickly became known throughout the Greek world, despite their differing dialects. They came from the shores of the Aegean and from Sicily, but above all from the islands. Lesbos, for example, in the north-east Aegean, and Keos, not far from Attica, were especially productive of craftsmen of words. Simonides of Keos, the first man to make a fortune from literature, composed for commissions from Thessaly, south Italy, and Sicily, as well as for 'customers' nearer his home island. Eventually he managed to become more or less the official celebratory poet of the great victories over the Persians in 480–79. Commissions for poetry of various kinds from the Theban poet Pindar came from as far afield as Macedonia, Rhodes, Sicily, and Kyrene (in Libya), as well as places nearer home.

Tragedy and comedy (Ch. 3) were astounding innovations, yet grew from within this culture. Theatre was in effect invented at Athens in the fifth century for a predominantly Athenian public. But this central locality did not stop it from spreading rapidly and easily through the whole Greek world. During the fourth century virtually every polis of any note built an auditorium for performances. Soon the makers were coming from Asia Minor, the Black Sea, southern Italy, and many parts of the Greek mainland as well as Athens.

Down to, say, 390 BCE the turbulent, triumphant Greek world was exuberantly productive of fine poetry, and many kinds of poetry. It also inaugurated highly worked prose literature of the kinds that we now call history (Ch. 4), rhetoric, science, and philosophy. The next hundred or so even more turbulent years, although a period of great prosperity and of creativity in the arts in general, was a relatively thin time for poetry, at least poetry other than drama. But it was a highly fertile and formative period for rhetoric (Ch. 6), pedagogy, and above all for philosophy (Ch. 5). Prose cannot be transmitted by memory in the way that poetry can, and it makes sense that this great age of prose literature was also the era when literacy first reached a relatively large proportion of the population—a third or more at Athens, still the cultural centre—and also became really widespread throughout the Greek world.

The hundred years from (roughly speaking) 360 to 260 saw a crucial and irreversible re-formation of the Greek world, which meant that in most important ways the southern mainland ceased to be the centre of gravity. To the west the Greeks of Sicily and southern Italy enjoyed a time of great prosperity and cultural activity; but at the same time they came under increasing pressure from the Carthaginians (Phoenicians in what is now Tunisia), and from various Italian 'tribes'. Charismatic leaders were imported from the 'motherland', and helped to hold up the tide, but it eventually proved irresistible. And one particularly ambitious power in central Italy became ever-increasingly dominant: Rome. Once the Romans had overcome the threat of the Carthaginians under Hannibal in the late 200s, the ensuing expansion of power and wealth was stunning: northern Italy, southern Spain, mainland Greece, and central North Africa had all come under Rome by 146 BCE. As the Greek historian Polybios, who spent much of his life at Rome, observed, this one city had become the

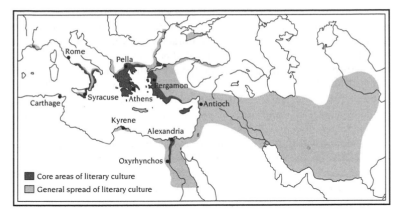

The world of Greek literature: 350–1 BCE

greatest power in the Mediterranean world in the space of some fifty years. Further territorial expansions into the Greek world in Asia Minor and the Near East continued, to culminate in the addition of the Egypt of the Ptolemies (last queen—Kleopatra) in 30.

But before sketching the development of the Roman period of the Greek world, we should follow first the awesome expansion of the Greeks to the East. The Macedonians, for long ethnically marginal in the north of Greece, developed a great military machine which overran the divided mainland during the 350s and 340s, under the leadership of King Philip. His successor, the charismatic, superhuman, and all-too-human Alexander, turned the Macedonian army against the empires to the East. Between 334 and his death in 323 he conquered not only the Near East (including present-day eastern Turkey, Syria, Israel, Jordan, Iraq), but also Egypt. He then went on into what are now Iran, Uzbekistan, Afghanistan, Pakistan, and even across the Indus. This vast, sudden empire broke up, of course, and some of it, especially in the further East, never became seriously part of the Greek world. But cities run by Greek settlers, and complete with the accoutrements of Greek life, such as the agora (civic centre), gymnasium, and theatre, were planted all over a vast area. At the same time the *koine*, a dialect based on that of Athens, became accepted everywhere. It is hard to know how many, or how few, of this far-flung diaspora ever became significant receivers of Greek literature; but texts have been found not only in (for example) Syria and Jordan, but as far east as Afghanistan.

During this period, which is standardly labelled Hellenistic, old Athens remained a cultural focal point, especially for philosophy and higher education. But other new centres flourished with rival cultural ambitions, for example on the island of Rhodes, and at Pergamon in Asia Minor and at Antiocheia (Antioch) in Syria. But Alexandria towards the western edge of the Nile delta (one of the many cities named after himself by Alexander) was to eclipse them all. Here the Macedonian dynasty of the Ptolemies founded their capital, which rapidly grew into a huge cosmopolitan melting-pot of some half-million inhabitants. The kings invested lavishly to turn it into the new cultural capital of the Greek world, attracting artists, scientists, and poets. During the 200s BCE there was an efflorescence of a new kind of wholly literary, self-conscious poetry (Ch. 7). While its receivers seem to have been well spread over the Greek world, its centre, and probably its core audience, was in Alexandria. The cluster of major poets came there from, among other places, Kyrene, Syracuse, Samos, Kos, and Soloi (south-east Turkey).

The learned 'post-golden' culture established in Alexandria and the other great centres of the Hellenistic world during the 150 or so years from the 280s BCE was sustained, with various lapses and resurgences, throughout the Greek-speaking world for another 500 years or more (Ch. 8). The receivers of literature that we happen to know most about lived in a scatter of places through Egypt, where their texts, written on the standard writing-material of papyrus, happen to have been preserved in the dry sand. It is interesting to find, for example, how well read and widely read were the citizens of the middle-sized town of Oxyrhynchos in the second and third centuries CE. It is true that little of their literature was contemporary or from their immediate world; at the same time, while the great classics, above all Homer, are predominant, there is also quite a lot from this long 'post-golden' world.

This long autumn of Greek culture produced little worthwhile poetry but plenty of interesting prose of a variety of kinds, mostly reflecting the centrality of rhetoric to education and to official public life. The modern questioning of the traditional canon of 'The Classics' has led to some lively revaluation of the literature of this era. The most important authors of the productive cultural scene known as the Second Sophistic (roughly 60–230 CE) came from all over the place, but they tended to gravitate to the cultural centres of Athens, Pergamon, Smyrne, and Ephesos (all these latter three are in Asia Minor). And, of course, many of them went to Rome.

But from now on the slope of the terrain is intermittently downhill. One might trace the beginnings of the end of the Roman world, and of the Greek world under the Romans, right back to the death of the philosophical emperor Marcus Aurelius in 180 CE. The usual kind of imperial and military history is told in terms of endless complicated power struggles and frontier wars; but the less extended and less contested worlds of literature were not in such turmoil,

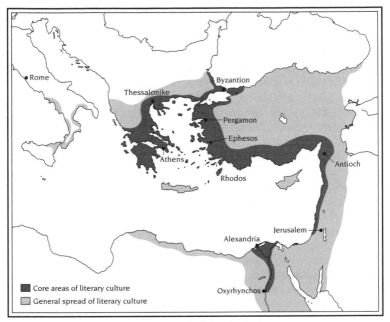

The world of Greek literature: 1 CE–end of the classical era

as the thousands of texts from the rubbish tips of Oxyrhynchos remind us. In both the Roman and the Greek worlds various interesting, and occasionally surprising, works emerge from the highly professionalized culture of the rhetoric schools. The recent repudiation of an established canon of 'Classics' has led to some interesting revaluations of the productions of this long, less brilliant era.

The Western, Latin half of the empire, based on Rome, and the Eastern Greek half, based on Byzantion (which was to become Constantinople, and then Istanbul) sporadically but inexorably grew apart. Yet the long twilight of the world of 'classical' literature was not so dissimilar throughout both. The pressure of new assertive powers, such as those of the Goths, the Vandals, and the Arabs, set up great whirlpools of insecurity. And the encroachment, and eventually triumph, of the absolute faith of Christianity, which also meant the growing importance in education of monks and clerics, was going to bring an end—as we can now see with hindsight—to the kind of pluralism that had been essential to Greek literature and to its Latin offspring (Ch. 8). One can pin-point key moments in the chronic debilitation of the 'classical' world, such as the official adoption of Christianity by the Roman authorities in 312, the first sack of the city of Rome in 410, the closure of the philosophy schools in Athens in 529, but this tends to hide the long, sporadic process. The overall effect was this: in 300 CE literature was still being widely read and copied, even though not a great deal was being created; by 550 CE, in the West entirely, and in the East largely, a literary 'dark age' had closed in. No one could claim that more than minimal literature was being made any more; and the vast quantities, from the tedious to the sublime, that had been created and disseminated during the previous 1,250 years was being neither read nor copied. By the time when, two or three hundred years later, there were, in their very different ways, literary revivals—in the West under Charlemagne and in the East under the emperors of Byzantion—the great bulk of both literatures had been irrecoverably lost—rotted, discarded, or burnt.

The twin sagas of how what survived of Greek and Roman literature did survive, separately until about the 1300s, and then in the reunion of the Renaissance, is another story. Most of the literature that was recopied by 900 CE has survived until today, though not all—there were further bottlenecks and bonfires. Most of the surviving plays of Euripides came through these hazards in only one copy, and it should not be forgotten how much failed to make it. The productions of many major makers did not survive at all except in tiny fragments quoted in other works; hardly anyone's *œuvre*, however great, has come through in its entirety. Whatever reached the era of the printed book, however, still exists today in multiple copies—and in electronic form. And the finds of papyri in the last hundred years and more have given us back a lot of lost Greek, and a little of Latin, though all too much of it is in tattered bits and pieces. The 'Literature' of this volume means inevitably the literature which has survived down to today, but it is worth remembering that this is very far short of being co-extensive with the literature which was known to its early receivers.

Greek literature has survived as texts, as the copied written records of the crafted words of its makers. It has not survived with any of their nurturing context; the dry core has been conserved without the surrounding appreciation of its receivers. It is rather like the survival of the skeleton of what was once a human who lived a life. The symbiotic creation and appreciation of the text, like the living body of the skeleton and its personal and social context, have to be painstakingly reconstructed, often (inevitably) with a fair degree of speculation. But without that original symbiosis of maker and public the literature would never have come into being in the first place. It is the mission of this book to say something about those shadowy, mostly nameless, publics of our great (though depleted) treasury of ancient Greek literature. To come alive in our far distant, far different worlds, the texts need the revivification of the audience, the readers and listeners who farmed and cultivated their growth. To develop the vivid image from the Italian poet, Cesare Pavese: although they are now rotted away, they were essential to the growth of the flowers we still pick and the fruit we still relish.

Greek Literature

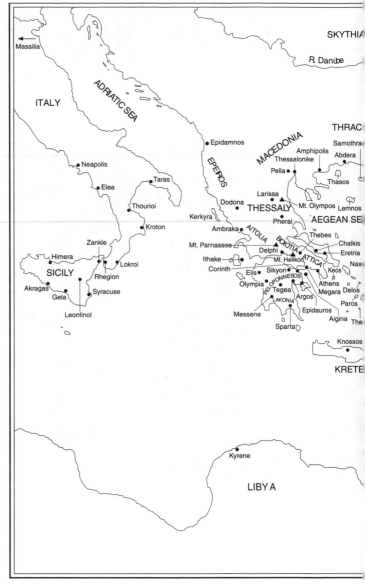

The Greek World: chief places mentioned in the text

Chaersonesos

Istros

BLACK SEA

KOLCHIS

Sinope

Byzantion

Herakleia

Trapezos

Chalkedon

ARMENIA

Kyzikos

Lampsakos

Mytilene

Troy

AIOLIS

MYSIA

PHRYGIA

Pergamon

Samosata

Lesbos

Kyme

Smyrne

Sardis

R. Euphrates

Teos

IONIA

Chios

Kolophon

LYDIA

Ephesos

Soloi

Miletos

KILIKIA

Antioch

Samos

Halikarnassos

Kaunos

Damaskos

Knidos

Kos

Kition

Rhodos

CYPRUS

Berytos

Tyre

PERSIA →

Gadara

MEDIA →

Alexandria

Naukratis

Heliopolis

EGYPT

R. Nile

Oxyrhynchos

1 | The spring of the muses: Homer and related poetry

OLIVER TAPLIN

> Thence form your Judgement, thence your Maxims bring,
> And trace the Muses *upward* to their *Spring.*
>
> (Alexander Pope on Homer)

Archetypes and antitypes

The rosy fingers which heralded the extraordinary era we know as 'ancient Greece' first gradually spread between about 900 and 700 BCE. The sunrise is quite distinctly marked, though, by the ascent at some time within a generation either side of 700, of the two poems: *Ilias*, the poem of Ilios (Troy), and *Odysseia*, the story of Odysseus—in English the *Iliad* and the *Odyssey*. It is astonishing that we should have such early poems preserved at all, let alone that this dawn of Greek literature should bring into the light not one but two great archetypal epics. For the whole of the ancient Greek—and Roman—worlds they established the large-scale narrative poem about great men of the past as the foundational genre. And they established the long, rather complex line of the dactylic hexameter as the most venerable verse-form.

These poems would never have come into existence if there had been no public for them, if there had not been people to stimulate them, hear them and appreciate them. So who was this poetry for, our earliest 'Western' poetry? Who were the people who made the poet—or poets—who made the *Iliad* and the *Odyssey*? Richard Bentley (the great Cambridge scholar) in 1713, reckoned he knew: 'Take my word for it, poor Homer . . . wrote a sequel of songs, to be sung by himself for small earnings and good cheer, at festivals and other days of merriment; the *Ilias* he made for the men, and the *Odysseis* for the other sex.' In 1985 Joachim Latacz (a distinguished professor at Basel) is no less assertive: 'the singer could find an appreciation for such an artistry only among those from whose manner of life it originated ... among the nobles ... Homer could not have made clearer the natural link between nobility and heroic song, nor could he have declared more clearly his own membership in this social sphere.' As this direct contradiction indicates, the straight truth is that we can say next to nothing *for certain* about the original circumstances of production of our two poems, neither about their audience nor their author nor their context of communication. For a start, they come from a time well before any kind of firm external historical record. But this is no reason for giving up and regarding it as a waste of time to ask who Homeric poetry was for, and what it meant to them: there are still aspects of context and performance that are likely, plausible, interesting. There is still, as this chapter hopes to show, much worth saying, even though it is not 100 per cent proof definite or definitive.

The prime evidence for Homeric performance and production is bound to be the poems themselves. And there is an unavoidable circle of argument here: we interpret the poems to reach an idea of the audience, and then we feed this audience back into the interpretation of the poems. Both Bentley and Latacz have all too obviously done just that. But provided we are aware of the problem, it does not vitiate the whole project: it is still worth searching for the interactive arcs which are most suggestive, most interesting, and which fit best with external considerations. We have to be especially careful, however, with the representation of poetry as performed and appreciated within the poems themselves. This can be suggestive and illuminating, provided we keep in mind always that the poems are creating fictional worlds, set in the heroic past. The internal audiences should not be treated as direct or 'literal' evidence for the world of the external audiences—though that does not mean that there is *no* relationship between them. It is a further problem that the poet-narrator himself never ever comes out of the fictional world into the real world, or even what purports to be the real world. 'Homer' never in any way declares who he is, where he comes from, or who he is making poetry for. Even if he did, we would have to treat the declaration with care—it need not be literally true—but he has covered his own tracks so completely that this question does not arise. More than in almost any other poetry, the craftsman suppresses his own presence, and effaces his own identity.

One big question left open by this self-concealment is whether the *Iliad* and *Odyssey* are the work of the same poet. Nearly all ancient Greeks—though not all—believed that they were, and that his name was Homer, or rather *Homeros*. But modern scholarship has still not been able to settle this basic question of authorship decisively. In view of the way that the epics depend on a long poetic tradition (see pp. 12–13 below), and of the way that they may well have been preserved at first through performance, rather than as a fixed text (see p. 32

below), it is even open to question how far the modern concept of authorship is appropriate at all. While I am inclined to believe, though with no great confidence, that they *are* both fundamentally the work of one poet, the important point that seems to me beyond reasonable doubt is that they were created for very much the same audiences and occasions. While they are simultaneously highly similar in some ways and different in others, the differences are pervasively complementary. This is especially clear with the *Odyssey*, which has the Trojan War as its immediate past, even as its point of departure—when Odysseus tells of his various adventures he begins 'Leaving Ilios, the wind took me . . .' (9. 39). The other great heroes, alive or—all too many—dead, are very much the same characters as those in the *Iliad*. More than that, the experience of the war as both glorious and destructive, magnificent yet full of suffering, emerges as quintessentially similar. When Odysseus is listening to a narration of his greatest deeds at the sack of Troy, instead of glorying, he weeps:

> The tears trickled down and drenched his cheeks.
> As a woman might weep as she clasps the body of her beloved
> husband, who has fallen before the eyes of his whole people,
> trying to keep off the cruel day from his land and its children;
> she sees him in his death throes, and twining herself around him
> shrieks in keening lament. But her captors come up behind her,
> and beat her across the back and shoulders with their spears,
> as they are seizing a slave for a life full of grief and labour,
> and her face is wasted, her cheeks wracked with pitiful streaks:
> so Odysseus shed tears, drops of the water of pity.
>
> (*Odyssey* 8. 522–31)

This is very like the suffering of the Trojans in the *Iliad*, and especially of Andromache—not exactly the same, but tapping the same sensibility.

Throughout their existence most readers and audiences of one poem have seasoned their appreciation of it with their knowledge of the other. More clearly the *Odyssey* feeds on the *Iliad*, and it is generally regarded as the later poem, a kind of sequel. But there are also places where the *Iliad* appears to draw strength from the *Odyssey*. Thus it is Odysseus (who twice calls himself in a unique turn of phrase 'the father of Telemachos') who in the first sequence of the *Iliad* takes Agamemnon's special prize, Chryseis, back to her father, the one and only return-home narrated in the poem. And Odysseus already has the three epithets which are unique to him, and which capture the qualities which will see him through the *Odyssey*: 'much-subtle', 'much-enduring', and 'much-devising' (*polymetis*, *polytlas*, and *polymechanos*). These epithets belong to the antitype of the direct, 'fast-footed' Achilles. It is revealing that both of them were offered as central figures to the early Greek audiences (later Greeks had serious scruples about both, especially the deceitful Odysseus). Achilles is uncompromising, overt in his feelings, unhesitatingly ready to die in order to make good his failings: Odysseus, the great survivor, is subtle, always ready to temporize, to disguise, and to lie. Achilles speaking to Odysseus, insists:

> I detest that man as much as the doorway of Hades,
> who hides one thing inside and declares out loud another.
> *(Iliad 9. 312–13)*

But Odysseus is the great specialist at just that. On Ithake (in Latin Ithaca) Athene drops her disguise to acknowledge a man after her own heart:

> You are outstanding among men for clever and devious words,
> while I am the greatest god for cunning and for conning.
> *(Odyssey 13. 297–9)*

The archetypal antitypes go far beyond the two heroes. The *Iliad* tells directly of only a few crucial days out of the whole Trojan War; and it is almost entirely set, claustrophobically almost, at Troy. At the same time, the poem extends understanding towards a wide range of characters, and to both sides in the war. While the *Odyssey* narrates only a small number of days directly—those leading up to Odysseus' return and revenge on Ithake—it covers, by means of flash-backs, a wide spread of places, including the varied story-worlds of Odysseus' adventures. And his adventures (and those of Menelaos) are spread over some ten years. Yet, for all its range of time and place, the *Odyssey* is centred on one man and his close associates in a way quite different from the multiplicity of the *Iliad*.

The *Odyssey* is fundamentally a crime-and-punishment story: the good and the likeable triumph, and the wicked are in the end brought low. It all moves towards reunion and the establishment of a stable and peaceful society, even though that is not fully achieved by the end of the poem (the eventuality is prophesied). The *Odyssey*'s overall direction is from suffering and disruption towards restoration and the united family. The *Iliad*, on the other hand, is not evidently a story of right and wrong; it tells of a world in which all suffer, and where the suffering is not apportioned by deserving. The finest people and the finest relationships—Achilles, Patroklos, Hektor, Andromache, Priam—are destroyed. The best gets wasted; anger and conflict rule human life. The prosperous and civilized city of Troy is to go up in flames; and by no means all of the leading Achaians will get home—and even fewer will enjoy the fruits of victorious peace. Two quite different views of the human condition, then, and yet somehow a pair, like non-identical twins.

Hesiod of Helikon

Before trying to get any further with reconstructing a context for Homer, it might be a good idea to turn to another poet, one who does locate himself in a kind of scene. For the Homeric epics are not our only works from this early period, and not even the only kind of archetypal hexameter poetry. There is also Hesiod, in Greek *Hesiodos* or *Heisiodos*. And he, by contrast, *does* 'come out' of his poetry. He even names himself, something that many (perhaps most) poets do not do:

> And one day they taught to Hesiod the beauties of song,
> as he was herding his lambs below holy mount Helikon.
> And this is what the goddesses said to me first,
> those Olympian Muses, daughters of mighty Zeus:
> 'You shepherds of the fields, you disgraces, pure greed,
> we know how to tell many falsehoods just like the real thing,
> and we know, when we so wish, how to sing truly'.
>
> (*Theogony* 22–8)

In other places Hesiod says precisely where he lives below Mount Helikon (the range of mountains between the central mainland plains of Boiotia and the gulf of Corinth). He also gives details of his family history, and even tells of participating in a poetic performance. We cannot be certain how much of all this is historically true, and how much is 'falsehood just like the real thing'. But it is offered as if true, and it is still revealing for us.

We have two poems from Hesiod, traditionally known as the *Theogony* and the *Works and Days* (abbreviated as *W&D*). Our texts have both accumulated some 'unauthorized' additions over the centuries after Hesiod, especially towards the end of each poem; but, even including these, they are far shorter than the Homeric epics. Quite a few other miscellaneous hexameter poems got attached to the name of Hesiod, but we know enough about them to be confident that they date from some time later than the two which we have (see p. 38 below). The *Theogony*, in about 1,000 lines, covers the origin and genealogies of some 300 gods (many in lists of course), and it all leads up towards the establishment of Zeus as the supreme divine ruler. The shorter *Works and Days* is a kind of discursive collection of wise advice, especially about good husbandry; it tells what a man should do to fit into the natural and moral order of the world. Unlike any other early hexameter poetry, *W&D* is addressed to fellow contemporaries, mostly to Hesiod's layabout brother Perses, and partly to the local lords whom he accuses of corruption. (It is worth registering here, since it will recur, that the word for 'lord' is *basileus*, often mistranslated as 'king', which is what it meant in later Greek.)

Although so different in tone and subject from Homer, Hesiod's poems are in the same hexameter metre, and in a pretty similar style and diction. There has been much dispute over which came first, but it may well be that the two poets were contemporaries, or at least their lives may have overlapped. Homer almost certainly came, though, from the other side of the Aegean Sea, from the middle part of the Asia Minor coast known as Ionia, near its border with the more northern part known as Aiolis. Even so, it is not impossible that they both participated in the same poetic occasions sometimes. The ancient Greeks certainly liked to believe that they did, and stories about a great 'Contest' between them grew up early, probably within a few generations of their own day. This sets up a kind of contest within the whole nature of poetry: the story-teller of glamorous champions versus the font of homely wisdom.

Hesiod and Homer get cited as a pair, as the twin founders of Greek poetry, and even of the Greek mentality. Herodotos in the later fifth century wrote, 'I think that Hesiod and Homer lived no more than 400 years before my time; and they were the ones who created the gods' family trees for the Greek world, gave them their names, assigned them honours and areas of expertise, and told us what they look like. Any poets who are supposed to have lived before Hesiod and Homer actually came after them in my opinion' (2. 53). Those early thinkers who set themselves up as purveyors of new wisdom (see pp. 139–40, 144 below) denounce their primal pair of rivals. Thus Xenophanes, for example (second half of sixth century): 'Homer and Hesiod attributed to the gods all the things which among men are shameful and blameworthy.'

So what might Hesiod reveal about the audiences of his world, and possibly though less directly of Homer's also? The most revealing passage comes well on through *W&D* when, after over 200 lines devoted to the agricultural year, Hesiod turns to sea-faring as a source of livelihood, and even profit. It is built up to with circumstantial 'autobiography':

> . . . just as our father, mine and yours, you stupid Perses,
> used to go to sea in ships in his search for a good living.
> And one day he came here, making the long sea-crossing,
> quitting Kyme in Aiolis, all the way in his dark ship,
> not running away from wealth ... but from foul poverty ...
> And so he came to settle near Helikon in a miserable village
> called Askre, harsh in winter, nasty in summer, good at no time.
> *(W&D* 633–40)

There are details here that are not predictable and most unlikely to have been conventional. The migration of Hesiod's father goes against the obvious tack by leaving the relative prosperity of Asia Minor (Homer's home territory), and heading up a valley from the fertile plains of Boiotia (later Greeks planted Askre with groves and turned it into a delightful sanctuary of the Muses). There follows rather a long introduction to what will be in the end the rather short section on seafaring:

> I shall show you the measures of the reverberating sea,
> uninitiated though I am in the skills of seamanship and boats.
> For as for ships, I have never ever embarked on the broad seas,
> unless you count to Euboia from Aulis (where the Achaians
> once waited through long bad weather when they had gathered
> a mighty expedition from Greece against Troy, city of beauties).
> From there I crossed over for the funeral games
> of strong-minded Amphidamas at Chalkis
> —and many were the prizes announced and displayed
> by the sons of that great man. I declare that there
> I was victorious in poetry and won a tripod with ring-handles.
> And I dedicated it to the Helikonian Muses,
> at the place where they initially set me on the path of clear song.
>
> (*W&D* 648–59)

We cannot know for sure whether this is all literally true or 'falsehoods just like the real thing'. But it does sound like the real thing, and there are no clear signals that this is fiction or merely traditional tales. It is a fact that bronze tripods (vertical-legged cauldrons) were the prestige prizes and dedications of the time, as is clear from excavations at Olympia. And there is no doubting that Chalkis on the island of Euboia was very prosperous in this era; it won a famous victory over the neighbouring Eretria, which is probably reflected archaeologically by the desertion of the major site of Lefkandi in about 700 BCE. Aulis is indeed a good harbour on the opposite mainland coast, and its place in the great epic tradition is taken for granted in Homer. There is even a joke here for those who know the local topography (the first joke in Greek literature?): the distance across the straits between Aulis and the coast of Chalkis opposite is less than 100 metres ('I shall show you the measures of the reverberating sea'!)

Last but not least, it was surely Hesiod himself who established the Muses, traditionally from Mount Olympos far to the north, on his local mountain, Helikon. He even seems to have coined, in his *Theogony*, their canonical nine names, and to have put the little river Permessos and the spring of Hippokrene on the poetical map. It was there, where he was grazing his flocks, that the Muses, as Hesiod claims, once appeared to him (see above), and gave him a magic staff of laurel:

> ... and they breathed into me a marvellous voice,
> so that I might celebrate [give *kleos* to] matters of the future
> and of the past. And they commanded me to sing poems
> of the family of blessed gods who live for ever,
> and first and last always to sing of them themselves.
>
> (*Theogony* 31–4)

(for *kleos* see further below and pp. 119–20)

Hesiod performed his poetry, then (or made out that he performed) at a big public occasion which attracted visitors and competitors. Competition can be good, he claims elsewhere (*W&D* 25–6) 'potter against potter, carpenter with carpenter . . . poet with poet'. This overlaps suggestively with a passing remark in the *Odyssey* (17. 384–5), listing certain kinds of craftsmen who are welcome anywhere: 'a seer or a healer or a carpenter in wood or an inspired poet who delights with his song.' So a picture begins to take shape of poets who travel, and whose venues include big public occasions where they can compete to win attention, prestige, and reward.

Why poetry at the funeral games of Amphidamas of Chalkis? Funeral games were meant to be a glorious memorial to the dead man; they were an occasion for his surviving relatives to be conspicuous and generous; and they were some kind of consolation for them. Mortality should not—the games declare—obliterate all delight from human life: life goes on. (The reason, I should add, why there is no poetry competition at the funeral games for Patroklos in *Iliad* 23, is because in the *Iliad* this state of mind is not fully achieved until the later scene between Priam and Achilles.)

In *W&D* Hesiod casts himself as a grim old bugger, tough, without illusions, worn down by hard labour, pessimistic:

> How I wish I didn't live in the Fifth Age of men,
> but had either died before or had been born later.
> For this is a race of iron now; and they shall not cease
> from toil and misery . . .
>
> (*W&D* 174–7)

But this does not mean that Hesiod's audience listened to him in order to get depressed. What does his poetry offer them, then? Explicitly: vivid wisdom, mythical and religious lore, and glorification of the gods, above all of Zeus. But there is an important passage in the *Theogony* which brings out a further, key reason for audiences to give time to this special form of discourse, poetry. Hesiod is talking of the behaviour and blessings of a good *basileus* (lord), and emphasizing the importance to him of the poet:

Sweet is the speech that flows from his lips,
for even if a man has sorrow in his breast fresh inflicted,
and is exhausted with grief, even so the poet, attendant of the Muses,
can sing the glorious achievements [*klea*] of the people of old,
and can sing of the blessed gods who are on Olympos;
and then he quickly becomes oblivious of his ills-of-heart,
and no longer dwells on his cares. Soon the Muses' gifts divert him.

(*Theogony* 97–103)

Poetry soothes, diverts, banishes angst—'Music for a while | Shall all your cares beguile'. This is why poetry is so important in a world which is as grim as Hesiod makes it out to be: it is still not *human* to dwell on our troubles and griefs the whole time. We need charms, delights, soothing salves, consolations to take our mind off them—such as poetry, music, becoming absorbed in a good story.

Aural and oral poetry

In the passage just quoted Hesiod alludes to two different kinds of poetry: poems about the gods—that is what he delivers in the rest of the *Theogony*—and poems about 'the glorious achievements of the people of old' (line 100, *klea proteron anthropon*—*anthropon* is not gender-specific). This is just the kind of poetry we have in the *Iliad* and *Odyssey*; and it shows that, however little travelled Hesiod was, and however godforsaken his village of Askre, he was well aware of a mainstream of epic poetry of the Homeric kind.

Hesiod refers to both kinds of poetry as conveyed live to their audience by the *aoidos* (poet-singer), who sings or recites. There is every reason to suppose that this is how early hexameter poems were composed and communicated. This is not only because Hesiod and Homer both use the same terms (*aoidos* etc.), and both speak of poets in performance, but because of the basic nature of their language and narrative techniques. It is now some seventy years since Milman Parry first demonstrated in a quasi-scientific way that both Homer's poetic diction and scene-construction, with their rich yet efficient range of formulae and repertoire of repeated sequences, are to be explained as the accumulated stock of generations of practitioners of oral poetry. Since then Parry's theory has been elaborated, strengthened, and generally accepted—and rightly so: Homer is the inheritor of a centuries-old tradition of oral story-telling. It is beyond reasonable doubt, that is to say, that Homer—and Hesiod too—learned how to be a poet by hearing and imitating performing poets, who had in their turn learned from the previous generation, and so on back through generations, even quite possibly back into the prosperous and powerful era of the so-called Mycenean Age some 500 years earlier.

No less importantly, Homer's and Hesiod's audiences will have learned to appreciate epic poetry by listening to performing poets. This is the way that they will have come to know the subject-matter and concerns of the tradition, its typically recurrent scenes, its basic strategies, and its special language. For the language of Homeric epic is far away from anything that was ever actually spoken at any one time or place. It amalgamates a mixture of dialects, incorporated over generations from different areas of the Greek world ; it also retains archaic words and grammatical forms that had gone out of spoken use long ago. Yet these are all mixed up with, and indivisible from, current words and forms, including phrases which had been coined by the particular performer, perhaps on that very occasion. If one were able to stick a little label on each half-line of Homer, coded with the time and place that that phrase had been first incorporated into poetry, it would make a thoroughly variegated and unpredictable kind of 'mosaic'. Yet this special poetic language will not have struck its hearers as artificial or outlandish, precisely because they knew it and expected it as the language of hexameter poetry. It is the language proper to the occasion that they will have assimilated from childhood. (A partial analogy might be the way that those brought up in a church where the Authorized Version of the Bible was the norm came to know its language and to regard it as special and appropriate to its context.)

It is crucial to the quality of Homer, and even of the less fluent Hesiod, that their audiences were already soaked in hexameter poetry of the traditional style. This helps to explain how what is for us the earliest Greek poetry can be of such high quality (to put it modestly). By keeping to and by departing from the expected patterns and priorities, the poetry can build on and exploit the audience's already rich experience. However 'archaic' these audiences in terms of standard chronological 'period', they were already trained in a highly developed tradition of poetry.

So far I have spoken exclusively in terms of live performances sung or recited before the audience; and Homer and Hesiod themselves allude to poetry exclusively in those terms. But what about reading and writing? There has been, and still is, a lively debate about whether the art of writing played a formative part in the composition of the *Iliad* and *Odyssey*. In fact at present (late 1990s) scholars are pretty evenly divided on the issue. The claim that Homer 'had the advantage of writing' (as it is often tendentiously put) is chronologically quite possible. The Phoenician alphabet had been adapted to Greek by the mid-eighth century, and by Homer's time (assuming somewhere between, say, 733 and 666 BCE) the skill was available and catching on. Several of our earliest specimens of Greek writing are, in fact, lines of hexameter poetry scratched on pottery. One from about 725 BCE is a beaker which refers to itself as the 'cup of Nestor'; and it has been claimed to be alluding humorously to the huge golden goblet (not the same word) which Nestor drinks from in *Iliad* book 11. But this heated scholarly discussion is all marginal to our present concerns, because, even if Homer himself learned to write, or if—as is much less unlikely—he was persuaded to let a skilled scribe transcribe his poetry (see p. 32 below) *the poetry was not made to be read*. There was no reading public. Even assuming a written version was in existence—perhaps to be studied by newly literate disciples?—it is still as good as certain that Homer conveyed his poetry to his public through performances.

EPIC GRAFFITO? This message, partly in hexameter verse, was scratched on a beaker found at Ischia in the bay of Naples at an early Greek settlement site, dating from 700 BCE or slightly earlier. Its allusion to Nestor has led some scholars to claim that it presupposes a knowledge of the Iliad.

It is often claimed that Hesiod used writing even if Homer did not. His authoritative editor, Martin West, argues this on the grounds that Hesiod's personalized poetry—'your father and mine, Perses' etc.—could not possibly have been performed by others or transmitted orally. But there is no reason why I should not recite feelingly a highly personal lyric by Hardy or Heaney; and, more immediately to the point, later classical Greeks happily recited the first-person poems of such individualized artists as Alkaios or Anakreon (see pp. 57–61 below). In later times visitors to Askre, such as Pausanias in the second century CE, were shown a time-worn sheet of lead with the *Works and Days* (or at least some of it) scratched upon it. This is a reminder of how unwieldy writing was back in the early days before papyrus was readily available from Egypt. It is absurd to think of Hesiod reading his script from sheets of lead, let alone his public carting home literally tons of poetry. Even if they were written on prepared skins or on wooden tablets coated with wax, the texts will still have been bulky and unwieldy.

There is no allusion whatsoever to writing in Hesiod, even though *W&D* deals with his own contemporary world. There is, however, one intriguing reference in the *Iliad*. In the course of a story about the past before the Trojan War, Bellerophon is sent away to Lykia by a jealous king:

> ... he sent him off with a consignment of lethal symbols,
> inscribing deadly designs inside a sealed tablet ...
>
> (*Iliad* 6. 168–70)

The way that these inscribed signs are treated with a kind of folk-tale mystery does not necessarily mean that Homer's audience had never encountered writing, because, since the introduction of writing into Greece was pretty recent, the poet would want to avoid sounding anachronistic. (It is highly unlikely they would be aware that a different kind of writing—Linear B—had been in use back in Mycenean times.) At the same time, this passage is not conclusive evidence that the poet knew about writing himself, still less that his public read his work.

Internal audiences

It is now time to turn to the explicit mentions and accounts of the performance of poetry scattered through the Homeric epics. We have to remember the examples of Bentley and Latacz and keep on our guard against treating these simply or literally: they are set in a past heroic world, and there is no guarantee that they are self-reflecting accounts of how the actual poem was (is) being delivered. But, via a more circumspect approach, the scenes may less directly yield some significant plausibilities (not certainties) about the production of the poems and their reception.

There are passages where groups, even maybe choruses, are portrayed as performing; but interesting though these are, they are marginal to the primary search which is for solo performers telling heroic stories. What is clear, though, is that poetry and music are mostly thought of as part of the good life, especially of feasting and festivity. So it is typical that they appear in three of the pleasant scenes on the great shield that Hephaistos makes for Achilles, a kind of microcosm of human life not dominated by war (*Iliad* 18. 494–6, 569–72, 604–5—the last passage is unfortunately caught up in a serious textual problem). It is in keeping with this that the *Iliad* portrays no solo performances of poetry for entertainment, not even at any feast of the Achaians or the Trojans: a world of war does not seem to be the place for epic poetry.

With one extraordinary exception. Achilles has been taking no part in the fighting for four days, and the Achaians are in such danger of disaster the next morning that they send a small group of negotiators to try to placate him. As they approach his encampment along the shore—

> they found him pleasing his spirit by playing a melodious lyre,
> an intricate instrument, fitted with a bridge of silver,
> which he had picked from the spoils when he sacked Eetion's city.
> He was pleasing his spirits by reciting the famous feats
> of men. Patroklos alone sat facing him in silence
> waiting for whenever Achilles should close his singing.
>
> (*Iliad* 9. 86–91)

The phrase for 'feats of men' (*klea andron*) is used in the *Odyssey* to refer to heroic epic, and it is close to Hesiod's phrasing at *Theogony* line 100 (see p. 30 above). It would be foolhardy to jump to the inference that in Homer's own world it was common—or even known at all—for young aristocrats to strum epic poetry to themselves for their own satisfaction or that of a few close friends. Is it any more justifiable to conclude that Homer's audience 'saw its own idea of the highest form of self-realisation reflected in this combination of warrior and artist' (Latacz)? In view of the absence of epic performance elsewhere in the warrior world of the *Iliad*, there might be a better, less literal interpretation. At this stage of the poem Achilles is, in effect, *not* a warrior; he is living in a kind of capsule of peacetime activities (like his men, the Myrmidones, who indulge in athletics and wander around—2. 773–9). So the significance of Achilles' singing heroic epic may be, I suggest, that this shows his awareness that he is staying out of the war, out of the world where the 'glorious achievements of men' are enacted (though the double irony is that by doing so he is winning his special place in epic). It is, then, because of this, and because Achilles is an aristocrat and not a practising poet, that, like some archaic Hopkins, he has no performance-context and no public.

The *Odyssey* is far more poetically self-referential, or metapoetic, than the *Iliad*: poets and their audiences are a constant theme. The epic is not more than a quarter of an hour old when Phemios is introduced, the poet who has to perform after the feast for the suitors on Ithake (*Odyssey* 1. 150–5). And not long after that:

> the celebrated poet was performing a poem for them,
> as they sat in silence listening; his story was of
> the disastrous homecoming of the Achaians ...
>
> (*Odyssey* 1. 325–7)

Penelope rebukes him:

> 'Phemios, you can perform all sorts of other soothing songs
> about the deeds of gods and of men, such as poets celebrate [give *kleos*].
> Sing one of these for them as they sit lulled to silence
> drinking down their wine. But stop this disastrous story . . .'
>
> (*Odyssey* 1. 337–41)

To her surprise, her son Telemachos comes to the defence of the poet: he is bound to sing what is 'newest', meaning both with recent subject-matter and with novel touches. Already here we have some features which can be plausibly transferred—at least wishfully—to the world of the poet and his audience: the celebrity of the poet, his association with festivity, his ability to bestow fame (*kleos*), the expectation that he will provide charms or soothings. Also note how even the rowdy, over-indulgent suitors sit in silence when the poet is at work. His ability to sing 'about the deeds of gods and of men' may suggest that he should also have poetry more like the *Theogony* in his repertoire. And this may also be implied when, towards the end of the poem, Phemios pleads with Odysseus for his life, saying that he sings 'for both gods and humans' (22. 346—he is spared on the grounds that he sang for the suitors against his will).

Poetry is also important among the Phaeacians (in Greek *Phaiekes*) on their remote island of Scherie, Odysseus' last port of call before he gets home. They are intermediate between the realities of Ithake and the fantastical world of Odysseus' stories, and they lead an almost utopian existence. They have a suitably talented poet, the blind Demodokos 'held in honour by the people'—'the god had given him more than to any other the gift to please with poetry, when his spirit might move him to perform' (8. 44–5). Demodokos can play to accompany dancing, and he can sing *risqué* stories of the affairs of the gods, which also 'please' (8. 368). But his central repertoire is heroic epic, which he performs after the feast. At the midday feast in book 8 he sings

> a tale of the famous feats of men [*klea andron*],
> picking up the track at a point famed [given *kle-os*] to the skies.
>
> (8. 73–4)

This turns out to be the story of a dispute among the leaders at Troy, significantly similar to the opening of the *Iliad*. Then in the evening, at the special request of Odysseus, he tells of the fighting at the sack of Troy: Odysseus weeps (see p. 6 above), which prompts King Alkinoos to urge Odysseus to tell his own story. Throughout these scenes there is much praise of the poetry for its sweetness and capacity to charm.

But there is another poet in the *Odyssey*, or at least an honorary poet. The loyal farmer Eumaios tells Penelope what it was like to listen to 'the stranger':

> 'as when one stares at a poet, who is divinely inspired
> to tell delightful stories to men, and everyone
> is happy to listen to him unceasingly when he sings—
> that's how that man entranced me . . .'
>
> (17. 518–21)

Earlier Alkinoos, on Scherie, had said to Odysseus:

> 'There is such beauty in your words, and also such wisdom;
> you have told of your toils . . . so skilfully,
> you're as good as a poet yourself . . .'
>
> (11. 367–9)

It was already late evening, after the feast and after Demodokos, that Odysseus began. While telling of the underworld, over two hours into his story-telling in 'real' narrator's time, he rather abruptly stops and says it is time for bed.

> And they all sat in silence throughout
> the shadow-filled hall, enthralled under the spell.
>
> (11. 333–4)

He is persuaded to take up the thread again ('this night still stretches ahead . . . we could stay wide awake till dawn . . .', lines 373–6). And when he eventually ends, they sit in enthralled silence again (13. 1–2). Always bearing in mind that this is all fictitious, and that it is set in a distant heroic and idealized world, there are still poetic or metapoetic assumptions that it seems safe to transfer as aspirations to the world of Homer and his audience—in fact it seems unreasonable not to: the beauty of poetry, its skilled musical accompaniment, its sweet delight, the way it charms its audience, the way it reduces them to spellbound silence; and the poet as someone who is held in special esteem, someone who conveys some special kind of wisdom as well as pleasure.

The 'Odyssey model'

If that much is 'safe', the next step might be to infer that, just as the *Odyssey* reflects the poets' aspirations for appreciation, so it reflects the actual circumstances of their performances. It is a tempting step, and one that has often been taken. Homer performed, it is claimed, for the eighth-century equivalents of Penelope's suitors and of the Phaeacian court; his public sat at the tables of lords or kings in their feasting-halls, surrounded by peers, henchmen, guests, and retainers.

There are serious objections to this, however. First, there is the scale of our two poems. On both Ithake and Scherie the performance lasts for one, two, or at most three hours. At that rate the *Iliad* or *Odyssey* would have taken a week or a fortnight of performances. This is not unthinkable—oral poets in Muslim societies observing Ramadan, for example, are known to perform evening after evening. Or maybe Homer's audiences were prepared to stay awake most of the night listening to his monumental poems—the possibility eagerly urged by Alkinoos? In that case three nights, or even two for the *Odyssey*, should have been sufficient. *But* . . . on both Ithaca and Scherie the poet is subject to interruptions and requests. He is at the beck and call of his noble patrons; at any moment he may be stopped and told to sing something quite different. For the *Iliad* or *Odyssey* to have come into existence, there must have been, I would insist to the contrary, an audience *willing to listen to the whole poem*.

Both poems add up to far more than the sum of their parts. The connections and interactions within them form such a network that any one section is seriously impoverished by being extracted or separated from the rest. Of course, it would still be possible to enjoy isolated sections; and this kind of performance of extracts may well have happened in Homer's own day. But there was no reason for the whole poems to have come into existence in the first place without occasions for performance in their entirety. So, if we are to salvage what I shall call the '*Odyssey* model' reconstruction of the primary reception, we have to suppose feasting noblemen who were a great deal more patient and persistent in their poetry-listening than the Phaeacians, let alone the suitors.

There is a way out of this problem that has been so widely advocated in the scholarship of the last fifty years, that I must, briefly, bring out its implausibility. This theory starts from the belief—a perfectly possible scenario, see p. 41 below—that the way that the poems ever got recorded was through their dictation by the poet to a transcriber. It is then claimed that this process can explain their scale and complexity: while in normal performance the poet delivered shorter bits to demanding aristocratic feasters, as in the *Odyssey* model, the process of dictation gave him the time, the thinking-space, and the opportunity to expand, and so to join separate pieces into the mighty whole that we enjoy. I cannot insist that this is impossible, but I find it very hard to believe that these hugely artful networks came into being, not for a living responsive audience, but for the sake of a material transcription, a load of scratched skins or whatever. So I do not believe that this 'dictation theory' should let the putative audience of kings and barons off the hook. If they comprised Homer's audience, they should have been not just ready, but eager, to listen for many hours without interfering in the subject-matter.

Another serious objection to them is that the poems can hardly be claimed to tell an aristocracy what they want to hear politically or ideologically. Although set in a world of great heroes, they examine and question traditional power-structures rather than ratifying or reinforcing them. Agamemnon in the *Iliad*, who is some sort of king-among-kings (or lord-among-lords) is, taken over the poem as a whole, a far from admirable role-model. It is his errors of judgement and his greed which start the troubles. The most quoted lines in favour of kingly authority (*Iliad* 2. 203–5) are spoken by Odysseus in the middle of a shambles caused by Agamemnon's mismanagement. And, once he has had his brief hour of glory in book 11, the 'king of men' has little part to play in the rest of the poem: his humiliating climbdown in book 19 is in fact the last time he speaks in the entire epic. On the other hand, Achilles is so individualistic and prepared to be so antisocial, that he cannot be claimed as an exemplar for any social group either. Hektor is admirable, but he is killed, and thus dooms his city, because he recognizes that otherwise people will say 'Hektor trusted in his own strength and destroyed his own people' (22. 107). In the *Odyssey* the local aristocracy of the Ithake area are the suitors, hardly a good advertisement. Odysseus, if only he could get home and settle down, would be, we are assured, a fine ruler, but at the end of the poem this is still only a promise, prophesied for the future. But the fact remains that during the poem he manages to lose all the men that he took to Troy with him, all twelve shipfuls. It is emphasized that this was their fault, not his; but this is hardly a story of successful leadership.

Many scholars seem to agree that the Homeric poems 'support' either traditional aristocracy or traditional monarchy. We have already met Latacz's predilection for the nobility: 'we do Homer no disservice in thinking he was encouraged and patronised by an aristocratic clientele (to whose class he himself may have belonged).' Richard Janko, for another example, writes of 'ideological support . . . to traditional images of authority'. To complete a trio of heavyweights, Ian Morris claims that the poems served 'as an ideological tool to legitimise elite domination, presenting it as natural and unchangeable . . . Throughout the poems the *basilees* are glorified, and the *demos* ignored to the point of total exclusion.' But none of this is validated by the actual poems. I have already pointed out what questionable figures the *basilees* and nobles often cut. As for the *demos*, the people as a whole, the usual word for them in Homer is *laos*, and the *laos* is constantly referred to and far from ignored. This does not (of course) make the poems 'democratic', any more than the nobles make it ideologically aristocratic, but it gives a real significance to the non-élite levels of society.

The *Odyssey* model of Homer's audience might still be defended by objecting that I am attributing an unfairly crude attitude to the eighth-century nobility. This is the poetry of suffering after all, it might be said in their defence, and we should not assume that they would be so simple-minded as to demand that all the kings and nobles are good and successful all the time. The poems are, indeed, set in an aristocratic world, and the prosperity of its societies is closely tied up with the authority and well-being of their rulers. The failings of individuals do not necessarily constitute an attack on the élite as a whole. But even accepting this, there remains a further argument against the *Odyssey* model—the most powerful and significant of all the arguments against.

In many parts of the world in modern and earlier times, heroic poetry of the great deeds of men of the past is and has been performed for audiences which are, as in the *Odyssey* model, gathered around those in power. These chiefs or potentates in the audience are normally taken to be the direct descendants of the heroes in the poems. Furthermore, this is explicitly spelled out in various ways, mainly through prophecies and genealogies. So the poets openly celebrate their living patrons by indicating that the poems are about their forebears. This kind of poetic celebration was familiar and important in ancient Greece: it is reflected, for instance, in the victory odes of Pindar (see pp. 64 ff. below). But such ancestral connections between the audience and the poem are conspicuously *absent* from Homer. There is a blank of allusions to future dynasties tracing their family-tree to Agamemnon or Odysseus or whoever, and no addresses—or references of any sort—to any particular individuals, however prestigious, in the audience. There is just one exception, the exception that accentuates the rule. In *Iliad* 20 the gods agree that they must preserve a certain mortal because he is due to have noble descendants, not an Achaian but a Trojan: Aineias. Once the family of Priam has been obliterated, says Poseidon,

> . . . mighty Aineias shall have rule over the Trojans,
> and his children's children, generations in future time.
> *(Iliad* 20. 307–8)

(No mention of Italy, of course—Rome and Aeneas (in Greek, Aineias) are still no more than a twinkle in History's eye!)

There are passing references to the future, to the era of the audience, in Homer, but they are not this kind of genealogy-related pointers to great descendants: on the contrary 'men nowadays' are dismissed as comparative weaklings. There are, however, scattered allusions to the origins of phenomena which are still to be seen in the audience's day—these are, in effect, forerunners of the aetiologies that have such a significant place in later poetry, Greek and Roman. There are references, for example, to an old tomb in the southern Troad surrounded by elm-trees (*Iliad* 6. 419–20), to the tomb of Sarpedon in Lykia (16. 671–83), or to the rock-formation on Mount Sipylos which is supposed to be Niobe turned into stone (24. 614–17—she is there 'now', says Achilles). In the

Odyssey there is an explanation of the strange rock-formations and double entrance of the Cave of the Nymphs on Ithake (13. 102–12—in classical times it housed a large dedication of ancient tripods). There are also references in both poems to tombs at Troy which will be seen by future generations. The Achaians raised one for Achilles and Patroklos,

> on a steep promontory above the level Hellespont,
> so it might be conspicuous, seen from far out at sea
> by people in the present and by generations in future time.
>
> (*Odyssey* 24. 82–4)

There are also a couple of interesting 'negative aetiologies'. In *Iliad* 12. 10–35 there is an elaborate explanation of how the gods eventually obliterated the Achaean camp on the shore at Troy. This alludes explicitly to times after the war is over, and strongly implies that Homer's audience would want to know why no trace survived of the camp (in contrast to the mighty walls of Troy). And in *Odyssey* 13. 125–87 it is explained how the gods turned the Phaeacians' ship into stone to make sure that they would not be seafarers any more after they had taken Odysseus home. This implicitly explains to the audience why they have never encountered them (though it did not stop the classical inhabitants of Kerkyra, Corfu, from claiming that their island was Scherie).

The important point is that these quasi-aetiologies and other forward allusions are pretty few and far between, and geographically scattered as well. We cannot highlight specific passages—with the exception of the descendants of Aineias at Troy—and claim that they are there to please particular dynasties or particular localities. A huge number of heroes and places are named, especially in the catalogues in book 2 of the *Iliad*, but none of them is given any obviously special treatment; and none seems to indicate the locality of an audience. If any specially emphasized catchments were to be claimed, they would have, I think, to be Troy and Ithake.

In later classical times all sorts of patriotic and territorial claims were made on the strength of allusions in Homer. But none of them had any explicit sanction. For example, the Athenians justified their claim to Sigeion, an important site at the mouth of the Dardanelles, on the ground that there is an Athenian contingent in the *Iliad*. But dozens of other places could make the same claim. The Athenians' rivals for control of Sigeion were from the nearby island of Lesbos, and no doubt they on their side pointed out that Achilles' beloved Briseis came from there, and that they were part of the ancient kingdom of Troy (*Iliad* 24. 544). One of the earliest external sources we have for the reception of Homeric epic involves a 'misunderstanding' of this very point about what might be called 'non-localization'. According to Herodotos (5. 67)

Kleisthenes, the monarch of Sikyon in the northern Peloponnese, during the course of a war against Argos in about 590 BCE, put a stop to the performance of Homeric epics at Sikyon because they were 'full of celebration of the Argives and Argos'. First it is not true—at least not in our poems—that Argos is given any special praise, as opposed to being frequently named; and secondly 'Argives' in epic, like 'Achaians', generally means Greeks as a whole rather than specifically men from Argos.

What is true, however, is that Sikyon is scarcely mentioned in Homer. Nor are some other places which were powerful and wealthy communities in Homer's own times, for example Corinth and Chalkis and Miletos—and indeed Athens. Homer does not even glorify his own homeland. However much the poet wandered around the place in the course of his profession, one might have expected some kind of special mention of the places of his 'home base', so to speak, and of their local dynasties. There were strong traditions in ancient times that associated him with Smyrne and with the nearby island of Chios, where there was a school of performers claiming descent from him (see p. 32 below); and there is no reason to disbelieve this tradition, which fits with the dialect-mix of the poems and with their familiarity with the Troy area. But these places, and indeed the whole area of Ionia, are given no special attention—in fact they seem to be positively disregarded in the poems. The nobility of Homer's own 'country' would, then, have found no ancestors or other boosts to their local pride in the poetry of their celebrated compatriot.

The 'Delos model'

This remarkable lack of 'favouritism', 'localism', or dynastic reinforcement in Homer is, then, a strong negative argument against the *Odyssey* model of an élite audience of indoor feasters. In fact, it might, I suggest, be turned to use as a positive pointer towards a different kind of audience and occasion altogether. It might suggest occasions where local differences were set aside, contexts of social integration rather than of local or class division. The Homeric poems are in a sense 'panhellenic'; and it has been becoming quite common to use this term of them (Greg Nagy has been especially influential here). This might not be the best word, however, since it is especially associated with later rallying of Greek unity in opposition to foreign 'barbarians'. Even in later times there were few occasions which were so fully panhellenic that there was a strict and universal truce for their duration; and even the most venerable of those, the great gathering at the sanctuary of Zeus at Olympia, was apparently local to the

Peloponnese back in the eighth century. So perhaps the term 'inter-communal', though less attractive, might be more accurate.

There were in the Greek world many gatherings which, while less all-inclusive than panhellenic, brought together a collection of communities which had some sort of geographical, traditional, or ethnic coherence. There were dozens of these inter-community festivals, mainly annual, all held in religious sanctuaries. At most (all?) there were athletic competitions—Pindar alludes to some twenty such prize-winning occasions. At some there were also competitions in poetry and/or music; and, even where there were not, artists might still take the opportunity to perform—we know that this happened at Olympia. There were enough such festivals each year for a travelling poet to give a good few performances, and to be well rewarded. Hesiod might, for example, have performed at big gatherings at Lebadeia, Thermopylai, and Delphi without travelling very far and without getting on a boat (the big local festival at Thespiai might have started because of Hesiod rather than before him). At such festivals there were often competitions for song-poems in honour of the local deity (hymns to Apollo at Delphi etc.). When there were contests for the performance of heroic epic, there is, however, no reason to think that there was any precondition that the narrative should include local allusions. Another kind of occasion where a large gathering from a considerable geographical area converged is funeral games; and we have Hesiod's explicit evidence for poetic competitions there (see p. 10 above). Another might be a big marriage—marriages are still an occasion for the performance of epic poetry in India and other parts of the world. Funeral games and weddings, being dynastic, might have encouraged elements of local praise, but not necessarily so. It is a crucial feature of all such 'pilgrimage' gatherings that they last for several days. In ancient Greece people used to travel surprising distances to them, and would camp out in tents. There were always sacrifices and feasting, as well as athletics and music. There was no need to rise early for work; and at many modern analogous occasions the performance of poetry goes on through the night. Typically it begins at dusk and goes on into the small hours.

There is no narration of any such open inter-communal gathering in the *Iliad* or *Odyssey* (though Nestor recalls a funeral games open to all-comers at *Iliad* 23. 629 ff.). There does, however, seem to be an oblique awareness of some such occasions. For example, at *Iliad* 20. 403–5 there is a simile alluding to the cult of Helikonian Poseidon: his sanctuary was at Mykale (between Ephesos and Miletos), and a gathering of all the Ionians from Asia Minor was held there. At *Iliad* 11. 698–9 Nestor tells of racing-horses sent to compete for a tripod in Elis, the place of the Olympic games. And at *Odyssey* 6. 162–5 Odysseus tells the princess Nausikaa how he once saw an astonishing palm-tree by the altar of Apollo on

SPECTATOR SPORTS. *This representation of the spectators of a chariot-race was painted in Athens c.580, but found in Thessaly. The inscriptions reveal not only that it was painted by one Sophilos, but that it is supposed to be the Funeral Games of Patroklos, the Iliadic companion of Achilles, whose name is also inscribed to the right.*

Delos. This small rocky island in the middle of the Aegean was celebrated as the birthplace of Apollo and Artemis: their mother Leto gave birth under a palm-tree that became a sacred symbol. It was here that the Ionians held a big festival for all those supposed to be of Ionian origin, including those from the islands, Euboia and Athens.

Delos is the cue for a key piece of external evidence, which, although it cannot be firmly dated, was very probably composed within a hundred years of Homer. This is a poem of over 500 hexameters which we know as the *Homeric Hymn to Apollo* (on these 'Hymns' see pp. 37–8 below). The first half celebrates Apollo's cult on Delos (and the second half, which may not be so early in date, his cult at Delphi). 'You have many temples and cults, Apollo', goes the poem,

> But you take special delight in the island of Delos,
> where the fine-robed Ionians gather themselves together
> along with their children and their decorous wives,

when they set up contests remembering to do you honour:
they delight with fistfights and with patterned dance and poetry.
Anyone coming upon the Ionians gathered there
might believe them to be unageing, undying gods;
he would see all their grace, and feel a deep delight
at the sight of such men and their fine-figured wives,
and their swift ships and all their splendid goods.

(ll. 146–55)

Here is the right kind of occasion, drawn from evidence outside the poems, an occasion—perhaps significantly?—unlike any within the poems. It is a delightful festive gathering which lasts several days; it brings together people from various and widespread communities. It is striking that the participants are not stratified by class; and that they include women as well as men. The rituals, athletics, and dancing took place presumably during the day; it would be in keeping with the comparative evidence from other parts of the world if the performances of epic poetry occupied the evenings and nights.

We can roughly calculate from experiments and comparisons that the *Iliad* and *Odyssey* would each take something between fifteen and twenty-five hours to perform in their entirety. The *Odyssey* falls very distinctly into two halves. The first part which has ranged across time and place and across 'levels of reality' ends at 13. 92, with Odysseus asleep on the Phaeacians' boat: from 13. 93 onwards the poem is set almost entirely on Ithake, and its events take up only six days. This could all be performed over two nights, with some intervals of course. Analogously the *Iliad* would need three nights. The first major internal division comes (according to me, at least) at the end of book 9 with the failure to mend the great quarrel of book 1. The other comes at the end of the great central day of the narrative which stretches all the way from the beginning of book 11 to midway through book 18, probably when Thetis arrives on Olympos at 18. 369.

A big occasion on the Delos model would, unlike the *Odyssey* model, have provided an audience in a tolerant communally spirited mood. This would have given some poets the opportunity and the impetus to grow their poems from shorter lays of one or two hours long into monumental epics. Of course the poets (including Homer) may well have performed shorter poems for other occasions; they may well have sung sometimes at the feasts of lords and lordlings. But that is not how the *Iliad* and *Odyssey*, with their enormous scale and scope and internal complexity, came into existence. The primary, formative audiences, those who participated in the symbiosis that produced our two great epics, were not the commissioners of extracts and episodes, but participants in longer, more open occasions.

There is a problem in this reconstruction, however, though it is not, I think, insuperable. It is clear that the events at the big inter-communal occasions were competitive. How could there be a competition between epics the length of the *Iliad*? Well, if such a festival lasted six days, there would still be time for two *Iliad*-length or three *Odyssey*-length poems. Or perhaps most poets were content with just one evening/night for their poems? Perhaps each poet would tailor the length of his poem to his assessment of the audience's capacity; and maybe only very few poems grew to such a great length as our two. We have no evidence of other Greek oral epics as long as the *Iliad* and *Odyssey*, though it is true that poems as long and even longer have been reported from various parts of the modern world.

The people who went to these festivals for several days will have tended to be the better-off in their communities: note how the *Homeric Hymn* emphasizes the Ionian pilgrims' fine life-style. So this is not really a 'peasant' audience, nor is it like the menfolk-in-the-coffee-house who are found listening to some modern oral traditions. But they are still very different from the power-élite of the *Odyssey*-model. The occasion of the Delos-model is open rather than closed, inclusive rather than exclusive, communal rather than entrenched, various rather than homogeneous. It is also the archetype for the open-air audience, as opposed to the indoor audience, a distinction which will run through later Greek literature.

We have seen how those who believe in an élite aristocratic audience claim to find suitable assumptions and values reflected within the poems. So any search for internal reflections of this wider 'Delos-type' audience needs to be aware of its methodological insecurity. Nonetheless it is interesting to find it argued recently that both the housing and the diet of the heroes in Homer show no acquaintance with the actualities of the 'upper-class' life-style in the eighth century (let alone in Mycenaean times): it is, a 'bottom-up' view of grand living. I would also draw attention to the similes, which, as is obvious, contain many scenes of 'everyday life'.

The long and unpredictable similes (four times as many in the *Iliad* as in the *Odyssey*) have always been a favourite and much-imitated feature of Homeric poetry. Two characteristic examples. The Trojans, elated by their success the previous day are camping the night out in the plain:

> As on a moonlit night the stars blaze out most brightly
> in the heaven above, when the air stands still without wind,
> and the shapes of the slopes and the mountain-tops and trees
> are silhouetted clearly, and an infinity of air is unfurled;
> each star is distinct —and a glad feeling fills the shepherd's soul.
> So many blazed the watchfires which the Trojans had lit
> outside Troy, in between the ships and the rippling Xanthos.
>
> (*Iliad* 8. 555–61)

(Imagine this delivered to an audience sitting out under the stars!) Second, in the *Odyssey*, when Odysseus has been swimming desperately for two days and nights, he glimpses land from the crest of a big wave:

> As welcome as would be the first signs of reviving life
> to a family whose father has lain suffering from fever,
> weeks wasting away, and loathed death has brushed by him,
> yet finally—welcome the gods free him from disease,
> so welcome the woods and land seemed to Odysseus.
>
> (*Odyssey* 5. 394–8)

(At 23. 233–40, when Penelope at last has Odysseus restored to her, it is as welcome to land to shipwrecked sailors.)

The similes, like the Delos audience are various and inclusive, and are open rather than closed. First, they are not drawn from the world of *the* audience, but of almost any audience of almost any time or place. Very few are set in a particular locality, scarcely any in a particular era; and remarkably few are specific to any particular culture. This is essential to their fresh appeal. Secondly, the subject-matter of the similes is usually in distinct contrast with the surrounding narrative: they make vivid and intensify by means of difference no less than similarity. What the similes do for the audience is to make the narrative more vivid by drawing them into it through a picture that is different from the world of the poem, while being familiar (or at least not alien) to their own world. This mirrors in miniature the way that the whole world of the poem is simultaneously very different from the audiences' world, and yet also powerfully, spellbindingly similar. A few similes draw on the gods, and a few on the world of the very rich (an ivory ornament, a team of prize-winning horses), and a very few on the world of warfare; but the great majority draw on a peacetime 'ordinary' world of crafts, seafaring, weather, animals, agriculture, herding. It is not always a happy world—it includes hard labour, dangerous natural phenomena, marauding lions—but it is also often constructive, fruitful, and intensely beautiful.

A social-historical context

I have tried to avoid arguing from external history, if only because this is still an era of prehistory: we simply do not have the kind of detail and precision that would validate such an approach. On the other hand, it should now be worth the attempt to relate the reconstruction that has been built up of Homer's primary audiences at inter-communal festivals to what can reasonably be said about the social and political history of the time. Cramming a lot of history into a small nutshell is bound to involve over-simplifications, of course, but what kind of thing was going on in the Greek world in the decades on either side of 700 BCE?

The era of Homer and Hesiod was even more a time of radical changes than most (though it is true that in many ways the Greek world was in a state of perpetual revolution from about 800 BCE for the next 500 years and more). There was at this stage, however, an exceptional widening of horizons in every political and cultural sense—in some ways, the pottery decoration of 650 set beside that of 750 makes the point at a glance. Very generally and roughly

HUMANS AS PATTERNS. This huge bowl (well over 1 m. high), made to be a tomb-marker, typifies the geometric style of painting c.750 BCE. It was found at Athens, which specialized in this kind of art-work. Mourners are grouped round the funeral of a body carried on a chariot.

NEW MOVEMENT. This band from a jug-like vessel made in Corinth c.650 BCE demonstrates the great change in techniques of representation of movement and of the human figure from the geometric style of 100 years earlier. The battle in massed ranks might suggest the new hoplite warfare, and the aulos accompaniment is reminiscent of the war poetry of Tyrtaios (see pp. 74–5).

speaking, Greece in 750 BCE consisted of communities which were accreted round leaders, the powerful dynasties, the *basilees* who traditionally dominated power, wealth, and the sense of local identity. This is pretty much the world of Hesiod's *Works and Days*, though he registers protests. By 650 BCE a new, larger power-base had emerged, a citizenry—far from democratic, but with a developing sense of shared power and community. This was related to (though not simply caused by) a radical change in military practice. Instead of a few aristocratic champions with a mass of retainers, there developed co-ordinated ranks of those who could afford to be heavily armed in bronze, the hoplites. Power accompanied the indispensability of each hoplite to the security of the community. At the same time communities structured themselves into conurbations with surrounding agricultural areas, the city-state or polis of classical times. Laws began to be codified for the whole area; and, thanks to the new technology of inscription, they were recorded on stone or other imperishable material, beginning the transition to a time when legislation no longer rested in the minds of the powerful few. The civic centre (the agora) conglomerated, with suitable buildings and temples. The religious dimension of the polis was also expressed in local hero-cults (the cult of the powerful dead) and in major sanctuaries with competitive festivals, often located out in the countryside.

This was also generally an era of growth in population and prosperity. Hand in hand with this went the sending out of new settlements all over the Mediterranean world (*apoikiai*, usually called 'colonies', but the word brings the wrong baggage). This important change led both to an increase in mobility, trade, and travel, and to a new awareness of what it is that binds scattered communities together. This relates to the way that certain mainland cult-centres became of the first importance. The Olympic games developed from a gathering for Peloponnesians to an occasion open to all Greeks, including those from the coasts of what are now, for example, Ukraine, Libya, and France, let alone Turkey, Cyprus, Sicily, and Italy. And the oracle at Delphi gained a special authority as an authorizer of these overseas settlements—and as the recipient of thank-offerings for display. Archaeology suggests that this was the very period of the first growth of the big inter-communal festivals (avoiding the term 'panhellenic'—see p. 23 above). Olympia explodes in activity in the mid-eighth century; Delphi and Delos two or three decades later; and many of the other main sanctuaries leave traces of substantial development around 700 BCE.

People are likely to have brought to these festivals at this period a new sense of civic polis-identity, combined with a co-operative yet competitive interaction with the other participant communities. News and ideas about politics, trade, and travel will have been exchanged. Temporarily away from the constraints and power-structures of their home communities, they will have had the opportunity to discuss and think about political, social, and cultural issues. We have here, in fact, the germ of that extraordinary combination of shared Hellenism with fierce inter-city conflict which is so characteristic of the great age of ancient Greece. The common religion and culture cut across political and military boundaries to a remarkable extent. Whatever their enmities, they share the gods, the athletics, the architecture, and the art. And they share poetry. It is here that the non-local amalgam of the 'dialect' of hexameter poetry becomes really important. And this is, I would claim, the context for the absence of 'localizations' in Homer: the poems do not give prestige and advantages to some participants over others. This may be less true of Hesiod, with his Boiotian colouring, but even his poetry is largely 'unpartisan'.

And 'ideology'? I have argued that the poems do not bolster the *basilees*: on the other hand, they do not advocate their overthrow either. The 'people' (*laos*) in Homer are important—more important than is usually recognized—but there is no message that they should have more power. The poems seem to emerge, rather, as a kind of opener of discussion, an invitation to think about and to scrutinize the structures and allocations of power and of respect. Thus, while everyone within the poems agrees that honour—the key Greek word is *time*—should be given where honour is due, they do not agree on the criteria for its allocation. So while Homer does not positively advocate any particular kind of political change, this is surely not the poetry of political conservatism or retrenchment either. It is part and parcel of an era of radically widening horizons; and it is a catalyst to change.

Setting Homer on the classical pedestal

It is a historical fact that the *Iliad* and *Odyssey* got written down. At the time of the great Alexandrian editors (see pp. 216–17 below) many cities throughout the Greek world had their own transcriptions, all slightly different. I have already argued that the poems were not created through writing, let alone for reading. It still remains a real possibility that they were dictated by the poet himself to an expert in the new craft of Phoenician-type inscribing. Another possibility is that a disciple or disciples learned the poems by heart, and that they were handed down orally until the technique of writing and the supply of papyrus were more developed. There was on the island of Chios a guild of Homer experts who called themselves the 'Descendants of Homer' (*Homeridai*). Perhaps the early Homeridai tried to act as human tape-recorders and to preserve the poems as close as they could to word perfect? It is widely objected that over the course of 100 years or more the poems would have become inevitably more and more altered, consciously or unconsciously; and it is true that most oral performers who claim that they are repeating a poem word for word are in fact making considerable changes. The 'oral transmission' theory (which I am inclined to believe myself) has to suppose either that the disciples of Homer had genuine aspirations to achieve perfect recording, or that the poems went on being developed, to a greater or lesser extent, during the first generation of their 'recording'.

Whichever of these models is right, dictation or oral transmission—and there do not seem to be any serious alternatives—it has been generally (generally, but not universally) agreed in recent times that the poems which we have are pretty close to those created by Homer, along with his audiences, in about 700 BCE. We know from the local city-transcriptions and from early papyri (third-century BCE) that there were a lot of small variations—a couple of lines added in one, a line missing in another and so on—but by before 500 BCE it is highly likely that the text was already fixed much as we have it. One reason for supposing that this version was close to Homer's version is that the poems we have are so highly crafted, and so highly integrated both on a large and a small scale—they must go back to a high point of creative symbiosis. This is admittedly an aesthetic claim, and it used to be much disputed, especially in the nineteenth century; but it is now widely agreed. The two most significant exceptions are raised in the next paragraph. The other main reason why most experts believe that the texts were not pervasively developed or changed in the 200 or so years between 700 and 500 is that there is so much in the poems which comes from the eighth century in terms of material objects, social world, and linguistic features, and so little (merely an occasional line) which betrays any sign of coming from after, say 660 BCE.

There are two major exceptions, one in each poem, to the claim that the texts which were more or less fixed by 500 BCE went back to Homer's versions. The 579-block of the *Iliad* which we know as book 10, or the *Doloneia*, is full of differences of language and tone from the rest of the poem. And, while it has been made to fit its slot in the *Iliad*, the rest of the poem makes no reference to it whatsoever. If it was added to Homer's *Iliad,* that must have been done early in the transmission and by a powerful authority; and an ancient tradition said it was added by the sixth-century ruler of Athens, Peisistratos. But this may well be only a reflection of the later cultural authority of Athens: the Homeridai are more likely to have been responsible. The other big problem, which is the ending of the *Odyssey,* is quite different. While some have traced the starting-point of their reservations and disappointments some 620 lines back from the end, as soon as Odysseus and Penelope are finally reunited in bed, there is much that is important and integral in the first half of book 24. It is in the last 200 lines, where the relatives of the dead suitors confront Odysseus, that are full of ever-increasing staggerings in both language and narrative techniques. The theory that something went wrong with the actual original recording, for example that the poet's health deteriorated, seems a real possibility. In any case, the widespread agreement among experts that these two major problems are on a different level and scale from any others is some indication of how the rest has a consistently high aesthetic quality.

Even supposing that the *Iliad* and *Odyssey* were set down in writing back in the poet's lifetime(s), somewhere not long before or after 700 BCE, there is no reason to think that they were ever appreciated by being read as opposed to being performed for at least 200 years after that. The text existed for learning from and for checking, not for 'receiving'. There seems to have been, however, an important division in the reception of Homer somewhere in between 700 and 500 BCE, as has been brought out by Walter Burkert. Before about 600 there

ILIADIC INSPIRATION. This florid plate, painted c.600 probably in Rhodes, shows a battle scene which seems to be directly inspired by the Iliad *(though this has been disputed). The two warriors are labelled Menelaos and Hektor and they are fighting over the corpse of Euphorbos. This particular dual is narrated in book 17 of the* Iliad.

is not one certain allusion to Homer in another poet; there are plenty of references to epic, to its values and diction as well as its stories, but not specifically to Homer. It is similar with the visual arts: while there are many seventh-century representations of heroic episodes, none points unequivocally to a telling in Homer—though there is an outcrop of vase-paintings of the blinding of the Cyclops Polyphemos in the mid-seventh century, which is arguably inspired by our *Odyssey*. In other words, our two epics do not seem to have stood out in the seventh century. The first clearly Homer-inspired visual art in my view (though disputed) is a plate, probably painted on Rhodes in *c*.600 BCE, which shows a precise moment at *Iliad* 17. 106 ff.

The Delos half of the *Homeric Hymn to Apollo* (see p. 43 above) may well date from about the same time as this, or not long after. Near the end of this the poet addresses the young women of Delos who dance a special, famous dance to Apollo, and tells them that if anyone ever asks them which performer they take to be the best of those who visit Delos,

> . . . you should all answer firmly for me:
> 'he is the blind man, his home is [*oikei*] in craggy Chios;
> and his poetry shall all stand as the finest for future times.'
>
> (ll. 169–73)

Either the poet is pretending to be Homer (for this poem is certainly not by the poet of the *Iliad* or *Odyssey*); or Homer still 'lives' in Chios through the skills of the Homeridai; or, as Burkert has proposed, the verb *oikei* is past and means 'his home used to be', in which case we have a performer of Homer advertising his master-poet. Whatever the right explanation, we have here the earliest trace of what became the 'Homer Myth', a collection of stories, with variations, which grew up around the 'biography' of the shadowy Poet himself. The blindness, for example, which was most likely derived from the blind Demodokos in the *Odyssey*, and the home-base on Chios, which cannot be derived from the poems, are central features of this Myth. Another, that he died on the island of Ios after failing to solve a riddle posed by some boys (the answer was 'lice'!) was already current by the time of Herakleitos in about 500 BCE.

By 500 BCE the situation is completely different from 100 years earlier. Homer is by then *the* Poet, the father-figure of Greek culture, the staple of basic education. Simonides can say

> The poet from Chios said one thing which is the most beautiful:
> 'Like the generation of leaves, such is that of men also'

and everyone knows that he is alluding to *Iliad* 6. 146. Allusions to Homer in the visual arts, as well as in poetry, have by now become common, even standard. The proto-philosophers (or 'performers of wisdom'—see pp. 138 ff., below) attack Homer in the process of setting themselves up as alternative authorities. 'From the beginning following Homer, because they have all learned . . .' began an attack by Xenophanes; Herakleitos complains: 'Homer deserves to be thrown out of the public contests and given a beating' (presumably meaning recitals of Homer at contests). By the early fifth century we begin to get proto-scholars defending Homer against such attacks, especially by allegorizing his stories ('Achilles represents the sun, Hektor the moon . . .' to give a wild but early example).

It was probably during the sixth century, then, that competitions in the recitation of Homer and other traditional epics—as opposed to competitions in performing new poems—became established at many of the festival occasions. The performers were called 'rhapsodes' (*rhapsodoi*, probably meaning 'stitchers of song'); and their art was to be practised for another 700 years or more. Some of the leading rhapsodes were Homeridai from Chios, but they had no monopoly. They never, so far as we know, performed poems of their own, only the fixed texts of the great masters of the past; and, unlike the creative oral poets, they had no musical instrument. They could become celebrated and win good prizes, although intellectuals tended to be supercilious about them and their showmanship. It is an index of Homer's growing prestige in the mid-sixth century that when Peisistratos, the ruler of Athens, put together a special new Athenian festival to be celebrated every four years, the great Panathenaia, he included a rhapsodes' competition in the official programme. We hear disproportionately much about this Athenian competition because of the Athenian domination of our sources. It is interesting to gather, though, that only Homer—and that seems to have meant the *Iliad* and *Odyssey*—was permitted at the Panathenaia.

It is, ironically enough, Homer's greatest detractor, Plato, who gives us our best external account of an audience of Homer—though this too is liable to some distortion of course. In order to build up his kind of Philosophy (see pp. 154 ff. below) as the only true access to wisdom, Plato has to discredit other traditional claimants, including poetry, and above all The Poet. In his brief dialogue, *Ion*, he does this by having Sokrates expose the rhapsode Ion (from Ephesos) as not only stupid and conceited, but also as a passive rather than active link in a kind of magnetic chain of inspiration within which even Homer is the transmitter, not the source. In the dramatic setting of the dialogue, Ion has just won the rhapsodes' competition at the festival of Asklepios at Epidauros, and is now in Athens in the hope of winning at the Panathenaia. Sokrates establishes that Ion is in a high emotional state when he performs emotional scenes (thus fudging, as Plato always does, the distinction between the emotion of a performer and that aroused in real life):

> 'Really, Ion! Can we possibly maintain that this man you describe is in his right senses? Here he is, adorned with ornate clothing and a golden garland, and yet he is weeping amid an atmosphere of sacrifices and festival, even though he has lost nothing. Or is he frightened, while standing in the presence of over 20,000 well-disposed people, although no one is trying to rob or harm him?' (535d)

And you realize, asks Sokrates, that you produce the same effect in the spectators? 'I most certainly do', replies Ion, 'I look at them from up there on the platform, and there they are weeping and staring wildly and feeling amazement in tune with the words . . .' (535e). And he adds, with the kind of commercialism that Plato despised, that if he can make audiences cry, then he will laugh all the way to the bank, while if he makes them laugh, he can cry goodbye to his money. It is Plato's aim to discredit the experience of audience, performer, and poet alike. In the process, however, he captures the ability of Homeric poetry, well performed, to grip the attention and to move a live audience, even in Athens some 300 years after it was first made.

In the wake of Hesiod and Homer

By the time of Plato, and from then onwards, epic poetry meant the *Iliad* and the *Odyssey* far above every rival. This is clear from references in our sources, from papyri discovered in Egypt, and even school exercises. But it would be quite wrong to suppose that back in the seventh century Homer already over-shadowed the whole genre. There were other epics all along, and some of them must have been popular in their time. When Hesiod, going through the five ages of mankind, tells of the bronze age of heroes, he implies that two great wars dominated:

> Foul war and fearful fighting killed them off,
> some around seven-gated Thebes, in the land of Kadmos,
> as they fought over the flocks of Oedipus,
> while it drew others in ships over the great gulf
> of the sea to Troy for the sake of fair Helen.
>
> (*W&D* 161–5)

But, both before Homer and after, oral poetry must have told all sorts of other epic narratives as well as those of Thebes and Troy, tales about the Argonauts, for example, Herakles, Meleagros, and the rest. The visual arts in the seventh century, and to a considerable extent in the sixth and fifth as well, show that many other heroic stories besides Homer's were well known. Quite a few texts of these survived to reach the great Library at Alexandria in the third century BCE; but we now have only scraps and fragments, and all too little information about them.

Some of the epics which were recorded got attached to the name of Homer, although few were seriously considered as really his work. Aristotle comments on how inferior they are to the *Iliad* and *Odyssey* in their structure and narrative technique; and the fragments we have appear to confirm this. A large group of these epics were later set in a kind of sequence which was known as the *Kyklos* (or *Cycle*), running from the beginning of the world down to the end of the age of heroes. Some were clearly designed to fit round the *Iliad* and *Odyssey*: the *Aithiopis* even began with the last line of the *Iliad*—'So they buried Hektor; and the Amazon princess arrived . . .'. But, even if they were not brilliantly told, they provided a rich repertory of good stories for later visual arts and for literature, especially tragedy.

Yet other hexameter poems got connected with the name of Hesiod. The most interesting, usually known as *The Catalogue of Women*, was far more widely read in antiquity than the *Kyklos*, as is shown by finds on papyrus. It told of the dynasties that were founded by gods' mating with mortal women, and was known, from the recurrent transitional phrase *e hoie*, meaning 'or like the woman who . . .', as the (plural) *Ehoiai*. It purported to continue the *Theogony*, but was probably composed piecemeal as late as the sixth century. We happen to have preserved some 480 lines of martial epic which were incorporated in the *Ehoiai*, which tell of the battle between the Theban Herakles and the Thessalian Kyknos. The piece is known as the *Shield* because of its long description of Herakles' shield (like that of Achilles in *Iliad* 18). It hardly seems subjective to say that this is dreary doggerel; and, if it is at all typical of sixth-century epic, it accentuates the quality of Homer.

As well as poetry that told of the feats of great men, there was also always poetry about the gods, like the *Theogony* or like the *Battle of the Gods and Titans* in the *Kyklos*. And there was poetry which included both, like the *Ehoiai*. Some actual examples of 'gods-poetry' survive (a change from all these fragments!): we have a miscellaneous collection which is known as the *Homeric Hymns*. Quite a few are less than ten lines long, and are no more than an invocation; but the longer ones, which are attractive poetry in their own right, tell stories of the exploits of the particular god who is being honoured. Most are probably pretty late in date, some even later than the fifth century. But it is reckoned that the *Hymn to Hermes* (who steals the cattle of Apollo) and the *Hymn to Aphrodite* (who becomes the mother of Aineias by seducing the Trojan Anchises on Mount Ida) are relatively early. We have also already met the *Hymn to Apollo*, with its division between Delos and Delphi. Most interesting of all and perhaps earliest is the *Hymn to Demeter*, which tells of the goddess' sorrow on losing her daughter Persephone, and the ecological disaster it caused, leading on to the foundation of her cult at Eleusis near Athens.

Thoukydides (3. 104) refers to the *Hymn to Apollo* as a *prooimion*, a 'prologue' or 'overture', and the same word is used elsewhere of such 'hymns'. But it is hard to see how the longer examples, which would take the best part of an hour in performance, could have been only a 'warm-up' for something else. They might well have been performed, however, at the opening of festivals. While very different from large-scale epic, they share many of the same traditions of diction and narrative technique; and they are a warning against setting generic descriptions too narrowly.

After 500 BCE hexameter poetry is still to have a long history in Greek literature, and then in Latin. But from now on every poem was aware that it was, in varying ways, in the wake of Homer and Hesiod. Several early 'performers of wisdom' put forward their ideas in hexameters, sometimes in explicit rivalry (see pp. 143–4 below). In Hellenistic times the subject-matter of 'didactic epic' became less ambitious and more directly factual (see pp. 228 ff., below). But it was yet to find new life in two great and very different Latin descendants, Lucretius and Virgil's *Georgics*.

Returning to narrative poems that tell of great feats, there were plenty in between 500 BCE and Virgil's *Aeneid*, though the only significant one to survive intact is Apollonios' *Argonautika* (see pp. 223 ff. below). There are within this period two important changes away from the Homeric tradition and manner. One is a growth in overt self-consciousness. The epic, and the hexameter metre, are no longer the 'natural', unchallenged medium of poetry; they have to locate themselves in the literary scene. The other is a movement towards a more literal, geographical 'localization'. There had been, in fact, quite an early poem, traditionally attributed to Eumelos, which set out to put Corinth on the heroic epic map. In the mid-fifth-century Panyassis, a relation (uncle?) of Herodotos, composed an epic about Herakles, which paid special attention to his adventures over in Asia Minor. Antimachos, soon after 400 BCE, was very aware of how his native Kolophon was in the heartland of Homer country. He was a quasi-professional Homer expert who worked his scholarship into his poetry, anticipating the practices of the Alexandrian era.

To conclude with, there is a five-line fragment from the later fifth century which epitomizes the great change from the open unselfconsciousness of performed epic to a written text which is searching for metaphors to express its metaliterary self-location. This is by Choirilos of Samos, from an epic about the mythical origins of the Persians, and tracing them down to the great Persian Wars:

> Ah, happy he who in that era was expert in poetry,
> a servant of the Muses, when the meadow was still unscythed.
> But now when everything has been apportioned out,
> and the crafts all have their own spheres, we are left behind,
> like the last off the starting-grid. And though
> I glance all round, I can not light on any new chariot to harness.

2 | The strangeness of 'song culture': Archaic Greek poetry

LESLIE KURKE

. . . As I know how to lead off the lovely choral strain of Lord Dionysos,
The dithyramb, when my brains are blitzed with wine.

(Archilochos)

> Let the lyre sound its holy strain, and the reed pipe (*aulos*),
> And let us drink, when we have gratified the gods with libations,
> Saying things full of grace to each other,
> And fearing not at all the war of the Medes.

(Theognis)

I breakfasted, having broken off a bit of slender honey cake,
And drained my cup of wine. And now I delicately pluck the lovely Eastern lyre,
Celebrating the festivity (*komos*) with a dear and dainty girl.

(Anakreon)

> O Mistress Muse, our mother, I pray you,
> In the holy month of Nemea
> Come to the hospitable Dorian island of Aigina, for beside the water of
> Asopos wait young men, craftsmen of honey-sounding celebrations (*komoi*),
> longing for your voice. And different achievements thirst for different things,
> but athletic victory most loves song . . .

(Pindar, *Nemean* 3. 1–7)

These diverse snippets of poetry (ranging from the mid-seventh to the early fifth century BCE) evoke for us the strange world of early Greek 'song culture', in

The following standard abbreviations are used in this chapter: *PLF* = E. Lobel and D. L. Page (eds.), *Poetarum Lesbiorum Fragmenta* (Oxford, 1955); *PMG* = D. L. Page (ed.), *Poetae Melici Graeci* (Oxford, 1962); *SLG* = D. L. Page (ed.), *Supplementum Lyricis Graecis* (Oxford, 1974); W, W^2 = M. L. West (ed.), *Iambi et Elegi Graeci*, 2 vols. (2nd edn. Oxford, 1989–92; W^2 = 2nd edn. specifically).

which sung and recited verse were an integral part of daily life. In this world, song was only imaginable as part of live performance in a particular context, where it forged a powerful bond between singer/speaker and listening audience. Many of the elements of this living song culture (which endured at least until the end of the fifth century) had already been lost or forgotten by the time Greek scholars of the Hellenistic Period organized definitive editions of the early poets, so that we cannot entirely rely on their categorizations and genre distinctions. Instead, we must attempt to reconstruct an older system from what we know of the social context, scattered reports about performance, and the internal evidence of the poems themselves. Modern scholars have been aided in this endeavour by the discovery and publication of substantial papyrus finds in this century: perhaps for more than any other domain of Greek literature, the understanding of early Greek poetry has undergone a revolution as a result of such papyrus finds. From the publication of substantial texts around the turn of the last century (e.g. Alkman's Partheneia and Bakchylides) to the appearance of fragments of Simonides' Elegy on the Battle of Plataia in 1992, papyri have vastly increased our corpus of lyric texts and thereby allowed us to piece together an alien system of poetry in performance. Given the scanty and fragmentary nature of the remains, any reconstruction must be tentative and hypothetical; yet it seems worth the effort of historical imagination to try to hear again the distant strains of early Greek song culture (what is conventionally—and loosely—designated 'Greek lyric poetry'). In this effort, we must avoid two misconceptions. First, that the 'age of lyric' succeeded the 'age of epic' as an organic development of the Greek spirit (to be succeeded in turn by the Hegelian 'synthesis' of tragedy). Second, a more serious misconception: we cannot expect ancient Greek lyric to conform to our modern assumptions of what lyric should be. In the modern era, lyric has become the form of poetry *par excellence*, the most private and intense expression of emotion by a speaking subject, often linked to the confessional 'I' and valued for the authenticity of feeling expressed. Because Greek lyric poets are found 'speaking' for the first time (almost) in the first person in their texts, there is a great temptation to assimilate them to modern notions of lyric subjectivity. Thus, it is often said that with archaic Greek poetry, the individual 'I' first emerges onto the stage of history, with lyric subjectivity inexorably succeeding the objective form of epic as the Greek spirit develops. Both of these claims (lyric as the invention of the self, and the organic development from epic to lyric) are romanticizing modern projections that fail to take account of the cultural specificity and difference of ancient Greek poetry.

The diachronic development from epic to lyric is, in a sense, a mirage produced by certain technological developments in ancient Greek culture. For the study of comparative metrics reveals certain lyric metres to be of immemorial antiquity (songs the Greeks were singing before they were Greeks), while the Homeric poems also provide representations of embedded lyric performances (harvest song, wedding song, paian to Apollo, *threnos* or mourning song). Thus, epic and lyric must have coexisted throughout the entire prehistory of Greek literature. What suddenly enabled the long-term survival of lyric in the period under discussion was, paradoxically, the same technological development that ultimately ended the living oral tradition of epic composition-in-performance: the invention of writing. It was, then, an accident of technology and not the necessary development of the Greek spirit that caused lyric to 'succeed' epic in the literary remains.

But if lyric poetry depended on the advent of writing to survive, it was very much an oral medium for the whole period under discussion (and this brings us to our second misconception). Greece down through the fifth century has aptly been described as a 'song culture', in which everyone sang and knew songs, and there was a highly elaborated system of songs for different occasions. In such a culture, all song-making and performance are 'embedded'—that is, intended for performance in particular public (often ritualized) contexts. Such 'embedding' makes ancient lyric radically different from our modern notion of lyric as the personal outpourings of a poet, written in private to be read in private by individual consumers. According to John Stuart Mill's familiar dictum, in the modern era eloquence is meant to be heard; poetry overheard. Greek lyric, in contrast, was always intended to be heard, not overheard.

What then was the purpose of such poetry in performance? Beyond whatever particular purpose it performed (for example, prayer to a god, celebration of marriage, mourning at a funeral), embedded song served in general as a means of socialization and cultural education in the broadest sense. In a largely oral culture, with no institutionalized schools and only minimal state structure and intervention, poetry in performance was a vital way of transmitting to each individual their store of cultural knowledge, the values to be espoused, their proper level of expectations and aspirations, and their social roles. That is to say, embedded poetry was one medium (along with, for example, family, military service, and forms of commensality) for constructing individuals as social subjects. This formative process applied to both the singers and the audience of early Greek poetry, since, throughout most of this period, the singers would have been non-professionals and members of the same community as their listeners, whether that community be the entire city or a small group of 'companions' at the symposium.

Indeed, it seems likely, given the cultural work of socialization performed by poetry in context, that the particular formation of the Greek poetic system was linked to and partly conditioned by the rise and development of the polis in this same period. The polis, or city-state, emerged as the characteristic structure of Greek community some time in the eighth or seventh centuries (cf. Ch 1, pp. 29–31). The polis was not just a built town, but the indissoluble union of city and territory (*chora*), in which the inhabitants felt themselves to be fellow 'citizens'. The constitution of the polis depended crucially on the abstraction of law and office from individuals and the notion that all citizens (however the citizen franchise might be defined) should participate in communal decision-making. In these terms, the polis is more properly understood as 'state' than 'city', and the eighth to sixth centuries as the critical period of Greek state formation.

In this same period, we find a proliferation of what appear to be new poetic genres and occasions. Thus, for example, in addition to paian, wedding song, and *threnos* (already evident in the Homeric poems), such genres as partheneion ('maiden song'), dithyramb (a cult song for Dionysos), and epinikion (a song celebrating athletic victory) developed, and all three in different ways served the interests of the civic community (as we shall see). Other genres of poetry seem to have taken their distinctive form in this period, if not *in the service of* the polis community, then *in reaction to* it. Because of this mutually informing relation of polis structure and poetic system, the remains of archaic lyric (scanty though they are) provide us with a precious view of competing values and ideologies in the period of Greek state formation (on which more below).

These two facets of early Greek poetry—its performed and performative nature within a living 'song culture'—have an important corollary: that we cannot take the 'I' of Greek lyric to be the biographical poet. There is, first, the evidence of other 'song cultures' around the world, in which the singer often adopts a persona well known to other members of the community, though he or she sings in the first person. We encounter precisely this phenomenon in Greek poetry when Aristotle mentions offhand that two first-person poems of Archilochos of which we have fragments were in fact spoken in the persona of 'Charon the carpenter' and 'a father speaking to his daughter' respectively (Archilochos, W^2 frr. 19, 122). Since we do not possess the whole of either poem, we cannot know whether the speakers were explicitly named, but without Aristotle's *obiter dicta*, we might have been tempted to take the speaker of both poems as the historical Archilochos himself. A similar situation pertains to certain first-person fragments of Alkaios and Anakreon which happen to contain words with feminine endings to characterize their speakers (Alkaios, *PLF* fr. 10B; Anakreon, *PMG* frr. 385, 432). These poems, because they cross gender lines, clearly exemplify instances of the poet speaking in the persona of another, but they should make us cautious about the rest of the poetic production from this period. How often did the poets of Greek iambic, elegy, and melic (see below for these terms) speak in a fictive persona, which, because it was gendered male, is otherwise unmarked in our texts?

The second aspect (what I have referred to briefly as the 'performative' nature of Greek poetry—its power to form singers and audience alike) provides even more compelling arguments for scepticism about the lyric 'I'. If comparative evidence shows us that the poet's 'I' *can* be a fictive persona, the consideration of the cultural work of poetry in performance suggests that in a sense it *must* be. For the poet's speaking 'I' must always have served the needs of genre and occasion, constituted so as to make the most compelling appeal to the audience while achieving the needs for which the poem was being performed.

Indeed, we should probably think of different poets or poetic names, at least in the first half of the period under discussion, not so much as authors but as traditional authorities, personae to be occupied by any composer/singer who wanted to speak from that ideological place. Thus, for example, the 'Theognidea' (a collection of brief elegiac poems running to about 1,400 lines) has traditionally been taken to contain an authentic core of poems by a historical 'Theognis', around which has accreted the detritus of generations of lesser poets imitating him. Instead of thus dissecting the corpus, we might think of 'Theognis' as the name for a particular ideological position—a disgruntled and alienated aristocrat inveighing against the evil developments in his polis to an audience of fellow symposiasts. Such a model would account for the fact that references to historical events in the Theognidean corpus seem to range from the late seventh century (the probable date of the tyrant Theagenes) to the Persian invasion of 480 BCE, as well as for the occurrence of poems otherwise attributed to Solon, Tyrtaios, and other elegists in the Theognidea. That is, we should perhaps imagine an ongoing process of composition and performance as 'Theognis', extending over two centuries and many parts of the Greek world. An even clearer example of this kind of ongoing composition in a persona is provided by the Anakreontic corpus. This light playful sympotic verse continued to be composed in the persona of Anakreon for many centuries, and it is often hard to tell where 'Anakreon' ended and the Anakreontics began.

This model of authority in place of authorship has two implications in turn. First, questions of authenticity—is this poem by the 'real' Theognis or Anakreon?—are not necessarily appropriate. Such questions are the product of a literate age, an age of books, and may well be alien to a living song culture. Second, we cannot necessarily reconstruct individual poets' biographies from their work, since they were always speaking in a persona suited to the generic occasion and calculated to make an appeal to the audience. Thus it may be that the historical Archilochos was a mercenary, that the historical Hipponax had problems with impotence, and that the historical Anakreon loved wine and boys, but we cannot safely assume these 'facts' based on their poetic production.

It should also be acknowledged that over the course of this period a shift took place from traditional authority to authorship, a shift that corresponded to a change in the conditions of production of lyric poetry. One contributing factor in this shift may have been the rise throughout the Greek world of the monarchical rulers conventionally known as tyrants. The term 'tyrant' was originally a neutral one, borrowed from Lydia to designate any sole ruler whose authority was not hereditary or constitutionally sanctioned. In the late seventh century, such tyrants appeared in Corinth, Sikyon, Megara, and Mytilene, while the sixth century saw tyrannic regimes established in Athens, Samos, and many of the Ionian cities. By the early fifth century, the 'age of tyrants' had largely passed for most of the Greek world, but the great warlords of Sicily were still founding their dynasties in the West. Historians debate the causes and effects of this wave of tyrannies, but one thing is certain: the tyrants emerged on the stage of history as the first distinctive individuals, partly because they fostered their fame and renown through the patronage of poetry. Thus, in the first 100 years of the period 650–450 BCE, poets were not professionalized, and they generally lived and worked in their own communities (for example, Archilochos, Hipponax, Kallinos, Tyrtaios, Solon, Stesichoros, Sappho, Alkaios). This began to change in the second half of the sixth century, when poets like Ibykos and Anakreon travelled abroad to join the court of Polykrates, tyrant of Samos. Ibykos and Anakreon were intermediate figures, not fully professionalized, nor yet said 'to work for pay', but affiliated with a powerful tyrant in a patronage relationship. With Simonides in the next generation, this process of poetic professionalization was completed. Simonides, we are told, was the first to accept poetic commissions from individuals 'for a fee', and he appears to have travelled all over the Greek world, wherever his various commissions took him. The lyric poets of the next generation, Pindar and Bakchylides, were fully professionalized itinerant craftsmen. Such professionalization radically altered the relation of the poet to tradition and to his audience, for it put a premium on his special, individual poetic skill (*sophia*). Because patrons were paying for the particular artistry of Simonides, Pindar, or Bakchylides, these poets emerged from the mists of tradition as the first true authors (though even in this case, Simonides remained a magnet for a whole tradition of terse and witty epigrams attributed to him throughout antiquity, so that we might say that he was both an author and an authority).

Taxonomies of song in context

In short, ancient Greek song culture was radically different from anything our modern notions about lyric poetry might lead us to expect. How, then, can we come to understand the highly elaborated system of Greek genre and performance on its own terms? Let us imagine we are anthropologists, visitors to an alien culture attempting to construct a taxonomy of native categories and performance genres.

CHART. Genres of Greek poetry and their performance contexts

	Symposium	Public Sphere
Iamboi (recited)	?	At festivals (?) Archilochos, Hipponax Semonides, Solon
Elegy (recited or sung to *aulos*) [Ionic colouring]	Brief erotic, advice poetry Mimnermos, Kallinos, Theognis, Simonides	Historical Narrative Military exhortation Tyrtaios, Solon, Simonides
Melic (sung to lyre)	Monody [local dialects] Sappho, Alkaios, Ibykos, Anakreon	Choral/Public [Doric colouring] Alkman, [Stesichoros], Simonides, Pindar, Bakchylides

Within the Greek system, genre correlated with occasion and performance context, as well as with formal features. We may think of these as two axes of differentiation (see Chart). Perhaps the most significant contexts for performance were (*a*) the small group of the symposium and (*b*) the public sphere of the city. The opposition of these two only approximately corresponds to our 'private vs. public' (since, in a sense, 'private' was an inconceivable category for the Greeks), but these terms may be helpful in conceptualizing the difference.

In the archaic period, the symposium (Greek: *symposion*) that followed the communal meal came to be the main focus of attention and ritual elaboration for the privileged élite. At the same time, early in the archaic period, the Greeks adapted from the East the custom of reclining at banquet and symposium. This shift in banqueting posture crucially limited the number of people who could participate together in a symposium at a private house. In a normal house, the

HAPPY HOUR. A typical scene of a well-advanced symposion with music decorates the outside of this mid-fifth-century Athenian wine cup. The inebriated men are by now dancing to the accompaniment of the aulos *(double reed pipe), played by a professional woman.*

andron or dining-room (so called because the symposium was an exclusively male activity, forbidden to respectable women) could accommodate no more than seven to nine couches, so that the sympotic group was limited to fourteen to twenty-seven participants (two to three to a couch). Thus, in contrast to the Homeric representation of large groups of warriors eating together, the archaic period saw the development of small, tightly knit bands of 'companions' (*hetairoi*) who drank together.

As we know from literary remains and the evidence of vase-painting, there was a whole culture of the symposium. This generally included the consumption of wine mixed with water under the direction of a symposiarch or 'master of revels'; wearing of crowns and perfumes for all the symposiasts; the ready availability of sex with boys or hired women; drinking games like *kottabos* (a kind of ancient 'beer-pong'); and the *komos* or drunken rout with which the party often ended, when the revellers would spill out of the house and career through the streets with torches, singing and dancing. We get a clear idea of the ancient conception of the potential progress of a symposium from a fragment of a fourth-century comic poet, who puts into the mouth of Dionysos the sequence of 'kraters' or large bowls of wine and water mixed and consumed by the revellers:

Three kraters alone do I mix
for those who have good sense; one belonging to health,
which they consume first; the second belonging to
love and pleasure; the third belonging to sleep,
which, when they have drained, wise guests
go home. But the fourth is not still
ours, but belongs to hybris; and the fifth to shouting;
and the sixth to drunken revels (*komoi*); and the seventh to black eyes;
and the eighth to the policeman and the ninth to biliousness;
and the tenth to madness and the throwing of furniture . . .

> (Euboulos fr. 93, in R. Kassel and C. Austin (eds.),
> *Poetae Comici Graeci*, vol. v (Berlin, 1986))

Given the very real possibility that the symposium could degenerate into complete drunkenness and violence, the Greeks also established an elaborate code of sympotic etiquette, much of it purveyed in poetry performed in this context. This was one particular way in which song served an educative function within the symposium, but we should not limit its role to that. The élite symposium seemed to be most of all a play-space, exempt from the larger civic order, in which its participants could safely try on different identities and social roles. Through sympotic song, the revellers could momentarily mime a woman or a slave or a barbarian, even as such poetry also taught them how to be proper aristocratic *hetairoi*. The symposium as a space for role-playing and fantasy is perhaps best emblematized by the so-called 'eye-cups', ancient drinking vessels with large eyes painted on their exterior. When the drinker raised his cup to drain it, its eyes covered his own and presented to his fellow drinkers a mask. Thus Dionysos presided over the symposium not just as god of wine, but as the divinity associated with masks, altered states, and 'otherness'.

Poetry was performed either within such a small sympotic group (or *hetaireia*), which was often in competition with other small groups or with the city as a whole, or it was performed at a large public event in which the entire city (notionally) participated.

Such civic festivals were public holidays, often involving animal sacrifice and the distribution of meat; athletic and musical competitions; freedom from toil; and a general party atmosphere. Whether the performing choruses were male or female, it seems that both men and women comprised the audience, dressed in their holiday best and enjoying the elaborate spectacle of beautifully costumed chorus members singing and dancing in unison. We can get some idea of the experience of such festivals—though on a larger, 'inter-communal' scale—from a passage in the *Homeric Hymn to Apollo* describing an Ionian festival on Delos (cf. Ch. 1, pp. 23–8):

CUP AS MASK. It was a favourite conceit for the underside of Athenian drinking cups that they should reveal the representation of eyes so that the drinker would be covered by a kind of ceramic 'mask'. This particular vessel painted c.500 BCE is unusual in being in the shape of a female breast.

> But you [Apollo] take special delight in the island of Delos,
> where the fine-robed Ionians gather themselves together
> along with their children and their decorous wives,
> when they set up contests remembering to do you honour:
> they delight with fistfights and with patterned dance and poetry.
> Anyone coming upon the Ionians gathered there
> might believe them to be unageing, undying gods;
> he would see all their grace and feel a deep delight
> at the sight of such men and their fine-figured wives...
>
> (ll. 146–54)

These different performance contexts can often be correlated with different ideological positions expressed; symposium poetry often espoused élitist values, championing the supremacy of an aristocracy of birth, wealth, and status against the more egalitarian values of the civic community. Public poetry, even when it supported the claims of the élite, did so in terms of civic, egalitarian values. Thus, for example, choral poetry tended to assume that power in the city should be held in common, accessible to all citizens, and that all good citizens were moderate in wealth and needs.

In terms of formal features, our modern catch-all designation 'lyric' actually subsumes three different categories of poetry (based on metre, level of decorum, and style of performance—sung vs. recited). These are:

1. *Iamboi*: a category which included, but was not limited to iambic metre; *iamboi* were also composed in trochaic metres, and in epodes which combined iambic or trochaic verses alternating with dactylic rhythms. The defining feature of *iamboi* in this period seems to have been their coarse, 'low-class' content, sexual narratives, animal fables, and use for blame. There is dispute about their performance context, but many scholars take *iamboi* to be a kind of dramatic monologue performed at public festivals, perhaps originally associated with fertility rituals. *Iamboi* were apparently spoken, not sung.

2. Elegy: poetry composed in elegiac couplets (a dactylic hexameter followed by a shorter dactylic pentameter). All the elegy we have preserved from the archaic period shows a marked Ionic dialect colouring, suggesting that the genre of elegy developed originally in East Greece. Although in later antiquity elegy was strongly associated with funeral lament, there is no good evidence for this function in the remains of early elegy. Instead, there seem to have been two different genres of elegy: brief poems of advice and/or erotic sentiment probably performed at the symposium, and longer historical narrative elegies or poems of military exhortation probably performed at public festivals or on campaign. In style, elegy tended to be more decorous than iambic, but not as elevated as melic poetry. It appears to have been sung (though it could also be recited), perhaps to the accompaniment of the *aulos* (double reed pipes).

3. Melic: composed in lyric metres properly so called, melic is conventionally divided into monody (performed at the symposium) and choral poetry (performed in public for the civic community). Monody was sung by a solo performer, accompanying him- or herself on the lyre; choral poetry by an entire chorus singing (and dancing) in unison, to the accompaniment of a lyre (and sometimes perhaps also an *aulos*). Monody tended to be shorter and simpler in its metrical structure; choral poetry longer and more elaborate, both in diction and metre. The language of monody tended to conform to the local dialect of the composer, while choral poetry exhibited an artificial poetic dialect with a marked Doric colouring. Monody has traditionally been read as more personal, because (in our terms) it speaks to a small, 'private' group in terms of shared knowledge and shared values. Choral poetry tended to speak to and for an entire community on important ritual occasions, mapping both the unity and hierarchy of that community through the choral group.

This is, I realize, a very schematic account. In order to flesh it out, I will go through each category in turn, and briefly consider some poets whose work is characteristic of each genre.

Iamboi

The main iambic poets were Archilochos, Hipponax, and Semonides of Amorgos. Archilochos of Paros, conventionally dated to the mid-seventh century, composed in an array of iambic metres, epodic structures, and also in elegiac couplets. He is thus our first (preserved) multi-genre poet, revered in antiquity for the poetic skill which earned him frequent comparison with Homer and Hesiod. His poems range from the pensive seriousness of

> Heart, Heart . . . do not rejoice openly when you win,
> nor lament, downcast in your house when you lose,
> but rejoice at pleasant things and be annoyed at evils
> not too much, and know the rhythm that holds human beings
> $(W^2$ fr. 128, ll. 4–7),

to the beast fable of the fox and the eagle (W^2 frr. 172–81), to the obscene, 'Just like a Thracian or a Phrygian drinking beer through a straw, she sucked, bent over, also engaged from behind' (W^2 fr. 42).

The fragments of Hipponax of Ephesos (traditionally dated to the mid-sixth century) are more purely 'iambic', obsessed with food, sex, and excrement as they chronicle the picaresque adventures of a low buffoon in language generously mixed with Eastern loanwords. Thus in one fragment, a thievish speaker prays to Hermes,

> Hermes dog-throttler, Kandaules in Maionian,
> Companion of thieves, come to my aid here
> $(W^2$ fr. 3a).

Another fragment, preserved on papyrus, appears to describe a painful treatment for impotence set in a privy (W^2 fr. 92).

Greek tradition had it that Archilochos was set to wed Neoboule, but that her father Lykambes broke off the engagement. Archilochos responded with such a stream of scathing invective (apparently including the claim that he had had sex with both Neoboule and her sister in the precinct of Hera) that both the daughters of Lykambes took their own lives. We can take this story as a parable for the power of blame poetry and the social norms it enforces, for the names of the figures involved suggest that they were stock characters in an iambic 'mini-drama' performed at public festivals (the name 'Lykambes' shares a root with the genre name *iambos*, while 'Neoboule' meaning 'new plan' is apt for a fickle bride-to-be). We might imagine Archilochos in the persona of a rejected bridegroom, lampooning Lykambes and his daughters to the assembled civic community, which was united by the scapegoating of these stock characters.

We find precisely this story pattern repeated for Hipponax and his enemies, the sculptors Boupalos and Athenis. In this instance, we are told, Boupalos made an unflattering portrait of Hipponax, whereupon the poet dunned him with invective verse until he, too, committed suicide. And, indeed, the name Boupalos recurs in the scant corpus of Hipponax, for example, in the fragment, 'Hold my cloak—I'm gonna punch Boupalos in the eye' (W^2 fr. 120) and another which describes Boupalos in obscene and literal terms as a 'motherfucker' (W^2 fr. 70). The recurrence of very similar stories told about Archilochos and Hipponax suggests that the story pattern was somehow characteristic of the genre *iambos*. Indeed, some scholars have speculated that *iambos* was informed by a ritual pattern whereby a marginalized and abject persona succeeded in scapegoating others through the power of his invective.

The publication of the 'Cologne Epode' of Archilochos (W^2 fr. 196a) in 1974 has both confirmed and complicated this model of *iambos* and ritual abuse. The Cologne papyrus gives us the end of an epode describing the encounter of a young man and a girl in an isolated rural landscape. In the lost beginning section of the poem, the young man apparently expressed desire for sexual union on the spot, and, when the papyrus picks up, the girl is just ending a speech trying to dissuade him from such immediate gratification. A negotiation ensues in which the young man seems to promise that he will not 'go all the way', hints at the possibility of marriage later, and then, with a swift succession of first-person verbs, has his way with the girl in the meadow. The poem ends with his ejaculation, though it remains ambiguous (especially given the fragmentary state of the papyrus) whether this is with or without full penetration. Some modern scholars have read the poem as a charming and light-hearted erotic idyll, but such a reading does not account for a lengthy passage of scathing invective against Neoboule embedded within this encounter. The girl, at the end of her speech, apparently offers (her older sister?) Neoboule as an alternative for the speaker's desire (lines 5–8). In his speech in response, the speaker paints a blistering portrait of Neoboule in contrast to his virginal interlocutor:

> As for Neoboule—let some other man have her.
> Pah! She is over-ripe, and twice your age,
> And her maiden bloom has fallen away,
> And the grace she had before.
> For she does not . . . satiety,
> And, a maddened woman, she has revealed the limits of . . .
> Hold her off—to the crows with her!
> May the king of the gods not ordain
> That, having such a wife, I will be a source of joy to my neighbours.

> I much prefer to take you;
> For you are not untrustworthy, nor duplicitous,
> But that one is far too keen,
> And she makes many men her friends.
>
> (W² fr. 196a, ll. 24–38)

This contrast between the 'maddened woman' the speaker reviles and the dainty, innocent girl he seduces is central to the poem, and must figure in any interpretation of it. The other fact that is often ignored in discussions of the poem is that it is not simply a sexual encounter, but a narrative thereof offered to an audience, perhaps of male *hetairoi* (cf. W² fr. 196). As such, the epode itself works to destroy the reputation of the girl by impugning her chastity. Thus paradoxically, the narrative of events collapses the distinction between Neoboule and the girl, between the virgin and the whore of the speaker's representation. (In this sense, the whole poem serves to demonstrate how brief and fragile a girl's 'maiden bloom' is.) And, since the two females involved are apparently unmarried, their sexual shame redounds to the dishonour of their male *kurios* (or guardian)—their father, if he is living. On this reading, the 'Cologne Epode' is an example of iambic abuse, though of a more insidious and subtle kind than we might have expected. By itself, furthermore, it cannot definitively answer the question whether Neoboule, her sister, and Lykambes were real persons or stock blame figures.

With Solon the Athenian lawgiver (active around the turn of the seventh to sixth centuries), we see a shift in the function to which the public performance of iambic was put. Solon used iambic to defend his political programme (and this is indeed why the fragments were preserved in the texts of later writers like Aristotle and Plutarch). Thus he justified his reforms, the 'shaking-off of debts' (Seisachtheia) and abolition of slavery for debt, in the resounding W² fr. 36:

> Those things for which I drew together the demos,
> which of these have I stopped before accomplishing?
> She would best bear witness to these things in the court of Time,
> supremely great mother of the Olympian gods,
> Black Earth, from whom I once
> removed the boundary stones fixed in many places,
> she who was before enslaved, but now is free.
> And I led back to their god-built homeland of Athens
> many who had been sold, some unjustly,
> others justly, and others still who had fled
> under the compulsion of debt, no longer
> speaking in the Attic tongue, since they had wandered far and wide.

> And those who suffered shameful enslavement here,
> trembling at the habits of their masters,
> These I set free.
>
> (Solon, W² fr. 36, ll. 1–15)

But even here, Solon simultaneously drew on the traditions of iambic in using the humble sphere of beast fable for his final image:

> . . . making my defence from every side,
> I turned like a wolf among many dogs.
>
> (W² fr. 36, ll. 26–7)

We might thus view Solon as an intermediate figure, who adapted Ionian *iamboi* (both iambic trimeter and trochaic tetrameter) to a loftier style and content, and thereby (perhaps) made these metrical forms suitable eventually for Attic tragedy.

Elegy

Solon also composed elegies, both on public themes and in celebration of 'private' pleasures, so that his elegies seem to provide us with examples of both sympotic and civic forms. The other major elegists known from the period are Kallinos, Mimnermos, Tyrtaios (all traditionally dated to the seventh century), Theognis (seventh–fifth centuries), Xenophanes and Simonides (both late sixth–fifth centuries). Most of the extant poems of Kallinos and Mimnermos, as well as the entire corpus of the Theognidea, represent symposium poetry—short hortatory or meditative poems reflecting on the pleasures of life, love, and wine. A good example of this type is Mimnermos, W² fr. 1 :

> What is life, what is pleasure without golden Aphrodite?
> May I die when these things no longer concern me—
> secret love-making and honeyed gifts and bed,
> what sorts of things are the lovely blooms of youth
> for men and women. But when grievous old age comes up,
> which makes a man ugly and base,
> always evil cares wear out his wits,
> and he does not even rejoice when he looks on the beams of the sun,
> but he is hateful to boys and without honour among women.
> So dreadful a thing god has made old age.
>
> (Mimnermos, W² fr. 1)

The lengthier collection of the Theognidea (the only archaic elegy handed down by direct manuscript transmission) allows us to see more clearly the politics that inform such symposiastic verse. Framed as advice by an older man to a boy (sometimes explicitly named Kyrnos), the corpus can be read as a kind of survival manual for an imperilled aristocracy. Thus, in addition to advice on proper sympotic behaviour, the Theognidea returns obsessively to the dangers of associating with *kakoi* or *deiloi* (social inferiors) and the paramount importance of choosing the right companions, the *agathoi* or *esthloi*. A good deal of the impact of this Theognidean refrain derives from the implicit collapse of social and ethical categories in these terms: the *kakoi* are inevitably not just socially 'base' but morally 'bad', while the aristocratic *agathoi* or *esthloi* monopolize for themselves innate 'virtue'. In addition, the speaker of the Theognidea broods about the fact that riches are bestowed indiscriminately by the gods, and that wealth has even 'mixed the race', as impoverished aristocrats marry their daughters to rich commoners (lines 182–96, cf. lines 1109–13). Through it all runs an implicit narrative of the speaker's biography: a nobleman betrayed by his friends, robbed of his property and exiled, he remains the city's true sage and lawgiver, if it could only recognize and embrace him (e.g. lines 332a–4, 341–50, 543–6, 575–6, 667–82, 1197–1202). This leitmotif ultimately constructs a kind of god-given, naturalized authority for the speaker, precisely in the period when the nature and criteria for civic authority were most contested and up for grabs. We can imagine the Theognidea—or something very like it— being sung or recited at aristocratic symposia all over Greece, as speaker and audience alike constructed and reaffirmed their legitimate authority through performance. It is perhaps evidence for the panhellenic appeal and circulation of the Theognidea that even in antiquity there was doubt about Theognis' home city: was he from mainland Megara or its Western colony in Sicily, Megara Hyblaea? This uncertainty of origin made Theognis (whose name means 'descended from god') a figure for any beleaguered aristocrat in a troubled city.

In addition to such sympotic verse, we have evidence of another genre of elegy: longer historical narrative elegy probably performed at public festivals. Thus later authors attributed to Mimnermos a book called *Smyrneis*, which may have included a narrative of the founding of Kolophon, Smyrna's mother-city (W^2 fr. 9) and an account of a battle between the inhabitants of Smyrna and Gyges, king of Lydia (W^2 fr. 13, 13a). In like manner, Tyrtaios was said to have composed a poem called *Eunomia* or *Politeia*, while we also hear that Xenophanes of Kolophon 'composed a foundation of Kolophon and the colonization of Elea in Italy in 2,000 lines' (for Xenophanes, cf. p. 144). This may well have been a poem in elegiac couplets, which included Xenophanes, W^2 fr. 3, a denunciation of the 'useless luxuries' adapted by the Kolophonian élite from their neighbours, the Lydians. A late theorist, *On Music* provides evidence for the performance of sung elegy as part of the musical competition at festivals like the Athenian Panathenaia, and that public festival context conforms to the community these fragments seem to construct for themselves. For such narratives of foundation and battle speak to (and help forge) an entire civic community, while Xenophanes' brief fr. 3 suggests that this kind of elegy could also oppose from an egalitarian position the extraordinary status markers assumed by an internal élite.

The nature of such longer narrative elegy on historical themes has been clarified recently by the publication of fragments of Simonides' Elegy on the Battle of Plataia (W^2 frr. 10–18—Plataia was the great land battle against the Persian invaders in 479 BCE). This poem began with a hymnic prooimion addressed to Achilles (through which the poet linked the glory of the Greeks at Plataia with that earned by the heroes who fought at Troy). It continued (apparently) with an account of the march of Spartan (and other) troops from the Peloponnese to Plataia, and seems to have included a description of the order of the Greek troops for battle (for example, Corinthians in the middle, W^2 fr. 15). Beyond that, the extremely tattered and lacunose papyrus fragments make it difficult to say anything with certainty, though the poem perhaps contained embedded speeches of prophecy or exhortation (W^2 fr. 14?). Scholars have speculated that the poem was commissioned shortly after the battle, to be performed at a public festival in Sparta or perhaps Plataia itself (where those who fell in battle were honoured periodically with festival and offerings).

Finally, Tyrtaios' poems of military exhortation represent a somewhat different context for public performance. The fourth-century Athenian orator Lykourgos tells us that 'the Spartans made a law, whenever they went out on campaign, to summon all the soldiers to the king's tent to hear the poems of Tyrtaios, believing that thus they would be most willing to die for their country' (*Against Leocrates* 107). It seems that in the fourth century at least (and perhaps much earlier), these elegies were performed before the entire Spartiate army assembled (though we need not imagine it occurring on the very eve of battle). Like the Spartan custom of *sussitia* (public communal dining), this performance context extended the sphere of commensality to the entire citizen population. In this context, we can imagine the profound effect of verses such as:

> This is virtue, this is the best prize among mortals
> and the most beautiful for a young man to win;
> And this is a common noble deed for the city and the entire demos,
> whatever man, planting himself firmly, stands fast in the front ranks
> unceasingly, and forgets entirely shameful flight,

setting at risk his spirit and his enduring heart,
and, standing next to his neighbour, encourages him;
This one shows himself to be a good man in war.

(Tyrtaios, W² fr. 12, ll. 13–20)

Melic—(a) Monody

Like elegy, melic can be divided into poems performed for the small group of
the symposium and those performed at more public, civic occasions. As we
shall see, the opposition symposium—public sphere corresponded roughly
(but not exactly) to the traditional opposition of monody—choral poetry. The
major surviving monodic poets are Sappho and Alkaios (both traditionally
dated to the late seventh–early sixth centuries), and Ibykos and Anakreon
(mid- to late sixth century). Sappho and Alkaios were both from the city of
Mytilene on the island of Lesbos, and both composed in their characteristic
Aeolic dialect and lyric metres.

Alkaios' poetry constructed him as a Mytilenean nobleman, heavily involved
in the turbulent politics of his home city, where tyrants rose and fell; where
sympotic groups of 'companions' (*hetaireiai*) plotted and went into exile; and
where the poet and his group were betrayed by a former 'companion'. This was
Pittakos, whom at some point, the people 'established as tyrant, acclaiming
him greatly *en masse*' (Alkaios, *PLF* fr. 348). All this should sound very like the
implicit biography of Theognis, for both the elegy and Alkaios' melic were
poetry of the *hetaireia*, working to unite a small group of aristocratic co-
conspirators and to legitimate their claims to authority within the city. Thus we
find a similar range of themes in the Theognidea and Alkaian monody (though
the latter dealt more in particulars): drinking songs, affirmations of the importance of noble birth, bitter laments from exile, exhortation to companions to
maintain their loyalty and courage, abuse of tyrants and perceived traitors to
the group. Though often denigrated in modern times as more of a political
trouble-maker than a wordsmith, Alkaios was a poet of great power and precision. For example, in two lines that are almost an oxymoron in their juxtaposition of festive mood and grim reality,

Now one must get drunk, and even violently
Drink, since Myrsilos is dead.

(*PLF* fr. 332)

Sappho, Alkaios' contemporary, was the only female poet to make it into the
Hellenistic canon of the 'Lyric Nine', and, indeed, one of the very few female
voices preserved for us from antiquity. There is much scholarly debate about
what context we should properly imagine for the composition and perform-

POETS FOR A SYMPOSIUM. *This unusual vessel, a double-walled wine-cooler, was painted in Athens c.470 BCE and also has unusual subject-matter. The male and female poets represented are labelled as Alkaios and Sappho, the two great lyric poets from Lesbos.*

ance of Sappho's poetry. Almost certainly, some of her poems were originally composed for choral performance; this is likely for songs such as epithalamia (wedding songs), of which unfortunately we have only exiguous fragments. But most of the poems we have (and the publication of papyrus finds in this century has greatly increased the corpus) appear to be monodic and so raise the question of the nature of Sappho's group. Some scholars propose a female symptotic group or *hetaireia* which would have been the exact analogue of Alkaios' group. Others imagine Sappho as an educator of young women, who took girls before marriage and prepared them for this life transition. This reconstruction, in turn, has several versions, which run the gamut from high secular 'finishing school' to high religious 'initiation'. According to this latter model, Sappho was the leader of a *thiasos* of young women, engaging in ritual homoeroticism to prepare them for marriage. There is almost no reliable external evidence for any of these positions, so it is perhaps best to maintain a healthy scepticism.

Yet another approach to Sappho wants to see her as definitively different from all other Greek poets, in so far as her verse seems authentically personal and intimate—much more like our modern notions of lyric. Yet here I would reiterate what was said at the outset: *no* Greek poetry was composed as private, authentic utterance to be 'overheard'. Sappho's poetry too must have been composed for performance before a group. Instead, we might read the more intimate and personal quality of Sappho's poetry as a phenomenon of the marginalization and containment to the private sphere of women *as a group* in ancient Greek culture. Thus the poet spoke intimately to other women, with whom she shared the experiences of seclusion, disempowerment, and separation. Sappho's poems often spoke openly of love and longing for other women or girls, who seem to have been separated from the speaker by forces beyond her control. Because of this pattern of separation, memory played a much greater role in the texture of Sappho's poetry than that of the other lyric poets (and conjures up for us perhaps a stronger sense of the speaker's interiority). For example, in one (fragmentary) poem, the speaker seems to comfort another woman longing for a third:

> . . . Sardis. . . . often holding her mind here . . .
> When we . . . she honoured you
> like a far-conspicuous goddess,
> and she used to rejoice most of all in your song.
> But now she is conspicuous among
> the Lydian women, as, when the sun
> has set, the rosy-fingered moon
> surpasses all the stars; and it sheds its light
> equally upon the salt sea
> and on the much-flowering fields,
> And beautiful dew is shed,
> and roses bloom and soft chervil
> and flowering melilot.
> And wandering much, remembering
> gentle Atthis, with longing
> she consumes, I suppose, her delicate heart.
> But for us to come there . . . this is not
>> (Sappho, *PLF* fr. 96)

This poem is remarkable for the extended, almost epic-style simile that fills its three middle stanzas. Through the simile, the poem hollows out an imaginary space where the two women can be together in fantasy (just as they both gaze on the same moon). This reading is perhaps confirmed by the striking transfer of the epic epithet 'rosy-fingered' from Homer's dawn to the moon in the night sky. If epic represents the daylight world of men, this poem constructs a separate magical night-time realm for women.

Ibykos of Rhegion in southern Italy and his contemporary Anakreon of Teos on the coast of Asia Minor came from opposite ends of the Greek world to the court of Polykrates, tyrant of Samos. We are told that Ibykos composed long poems on mythological themes (like the earlier Western poet Stesichoros), but the few fragments we have look much more like monody. Thus Ibykos sang of love and the desirability of beautiful boys (appropriately for the pederastic context of the symposium), as in

> Eros again looking at me meltingly from under dark eyelids
> with all sorts of enchantments casts me into the boundless nets of Kypris.
> And I tremble at him as he approaches,
> like a yoke-bearing horse—a prizewinner who, come to old age,
> unwilling enters the contest of swift chariots.
>
> (*PMG* fr. 287)

or again

> O Euryalus, shoot of the grey-eyed Graces,
> and darling of the beautiful-haired Seasons, you Kypris
> and gentle-eyed Persuasion nurtured amidst blooming roses
> (*PMG* fr. 288)

This latter fragment seems to be an example of what Pindar and Bakchylides would later refer to as *paideioi hymnoi* ('hymns to boys'), which again probably had an important social function in context. It has been noted that the objects of such 'hymnic' praise were always young noblemen or dynasts, so that we might read the eroticism of these fragments as a conventional form of communal praise and affirmation of social pre-eminence. (Indeed, some have even read Ibykos, fr. 282, a long poem in honour of Polykrates, as an exemplar of this genre.)

Anakreon too seems to have composed for a small group of like-minded fellow symposiasts. Thus his themes are frequently the pleasures of love and wine in exquisitely turned verses, such as

> O boy of the maidenly gaze,
> I pursue you, but you do not heed me,
> unaware that you are my
> soul's charioteer.
>
> (*PMG* fr. 360)

or again,

> Bring water, bring wine, boy, and bring for us flowering
> crowns, since I go to box with Eros.
>
> (*PMG* fr. 396)

But we should not be fooled by Anakreon's light touch; there was a politics implicit in his sympotic celebrations, as his scathing attack on a social climber (*PMG* fr. 388) reveals. The language and imagery of Anakreon's attack on the low-class Artemon echo those of Theognis' lines bemoaning the fact that 'the base' (*kakoi*) have now become 'the good' (*kaloi*, Theognis, 53–60). This similarity is not accidental, for Anakreon, like Theognis, was much concerned with maintaining the purity and exclusivity of the aristocratic group, as it was threatened by the encroaching power of the city.

Melic—(*b*) Choral poetry and public poetry

Turning from monody to choral, public poetry, we immediately perceive a shift in formal features and level of style, as well as in occasion and social function. Choral poetry tended to be composed on a larger scale, with more complex metrical systems; more elevated, ornate diction; and (often) extended mythic narrative. Choral poetry was, furthermore, in some sense always religious poetry, whether performed as part of a ritual (like Alkman's partheneia) or more loosely dedicated to a particular divinity (like dithyrambs in Athens).

The earliest preserved choral poetry is that of Alkman (traditionally dated to the last quarter of the seventh century). Alkman composed 'maiden songs' (partheneia) which were performed at Sparta; papyrus finds have given us extensive fragments of one such poem and bits of another (*PMG* frr. 1, 3). Internal evidence suggests that the first Partheneion was sung by a chorus of ten or eleven girls while another girl performed ritual activities (offering a cloak or a plough to Orthia at sunrise). Such ritual conforms to the theory that in this instance, choral performance was part of an initiatory experience for the chorus members (or choreuts), perhaps marking a life-transition before their marriage. At the same time, performance of the partheneion also provided an occasion to put marriageable girls on display before the whole city, decked out in all their finery. The first half of this long poem, of which we have only fragments, narrated the story of the attempted abduction of the mythical daughters of Leukippos by a band of violent young heroes. This was offered as a paradigm of overreaching and transgressive failed marriage; thus a few gnomic lines from the myth admonished, 'Let no unwinged strength of mortals fly to heaven nor attempt to marry mistress Aphrodite.' The second half of the poem then shifted from myth to present actuality, from violent battle to girls' play and adornment, and in a sense from mythic transgression to ritual propriety. This latter half is remarkable for its carefully scripted but ostensibly spontaneous self-referentiality; the choreuts speak at length about their own ornaments and appearance and about their two leaders, Hagesichora and Agido, for whom they evince an erotic fascination. We might read this vivid erotic praise, sung by a chorus of girls before the entire civic community, as analogous to the *paideioi hymnoi* of Ibykos. Thus, the erotic interest voiced by the chorus could be said to represent the admiration of the entire community for these two (now nubile?) girls, but in a form that was safe because ventriloquized through the modest maiden chorus.

We should also note that the chorus of young girls seems to have staged in performance both the unity and the hierarchy of the community. For these ten or eleven girls represented their entire age cohort and the whole community (as their praise suggests), while they did so in clear subordination to the two leaders. Indeed, there is evidence to suggest that the name 'Agido' connects one of their two leaders with one of the two ruling houses of Sparta, the Agiad dynasty. If we are to imagine Agido as a young woman of this royal house, then the enactment and affirmation of social hierarchy through the hierarchy of the chorus would have been complete.

Stesichoros, who was active in Italy and Sicily in the first half of the sixth century, was traditionally numbered among the choral poets, but recent papyrus finds have made that categorization less definite. Stesichoros was known to have composed mythic narrative poems in lyric metres, but until the 1960s, we had only the most exiguous fragments preserved by quotation in other ancient authors. At that point, three Stesichoros papyri were published, one of which contained fragments of the *Geryoneis*. Calculations based on the size and layout of this papyrus revealed that the poem would originally have spanned 1,300 lines at least (remarkably long for a lyric poem; indeed, analogous in length to an entire tragedy). Such exceptional length (and certain odd metrical features) have caused scholars to think that Stesichoros' poems could not have been performed chorally. Even if true, this does not, however, mean that they were not *public* poetry, for one fragment of Stesichoros, at least, seems to have required a civic audience. In this case, what may have been the opening lines of Stesichoros' *Oresteia* asserted that its subject-matter was *damomata*, 'things common to the citizenry'. It was perhaps performed before an entire community by a solo singer accompanied by a miming chorus. We might then imagine Stesichoros' lyric productions as proto-dramas, which would well suit what we can deduce of his vivid narrative style and frequent use of direct quotation. For example, much of the *Geryoneis* appears to have been narrated from the point of view of Geryon, a monster killed by Herakles as one of his twelve labours. We even have a fragment which must have been spoken by Geryon's mother, begging her son to save his life (by flight?; *SLG* fr. S 13).

Another papyrus, published in 1977, has given us thirty-three virtually intact lines of a poem on the Oedipus cycle. In it, Iokaste spoke directly to her sons Eteokles and Polyneikes on the verge of war, urging them to divide their father's property by lot and thereby spare their house and city from destruction. The extended use of direct quotation (thirty out of thirty-three lines were spoken by Iokaste) would have made the poem particularly vivid in performance, while Iokaste's appeal on behalf of the 'city of Kadmos' (which did not figure in Homeric versions of the Oedipus story) may reveal something about the original civic audience to which the poem was pitched.

With Simonides, Pindar, and Bakchylides, we reach the final great period of choral lyric production (*c*.520–450 BCE). It is hard to say much about the choral poetry of Simonides, since so very little survives. For Bakchylides of Keos, however, major papyrus finds early in this century have given us substantial fragments of fourteen epinikia (poems celebrating athletic victories), as well as dithyrambs and paians. Bakchylides' dithyrambs were composed for different cities, including two for Athens. In Athens we know that dithyrambs were performed in competitions at the City Dionysia (cf. Ch. 3, pp. 84–91) and perhaps other festivals (according to the Parian Marble, the dithyrambic contests at the Dionysia were instituted in 509/8 BCE). For this competition, each of the ten Athenian tribes entered a chorus of men and a chorus of boys, each containing fifty members. They were elaborately and beautifully costumed and crowned, and danced with circular choreography as they sang to the accompaniment of an *aulos*. Such competition would have required rigorous training and would have involved 1,000 Athenian citizens and future citizens each year. As such, the dithyrambic contests played a major part in the citizens' choral education.

Like the Athenian tragic contests, instituted according to the traditional date some years earlier, the dithyramb was a song in honour of Dionysos, but like contemporary tragedy, that dedication seems not to have required Dionysiac themes as subject-matter. Thus Bakchylides' two known dithyrambs for Athens (18, 19) told the stories of Theseus' first approach to Athens as a young man, unknown to his royal father Aigeus, and of Io's wanderings after Hera transformed her into a cow. The former poem was constructed as a dialogue, with a single voice (perhaps the chorus leader) speaking in the persona of Aigeus, while the chorus responded in the role of representative citizens of Athens. The mood created was one of uncertainty and fear, as king and people alike apprehensively awaited the powerful but unknown individual who had exterminated the robbers and criminals lining the road from Epidauros to Athens (whom, of course, the audience knew to be Theseus). In its dialogic form, as well as in the asymmetry of knowledge constructed between characters and audience, this poem seems to show the influence of the contemporary genre of tragedy on more traditional choral song. It thereby told the familiar story of Theseus' youthful exploits in a novel way and allowed chorus and audience alike to unite in celebrating their national hero.

Bakchylides' exact contemporary was Pindar of Thebes (traditional dates 518–438 BCE), regarded by many as the greatest of the canonical nine Greek lyric poets. In his own time, Pindar was in great demand, receiving poetic commissions from all over the Greek world. By the Hellenistic period, his poems were collected in seventeen books (i.e. papyrus rolls of 1,000–2,000 lines each). He was thus a prolific poet who composed many different types of choral songs—hymns, paians, dithyrambs, partheneia, dirges, and epinikia among them. From papyrus finds, we possess substantial fragments of his paians and a few bits of hymns, dithyrambs, and parthenaia. All these poems exhibit Pindar's characteristic style: difficult, crabbed syntax; obscure transitions; very elevated diction; and elaborate, vivid metaphors and conceits. But all these qualities are shown to best advantage in his epinikia, of which four books survive through direct manuscript tradition.

Both Pindar and Bakchylides composed epinikia. Relatively speaking, we have a substantial corpus of this genre preserved: fourteen Bakchylidean epinikia from papyrus; forty-four Pindaric odes preserved through direct manuscript tradition. Epinikion, choral poetry composed on commission to celebrate individual athletes who had won at the panhellenic games, was a relative latecomer among the genres of Greek choral poetry (the earliest epinikion we know of was composed by Simonides in the 520s). We might understand it as an adaptation to the needs of a panhellenic élite (those with the money and leisure time to train and compete at the games), when their authority within their individual cities was no longer unquestioned. Athletic victory itself was one means of acquiring enormous prestige within the city and the aristocracy in general, but, as we know from Tyrtaios (W² fr. 12) and Xenophanes (W² fr. 2), the civic value of athletic victory could be challenged from an egalitarian perspective. Thus Xenophanes could contend in elegiac verse:

> For even if there should be a good boxer among the people,
> or one who is good at the pentathlon or wrestling,
> or in the swiftness of his feet—the very thing which is most honoured,
> of all the works of strength in the contest of men—
> the city would not on that account be more orderly.

But there would be little joy to the city in this,
if someone should win in competition beside the banks of Pisa [at Olympia];
for these things do not fatten the city's coffers.

(Xenophanes, W² fr. 2, ll. 15–22)

Against such challenges, epinikion affirmed the common value of athletic achievement. At the same time, it worked to reintegrate the victor who had so distinguished himself into his various communities. Thus epinikion praised the victor by representing him as an ideal member of his aristocratic class *and* of his civic community. Emblematic of this reintegrative function was the performance context of most epinikia: composed by a professional poet, the victory ode was sung in unison by a chorus of the victor's fellow citizens in his home town. Often the poem voiced by this representative chorus contained a myth which linked the victor's achievement with those of local cult heroes (as Pindar, for example, tended to use myths of the Aiakidai in odes for Aiginetan victors). Thus also much of the familiar rhetoric of epinikion, warning about human limitations and admonishing the victor 'not to seek to become Zeus' should perhaps be read in a political context. Such rhetoric served to reassure the victor's fellow citizens that he did not aim to use the extraordinary prestige acquired from athletic victory to wield undue political influence within the city. For example, Pindar could say, speaking in the 'generic first person' which voiced the sentiments proper to victor and poet alike:

I would desire beautiful things from god,
Striving for things that are possible within my age-class.
For finding the middle ranks blooming with more enduring prosperity throughout
the city,
I blame the lot of tyrannies;
And I am strained over common achievements. And the envious are fended off,
if a man, having taken the peak of achievement, plieś it in peace and avoids dread
hybris . . .

(Pindar, *Pythian* 11. 50–8)

Epinikion seems also to have served a panhellenic function, as we can deduce from the large number of commissions Pindar and Bakchylides received from Greek colonies, and especially from colonial rulers like the kings of Kyrene in Libya or the Greek tyrants in Sicily. Nearly a third of Bakchylides' extant epinikia were composed for colonial victors (including three for Hieron, tyrant of Syracuse), while twenty of Pindar's forty-four surviving epinikia celebrated victors from Greek cities in Italy, Sicily, and North Africa (of these, ten were commissioned by colonial dynasts or members of their immediate families). Just as Greek colonial citizens and dynasts competed avidly at the panhellenic games and made lavish dedications at Olympia and Delphi, so also they commissioned numerous epinikia from the most famous poets of mainland Greece. All three activities derived from the same impulse—the desire of colonials to assert their Greekness and to maintain a visible presence on the Greek mainland. For dynasts on the margins of the Greek world the aspiration extended further; they wanted to affirm the legitimacy of their rule as well as their rightful membership in a panhellenic élite. This participation on the larger stage of Greek history and culture was the real substance behind epinikion's promise, frequently proclaimed, to spread the victor's fame to the very limits of the earth.

In all these different contexts in epinikion, the poet's 'I' figured prominently, but it was a flexible persona, suited in each poem to serve the needs of the victor's reintegration and glorification (again we should not deduce anything about the historical Pindar or Bakchylides from their poetic self-references). Thus in the passage from *Pythian* 11 quoted above, the poet's 'I' voiced the sentiments of an ideal middling citizen, as he did again in *Nemean* 8 (composed for a private citizen of Aigina):

> Some pray for gold, others for a boundless expanse of land,
> But I pray to cover my limbs with earth when I have pleased the citizens,
> Praising the one who is praiseworthy, and showering blame on wrongdoers.
>
> (Pindar, *Nemean* 8. 37–9)

In contrast to this middling stance, the poet's 'I' espoused a very different position in odes composed for tyrants; thus both Pindar and Bakchylides ended major odes for Hieron by asserting the absolute pre-eminence of his 'kingship' and affiliating their own poetic skill and reputation with the dynast's status:

> The furthest height caps itself
> for kings. No longer look further.
> May it be for you [Hieron] to tread aloft for this time,
> As for me to the same extent to keep company with victors, being pre-eminent in poetic skill throughout all Greece.
>
> (Pindar, *Olympian* 1. 113–115b)

> O Hieron, you have displayed
> the most beautiful blooms of blessedness to mortals.
> But for one who has been successful, silence bears no ornament;
> Together with the truth of noble deeds, someone will hymn also
> the grace of the Kean nightingale.
>
> (Bakchylides, Ode 3, ll. 92–8)

The 'new music' and the end of the 'lyric age'

Pindar's latest datable epinikion was composed in 446 BCE. In a sense, this ode marks the end of the great age of Greek lyric poetry. After the middle of the fifth century, there was no single iambic, elegiac, or melic poet deemed worthy of canonization by the later Hellenistic scholars (though poetic composition and performance continued in all three forms). What then was the cause of the abrupt silencing of Greek song culture in our sources? I insisted at the outset that we should not impose an organic, developmental model on the diachronic sequence epic–lyric–tragedy, taking these genres to correspond to different phases of the Greek 'spirit'. And yet, the end of the 'lyric age' of Greece seems to correspond with the mature phase of Attic tragedy; should we not interpret this as an organic development?

As in the case of the apparent shift from epic to lyric, the processes involved were probably more complex and more historically specific than such an organic model allows. The appearance and popularity of Attic tragedy and comedy played a part, to be sure, for both genres appropriated lyric forms that had earlier been independent (including iambic, choral song, and monody; cf. Ch. 3, pp. 70–1). The domination of tragedy and comedy may have meant that gifted poets were drawn to these forms rather than to traditional lyric composition. In what may have been partly an attempt to compete more effectively with these synthetic genres, practitioners of other lyric forms (especially dithyramb) seem to have led a musical revolution in the last third of the fifth century in Athens. This was the period of the so-called 'New Music', characterized by an abandonment of strict strophic responsion in favour of looser, astrophic forms, a much freer mixing of different rhythms and musical modes (or scales) within a single composition, and the proliferation of notes at smaller intervals.

One prominent practitioner of the New Music was Timotheos of Miletos, active in the last third of the fifth century and beginning of the fourth. Timotheos added four strings to the traditional seven-stringed lyre, thereby allowing the performer to modulate between modes (or scales) within a single composition without having to adjust the strings. Timotheos composed dithyrambs and also lyric kitharodic nomes (in which a solo singer accompanied himself on the lyre). An extraordinary example of Timotheos' work in this latter genre came to light on papyrus in 1903; our oldest literary papyrus (dated to the fourth century BCE) preserves over 200 lines of Timotheos' *Persians*. This poem, probably performed at a Panathenaic kitharodic competition some time in the years before 408 BCE, vividly narrated the Battle of Salamis (480 BCE), and ended with a series of four quoted speeches by defeated Persians, ranging from the fractured Greek of a common Phrygian soldier to the solemn lament of the Great King. Just as the rhythm shifted from the dactylic hexameter of the opening line to iambic and Aeolic measures, so also the style of the poem fluctuated from baroque dithyrambic, full of compound adjectives and elaborate metaphorical conceits, to the restrained dignity of Xerxes' lament:

> But when the King looked upon
> his all-mixed force rushing to backturning flight,
> he fell to his knees and defiled his body,
> and spoke, swelling with misfortunes,
> 'Alas the destruction of houses
> and the scorching Greek ships, which
> have destroyed the ships'
> youthful strength of many men.
> But the ships will not convey
> them on their way back, but
> the smoky strength of fire
> will flare with savage body, and groaning griefs
> will come to the Persian land.
> (Timotheos, PMG fr. 791, ll. 173–86)

Timotheos' *Persians* was a *tour de force*, a kind of compendium of the whole tradition of lyric rhythms, styles, and generic forms. As such, it helps us understand the ways in which the New Music contributed to the end of a living performance culture. This was not because (as Plato and Aristotle would have it), this New Music was morally decadent and corrupting; it was rather that, in its very virtuosity, it required performance by *professional* musicians. It was nearly impossible for amateur singers and lyre players to re-create the rhythmic and musical complexity of Timotheos' compositions (or those of the other practitioners of the New Music). But in a world with only the most rudimentary musical notation, continued reperformance was the sole route to survival and eventual canonization. Thus paradoxically, the New Music, by radically pushing the envelope of traditional musical styles, permanently altered the conditions for musical performance within Greek culture.

Another factor in the demise of the 'lyric age' was a more general shift in the techniques and style of education in classical Greece (cf. Ch. 5, pp. 149–54). With the rise of the Sophists in the last third of the fifth century, education became increasingly privatized and professionalized. For the Sophists (along with their Athenian counterpart Sokrates) insisted that education required special knowledge and expertise on the part of the educators. By systematizing different fields of knowledge (like rhetoric, mathematics, astronomy, and grammar), the Sophists worked to disembed education from its traditional cultural context, a large part of which was the choral and musical education received in a living song culture. Instead, they offered training in special skills for a fee, so that education became more of a private matter dependent on an individual's resources. It is then no accident that in the debate over the 'New Education' staged between a father and a son in Aristophanes' *Clouds*, the event that precipitates the final quarrel is the father's request that the son sing him a song by Simonides (which the son rejects as too 'old-fashioned'). With the rise of the New Education, the traditional modes of lyric performance fell out of favour and into disuse. Along with these developments, the medium of writing began to make much more of an impact in the later fifth century. In this period, new prose genres such as medical treatises, history, and philosophy were composed to be read rather than performed, and so contributed to the specialization and privatization of knowledge.

We might understand all these processes as part of a shift in the nature of performance in the polis. Public poetry of all kinds seemed to play a much less important role in the city and the education of its citizens in the fourth century. It is well to remember that Attic tragedy and comedy, which in a sense displaced other lyric production, did not maintain their unquestioned pre-eminence for long. In fact, it appears that much of the energy and prominence traditionally accorded to poetry had shifted to another domain of performance—the rhetorical displays of the lawcourts and assembly (cf. Ch. 6, pp. 178–98). Political and forensic oratory became the sites for the negotiation of speaker and audience, for the collaborative construction of ideal community that had been the function of choral poetry in performance. With this development came also the split between public oratory and private literary production, which for the first time constituted a category of the 'literary' closer to our own. Thus lyric poetry lost its crucial involvement in public ideology and was relegated to the private sphere.

Paradoxically, this meant that what had been a minority voice in the 'lyric age'—the elegy and monody performed at symposia—came to be the bulk of the lyric poetry that was reperformed and preserved. For symposia and their entertainments endured, as the sphere of public poetry did not. Historical narrative elegy was replaced by prose history, and Solon, had he lived in the fourth century, would certainly have composed speeches instead of poems. It is no accident that many of the lyric fragments we have derive from the second- or third-century CE antiquarian Athenaios of Naukratis, who wrote the *Deipnosophistai* (*Scholars at Dinner*), of which an interminable fifteen books survive (cf. Ch. 8, p. 243). Conversely, with the exception of Pindar's epinikia, all the major fragments of choral lyric we currently possess came to light from papyrus finds in this century. This happy accident of preservation has thus restored to us a domain of public poetry in performance that was profoundly different from all that came after it in the Western tradition.

3 | Powers of horror and laughter: The great age of drama

PETER WILSON

The growth of tragedy from song culture

tragedy blossomed forth and won great acclaim, becoming a wondrous event for the ears and eyes of the men of that age . . .

(Plutarch, *Moralia*)

When the tragic flower first blossomed in Attic soil late in the sixth century it represented a major innovation on the horizon of Greek poetry and society. For the first time the familiar figures of myth—the men, women, and gods sung of by the Homeric bard and his successors—had miraculously come to life. They moved and interacted as real physical presences before the eyes; they spoke and sung directly to the ear of the audience; the new technology of the theatrical mask and costume introduced the possibility of total impersonation. A unique set of circumstances had produced a radically new kind of performance, and with it the first fully theatrical audience.

The origins of Greek drama remain obscure. But it is much more helpful to speak of a coalescence of different forces—historical, poetical, religious, social—whose combination was amazingly productive, and generated the phenomenon we know from its classical form. Among these, we should include the ancient tradition of 'poetry of occasion'. In the oral society of early Greece poetry was produced for specific and significant social and religious occasions—a song for the gods, or to praise a man's athletic achievements, to celebrate the founding of a new city, a wedding, a funeral, to inspire soldiers to battle. For this kind of poetry, the words were only one part of a complex performance involving singers, musicians, and, crucially, a group gathered for a social and religious event (see Ch. 2, esp. pp. 40–1, 42 on 'song culture'). It was only much later in the day of drama's life that the very idea of a 'reading public' was born. Even then (around the end of the fifth century), reading drama was still very much a minority activity. Drama was essentially a performance—a 'doing' (as the Greek word *drama* itself signifies), and a performance for the masses, for a huge public audience.

Another important ingredient in the early mix that led to drama is the specific promotion of poetic performance by the tyrants of sixth-century Athens (for the term 'tyrant', see p. 45), Peisistratos and his sons Hippias and Hipparchos (Hipparchos, though remembered for his promotion of the arts, was never himself the sole ruler of Athens.) Before their time Athens was something of a poetic backwater: by the early fifth century, it was well on its way to becoming the poetic magnetic pole of all Greece. Some of the greatest poets of the age were invited to Athens (among them the versatile Simonides of Keos and Lasos from Hermione), to practice their crafts and, no doubt, to foster local talent. As part of their aim to promote Athens as a cultural centre to vie with the other great states of Greece, the Peisistratids expended much energy on enhancing the city's programme of major festivals, especially the Panathenaia, Athena's great 'birthday party', and—crucially for the future of drama—the Dionysia, the wine god Dionysos' major city festival. Both of these came to have grand public cultural contests as a distinctive characteristic: competitions in the recitation of Homer and in instrumental playing and accompanied singing at the Panathenaia; and competitions of the new art-form of tragedy, and later of comedy as well as of dithyramb, Dionysos' special choral song, at the Dionysia.

Since classical tragedy and comedy are bound up intimately with the political forms of democratic Athens, it would be fascinating to know whether and in what ways drama served the city while still under the control of a tyrant. The shadowy, alluringly half-mythic figure of the Athenian Thespis (whence ultimately our 'Thespians') was regarded by later writers as in some sense the father of tragedy and inventor of the art of acting, and they placed his activities in the last third of the sixth century, in the period of Peisistratid rule. Thespis may well have presented his startling innovation to his fellow villagers in his birthplace, the region of Ikarion in northern Attica (in Greek, Attike), a place with which the god Dionysos had special associations (see p. 79 below). Likewise with comedy: there were certainly sixth-century predecessors to the riotous 'other face' of Dionysian drama, which tended to slink—but scarcely quietly—behind its more 'elevated' sibling of tragedy in terms of the official recognition and prestige it gained.

If Homeric epic was in some sense 'shared' by all Greece, a precious element in a broad cultural patrimony rather than the special possession of a particular place or people (see Ch. 1, pp. 22–3), the situation was very different with drama. There were other claimants to the title of the 'inventor' of drama. Dorian communities of the Peloponnese put forward claims to tragedy; Megara (a city between Athens and Corinth) and a number of Sicilian Greek cities had flourishing comic performances, perhaps as early as the mid-sixth century. But whatever the substance of these claims (and the whole idea of looking for a single 'inventor' is in any case probably misguided), they were soon over-shadowed by the inordinate success of the Athenian experiment. Drama rapidly became a characteristically Athenian phenomenon. In the long-term perspective of literary history, tragedy and comedy were the two great con-tributions of Athens.

That drama grew up in intimate connection with the worship of Dionysos is another of the early shaping forces behind it. The qualities of this ambiguous and elusive god, and specific elements of his worship, played vital roles in the developing art-form. The mask had long played an important part in his wor-ship. However, its transformation from an object of cult veneration represent-ing the god to a malleable instrument of identity-change on the head of actors and chorus was decisive.

The situation with music is comparable. Music was always central to the worship of Dionysos, as of many gods. The forms of religious music for Dionysos included especially 'orgiastic' tunes and instruments, the kind of thing he was imagined as bringing with him to Greece from his journeying in the east, in Lydia and Phrygia. These were played enthusiastically by his fol-lowers, be they ordinary mortal worshippers at his various feasts and festivals, or his special possessed female followers known as maenads, or his anarchic male entourage of satyrs—see pp. 89–90 below. This ecstatic, Dionysiac music plays an important role in tragedy: Euripides' *Bakchai* is particularly full of it, as we should expect in a play with a chorus of maenads devoted to their god, who is himself its protagonist.

> —And he cries, as they cry, *Evohé!*—
> On, Bakchai!
> On, Bakchai!
> Follow, glory of golden Tmolos,
> hymning god
> with a rumble of drums,
> with a cry *Evohé!* to the Evian god,
> with a cry of Phrygian cries,
> when the holy pipe like honey plays
> the sacred song of those who go
> to the mountain!
> to the mountain!

ACTOR COMMUNING WITH MASK. *This very interesting tombstone was only recently discovered on the island of Salamis near Athens. It may date from as early as 420 BCE. It evidently showed a youthful idealization of the dead man holding up the mask of a female role from tragedy. It is revealing for the importance of the mask as a symbol of acting and for the kind of 'communication' that was set up between actor and mask.*

> —then, in ecstasy, like a colt by its grazing mother,
> the Bakchant runs with flying feet, she leaps!
>
> (ll. 152–69)

Ancient scholars from at least Aristotle's time believed that drama developed out of the form of the singing, dancing chorus for Dionysos, as a lead figure stood apart from the group and began to engage in dialogue with it. But the chorus stayed with drama even when its stories no longer centred on Dionysos, and it remained a strictly musical core at its centre. The basic format of all classical drama, tragic and comic, is an interlacing of the stream of *song* (and dance) from the chorus with the *speech* of the actors, in the form of iambic verse. (See pp. 54–5 on the Athenian tradition of iambic poetry.) The fact that the chorus can draw on, and imaginatively mingle together, a wide range of musical forms that existed outside drama is one of tragedy's (and comedy's) great resources. The many funerary songs and laments of tragedy, for instance, will have drawn real intensity from their relation to forms of ritual song known to the audience. The choral lament or dirge (*threnos*) sung by the slave women of the household in honour of the dead King Agamemnon in the *Libation Bearers*, the second play of Aischylos' trilogy of 458 the *Oresteia*, offers a good example. Its language, and doubtless the music that once accompanied it, shows many features characteristic of the traditional lament, including repetition of words or sounds in the same place in the various metrical units of the song:

> We have come from the house, sent here
> to bring libations. Sharp blows rained on us.
> Look at these gashes on my cheek—
> they're new; but for a long time now
> my heart has fed itself on misery.
> We've rent the fabric of our clothes in grief,
> we've torn and crushed the veils around our breasts.
> These are disasters which bring no one joy.
>
> (*Libation Bearers* 22–31)

This musical dimension is almost entirely lost to us, but would have been a major component of drama's ancient impact. It was here perhaps more than anywhere else that a poet could exert a direct emotional influence on his audience. The Greeks (like most modern musical theorists) regarded music's power as working directly on the emotions, as largely non-rational in its effects. And the *aulos*, the set of double pipes whose piercing sound was the usual accompaniment of tragedy, was above all instruments the one believed to seize hold of the soul in a powerfully direct manner.

We can catch a glimpse of the power of the lost musical dimension of drama, and of the ways in which it could be flexibly used to hint at or underscore developments in mood and plot, from passages where the chorus describe their own song and emotional condition as they perform. In the first part of Sophokles' *Women of Trachis*, for example, the young women of the chorus are exhilarated at the prospect that Herakles is about to return from his long exile, and hence that their mistress and friend Deianeira, Herakles' wife, will be released from her unhappiness and anxiety. They strike up what is essentially a traditional wedding-song to greet the return of Herakles, so long absent that the idea of a 'remarriage' is not out of place (lines 205–15). In poetry and (we can safely assume) musical forms that draw on elements of Dionysiac worship, they then go on to modulate their song:

> I am raised up and I shall not
> reject the *aulos*, O tyrant of my mind!
> See how it excites me—
> Euoi!—
> the ivy now whirls me round in Backhic contest.
> (*Women of Trachis* 216–20)

Particularly striking here is the description of the Dionysian *aulos* as 'tyrant of my mind'. This imagined Dionysian music—which would surely have found an echo in the music heard by the audience from the stage musician—evokes the excitement that has taken over the chorus' minds. But as so often in tragedy, the excitement and joy summoned up at such times soon show a grim, dark side, the destructive side of the ambivalent god Dionysos. For at this very moment, it is not Herakles who appears, but his beautiful object of war-booty, Iole, the young woman who threatens to usurp Deianeira's position. Her arrival throws a darkly ironic shadow back on their opening 'wedding' song, which now takes on a very different meaning. As if realizing this radical change of perspective, the last few lines of the chorus' brief song 'change their tune' once more—this time to a hymn for the healing god, Paian (lines 221–3).

Passages like this hint at the enormous expressiveness of the music that is lost to us, but which for its audience was a fundamental part of the experience of drama. Whatever the original meanings of the terms, the second part of the words *komoidia* and *tragoidia* reminds us of the central importance of song and music (*oide* is a basic Greek word for 'song').

A special form of free speech

Whatever the relative importance of these and other ingredients in the early matrix of drama, by the time of our first texts (and even in earlier fragmentary remains) a quantum leap has taken place. In a short period the pioneers had developed the immensely sophisticated poetic performance with its many formal conventions that we find in Aischylos, whose *Persians* of 472 BCE is our first surviving tragedy, though he had been producing dramas for more than two decades by then. Among the pioneers we need to include in a sense the avid early audiences too: drama of this sort could only have succeeded and progressed so vigorously with the enthusiastic support and involvement of the audience itself.

Our first substantial evidence for comedy starts much later: the earliest example to survive in full is Aristophanes' *Acharnians* of 425. At the other end of the chronological scale, our last tragedy is Sophokles' *Oedipus at Kolonos*, produced five years after the poet's death in 406, although some scholars believe that the play ascribed to Euripides called the *Rhesos* is not by him but an early fourth-century successor. For comedy the situation is rather different, since we have examples of fourth-century Aristophanic comedy (the *Women in Assembly* of 393/2 and *Wealth* of 388) which show signs of incipient change in form and function. And in Menander's (in Greek, Menandros) plays from much later in the fourth century, we can perceive that a more radical change has taken place in comedy, away from the topical and political concerns of the fifth century. Our lack of anything but small fragments of tragedy of the later period prevents us from investigating the development of the genre, although we know that new works continued to be composed for production as vigorously as ever each year for more than two centuries. (See pp. 200–8 for subsequent developments in both comedy and tragedy.)

These dates are significant: they highlight the important fact that both tragedy and political comedy (what is often called 'Old' comedy) roughly coincide in time with the most energetic and turbulent period of Athenian history—and of Athenian democracy. Absolutely crucial to the growth and to the character of drama were the massive social, political, and historical developments that swept through Athenian society from the end of the sixth century. After the expulsion of the tyrants, Athens famously adopted a new form of political organization which placed an unprecedentedly large control of affairs in the hands of the *demos*, the 'people', as opposed to the well-born aristocrats who wielded power in most other Greek cities. With the reforms of Kleisthenes (about 508 BCE) that ushered in a significantly more democratic constitution, and subsequent increasingly 'radical' developments in the democracy at various points in the fifth century, old social and political relations were profoundly changed. The new institutions of the democracy made the adult male citizen population responsible for the running of the largest and most powerful city in Greece. All the major decisions touching the lives of the citizens, their families and dependants, were now technically in the hands of the mass citizen Assembly (*ekklesia*), while the new Council of five hundred (*boule*) prepared its agenda and executed its decisions. The third major institution of the democracy, and one for which the Athenians became famous (or notorious), was the system of people's courts (*dikasteria*), which met on around two hundred days every year. They were manned by large panels of citizen-judges (up to

2,001 in important trials), and they considered not only private legal quarrels but, more importantly, all major political trials (and there were many), as well as exercising extensive powers of control over the Assembly, Council, other magistrates, and political leaders. (For orators, see Ch. 6.)

The democratic citizenry in fifth-century Athens was thus loaded with unparalleled power; and with unparalleled responsibility. It was constantly called upon to make judgements of the utmost importance—who to make alliances and war with, who to elect to high office, whose advice to follow in the leadership of the city. And with the passing decades of the fifth century the responsibilities of the citizens increased on an exponential scale, as the city became the most prosperous and powerful in the Aegean. The successful repulse of the two major Persian invasions of Greece, in which Athens played a leading role, gave the newly democratic city a powerful psychological boost of collective confidence, and confirmed it in its adherence to the ideal of fierce independence and freedom that underpinned its notion of citizenship.

The defeat of Persia was influential at more than a psychological level, however. It allowed the Athenians to assume a position at the head of a defensive league of Greek states which was designed to repel further threats from the east. This league of allies initially had its centre on the sacred island of Delos at the heart of the Aegean; but, over the course of the four decades following the Persian Wars, it turned into the 'empire' or 'domination', a federation of subservient subjects under Athens' very firm control, its treasury of collected gold tribute now the temple of Athena on the Akropolis. Athenian citizens were now masters of an extensive and immensely powerful maritime league; and one which turned to increasingly repressive means of administration and control over its 'allies'—a term which became a hollow euphemism for 'subjects'. The city's expansionism gradually drew it into conflict with the other major power in Greece, Sparta and her allies, and the last thirty years of the century saw the protracted and exhausting war (which we call the Peloponnesian War) between these two states and former allies which ended in the defeat of Athens. The pressures of the war had exacerbated social tensions within Athens, especially between rich and poor, and between city-dwellers and farmers whose lands had been left to be ravaged by the invading Spartan army. As so often happens in long wars, conventional morality and accepted values tended to be abused in practice and questioned in theory.

Throughout this seismic period of immense political, social, and historical change, the Athenians made of their theatre, not a place of escapist entertainment, but a vast sounding-board: a place in which to expose, explore, and scrutinize the ramifications of this constant upheaval and change. With tragedy, this usually operated at a level of powerful generality: though the stories told in tragedy have a very concrete particularity about them, the medium of heroic myth also provides a notable sense of distance from the here and now.

Comedy's approach was much more 'full frontal': the burning social and political issues of the day could be opened up directly on the comic stage. Comedy set itself up as a watchdog of political safety, relentlessly questioning the wisdom of the leaders and the led alike—of prominent politicians, other poetic 'advisers' (especially tragedians) and thinkers, as well as of the *demos* itself, whose gullibility and waywardness were not beyond comedy's criticism. Comedy became a special form of political criticism, a striking instance of the democratic ideal of *parrhesia* or 'free speech'. This is made clear by an anonymous writer on political matters who lived in the age of old comedy, and whose views are so radically opposed to the democratic form of politics as to have earned him the name (from modern scholars) of 'the Old Oligarch':

> the democrats do not allow ridicule and abuse of the *demos*, to avoid being criticized themselves, but in the case of individuals they encourage anyone who wishes, in the sure knowledge that the individual is not as a rule one of the *demos* or the masses but someone rich, well-born or powerful. (*The Constitution of the Athenians* 2. 18)

Although his own political views have caused the author to ignore the ways in which comedy can also criticize the *demos*, this is a precious piece of contemporary evidence for its important function as a democratic institution of criticism and ridicule. Generally this comic representation of the city's preoccupations came with a sufficiently large dose of the ridiculous, the inverted, and the fantastic to ensure that its engagement with 'live' issues did not overstep the boundaries (including laws of slander) which marked out the proper place of criticism in the democratic city. Nonetheless we should remember that in his speech of self-defence before an Athenian court when on trial for his life in 399, Sokrates supposedly spoke of the many slanderers who had created the utterly false reputation for which he was now being condemned: 'the most unreasonable thing of all is that it's impossible to discover and reveal their names—except in the case of a comic poet' (Plato, *Apology* 18d).

A range of theatrical occasions

> Genuine Athenians are shrewd students of the arts and untiring theatre-goers
> (Herakleides (third-century travel writer), *On the Greek Cities* 1. 4)

Before looking further at the ways drama engaged with the concerns of its audience, it is worth while to talk in more concrete terms about just where and how they experienced their theatre. The principal audience in any discussion will be the one that gathered in spring each year on the south-east slope of the Akropolis in Athens in the open-air theatre in the sanctuary of Dionysos, in celebration of his 'Great', or 'City' festival. It is worth pointing first, however, to a couple of other places where, by around the middle of the fifth century, the theatre-hungry Athenians produced and consumed their drama.

One of these is the so-called 'Rural' Dionysia, the name 'Rural' contrasting explicitly with the 'City' of the major event in Athens. Rural Dionysia were held by the smaller units of which the entire region of Attica, town and country, was composed—the 'demes' or 'municipalities', of which there were some 139 in all. The demes were mini-communities with their own religious traditions and political institutions at a local level, and among the gods worshipped with enthusiasm in the demes, Dionysos had an especially favoured position. Given that most of these demes were in fact 'rural' in the sense that they were located in the countryside outside the urban centre, the prominence of Dionysos, a god who was more at home beyond the city walls and identified intimately with the vine grown there, should not come as a surprise. The farmer-protagonist of Aristophanes' *Peace* called Trygaios—'Vintager'—gives a position of prominence to Dionysia in a list of the pleasures brought back to the countryside by the return of peace:

> she has the smell of harvest, hospitality and Dionysia;
> of *auloi*, tragedies, the songs of Sophokles; of thrushes, and Euripidean verselets.
>
> (*Peace* 530–2)

There is also a strong tradition that puts the very earliest performances of both comedy and tragedy in a rural setting before moving to the city. I mentioned the possible activities of Thespis in Ikarion (a deme), which claimed to be the first home of tragic performances. This may have some basis to it: there was a myth which associated Dionysos' first appearance in Attica with Ikarion, whose inhabitants he taught the art of turning grapes into wine. In the fifth century they held a well-organized Dionysia of their own at which, unsurprisingly, tragedy was the premier event.

Other scraps of evidence, mainly archaeological, give us tantalizing glimpses of the kinds of performance staged at these local Dionysia, and so illuminate the bigger picture of the formation of a sophisticated theatrical audience in Attica. For instance, we know that in a number of demes the community's central meeting-place, its agora, also served as its theatre—a fact that underscores the inherently 'political' character of drama in the broadest sense. These performances will not have had the grandeur of the urban event, but that will have been counterbalanced by the pride that obviously went with staging a

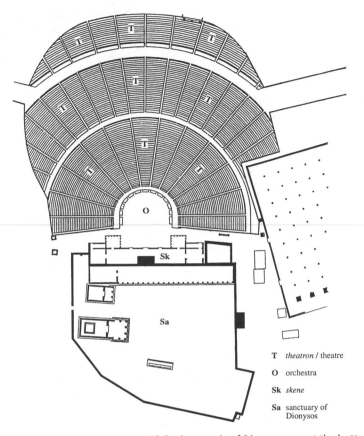

T *theatron* / theatre

O orchestra

Sk *skene*

Sa sanctuary of
Dionysos

THE SACRED SPACE FOR THEATRE. While the temple of Dionysos was at the bottom of the slope at the south-east corner of the Akropolis, the entire slope above was part of his sacred precinct, and became the area for the spectators of drama. Nearly all, if not all, of the great dramas of fifth-century Athens were first performed in this space.

dramatic festival and we should not assume that they were third-rate events. Some lucky inscriptional finds have made it clear that some of the really 'big names'—Sophokles, Euripides, and Aristophanes among them—produced their works in the demes, possibly (but not necessarily) as 'repeats' after an urban performance. If they *were* repeats, this is precious evidence for the formation of the very first 'repertory' theatre of sorts. The general principle of Athenian theatre was that every play was created for a single, non-repeatable occasion, for a fixed 'slot' at a particular festival in a particular year, so that the idea of reperformance was foreign to this culture of the occasion. We are told that after the death of Aischylos the Athenians passed a law permitting the reproduction of his works: a recognition (if true) of his unique status not just as a 'literary classic' but also as an 'educator' of the city. It was only later, in the 380s, that performances of 'old' tragedy and comedy became a regular feature of the City festival. So the Rural festivals may have played an important role in fostering what was clearly a high degree of familiarity among the audience with their drama.

By the late fifth century there was also a large-scale Dionysia in the Peiraieus, technically a deme but scarcely 'rural', since this was Athens' massive and cosmopolitan port-town. Sokrates made a special effort to leave his usual urban haunts when Euripides was competing at the Peiraieus, and for once he was not isolated in his enthusiasm. We hear from Plato of those 'spectacle-lovers' who 'run around to all the Dionysia, never missing one either in the towns or in the country-villages' (*Republic* 5. 475d). Some at least of these 'local' events clearly anticipated an audience made up of more than just their own community. The Peiraieus theatre probably held over 5,000 spectators, and there are some indications that demes co-ordinated their timetabling so as not to have their Dionysia clash, no doubt so that people (and performers) could move from one to another.

Another Dionysiac festival, called the Lenaia, was held in late January, roughly two months before the City Dionysia, which took place in early spring. (The name 'Lenaia' comes from the Greek word for a wine-press, an essential piece of technology in the worship of Dionysos.) This too was a festival of the city as a whole, but a less grand occasion than *the* City Dionysia. It too was probably held in the theatre under the Akropolis (although this, like just about everything else to do with the festival, is a matter of controversy). This would make sense for our understanding of a comedy like Aristophanes' *Lysistrate*, which was a Lenaian comedy. A central plank of Lysistrate's plan in this play to force the men of Athens to end the war is the seizure of the Akropolis by the women of Athens; and this ancient, natural fortress, charged with political, religious, economic, and historical significance, almost becomes a member of the comic cast. The effect would have been that much greater if the actual Akropolis formed a natural backdrop to the performance, looming at the backs of the audience.

From an audience perspective, a number of features of the Lenaia were revealingly different from the City Dionysia. While tragedy was clearly the 'senior' performance at the City Dionysia, comedy seems to have had the upper hand at the Lenaia. Of the eleven surviving comedies of Aristophanes, five were certainly or probably performed at the Lenaia. This is in keeping with the less grand character of the festival. January was no time for travel in Greece, so the large numbers of foreign visitors who attended the City Dionysia will not have been present then. Without these 'outsiders', and at a time of year when people were starting to give some thought to what was to come in the militarily and politically more active half of the year in spring and summer, the Lenaian audience had a more domestic focus. As much is clear from a passage of Aristophanes' *Acharnians*, which also throws important light on the claims of comedy—in competition, as often, with tragedy—to a role as a mouthpiece of serious advice for the city.

Acharnians was produced after more than five hard years of war with Sparta which had seen much of the countryside destroyed, including the ancient farmlands of Acharnai, a deme whose angry, bellicose old men form the chorus of the play. The comic hero, Dikaiopolis—'Mr Just City'—is forced to defend himself before these men, his head, quite literally, on the chopping-block, for having dared to negotiate a private peace for himself and, what's more, for suggesting that the Spartans 'are not entirely responsible for our troubles' (line 310). This is the kind of remark that may well have been historically and politically true, but could only ever be uttered on the comic stage.

> Do not be indignant with me, members of the audience,
> if, though a beggar, I speak before the Athenians
> about the city in a comedy.
> For even comedy is acquainted with justice.
>
> (ll. 497–500)

('*trugedy*', the word Aristophanes uses for 'comedy' here, is a punning formation based on the word for 'grape-pressings' and is clearly meant to make a proud stand beside its more elevated rival, 'tragedy'.)

Dikaiopolis goes on to preface his 'shocking but just' advice for the city with the remark that

> This time Kleon won't allege that I'm
> slandering the city in the presence of foreigners,

for we are just ourselves and it's the Lenaian competition
and there are no foreigners here yet;
neither tribute money nor troops have come from the allied cities
   [as they would two months later on the occasion of the City Dionysia].
This time we are alone, ready-hulled;
for I reckon the metics as the civic bran.

(ll. 502–8)

Kleon was the leading politician of the day, and Aristophanes had already crossed him because of an attack in an earlier comedy, perhaps stinging him to launch a counter-attack in the courts. This sort of comedy was, then, no harmless entertainment cut off from consequences in the 'real' world. Kleon's complaint seems to have taken the form of a claim that the poet had been excessively critical of the city and its leaders (i.e. himself) before an 'international' audience (the City Dionysia is implied) at a time of war when 'solidarity' before outsiders was paramount. So in this play for the Lenaia, where there were no foreigners present (on the metics or 'resident foreigners' see below), the comic character Dikaiopolis puts forward his author's rejoinder at the same time as he makes his own self-defence before the Acharnians. Audiences shape the way drama can speak.

One last (and somewhat neglected) context in which the Athenians consumed their drama: this is the very different, much more 'private' world of the (largely) upper-class drinking party known as the symposion. Here wine, conversation, pleasurable indulgences, and solo performances of various kinds circulated freely (see pp. 46–7). It had for centuries been part of the rules of the symposiastic game to be able to show off one's culture by singing a poem of some recognized master, and it is clear that some parts of tragic plays found their way into this intimate world of small-scale 'reperformance'. Given that every tragedy had a chorus of fifteen men, who had spent some months in rigorous physical and mnemonic training to learn its complex dance-songs, we should probably imagine those with such experience as important in this kind of (partial) reperformance. It is clear that an upbringing in the ways of *choreia*, the dance-and-song-culture of choral performance, was to some extent the reserve of those with the time and leisure to devote to it; and this group overlapped significantly with the kind of people who attended symposia. A story told about the defeated Athenian army in Sicily at the disastrous close of the expedition there in 413 BCE throws a fascinating ray of light on this different means of disseminating knowledge of tragedy. Some of the Athenian soldiers who were being held prisoner in the quarries outside Syracuse are said to have won their freedom by singing Euripidean songs to their Euripides-mad Sicilian captors.

The programme of the great Dionysia

The time, wealth, and level of administrative sophistication the Athenians devoted to their premier festival of Dionysos speak volumes for the importance they attached to their drama. For the best part of a week in spring the city effectively suspended all other official business. The democratic Assembly, the Council, and courts did not meet during the festival. By means of a major civic institution known as the *choregia* (literally 'leadership of a chorus') Athens required a minority of its rich élite to fund the organizational and performative 'heart' of drama, its chorus, as a form of highly honorific obligation. These *choregoi*, a kind of ancient version of the film producer—and with all the arrogance and self-interest shown by some of their modern counterparts—lavished vast sums of their wealth on drama. We hear of costumes with gold thread, gold crowns for their chorus members, specialized dietary regimes for the months of training, upkeep, and pay during this period, the hiring of various experts and of training-grounds. Individual *choregoi*, who were themselves competing for the prize, spent genuine fortunes on an evanescent event lasting only for part of a single day. And to these sums the city itself added more for the large numbers of beasts for sacrifice (over 200 bulls in one year), for the pay of the actors, prizes for poets, actors, and *choregoi*, and for the upkeep of the theatre itself, including, for most of the classical period until a stone theatre was built during the fourth century, the construction of temporary wooden benches for the bulk of the audience.

Certainly by the fourth century there were extensive regulations covering every aspect of the festival's organization, the conduct of its participants, the award of prizes, even to some extent, the behaviour of its audience. This was an occasion of truly mass participation, the largest annual gathering in Athens, and more than twice the size of a full Assembly. At somewhere between 15,000 and 20,000 strong, the comic hyperbole that describes the theatre audience as 'countless myriads' (*Wasps* 1010), 'the great crowd of people, thousands of discerning spectators' (*Frogs* 676), becomes perfectly intelligible. It is clear that it was never difficult to fill the theatre to its capacity, and this close-packed environment will have helped generate a shared, collective character of response to the emotional horrors of tragedy and the humour of comedy. Under such conditions strong emotions are infectious and readily and rapidly transmitted through a large crowd—and so too is laughter. The excitement and tensions created in such a gathering were high, and only increased by consumption of Dionysos' special gift, wine. We know of a law that prevented people taking advantage of these circumstances by, for instance, making attacks on their personal enemies. A man called Ktesikles was actually put to

COMIC SPONSORS. This extremely interesting and well-painted vase, produced in Taras in southern Italy in c.380 BCE, was first published in 1991. It shows a scene from a comedy with stage doors, costumes, masks, etc., but includes a figure on the left (labelled Aigisthos) in full tragic outfit. On either side of the slave posturing on a wool basket are two men with the label 'choregos', evidently representing the wealthy citizens who put up the money for dramatic performances.

death by a democratic court for striking an enemy with a whip as he took part in the procession. Questions of social order and status were a significant issue in the overall structure and conduct of this great festival, just as they also lay at the heart of the drama that was its most remarkable feature.

Although much of the elaborate programme of events is obscure to us, we know enough to form an idea of the grandeur and sense of display that permeated the occasion. Formal proceedings began, on the first of some five days, with a huge procession, made up of representatives of various segments of Athenian society, including of course adult (male) citizens; metics (both men and women); deputations of the states of the empire, during the period of Athenian hegemony; young Athenian men on the point of manhood and citizenship known as ephebes; the city's officials; the *choregoi*, and probably their competing teams. Opinion divides as to the involvement in the procession of Athenian women of full status. Some believe that the figure of the *kanephoros* or 'basket-carrier' who led the whole procession carrying the sacrificial knife hidden in the ritual basket, was the sole representative of the female half of the Attic population, while there is on the other hand some evidence (see Menander, fr. 55) to suggest that at least by the later fourth century women took part, if only in the capacity of spectators of the passing procession.

This procession performed a number of important functions. It not only conducted the effigy of Dionysos to a position of honour in the theatre or sanctuary. It also conveyed to the sacred altar of the god the animals to be slaughtered and consumed. The blood of hundreds of beasts was made to flow each year, and as Paul Cartledge has recently put it, 'the prospect of state-subsidised entertainment (and instruction) coupled with a beef supper liberally lubricated by Dionysos' special juice might have been a very attractive proposition indeed'. But the procession also had the important effect of dramatizing a sense of the community's identity, of producing a kind of social map on which each of the various groups represented had their 'proper' place and role, symbolized in part by what they carried and wore in the procession. The metics, for instance, were marked out by a special crimson robe, and they seem to have carried various utensils that symbolized their secondary and perhaps their 'productive' role in the community (bowls, water-pitchers). We hear of citizens simply dressing as they chose and carrying a wineskin, in honour of Dionysos no doubt, but such a show of piety would also have allowed these citizens, for whom the festival was principally designed, to refresh themselves on the way.

That the representatives of the allied states were granted a prominent place in the procession adds a significant dimension to the whole event, and distinguishes it sharply from the Lenaia. These non-Athenian Greeks, many of whom will have travelled long distances to reach the festival, were also required to deposit the tribute they paid to the imperial project led by Athens. This took place during another, special preliminary to the tragic competition, and it may be they even had to deliver it, ingot by ingot, in the orchestra of the theatre, before the assembled audience. Such an affirmation by Athens—perhaps 'dramatization' is the right word—of her position of power and control stands as a striking prelude to the tragic dramas that followed. For in the world of tragedy, the immense confidence that feeds such grand military and imperial projects is so often open to doubt, or shown to lead precisely to tragedy.

The disastrous ambitions of the Persian King Xerxes are the clearest case. At the start of the *Persians* the chorus of Persian elders sings of the military success and confidence of the great king and his people:

For divine fate has prevailed since
it enjoined the Persians to wage wars,
which destroy towers, ramparts,
and the glad tumult of horsemen,
and cities overthrown—
When the vast ocean was foaming,
by the winds boisterous whitened,
then they learned, trusting to cables
and to pontoons which convey men,
to scan the sacred sea.

(ll. 93–106)

But they immediately go on to think of the 'cunning deception of god' that leads men astray—a lesson they and their king will learn to their cost. Later in the play, the ghost of Xerxes' dead father, Dareios, draws a general moral from the Persian loss that could also have powerful resonance for the one-time victors over Persia, the Athenians themselves, on their way to becoming empire-builders: '. . . and let no one, scorning his present fortune, in lust for more, ruin his great prosperity' (ll. 824–6).

It is not only 'barbarians' in tragedy who demonstrate such behaviour. Aischylos' Agamemnon shows signs of a similar mentality and action. In the *Agamemnon*, he is very much a 'leader of ships' (*Agamemnon* 1227, cf. 96–8, 166–7), just as Athens was in 458 very much a 'leader of ships' in the Aegean. The king's maritime enterprise against Troy is depicted not as a simple pious exaction of justice, but as an act of terrible violence to the city itself, its crops, cattle, property, and religious places, bringing destruction to his own army, and of course to his own family. In its unforgiving focus on the suffering inflicted by war, particularly on the innocent and weak, Euripides' *Trojan Women* of the other end of the fifth century (415 BCE) obliterates any residual glamour that such warfare and imperialism may have had.

The competitions that formed the climax of the Dionysia occupied a full three or four days, and brought the city to the theatre from dawn till dusk. Simply being a diligent and attentive member of this audience will have been physically exacting, to say nothing of its emotional and psychological demands. Remember also the immense athleticism needed on the part of citizens for participation in one of the choruses—tragic, comic or dithyrambic—at the centre of these contests. That actors and chorus-members trained so hard and long, in particular to produce an ample volume of sound, clear articulation, and (in the case of the chorus) accurate delivery in unison, shows how important it was felt to be that everyone in this massive audience should be able to pick up the finest details of each performance. And that the Athenian audience was a sensitive (and exacting) critic is shown, for example, by the harsh treatment (especially the comic ridicule) the tragic actor Hegelochos received when he slipped up in enunciating a line of Euripides' *Orestes* (line 279), so that 'once more I see the calm after the tempest' came out as 'once more I see the weasel from the tempest'.

A comic chorus of birds imagines the useful fantasy of spectators having wings with which they could flit off when bored by tragedy (a bias we expect from comedy) and come back in the afternoon (Aristophanes, *Birds* 786–9). Weariness and hunger were doubtless part of the theatrical experience, the latter staved off by provision of snacks in the theatre—when the acting was particularly bad, as Aristotle tells us, suggesting that absorbed involvement was the norm. Theophrastos' caricature of 'The Man lacking perceptivity' (or simply 'The Dolt') demonstrates this quality by being the sole person asleep all throughout the performance, and being left behind when everyone else has gone.

We should not pass too quickly over the very fact that for the Athenians drama was an essentially, and intensely, *competitive* event. It was judged by a carefully selected panel of citizen judges whose actions could later be legally scrutinized for their propriety. And it is clear that the audience as a whole felt the panel of judges should take notice of its own collective view, as expressed (so Plato and others inform us), by whistling, shouts, hissing, and kicking against the wooden benches. The same idea is reflected in comedy through the god Dionysos' response to Euripides' indignant question, when he has been overlooked by Dionysos in favour of Aischylos in his judgement of the 'battle of the poets' in Hades:

> EURIPIDES: And do you dare look in my face, after that shameful deed?
> DIONYSOS: What's 'shameful', if the audience think it not so?
>
> (*Frogs* 1474–5)

Built into the whole experience was the sense that every individual tragic treatment of the mythic heritage, and every fantastic comic vision, was pressing its claims, giving its 'advice' and its pleasure directly alongside other, competing visions. This tendency to invite multiple and competitive views of the city in its drama is perhaps one of its most democratic qualities. It is also a sobering thought, from our historical perspective, that the competitive structure of Athenian drama consigned many works to oblivion after an unsuccessful appearance. Euripides' *Medeia* was lucky to survive its placement *third* in the contest of 431. This should make us wary of forgetting the many other poets who were involved in the fierce competitive culture of the Athenian dramatic festivals, but whose work did not survive the perilous path of transmission through antiquity and beyond, except in the most fragmentary form. Success-ful contenders from the fifth century include Ion of Chios, Sophokles' son Iophon and the Agathon immortalized in Plato's *Symposion*. While the fourth century—long regarded as a period of rapid decline—produced poets like Asty-damas and Theodektes who were much admired and long reread. The situation is even more extreme with comedy, given the survival in substantial form of only a single fifth-century poet. But Aristophanes' direct predecessors and rivals, Eupolis and Kratinos in particular, were giants in the field (the latter won six first prizes at the City Dionysia, three at the Lenaia), doing much to forge the very shape and content of Athenian political comedy.

Dithyramb was the first event on the programme (see Ch. 2, p. 63). Dithy-ramb had for decades contained elaborate narratives of stories largely or entirely unrelated to its recipient god, Dionysos, and was in this parallel to tragedy, which to some ancient observers already seemed to have 'nothing to do with Dionysos'. And there was a fair degree of productive influence between genres at the Dionysia from an early date. One dithyramb by the great Kean poet Bakchylides—his *Theseus* (poem 18) of as early as *c.*490 BCE—is a dialogue, in song, between a chorus of Athenian citizens and their leader, the mythical King Aigeus, father of Theseus. This generic mixing has its counterpart in an aspect of the audience's perspective that it is difficult, if not impossible, for us to re-create imaginatively: the experience of witnessing a set of performances in four very different but related styles over a number of days—dithyramb, com-edy, tragedy, and satyr play.

Thus, even before their drama had begun, the Athenians had been inundated with twenty sung narratives of divine and heroic mythology in these dithy-rambs. Moreover, the emotional and psychological temperature had been fur-ther raised by the keen competition between the tribes for the prize in these two events—and it has been argued that the audience in the theatre was actu-ally arranged into wedges of seats belonging to each of the ten tribes. The next day was (probably—again, most details are open to debate) entirely com-edy's: five individual plays by different poets. The next, and climactic, three full days were for tragedy. Or rather, for tragedy and satyr play. For most of the classical period, each of the three tragedians chosen to compete (a decision resting in the hands of a leading city official, the Arkhon Eponymos) presented their audience with three tragedies followed by a single satyr play. In Aischylos' day, the three tragedies often formed a trilogy in the strong sense that they presented a continuous, connected narrative sequence, as in the case of our sole surviving example, the *Oresteia* (made up of *Agamemnon*, the *Libation Bearers*, the *Eumenides*). Even the satyr play, the *Proteus*, may have had some connection to the tragic story—though a somewhat oblique one, since it seems to have dealt with an episode in the return home from Troy of Agamemnon's brother, Menelaos.

It is important to recall the arrival of the satyrs at the end of every grand and gruelling tragic production. Satyr play—'playful tragedy' as one ancient critic dubbed it—shared with tragedy its heroic cast, as well as much of its language and conventions; and the actors may well have used the same costumes they wore in the immediately preceding dramas. But to these were added, in every case, a chorus of satyrs, those mythical ithyphallic creatures of the wild, half-man and half-beast (equine or caprine) who frequently attended Dionysos. Hedonists and masters of misrule, obsessed with wine and the pursuit of all physical pleasures, the satyrs also show a surprising intellectual curiosity—they are experimenters and explorers. A common motif of their drama was the 'discovery' of important items of culture: musical instruments, products of metal-work, fire, perhaps even woman herself (Pandora). They were also instrumental in conveying the great gift of Dionysos—wine—and the means of its produc-tion to mortals. As Richard Seaford has put it, 'The satyr is an ambiguous crea-ture, cruder than a man and yet somehow wiser, combining mischief with wisdom and animality with divinity.'

It is very difficult for us to gauge the impact on the audience of this satyric finale, but the sudden change of gear, the injection of riotous Dionysiac satyr-dom into the elevated world of heroic tragedy, must have served an important psychological function. Emotional 'release' from the intensity of long hours of tragedy is too simplistic an explanation by itself, though surely one factor behind this arrangement. The satyrs' energetic and grotesque explorations of the machinery of Greek culture will have been another important attraction of this fourth Dionysian performance. And another, the way in which it brought performers and audience alike into an intimate relation, at the end of each day, with a more joyous, boisterous, masculine, and rather less threatening side of the worship of their god.

The City Dionysia alone thus needed five new comedies, nine new tragedies plus three new satyr plays every year (not to mention the twenty, much shorter, dithyrambs)—most if not all of which, it was normally expected, would never be performed again. This demand for so many entirely new large-scale per-formances was something unusual in the context of ancient Greek poetic pro-duction. By the start of the fifth century epic was predominantly a genre of the reperformance of a limited number of canonical classics (see pp. 35–6). There was to be sure a vast range of poetic composition taking place in connection with all manner of social and religious occasions, but the 'literary' culture of classical Athens represents a quite new direction and scale of production. Unusual too is its propensity for innovation and diversity. We have already seen the radical nature of tragic form as *drama*, as myth 'made live'. In fact, all of its distinctive features are innovatory: its deployment of many formal elements which, though found in separate usage previously, were never combined as they are in the complex manner of drama (choral song, including a range of formal hymns and other songs from specific contexts, like victory songs, wedding songs; iambic verse; the mask and so on).

Also innovative was the technology of the stage itself, a completely new space which encouraged experiment. By about 460 the major step had been taken to introduce at the back of the open acting and dancing area a stage building, or screen (*skene*), with all the possibilities it offered as a device to represent the face of any manner of buildings (royal palaces, caves, military encampments, the homes of 'ordinary' citizens). This introduced a powerful dynamic between closed and open spaces, between the visible and the invisible. Soon a device to reveal the secrets of this interior space was developed (the *ekkyklema*); another (the *mechane*) to exploit the upper register usually reserved for gods over the top of the stage building. The stage-front itself probably saw the development of illusionistic scene-painting on movable and 'disposable' panels. All of these innovations may seem tame to a modern audience brought up on the hyper-technological entertainment culture of films or musicals, but they must have been radical, even shocking innovations in their time. From the comic side, the demand from the audience for constant originality and innovation is formulated by the chorus in Aristophanes' *Women in Assembly*:

> Make sure your plans
> are quite original in word and deed.
> (This audience hates to see old stuff served up again!)
> (ll. 578–80)

The drive to innovation and experiment evident in the Athenian theatre parallels the restless energies of Athenian society as a whole in this period. The stereotype of the Athenian character put in the mouth of a Corinthian by the historian Thoukydides surely has some core of truth: 'given to innovation and quick to form plans and to put their decisions into action . . . bold beyond their strength, risk-taking beyond their better judgement . . . ' (1. 70).

The spectators, the chorus, and the drama

When they referred to themselves as an audience the Athenians tended to use the term *theatai* or the related *theomenoi*—'spectators' or 'watchers'; their theatre, the *theatron*, was literally 'the place for watching'. This emphasis on the 'spectatorial' is crucial. Much of drama's power lay in its emphatically visual quality, on the shared experience of its *theatai* in witnessing what went on on stage. And drama was, in an important sense, also a communal act of 'self-regard'.

In its shape and size, the *theatron* focused and intensified the attention of an unprecedentedly large group. Plato writes of 'more than thirty thousand Greeks' in the theatre, and even when modern scholars have deflated this exaggeration by as much as half (see above pp. 84–5), we are left with a gathering on a vast scale by ancient standards. The audience sat in a slightly more than semicircular space that fanned out, probably in wedge-shaped blocks, from the level area where chorus and actors performed. The rows of seats were fairly steeply raked up the natural hillside, so that the considerable distance separating those seated towards the back and the acting area did not adversely affect their line of vision. This spatial arrangement also meant, significantly, that the audience 'looked at itself' to a large extent. In the bright open-air theatre in the early Athenian spring the *theatai* could very easily see their fellows all around and opposite them. This physical reality of 'self-observation' was matched by the nature of the performances: the business of 'self-scrutiny' was at the heart of classical dramatic experience.

As I have already stressed, the technology of the stage encouraged visual experiment. Although we depend on the meagrest sources to conjure up the visual dimension of drama, it is abundantly clear that a good deal of the impact of both tragedy and comedy was visual. Dramatic costume was an object of special fascination and, particularly in the case of comedy, sometimes of stunningly ingenious construction (one can only wonder at the dress that brought to life comic choruses of cities, frogs, birds, waspish judges, islands . . .). The costumes of tragedy may have presented the Athenians with a degree of lavishness and exotic luxury they did not often see, given their supposedly austere habits of normal dress. The luxury of Persian and other 'barbarian' ways was paraded before them, the majesty of the gods themselves evoked, the wealth and splendour of heroic kings, queens, and tyrants. 'Silver vessels and rich purple fabric are suitable for tragedies, not for life,' as a fourth-century comic poet puts it (Philemon, fr. 105).

But the visual dimension of drama and dramatic costume in particular were much more than a matter of dazzling the eye. Costume was a crucial resource for evoking the other peoples and other places where dramas were set, and as the genre developed, the very business of taking on a costume and playing a role itself became an increasingly fruitful thematic device. Euripides notoriously dressed some of his heroes in rags, and used this 'shock tactic' to pursue dramatic reflection on issues such as the gulf between appearance and reality, between innate character and socially constructed status and identity, on the nature of fiction itself. His *Helen* is the most breathtaking example, with its 'two' Helens, one phantom, one real, its royal Menelaos in rags, its escape plot involving disguise and deception. Drama here used its own conventions to reflect on and, at least by Euripides' day, to question the conventional in society.

In many comedies on-stage role-playing and costume change are central to the plot. Athenian women elaborately disguise themselves as men, even take a comic lesson in how to speak and 'act' like men in order to infiltrate the Assembly and so take power in the city (*Women in Assembly*). Their leader, Praxagora—'Mrs Public Action'—has called them together in the opening scene, with all the 'props' of male attire, filched from their husbands—men's shoes, walking-sticks, cloaks; one has even let her under-arm hair grow and tanned her skin to look more masculine. But women have no experience in public speech:

> But that's precisely why we've gathered here,
> to rehearse our lines before the meeting starts.
> So get your beard attached without delay,
> And likewise anyone else's who's practised speaking.
> (ll. 116–21)

Dionysos himself in the *Frogs* dresses up as Herakles (if not very convincingly) to descend, as Herakles had, to Hades. In a spectacularly self-consciously (meta-)theatrical manner, Dikaiopolis in the *Acharnians* rifles through Euripides' entire theatrical wardrobe and comes away as the tragic hero Telephos so that he can speak with added pathos as a wronged beggar-king before the angry Acharnians. In tragedy, Orestes regularly uses disguise in order to pull off his planned murder of his mother and her lover and restore himself to power in Argos—dressing up, in Aischylos' *Libation Bearers*, as a visiting stranger 'with all the equipment' and even talking of putting on an accent, 'imitating the speech of Phokian language' (lines 560, 564). In Sophokles' *Philoktetes*, under Odysseus' direction a sailor stages an elaborate 'mini-drama' to try to deceive the wretched Philoktetes into leaving Lemnos with them. The manipulative and deceptive potential of role-playing is explored here, and it is, significantly, rejected by the outcome of events. Although tricked by this 'plot' into leaving, Philoktetes' departure is prevented by an attack of his painful illness at the last minute, and the experience of witnessing this at close quarters profoundly troubles the young Neoptolemos:

NEOPTOLEMOS: It's not just now a powerful kind of pity for this man
has come upon me; it started long ago.

PHILOKTETES: Take pity on me, boy: don't make yourself the object of men's abuse for tricking me.

(965–8)

Neoptolemos is so moved by this spectacle of suffering that he confesses the deception and promises to stand by the old hero against all the demands of his superiors and the needs of the Greek army.

Role-playing (appropriately) permeates that most Dionysiac of dramas, Euripides' *Bakchai*. The god of the mask himself masterminds the whole drama as its 'stage manager' from the first words of the prologue when he announces he will himself be disguised as a 'Lydian stranger' (lines 1–5). Under the influence of the 'new' god the old former king Kadmos and blind seer Teiresias dress as bacchants. And, at the critical question of the 'stranger'—'Are you not eager to be a spectator of maenads?' (line 829)—the young king Pentheus, enemy of the god, submits himself to an elaborate 'cross-dressing' as a woman on stage, under the god's direction. In fact his disguise will prove worthless, and he himself, perched in a pine-tree, will become the object of the attention of all, and the centre of a horrific and 'real' drama, not its distant spectator (see esp. line 1075).

Complete inundation by the visual image, especially the moving image of film and television, is so much part of the modern Western cultural experience that it requires a great effort to imagine the profound psychological impact of seeing the 'theatricalization of myth' for the first time, to see those familiar but distant figures of myth and religion live and breathe before the eye. This radical shift into a form of performance that Plato would later call 'full *mimesis*'—('imitation')—see p. 166—escalated to an altogether new level the intensity of the emotional charge of Greek poetry. And conservative critics like Plato regarded this as a seriously invasive psychological and moral threat for its audience, at best allowing them to indulge in 'shameless emotions'. We hear of audiences spellbound, or weeping at the performances of epic (see p. 36), where the only visual impact was that conjured up in the imagination of the listeners. But drama took the further, enormous step of enacting and *showing* the actions of its heroes. The accounts we hear of the audience's response are correspondingly more intense. *Theatai* are 'stunned' or 'struck'. Aristophanes' comic Euripides accuses Aischylos of 'blasting them out of their wits and astounding them' (*Frogs* 962). One of the most famous tragic actors of the late fifth century, Kallipides, supposedly prided himself on being able to fill the seats with weeping multitudes (Xenophon, *Symposion* 3. 11) An apocryphal story even tells of women miscarrying in fear at the sight of the Erinyes in Aischlyos' *Eumenides*. Even though apocryphal, stories of this sort suggest the remembered or imagined impact of such spectacles on their original audience.

There were of course limits on what was shown. Physical violence on stage was slight, though not unknown. Aias in Sophokles' *Aias* delivers his last, immensely moving speech to an empty stage (the chorus having, ironically, gone off in search of him), and at its end he throws himself on the sword he has planted upright in the earth.

> The slayer stands so it will be its sharpest, –
> if I've the time for such a calculation:
> a gift of Hektor, the most hated man of all
> I ever met, most loathsome to look upon.
> So it stands fixed in the enemy soil of Troy,
> freshly sharpened by the iron-devouring whetstone.
> I fixed it there, and carefully set it out
> to bring this man the comfort of quick death.
> So, I am well equipped.
>
> (ll. 815–23)

Whatever was actually shown to the audience, this is certainly an on-stage suicide, and the great body of the dead hero remains there for much of the rest of the play, to be fought over by his brother Teukros and his enemy Agamemnon.

The acts of most extreme violence, especially those of death (as in the case of the women who go inside to end their lives) or mutilation (as in the case of Oedipus' self-blinding) are nearly always concealed from the audience's gaze by taking place behind the stage-front. But such concealment at the critical moment has the effect of intensifying their impact; and what is not shown on stage is described after the fact by messengers, often at great length and in vivid detail. 'How? Tell us, how?' is an often-repeated request of the chorus on hearing the report of a death, and it triggers a verbal cavalcade. The messenger from inside the palace where Oedipus has blinded himself frames his account with' these words:

> What deeds am I to tell of, you to see! . . .
> He shouts for someone to unbar the gates
> and to display to Thebes the parricide. . . .
> . . . these wounds are greater
> than he can bear—as you shall see; for look!
> They draw the bolts. A sight you will behold
> to move the pity even of an enemy.
>
> (*Oedipus Tyrannos* 1224, 1287–8, 1293–6)

A complex interplay between the visual and the verbal is crucial to drama and its power.

At their tragic performances the Athenians gathered together to witness 'grand' but terrible actions: violence and suffering of all kinds; the trampling underfoot of accepted values; the abuse of social relations, especially troubling when, as so often, they are those especially strong ties that should bind *philoi* or one's 'close circle' of family and friends together. Rather, brothers fight and kill one another, parents kill children, and children parents, wives deceive and kill their husbands. And yet there was benefit to be derived from such things: the power of horror, and of fear, could be beneficial. A sense of order, of the proper boundaries to be observed in relations with one's fellow man and with the gods, could be built, in part, from a controlled contemplation of their disruption. The general point is made by the Erinyes (Furies) in the concluding play of Aischylos' great *Oresteia*. Turned at last from their fury at their defeat in the trial of Orestes by Athena's persuasion and her offer of an honoured role in the city of Athens as promoters of fertility and civil order, the Erinyes are given the right to exercise for the good of the city of Athens the principal of 'beneficial fear'. They sing of 'a place where the terrible is good and needs to stand as silent guardian on watch over the mind' (*Eumenides* 517–19); and, when Athena remarks at the very close of the trilogy on 'the great advantage for my citizens from these terrifying faces' (lines 991–2), we might think too of the advantages being gained by the citizens of Athens in their theatre from these 'terrible faces' of tragedy.

As the earliest critics of drama pointed out, and as Athenian audiences knew from the start, this beneficial spectacle of suffering and disorder was also *pleasurable*. There is a pleasure to be derived from confronting disaster, terror, and crises personal and public that are without any real comfort or practical solution, from having extreme, dangerous emotions aroused, temporarily and artificially, in a 'safe' environment, the context of the special time of the Dionysiac festival; and from experiencing all this in a highly wrought artistic form of language, of crafted speech and song, that was full of poetic beauty and power.

In this connection, one of the important roles of the chorus is to act as a kind of 'internal audience'. They are always close, physically and emotionally, to the horrors of each drama. Often they are tied to the suffering protagonists by powerful bonds of loyalty, dependence, and friendship. And yet, like the audience, however much they are affected by the fate of the individual heroes, they themselves are immune from serious danger. Though they often have good cause for fear during the course of a play—the women of Aischylos' *Suppliant Women* are the best example, pursued as they are by their violent and threatening cousins—choruses never die and are seldom in direct physical danger. They spend much of the time watching, commenting, responding, both emotionally and rationally, to what they see and hear. And in this they offer the audience a set of possible models for their own responses. The views of the chorus are only ever partial, as they have no special access to some greater knowledge or higher truth: it is wrong to see them, as was once fashionable, as 'ideal' spectators, or even as the 'voice of the community'. They do sometimes represent a generalized response of a wider collective, a kind of normative or expected reaction, but more often than not they are made up of groups who could have no real say in the formation of 'community opinion'. They are very often women, sometimes slave women, or foreigners, or frail old men well beyond their physical prime and perhaps even marginal politically, or even, rarely, divine or semi-divine creatures (such as the Okeanids of Aischylos' *Prometheus*). It is only very rarely that they are the kind of adult male members of a citizenry that we might expect to serve as the mouthpieces of an authoritative, communal view.

Important unwritten 'rules' govern just how much distance there needed to be between the world of the contemporary audience's immediate experience and the world of tragedy. The worst horrors of tragedy were not allowed to come too close to Athens: tragedy, on the whole, happens elsewhere. Early in the century, the tragic poet Phrynichos produced his *Destruction of Miletos*, a 'historical' tragedy which dealt with the capture and annihilation of the Ionian city of Miletos by the Persians only a year or two earlier. Miletos was a city with which Athens had close ties of kinship and culture, and its destruction was a matter of collective grief and, since they had given little assistance in the hour of need, probably of guilt. This subject proved quite literally 'too close to home' to be turned into tragedy for the Athenians. Herodotos tells us that the entire audience in the theatre burst into tears, the work was banned and the poet heavily fined 'for reminding the Athenians of troubles close to home [*oikeia kaka*]' (6. 21. 2).

The scenario of Phrynichos' play was perfectly 'tragic'. At its centre was the destruction of a city, with the intense pathos that evoked for the city-centred Greeks, the obliteration not only of lives, but of ancient traditions, its famous temples and oracular site, noble public buildings, roads and ancestral lands; the horror of enslavement for women and children, and of death for men. In later tragedy the city of Troy would return time and again to the stage as the iconic example of the sacked city. But unlike Troy of the heroic age, Miletos was a Greek city firmly within the contemporary orbit of Athens, and the spectacle of its destruction on stage lacked the necessary 'safety gap' that could make the intense emotion pleasurable and valuable for its audience.

Herodotos' account of an audience response to a specific drama very early in the fifth century is precious indeed. Its stress on a shared, basically undifferentiated emotional reaction is striking, and is confirmed in general terms by one of the (highly parodic and exaggerated) 'character types' sketched by Theophrastos over a century and a half later. This 'Disgusting Man' (11) is described as the type who when 'at the theatre will applaud when others cease, hiss actors whom the rest of the audience appreciate, and raise his head and belch when the theatre is silent so that he may make the spectators look around.' What makes this so effective an example of 'disgusting' behaviour is the way that it so ostentatiously and systematically runs against the grain of the group theatrical mood and response. This was a collective and communal experience.

Such other evidence as we have suggests the Athenian theatre audience as a whole could also have a generally active, noisy, demanding, even unruly character, so much so as to have needed a special kind of 'theatre police' (*rhabdouchoi* or 'rod-bearers') to maintain order. 'Audience participation' was especially important for comedy, and in more than the form of the punctuating rhythm of laughter at the right moments. Applause is actively solicited, for instance, for their poet by the chorus of *Knights*:

> raise a great tumult for him and send him
> a good hearty Lenaian clamour,
> so that our poet can depart rejoicing and successful,
> radiant with gleaming . . . forehead.
>
> (ll. 546–50)

At other times, however, the instruction is to pay attention or not to interrupt, 'to restrain yourselves and not hiss' (Timokles, fr. 19) as a character tries to explain something. The audience as a whole—and its representative panel of judges in particular—is regularly cajoled, bribed, flattered, or threatened into voting for a comedy:

> I'd like to make a little suggestion to the judges:
> let the wise, mindful of our wisdom, vote for me;
> let those who enjoy a good laugh, vote for me for my jokes;
> so it's basically all of you I'm telling openly to vote for me.
>
> . . . .
>
> Don't perjure yourselves, but always judge the choruses fairly.
> Don't behave like bad whores who can only ever remember their last customers!
>
> (*Women in Assembly* 1154–7, 1160–2)

'Cued' responses were sometimes vital to the progress of the play, as when at the start of the *Wasps* a slave has the audience guess who it is who is suffering from the 'strange disease' inside the house (lines 67–73). The fact that these 'guesses' are preserved in our texts of the play, and that they are prompts for jokes at the expense of the (well-known) figures who make them, shows that the scene was not really one of impromptu interaction between stage and audience; but it also suggests that more and less formal levels of this interaction were invited rather than avoided in comedy.

A theatre for political issues

Nietzsche wrote that 'the Athenians went to the theatre in order to hear beautiful speeches', and although not the whole story, this captures an important truth which needs to be set alongside the visual impact of drama: most of its serious work was done with words. The use of crafted speech in public contexts of debate and performance was central to all Greek society, from at least Homeric times on (see Ch. 6). And classical Athenian society gave an especially privileged place to the spoken word, for the institutions at the heart of its democracy were run by words. Crafted speech was so vital to the operation of the democracy that it has been aptly dubbed 'the political tool *par excellence*' (Vernant). In the Assembly, the Council, and the elaborate court system, all the major decisions affecting the most powerful city in Greece, as well as the lives of many beyond it, were taken by citizen 'audiences' after weighing up the arguments put before them by speakers. As the democracy developed there developed with it an increasingly sophisticated culture of speech makers and consumers, of arguers and assessors of argument. This is a vital part of the context in which we need to place drama's relentlessly argumentative character, its obsession with words.

This is no dry, intellectual or purely rhetorical concern. Rather, drama itself was for the Athenians a political institution (in the broad sense of 'political') which could focus attention on the meaning of complex key terms in the city's political language, and scrutinize the power of language in operation, either in the serious key of tragic debate or through the absurdist debunking of comedy. Drama became a forum where the huge, unwieldy, and often unanswerable questions generated by the rapid changes in society in the fifth century could be raised. Those changes set the Athenians on a psychological course that veered between euphoric confidence and deep-seated self-doubt, and it was above all in their drama that they found a place to confront and explore these tidal shifts.

Tragedies often centre around a key social concept, or set of concepts: 'justice' in the *Oresteia*, 'power' in the *Prometheus*, 'law' or 'custom' in the *Antigone*, 'desire' and 'self-restraint' in the *Hippolytos*. And all the resources of tragic language, with its immense powers of allusion and compression of meaning, set up a kind of 'debate' through each drama around these key concepts and show a fight taking place over the meaning of the words characters use. For instance, the radical conflict of the *Antigone* is explored through language which, ironically, shows that the opposition between Antigone and Kreon is not in fact absolute, that neither of the two opposed attitudes can by itself be right until it grants to the other its due place. Throughout the play, Antigone appeals to a concept of religious custom to justify her burying the brother who had died leading an army against his own city. Hers is a notion of religious custom attached principally to the family, and centred around the private, domestic hearth and the cult of the dead (lines 452–60, 519, 908). At the same time, the leader of the city, Kreon, justifies his edict requiring the death of anyone who attempted to bury the 'traitor' by appeal to the law—the law of the city and its gods. However, even as they stand against one another in irreconcilable opposition, Antigone and Kreon use the very same language to describe the principles they support. For Antigone, the term *nomos* means the 'custom' of burial and respect due to the family's dead: to Kreon the very same word is the 'law' of the city. The two use the same terms to describe sharply opposed ideals. Yet the very fact that they do so suggests to the audience that their positions in fact converge—or must converge—at a certain point. It is characteristic of tragedy that this full recognition of the multiplicity and complexity of meaning and values is only achieved by the audience, not by the protagonists themselves (hence much 'tragic irony'). Sometimes the clash of meanings and values that is played out in this way is also a clash of the past with the present, of an older principle with a more 'modern' one. This to some extent is the case with the *Antigone*. For the 'law' which Kreon endorses is very much a civic law, a law of a polis (Thebes) which also has magistrates and generals and is at least to some extent reminiscent of the contemporary city of Athens. By setting up a drama of language in this way between past and present tragedy will have been a very productive means for its audience to reflect on the nature of concepts central to their lives in a world of great change. One could not easily institute a debate in the busy practical democratic Assembly on the changing nature of justice, or on the conflicts developing between the claims of the family and those of the city.

At the most basic level of form drama shows its attachment to a culture of speech-making and debate: from the rapid-fire exchange of single lines of continuous dialogue (known as *stichomythia*), to the scenes where characters deliver long, rhetorically complex speeches to explain their position and justify their actions, often answering one another point for point like opponents in an Athenian court (see below, p. 178). The most famous example is one of the earliest and most influential of all tragedies, the fully-fledged 'court-room scene' in the third play of the *Oresteia* of Aischylos. Here the very creation by the goddess Athene of one of Athens' courts, the Areopagos, is depicted in mythic time, its first case the trial of Orestes for the murder of his mother. Athena selects 'the best of my townsmen . . . to decide this issue in accordance with the truth' (lines 487–8), and they listen in silence to the arguments of Apollo for and of the Erinyes against Orestes before casting their votes. The debate as to whether killing a husband, father, and king is worse than killing a mother, is made to turn on the nature of 'parentage', with Apollo claiming that the father is in fact the 'true' parent of the child ('the parent is the man, who mounts'), the mother little more than 'a stranger who preserves a stranger's offspring'. However we are to imagine the impact of such arguments on a fifth-century Athenian audience (and there are good reasons to believe they may have found them more credible than we can easily imagine), it is clear that the dramatization of the process of decision-making serves an immensely import-ant function for the city of Athens. This tragic myth of origins serves to exalt the majesty of an important institution and its power to resolve conflict, a conflict that threatens to engulf all Athens in violence. And this it does at a time (458 BCE) when the real city of Athens was still shaken by threats of internal discord following on recent further democratic reforms of its institu-tions, including the very court of the Areopagos. The mythic story thus served to stress the vital importance to the citizens of taking their democratic responsibilities as assessors of arguments seriously indeed. And it also serves to warn that the operation of such institutions was always perilously fragile, that persuasion was never far from violence, and that clear decisions acceptable to all parties were never easily won.

Nearly half a century later tragedy still continues to show its concern with the power and problems of language. In Euripides' *Trojan Women* of 415 there is, however, little or no sign of the cautious optimism or pride of the *Oresteia*, and the audience is, as often in Euripides, left with an overwhelming sense of the failure of argument and debate to achieve justice. In the central scene of the play Menelaos judges the case for and against his errant wife Helen. Helen speaks first, defending herself before her husband, the captive queen of Troy Hekabe, and the women of the city about to be carried off to slavery. In a rhetorical *tour de force* Helen blames Hekabe herself for the misery about them for having given birth to Paris, her seducer; and supports this with an assertion that the goddess Aphrodite is to blame, and none can fight a god. Hekabe answers these arguments with a rationalizing attack on the story of the judge-ment of Paris: 'Why should the goddess Hera have such a desire for the prize of beauty? . . . or was Athena hunting for a marriage among the gods—who sought from her father the gift of virginity, and fled the marriage-bed? Don't make the goddesses out as fools to give your crime a fine appearance' (lines

976–82). Deploying a word-play (impossible to capture in translation) based on the similarity in sound between the name of the Greek goddess of desire, Aphrodite, and a word for folly, *aphrosyne*, the queen shows herself just as adept as Helen in all the modern techniques of rhetorical argumentation:

> You looked at him, and sense went Cyprian at the sight,
> since Aphrodite is nothing but the human lust
> named rightly, since the word of lust begins the god's name.
>
> (ll. 988–90)

Eastern wealth and men, she adds, were what Helen wanted, not a return to her Spartan husband (lines 991–1022). These speeches reflect the interest in the specialized and controversial techniques of argument refined by experts in late fifth-century Athens, masters of rhetoric known (mainly by their detractors) as Sophists, who claimed to be able to argue any case, to defend seemingly indefensible and controversial positions (see pp. 127–8 and 149–52). They show the medium of public debate infected by a cleverness and rhetorical skill whose logic is perversely divorced from the real moral issues at stake. Menelaos at first concurs with the chorus' judgement that his wife must die, only to retract his decision to stone her at once with the promise to put her to death when back in Argos. Yet, as the audience knew from their *Odyssey* and, like the internal audience of this scene, from the behaviour of Menelaos when faced with his beautiful and persuasive wife, Helen will live on unpunished. In the end all the sophistications of rhetorical language fail to secure the least punishment for the woman who is held to have caused the extreme suffering seen all through the play.

Comedy also made extensive use of the forms of public debate to press its own claims as a voice to be heard in the public realm. We looked earlier at the scene of the *Acharnians* in which the comic hero Dikaiopolis defends himself before a 'jury' of angry old farmers, drawing on all the reserves of poetic technique—comic and tragic—to put advice before the audience concerning the contemporary political scene that was in its way fundamentally as serious as the lessons of tragedy. The *Wasps* on the other hand is entirely centred on the political institutions of Athens, in particular the system of popular courts. The chorus is made up of old men who fill their panels, taking their daily pay of 3 obols and lording it over anyone who comes before them:

> If you thoroughly inspect us, you will find in all respects
> That in way of life and habits we are very much like wasps.
> In the first place, there's no creature, once provoked,
> More sharp-spirited than we, none more cantankerous.
>
> .   .   .   .

And to make a living we are very well equipped,
For we sting everybody and procure a livelihood!

(ll. 1102–5, 1112–13)

For all the mileage that is made from parodying the foibles of the Athenian court system, and especially of its judges as obsessive, power-hungry vindictive men in it for money rather than from a sense of civic duty, the most potent critical fire in this comedy is directed at misguided citizens like Philokleon ('Kleon-lover') and the politicians (Kleon above all) who misguide them with their flattering rhetoric. Far from being the mighty Zeus-like (line 619) man of power that Philokleon fondly imagines he is as he sits in court, in reality, his son argues, he is a slave, receiving a pittance while the politicians who hoodwink him put away massive bribes (see esp. lines 665–72, 682–5, 703–11). At the core of comedy's powerful and complex political criticism are the concerns of speech and persuasion: 'You're bamboozled by that kind of speaking, and so you choose that kind of speaker to rule you' (line 668).

One of the most important formal features of old comedy that permitted its poet to address his audience more directly, often on matters of contemporary political and poetical concern, was known as the *parabasis*—literally the 'coming forward'. This occurred after the main conflict of the play had been established. The actors have left the stage and the chorus, probably through its leader, adopts the stance of its poet, and often his very voice. Although to modern eyes this can seem a rather odd interruption of the dramatic flow, it has the effect of powerfully linking the world of the drama with that of the external world of political and social reality. In the *parabasis* of the *Acharnians*, for instance, we find in addition to further abuse of Kleon—

> never shall I be found
> to be, like that man, a wretch and a bugger
> in matters of state
>
> (ll. 663–4)

—a claim for the poet's powers in a more 'choral' voice:

> Fame concerning his daring has already reached so far that,
> When the Great King tested the Spartan embassy,
> He first asked them which side prevails with ships,
> And then which side this poet rebukes;
> For he said that these men have become much better,
> And would triumph in war, possessing this counsellor.
>
> (ll. 646–51)

Comedy established for itself a place in the city from which it could exercise the twin ideals of *isegoria* and *parrhesia*. Basically, these are respectively the equal right of any citizen to speak and give advice; and an ideal of 'open speech', a willingness to bring any matter, however sensitive, before the people. It is no coincidence that comedy was given a formal institutional place in the competition of the City Dionysia in 486, a year known for important democratic reforms in the city, including the introduction of ostracism, a means for removing a political 'tall poppy' by a mass vote of the citizenry.

Who was there?

All that we have seen thus far of drama's context and content shows us a poetry aimed at the citizens (the *politai*) of Athens, at those for whom the weighty matters of responsibility, of leadership and judgement were intensely live issues, and for whom the control of language was crucial because they alone in the community exercised the power of using language 'politically'. Much else supports this idea that the citizens were the 'target' audience of drama, that it was their own special form of education, self-scrutiny, and entertaining reflection. In comedy, for instance, speakers often address the audience as 'Men of Athens', the same expression employed in the Assembly and courts where none other than fully fledged citizens were allowed. And the fact that citizens (only) could receive a small cash distribution from their local deme administration to assist their attendance in the *theatron* also very strongly suggests that this was perceived as a kind of civic duty directly analogous to sitting as a judge in a court or attending the Assembly.

Of course the audience could never literally constitute the citizenry of Athens. Although the theatre was very much larger than the space where the Assembly met, it did not have the capacity to admit the entire citizen body. Also, we have seen that foreigners attended in some numbers; and we know that men sometimes took their sons with them (an early inculcation in some of the 'big issues' of adult life). On the other hand, it is also clear that some Athenians were unable to attend. We should remember that some Attic farms were more than thirty miles from the city. In this connection, the long Peloponnesian War (431–404) made a powerful impact on the theatre audience and hence on the nature of theatre itself and the drama it left behind. The official Athenian policy, to abandon the countryside each spring to the enemy and depend largely on imported grain and the power of the navy, saw thousands of country-dwellers move inside the city walls. The most obvious theatrical response to this change is Aristophanes' *Acharnians*, which takes this calamity as the starting-point for its pro-peace fantasy, and this helps explain its idealization of the rustic life.

Nor was the theatre audience an entirely undifferentiated mass of democratic equals. There were front-row seats reserved for important officials, military and civic, for priests, foreign dignitiaries, and men honoured by the city for special services. There also seems to have been a special zone marked out for the fifty presiding members of the Council; and possibly for the year's 'ephebes', the Athenian adolescents on military service just prior to becoming full members of the adult, citizen community. The special place physically accorded the ephebes in the theatre has generated interesting speculation about the orientation of tragedy in particular around 'ephebic' concerns. It is certainly true that many tragedies seem to speak of the problems and perils facing a young man on the point of adulthood. One thinks of the depiction of Neoptolemos in Sophokles' *Philoktetes*, the young 'cadet' faced with his first serious 'campaign'; or of the numerous tellings of Orestes' ordeals, ever returning to the stage to claim his proper place at the head of his household and city, but having to do so through the extreme and deeply problematic path of matricide, a crime whose justification seems less and less sound as its tellings proceed across the generations of tragic poets. Another 'difficult ephebe' is Hippolytos, the companion of Artemis and eternal hunter (a very ephebic activity), whose refusal to recognize Aphrodite and take on the responsibility of adult sexuality (that is, to cease to be an ephebe) is an important element in his tragedy. At the very least a strong case can be made for the impact on tragic drama of this special segment of its audience.

Despite this clear civic focus of drama, it is one of the extraordinary characteristics of the tragic stage that its plays were regularly set in places other than Athens and populated by non-Athenians. This means by non-Athenian Greeks—Thebans and Argives figure most prominently in our surviving plays—and by barbarians, whether from the very edges of the Greek world, like Thrace, or well beyond it, as with the many Persians, Phrygians, and Egyptians who appear. It also means by non-Athenian women; and in general by figures whose social status put them above (kings, tyrants, even gods) or below (slaves) the level of the Athenian citizen. Some of these groups, we have already seen, were sometimes part of actual dramatic audiences in Athens. It remains to see how far this inclusion of 'others' in the audience and drama of Athens may have extended.

Part of the explanation for the fact that most tragedies are not set in Athens is the 'safety-gap' argument (see p. 97 above). Not only did this arrangement give Athens the satisfaction of seeing tragedy happen off their soil: a more rigorous, even relentless examination of social and moral problems was possible if they were not seen to form part of the city's own mythic past. The other side of this coin is the way that when Athens or Athenians do appear in tragedy, it is generally in a highly positive light. The end of the *Eumenides* is the classic example, as the polis of Athena emerges as the place where the disastrous history of self-destruction of the royal house of Argos can at last be resolved. A less subtle case is the way the venerable epic story of the 'Seven against Thebes', the campaign of Oedipus' son Polyneikes and his followers to recover power in his ancestral home, acquires in Euripides' *Suppliant Women* an entirely new sequel in which the Athenians now take centre stage, in the capacity of protectors of the weak and defenders of the sacred rights of burial. But as ever with tragedy, things are not quite so straightforward. We need think only of the way that, after the terrible murder of her own children, Medeia flies off from Corinth, entirely free from punishment, to a safe haven prepared by her earlier in the drama—in Athens!

We can safely rule out the presence of non-Greeks in the theatre audience. As Edith Hall demonstrated in her classic study, 'the barbarian' in tragedy was a figure of the imagination created for the tragic stage, a negative embodiment of Athenian civic ideals. 'Barbarians' as a group perpetrated all the social and political crimes like incest, polygamy, sacrilege, despotism, and having women in power in strict opposition to which 'the Athenian' defined his own ethical and political position. Once again, the Athenian remains the proper recipient of the dramatic message.

The case of metics is significantly different, as is that of slaves. Metics were almost certainly in the audience, perhaps in some numbers, given that many were city-dwellers. Metics were non-Athenians, immigrants usually from other Greek cities who had certain rights of residency in Athens, but no political rights, and various obligations to the city, including a special poll-tax. By the middle of the fifth century the metic population was large, and it played the leading role in conducting Athens' burgeoning trade and commerce. 'Metic issues' are central to a number of tragedies. In Aischylos' *Suppliant Women*, for instance, the Greek city of Argos, which despite being ruled by a king is depicted in markedly democratic colours, is faced with the weighty problem of whether to extend help to a group of outsiders. The Danaids, the daughters of Danaos who have some hereditary claim to the support of Argos through their Argive ancestor Io, have fled there from Egypt to escape the violent courting of their cousins. It is clear that to help them will involve the community in war, but the Argive assembly is shown as accepting this possibility and granting the young women a kind of metic status (line 609, cf. lines 994–5). This decision is presented as morally upright, but the fact that these 'metics' will indeed prove such a source of trouble for the city makes of the tragic treatment a complex rumination on the values and dangers of dealing with such outsiders.

The Erinyes of the *Eumenides* offer perhaps the best example of the issue as to how to incorporate potentially troublesome, and beneficial, outsiders. Athena's solution to their continuing anger after the acquittal of Orestes is to find a place of honour for these ancient goddesses within the city that will see their powers turned to the benefit of the city:

> I foresee—the flowing course
> of time will bring greater honours
> to these my citizens, and if you have a place
> of honour by the palace of Erechtheus
> an endless line of men and women will present to you
> gifts you would never get from any other race
>
> (ll. 852–7)

In Athena's own language this offer transforms the Erinyes into 'metics':

> Now you,
> descendants of Kranaos, keepers of this city,
> you must lead these honoured immigrants [*metoikoi*];
> the citizens must learn to understand
> their riches
>
> (ll. 1010–13, cf. l. 1018)

And as a visual marker of this new condition whose significance would not escape the audience, when the Erinyes participate in the great procession with which the entire trilogy closes, they put on crimson robes and march off stage, just as 'real' metics did when they joined in the most important procession of Athenian religious life, that of the Panathenaia. What metics in the audience made of this we can only speculate. Were they honoured at the analogy that saw their status-group depicted as a source of prosperity and security for the glorious future of Athens? Or, rather, offended by the reminder of the manipulation and degree of control exercised over them, at the extent to which for all the benefits they brought the city, they were firmly placed as 'second-class' citizens? This seems to be another case where the presence of this significant group within society, and within the theatre audience, has affected the concerns of some dramas, but where the 'message' is still principally for those with the power to make real-life decisions, with responsibility for managing the city and all its inhabitants.

Much the same point could be made for that even more silent and powerless group in Athenian society, slaves—we know some to have been in the theatre, but only in the capacity as attendants of their masters. In real life, slaves had virtually no agency. They were the legal possessions of their owners, and regarded by some at least in dehumanizing terms as little more than mechanically useful items of property, 'by nature' incapable of the power of judgement that was central to the identity of the free citizen. Yet they have an extraordinary prominence in drama, tragic and comic, where they can take on active roles of great consequence. It is easy not to notice how challenging a figure the slave Xanthias is in Aristophanes' *Frogs*. His prominent and active role appears to be an innovation in the comic tradition, where slaves' principal functions had hitherto been to set the scene in expository prologues, and to serve as objects of 'amusing' physical and verbal abuse. Xanthias, however, dominates his own master, Dionysos, makes a fool of him, and ends up having him beaten by the doorkeeper in Hades. This innovation in the comic slave may in part be a response to the fact that in the previous year a large number of slaves had been freed because of their contribution as rowers to the desperate Athenian war-effort in the battle of Arginousai. The Athenians may have been forced to reassess the possibilities of this largely silent group, even to question the 'naturalness' and permanency of that sharp and deep divide between free citizen and slave.

The prominence of slaves in tragedy suggests that here too drama was a means for 'thinking through' issues that found little scope for expression elsewhere. And, although from the mouth of a comic caricature and not the real poet, the Euripides of Aristophanes' *Frogs* claims he was 'doing the democratic thing' (line 952) by letting the slave talk as much as mistress, master, young woman, and old. The shepherd-slave of Sophokles' *Oedipus Tyrannos* is revealing here. For this man is a crucial link in the drama of Oedipus' life, and vital to his knowledge of it. Only he knows the secret of Oedipus' birth, because against all the normal expectations of the proper behaviour of the slave, he had taken the momentous decision, entirely on his own account, to ignore the order to expose the baby Oedipus. Similarly with the Nurse of the *Hippolytos*, a slave with dangerous rhetorical proficiency (see esp. lines 433–81) who takes the initiative, explicitly prohibited by her mistress, of revealing Phaidra's passion to Hippolytos, with all the tragic consequences that follow.

A few contemporary voices claimed that Athenian democratic conditions had obliterated or at least blurred the distinction between free citizen and slave. We should take such claims with much more than a grain of salt, but the important point, as far as drama is concerned, is this: the new, more open conditions of Athenian democratic society had shaken social expectations and accepted norms to such an extent that claims of this sort could at least be made—and that there was less complacency about the (supposedly) 'natural' order of social status.

Women at the theatre?

I have left the most intriguing and difficult case till last. Were women part of the theatrical audience in Athens? And if they were, what impact did their presence have on the works produced there? Were they close to the model of the male viewer, active participants in a moral, emotional, and intellectual event that was central to their lives as Athenian citizens? Or was their involvement more akin to that of the metic or slave, in that their 'presence' as a hugely significant sector of society at large had a major influence on the images shown in the 'mirror' of drama, while those images were still intended for an audience of citizen viewers?

We can begin from one point of certainty. Women made no contribution to the theatre in an active, creative capacity. There were no female tragic or comic poets in the classical period, no female actors. Medeia, Klytaimestra, Phaidra, the hundreds of 'young women' chorus members, goddesses, and slaves who crossed the stage were all acted by men, an extraordinary case of cross-dressing (fitting for Dionysos) on a grand scale. Nor so far as we know did women play any other part in the organization of the contests, as producers, musicians, trainers, or the like. In this most basic sense drama was 'men's work', and the words of every impassioned female in drama were the words of men, from a male mouth.

We simply are unable to answer the 'hard', factual question as to whether women were present in the audience. For decades scholars have squeezed the same few pieces of evidence for all they might offer, but the result has only been a lack of consensus; and a genuinely ambivalent picture emerges. At a minimum it is possible to say that, if women did attend the theatre, our sources are surprisingly unclear on the fact (whereas they are not on the matter of foreigners, for instance). And this is significant in itself. For it is consistent with a general policy of silence with respect to 'good' Athenian women, a policy most famously formulated by the Thucydidean Perikles in his address to the war widows: 'Great is your glory if you do not fall below the standard which nature has set for your sex, and great also is hers of whom there is least talk among men whether for praise or in blame' (2. 45).

A glance at a couple of the more important pieces of 'evidence' will show just how elusive an answer to this question is. The relevant texts are from comedy and Platonic dialogue, and are thus both very slippery and far from straightforward as evidence for what actually went on in the theatre. Comedy is in the habit of totally reshaping reality for its own ends, while Plato is notoriously biased against theatre, indeed against nearly all poetry, on broadly moral grounds. In a scene of Aristophanes' *Peace*, Trygaios' slave is throwing barley-groats to the audience at his master's instructions, in part because a sacrifice is about to take place, and grain was thrown as a preliminary ritual act at sacrifices, but in part also in keeping with the comic practice of getting the audience on side by distributing 'refreshments', usually fruit and nuts. The slave informs his master that 'there isn't a man in the audience who doesn't have barley' (and, crucially, the Greek word for 'barley' is also slang for 'penis').

> TRYGAIOS: But the women didn't get any.
> SLAVE: The men will give it to them tonight!
>
> (ll. 966–7)

From this some deduce that women were there in the theatre, but perhaps out of reach of the ballistic barley, at the back or far edges. Equally energetic are those who argue it proves they were *not* there, and that it shows rather that they were at home (where their husbands would return to 'give them their barley' after the performances were over). Supporters of this last line cite a passage from the *Women at the Thesmophoria* where a woman complains about Euripides' 'misogyny':

> Where has he not yet slandered us women, wherever
> there are audiences, tragedies and choruses,
> calling us adulteresses and man-crazy,
> wine-tipplers, traitoresses, chatterboxes,
> good-for-nothings, the scourge of husbands.
> Now as soon as they come home from the benches
> they give us suspicious looks and immediately start searching
> the house for a hidden lover.
>
> (ll. 390–7)

Firm foundations cannot be built on such shifting comic ground. And the 'strongest' passage of Plato is hardly more secure. It is from a dialogue largely devoted to an attack on rhetoric, the *Gorgias*. Sokrates argues that poets are rhetoricians, and he dismisses what they do as 'a kind of rhetoric directed at a public composed of children together with women and men, slave and free' (502d). Even this seemingly clear reference to an audience that includes women turns out to be elusive, for Sokrates does not connect it specifically to Athens, nor specifically to dramatic audiences. More importantly, it is clear that Sokrates' overarching desire to tarnish poetry and the performing arts in general has determined the kind of audience he alleges or imagines it to have— a hotch-potch which mixes men up with the less than fully human (slave) and the irrational (child, woman).

Apart from passages like this, we depend largely on the more general images that can be formed of the character of Athenian society and of the festival. These tend to be divided between two schools. There are those who stress, as I have, the largely 'political' character of the occasion, and the general tendency of Athenian society to limit the occasions on which women, especially unmarried girls, appeared in public. And on the other hand, those who stress the 'sacral' nature of the occasion, and the fact that it was precisely in the area of religion that women participated and could even play prominent public roles. Although we cannot answer the factual question, framing it encourages us to make valuable reassessments of our assumptions concerning the nature of ancient theatre and society.

We are left with a powerful sense of paradox. For while Athenian society did maintain a high degree of silence about its women, and liked to think of them remaining in the shadows of their 'proper' place inside the household, it filled its stage every year with women, including many young women, speaking in public, taking all manner of decisions on their own account, and putting their decisions into action—and not infrequently, actions of the most transgressive kind, like the murder of their own husbands and children. Our 'safety gap' argument comes into operation here too. Women on the tragic stage are very rarely 'Athenian' women. They are distanced by mythic time, by place of birth, by their excessively high (divine, royal) or low (slave) status. Apart from Kreousa, the daughter of the mythic King Erechtheus, and the crucial link in transmitting the line of male Athenian kings and proto-citizens (see Euripides' *Ion*), the only example of Athenian tragic women that we know about falls into the special category of 'sacrificial virgins'. They are Kreousa's sisters, the so-called 'Erechtheids' who died, apparently willingly, to save their city from destruction (their story was told in the *Erechtheus* of Euripides, of which important fragments survive). Far from being transgressive females they are thus highly conformist in their devotion to the future of their political community.

Comic Athenian women are a slightly different matter. We have perhaps one or two examples of 'real' Athenian women named in comedy (where hundreds of real Athenian males are regularly named, and regularly for abuse). But the most promising exception proves the rule, since it is Lysistrate, and her 'real life' equivalent was a priestess of Athena, an entirely honourable and public function. Comedy does however present generic Athenian women with all the stereotyped vices ascribed by men to their sex—addiction to drink, adulterous sex, and deceit. And while the goals of the schemes they devise, like the peace plans of the *Lysistrate*, often seem to 'make sense' and strike a sympathetic note with their audience, it is the very impossibility and fantasy of the means they use to promote them—sex-strikes, women taking over power, and the like—which make them possible in comedy.

However, just as non-Athenian men in tragedy offered useful models for the Athenian viewer through which to pose questions to himself, so with these 'other' women. Tragic women provide an immensely rich array of types and scenarios for Athenian men to think through, to worry at, or to wish away some major problems. A recurrent concern of Greek literature, and an obsession of Greek society in general, is the continuity and purity of the male line of each free man's household (*oikos*). The anxiety is at least as old as Homer, with Telemachos' reply to the disguised Athena's question as to whether he is the son of Odysseus:

> My mother says that I am his child, but I
> do not know. Never yet did any man himself know his own parentage.
> (*Odyssey* 1. 215–16)

This concern certainly did not disappear in fifth-century Athens. Far from it, for now the prize of citizenship, which depended on legitimacy of birth, was so much the greater. This is an important background to the prevalence on the Athenian stage of so many tales of threatened childlessness and the end of family lines (*Ion, Antigone, Seven against Thebes*), of dysfunctional marriages and the dangers of adultery (*Oresteia, Hippolytos*).

Women in tragedy also act out to the full the male belief that womankind was excessively given over to the passions, much more prone to being overwhelmed by them than men, whose control of their passions was an important cultural ideal. Thus figures like Phaidra and Stheneboia are shown as victims of excessive desire (*eros*) in a way men on the tragic stage never are. Comparable are the many scenes where women give full rein to the expression of the intense pain and suffering that is peculiarly theirs as women—as victims of male violence in war (*Trojan Women, Hekabe*), as wives and child-bearers (*Medeia*, Klytaimestra in *Agamemnon*), as grieving mothers and lamenters for the dead (Euripides' *Suppliant Women*). These passions were attended in real life by fear and in some cases (public lamentation, for instance) they were subject to legal control. In drama they were given full expression, and the disasters that followed from them (particularly in the case of female desire) may have served to confirm the audience in their belief in the need to maintain a vigilant control over their real-life expression. But they perhaps also permitted men to experience, vicariously, the force of such passions that in the ordinary course of their lives they resolutely suppressed. This more complex response to the 'female' in tragedy suits a performance for a god of ambiguous gender.

Another important set of issues whose dramatization is made possible by tragic women are those concerned with conflict between the public and private dimensions of life; where the political, military world of the city at large comes into conflict with the family, with its own partly independent needs and traditions. The city and family, polis and *oikos*, were certainly not a sharply opposed pair of entities in Athenian life. The city was in an important sense made up of the many separate households, and to be a citizen required a man to be the head of a household. However, as Athens grew as a force in the wider Greek world and devoted more and more of its energies (including the lives and land of its citizens) to grand military and civic enterprises (above pp. 94–5), areas of sharp tension between the public and private realm did emerge. In tragedy when women act 'out of place', beyond their 'proper' domain of the household, they often do so because they perceive some threat to it. And so they come forth from the stage building which so often represents the household (*oikos*), into the space before it which is a kind of no man's land between the private and public realms. Antigone explicitly signals her entry into this area for the purpose of discussing her seditious plan with her sister Ismene; both of them, as unmarried young women, are transgressing the moment they enter this place:

> I summoned you here outside the gates of the courtyard
> because I wished you to hear this alone.
>
> (*Antigone* 18–19)

Antigone remains out of place by venturing even beyond the city walls to tend to her dead brother's body (while the 'good' sister Ismene returns indoors). Yet in the outcome this transgression by the young woman against the order of the city in defence of the family is shown to have been to the good of the city itself, since it protected it from the pollution of an unburied corpse. (And, in a further irony, it turns out to have been detrimental to the continuity of her own family, since her actions led her knowingly to her death, in the face of pleas to desist from her sister and promised husband.)

This curious combination of benefit and danger in the tragic woman is not confined to Antigone. Even a figure like Klytaimestra, who must in many ways have seemed a nightmarish creation to the husbands and campaigning soldiers in the audience, is not without her complexity and even her claims for sympathy. She is of course the adulteress, the murderer—wielding a sword, like a man—of her own husband, the king; and she shows an 'unnatural' craving for the male prerogatives of power, and an equally 'unnatural' ability to acquire them through her intelligence and rhetorical skill. All of this makes her a clear 'negative paradigm', a model of the transgressive woman that plays on some of the most deep-seated male fears. And yet she is, for all that, allowed to make an eloquent defence of her actions, a crucial part of which is the claim that she was acting in response to the attack on 'the glory of our household' (*Agamemnon* 208) by Agamemnon who,

> not caring a thing about it, just as if an animal was dead
> from his abundant flocks of fleecy sheep,
> killed his own daughter, dearest fruit sprung from
> my labour-pangs, to charm away the winds from Thrace.
>
> (ll. 1415–18)

Even though an Athenian male in the audience would hardly have seen this as a justification for the queen's actions, the play does allow the argument to be heard, and it supports her general claim in the way it shows Agamemnon's great public, civic enterprise at Troy as a brutal and impious act of wanton destruction (see above p. 87). So too it allows Klytaimestra to voice her resentment of the sexual inequality that allows the husband to have his concubines while the wife must remain faithful (cf. esp. lines 1437–43), a situation that was the norm in Athenian society.

Tragedy is full of such apparently unacceptable behaviour and arguments from the mouths of 'women'. Even if real women were not there to hear them, these perhaps more than anything else left their audience with the most challenging of all their dramatic lessons.

4 | Charting the poles of history: Herodotos and Thoukydides

LESLIE KURKE

History before prose/Prose before history

Herodotos and Thoukydides, the two fifth-century practitioners of history whose works survive, together defined the parameters of history for the Western tradition. Thus, though the books they wrote are in many ways very different, they need to be read and considered in tandem. In the modern world, the relative respect and attention the two have received tend to correlate directly with contemporary notions of what history is or should be. When 'scientific history' was in vogue (mid-nineteenth to mid-twentieth centuries), Thoukydides was a hero of objectivity and accuracy, while Herodotos was denigrated and pitied for his *naïveté* and childlike story-telling. In more recent years, in the wake of the postmodernist contention that all truth is constructed, multiple, and unstable (as well as with the rise of social and cultural history and anthropology), Herodotos has come into his own as a model for cultural relativism and 'thick description', while we have become more and more uncomfortable with Thoukydides' pose of sublime objectivity. In the event, none of these modern stereotypes does justice to Herodotos and Thoukydides; we must instead, as far as we can, try to reconstruct the historical, intellectual, and cultural climate in which the two produced their remarkable texts.

Herodotos came from the Dorian city of Halikarnassos (modern Bodrum, in south-west Turkey). We are told that he was born around 484 BCE. He probably came from a prominent family and, to judge from the name of his uncle Panyassis, one that had intermarried with the native Carian population. We are told that he was exiled from Halikarnassos for his opposition to the tyrant Lygdamis, and then spent some time on the island of Samos. He also seems to

The fragments of the Greek historians are cited from F. Jacoby, *Fragmente der griechishen Historiker* (Leiden, 1954–69), conventionally abbreviated *FGrH*.

have spent time in Athens, and eventually participated in the panhellenic foundation of Thourioi in southern Italy in 443 BCE. This settlement ultimately failed because of civil strife between those of Dorian and Ionian ethnic affiliation within the city, a process which Herodotos could well have witnessed first hand. It is also usually assumed, based on the text of the *Histories,* that Herodotos travelled widely in Egypt and the Near East, though other scholars deny that he travelled at all, pointing to the mistakes and inaccuracies in his descriptions of foreign lands and peoples. I would contend that this is a sterile debate, in which both sides apply to Herodotos an anachronistic standard of accuracy or truth. We must accept the fact that we simply cannot reconstruct in detail exactly where Herodotos travelled from his text.

This is about all we can say about Herodotos the man (much of it already ancient conjecture). As for the *Histories* itself, the date of its composition is still very much an open question. All we can do is establish rough parameters. An odd speech in Sophokles' *Antigone* (lines 904–15) seems to be an imitation of a story Herodotos tells about the Persian wife of Intaphrenes (3. 119). If this speech is genuine and based on a Herodotean model, parts at least of Herodotos' narrative would have been known in Athens around 442/1 (the probable date of *Antigone*). We cannot, however, assume that the story was already fixed in written form at this time. As for the date of completion, the latest events referred to in the *Histories* fall in the first few years of the Peloponnesian War, so that scholars have traditionally assumed the completion of the *Histories* (and even Herodotos' death) by approximately 425 BCE. This span of at least fifteen years suggests a long process of composition, perhaps in oral form, over an extended period of time.

With the recent discovery of fragments of Simonides' Elegy on the Battle of Plataia, we confront the fact that historical narrative very likely existed in Greece before 'history'. Indeed, it has been suggested that one of the proper generic forms for elegy in the seventh–sixth centuries was extended narrative of the foundation, mythic traditions, and recent history of individual cities, performed at public festivals for a local civic audience (see Ch. 2, pp. 55–6 above). Such narrative elegy may account for some of the poetic production of Mimnermos, Kallinos, Tyrtaios, and Xenophanes, though almost all the texts of this genre of elegy have disappeared, overshadowed by the rise of prose history. Another practitioner of this genre may have been Panyassis, the uncle or cousin of Herodotos, who, we are told, composed 'a history of Ionia, in pentameters, dealing with Kodros, Neleus, and the Ionian colonies in 7,000 lines'. In the literary development from Panyassis to Herodotos, we see a shift from poetry to prose, which entailed simultaneously a shift in audience addressed.

Yet the fact that archaic poetry comprehended historical narrative publicly performed should make us wonder all the more about the development of prose history. Contrary to our assumptions, history does not require prose, nor is it self-evident that prose is the 'natural' medium for genres such as history or philosophy. We must therefore ask why prose genres first developed in Greece, and what the models were for Herodotos' remarkable undertaking. For Herodotos, the 'father of History' (as Cicero called him), conceptualized and wrote his work before 'history' existed. What, then, did Herodotos think he was doing? And why in prose?

Before Herodotos, we know that Herakleitos, Anaximander, and other Ionian *physiologoi* or 'writers on nature' wrote prose treatises (see Ch. 5, pp. 143–6). There were in addition (according to the first-century BCE critic Dionysios of Halikarnassos) a large number of prose writers who were earlier or contemporary with Herodotos, including Hekataios of Miletos, Akousilaos of Argos, Charon of Lampsakos, Hellanikos of Lesbos, and Xanthos the Lydian. They are shadowy figures to us, for whom only fragments and sometimes book titles are preserved. Yet even this is enough to give some sense of their themes and topics: these writers composed prose accounts of mythology (in all probability rationalized), genealogies, local histories, histories of individual peoples (entitled, for example, 'Persian Things', 'Lydian Things', 'Greek Things' (*Persika*, *Lydiaka*, *Hellanika*)), Annals or *Horoi*, and geographical treatises (the *Periegesis* or *Periodos Ges*). In his topics, Hekataios (the only one from Dionysios' list of earlier writers Herodotos mentions by name) is representative of the whole group: he wrote two books, a *Genealogiai* and a *Periodos Ges* (in two volumes, 'Europe' and 'Asia'). The first sentence of Hekataios' *Genealogiai* sounds the same self-confident critique of earlier traditions that occurs later in Herodotos and Thoukydides: 'Hekataios of Miletos narrates (*mutheitai*) thus; I write these things as they seem to me to be true. For the stories (*logoi*) of the Greeks are many and ridiculous, as they appear to me' (*FGrH* 1 F 1a). Wherever we have fragments of these authors, their dialect is Ionic, whether they derive from Ionian, Aeolian, or Dorian cities, suggesting that Ionic rapidly became the proper dialect for the early *logopoioi* ('prose writers' but also 'narrators of *logoi*, stories'). The fact that Herodotos (from Dorian Halikarnassos) composed his *Histories* in Ionic affiliates him with this group of writers, as also his use of the term *historie*, 'research, enquiry', does. It is to this word that we owe the term 'history'.

It is worth quoting the assessment of Dionysios of Halikarnassos on what distinguishes Herodotos' work from that of his predecessors and contemporaries among the early Ionian historians:

All of these showed a like bent in their choice of subjects. . . . Some wrote treatises dealing with Greek history, the others dealt with non-Greek history. And they did not blend together these histories (into one work), but subdivided them by nations and cities and gave a separate account of each, keeping in view one single and unvarying object, that of bringing to the common knowledge of all whatever records or traditions were to be found among the natives of the individual nationalities or states, whether recorded in places sacred or profane, and to deliver these just as they received them without adding thereto or subtracting therefrom, rejecting not even the legends which had been believed for many generations nor dramatic tales which seem to men of the present time to have a large measure of silliness . . . . In contrast to these men, Herodotos of Halikarnassos . . . expanded and rendered more splendid the scope of his subject matter. Not deigning to write the history of a single city or a single nation, but forming the design of comprising within a single treatise many varying deeds of people of Europe and Asia, he started with the Lydian empire and brought his history down to the Persian Wars and narrated in a single work the history of the intervening period . . . (Dionysios, *On Thoukydides*, ch. 5, trans. W. K. Pritchett)

Dionysios' remarks suggest that Herodotos shared the methods and interests of his predecessors and contemporaries, but conceived his work on a much more global scale, synthesizing different strands of local and ethnic history into a complex whole.

Between orality and literacy

Like the other Ionian *logopoioi*, Herodotos' work took shape on the cusp between oral tradition and written record. Throughout the period of the Ionian historians (approximately down to the time of the Peloponnesian War), Greece was still largely an oral culture, reliant on traditional oral means of preserving and transmitting knowledge and social norms. Thus, when the *logopoioi* researched the distant past—in the form of founding stories, genealogies, or the ultimate causes of Greek–Barbarian conflict, which Herodotos traced back to Kroisos—they were almost entirely dependent on oral traditions, story, and anecdote. Herodotos might, of course, have had at his disposal the written texts of all the *logopoioi* who preceded him, but significantly, he maintains a fiction of pure orality. He never cites earlier written 'researches' as such, although we know from several later authors that on many occasions (especially in his account of Egypt) he borrows from Hekataios (according to one source, even

Herodotos' striking formulation 'Egypt is the gift of the Nile' comes from Hekataios).

And just as the *logopoioi* depended to a great extent on oral sources, they probably presented their work in oral form, even while they also committed it to writing. Such a model of combined oral and written dissemination is implied in Hekataios' opening sentence, which uses first the solemn Homeric verb *mutheitai* ('Hekataios speaks thus authoritatively . . . '), then immediately shifts to *grapho* ('I write'). Late sources (Plutarch and Lucian) preserve accounts of Herodotos' oral performances at Olympia or Athens. Their portrayal of Herodotos' activities is heavily influenced by the slightly later practices of the Sophists (Hippias, for example, famously gave oratorical displays at the panhellenic festival at Olympia; cf. Ch. 5, p. 150), and yet, given what we can reconstruct about Herodotos' sources, period of composition, and milieu, the idea of some kind of public performance is not implausible. Especially if we envision Herodotos' text taking shape over a period of decades, it is easy to imagine him honing and polishing different parts of his narrative through oral performance. At some point, though, Herodotos committed the entire narrative to writing, thereby producing a mammoth, comprehensive text that was itself far too long for public performance (modern estimates of the time required to read the *Histories* aloud range from twenty-four to fifty hours). It needs to be emphasized that, at the time it was composed, Herodotos' text was uniquely and prodigiously long (about twice as long as the *Iliad* or *Odyssey*). The comparison with the Homeric poems may well be relevant, for in their case we possess oral compositions that had over time become too long to be contained in the performance context of a bardic recitation accompanying a feast (see Ch. 1, pp. 18–27). It may be that Herodotos was partly inspired by the scale of Homeric epic.

In Herodotos' first sentence we find evidence both for his Homeric conception of his project and for the convergence of oral and written methods that shaped his text. Herodotos begins, 'This is the display of the research *(historie)* of Herodotos of Halikarnassos, in order that the things done by men not become faded in time *(exitela)*, nor the great and marvellous deeds, some displayed by Greeks, others by barbarians, come to be without fame *(aklea)*, both the rest and why they came into conflict with each other.' Herodotos' choice of the adjective *aklea* ('without fame') links his work with the tradition of epic poetry, which characterizes itself as *klea andron*, 'the fames of men'. *Kleos*, 'fame' (derived from the verb *kluein*, 'to hear') is essentially *oral* remembrance preserved through time, the highest aspiration of the Homeric heroes (see Ch. 1, pp. 16–17 above). In addition, Herodotos' formulation 'this is the display of the research' *(histories apodexis hede)* puts the emphasis on the public oral performance of his findings; indeed, the verb from which the noun *apodexis* is derived itself occurs in the same sentence, to characterize 'the great and marvellous deeds *displayed*' by Greek and barbarian alike. This verbal repetition implies that Herodotos' work is a significant public performance, on a par with the great deeds it chronicles.

But if these terms affiliate the *Histories* with heroic epic and oral forms of commemoration through performance, other elements of the preface align Herodotos' text instead with written monuments. Thus the adjective 'faded' (*exitela*), which is co-ordinated with *aklea* in a parallel clause, is a metaphor apparently derived from the Greek practice of highlighting the letters of inscriptions with bright-coloured pigment to make them more visible. *Exitelos* describes the fading of the pigment, so that from a distance the inscribed letters seem to disappear. Along with this term, we should note the slightly odd syntax of the first clause of the sentence: Herodotos does not say, 'Herodotos of Halikarnassos displays (or displayed) these researches.' Unlike Hekataios before him or Thoukydides after him, Herodotos is not himself the subject of his first sentence; instead his name figures in the genitive, with the presentifying deictic *hede* ('this here present') attached to the noun *apodexis*. This construction resembles nothing so much as the form of early inscriptions, which 'speak' from the position of the object inscribed, while they characterize their absent owners in the genitive and the third-person ('this is the cup—or the tomb—of so-and-so'). That is to say, the syntax of Herodotos' first clause is predicated on the connection made between reader and text in the absence of the author.

The echo of epic *kleos* in Herodotos' first sentence is significant, and points us towards many other affiliations and influences on his project besides Ionian *historie*. We can see Herodotos' epic aspirations in his monumental narrative of a great war between East and West, as in particular moments like his catalogue of the invading Persian forces (7. 61–99), and his characterization of the twenty Athenian ships sent to assist the Ionian Revolt as the 'beginning of evils' (5. 97. 3, echoing the characterization of Paris' ship that carried off Helen in the *Iliad*). In addition, it is worth noting that while Herodotos only ever mentions two Ionian *logopoioi* by name (Hekataios and Skylax of Karyanda), archaic poets and sages figure prominently in his text. Thus Herodotos mentions five of the canonical nine lyric poets (Alkaios, Sappho, Anakreon, Pindar, and Simonides; cf. Ch. 2, pp. 57–66), as well as Archilochos, and Arion who, he reports, first composed and taught dithyrambs in Corinth. Even more striking, Herodotos' first book contains extensive anecdotes about six of the traditional Seven Sages (Bias of Priene, Pittakos of Mytilene, Thales of Miletos, Chilon of Sparta, Periandros of Corinth, Solon of Athens, while the seventh, Anacharsis the Scythian, figures prominently in bk. 4). Most famously, the encounter of Solon and Kroisos early in book 1 is widely agreed to be programmatic for the work as a whole, even while significant echoes of Solon's own poetry have been detected in the speeches Herodotos puts in his mouth. If Solon is to be read as a mouthpiece for Herodotos (as many have argued), perhaps we should see that ventriloquism as part of Herodotos' own competition with the Sages as 'performers of wisdom' (cf. Ch. 5, pp. 140–3). Herodotos' text vies with these figures even as it appropriates their authority.

The *Histories* furthermore includes a great deal of material that might have circulated for a long time in purely oral form, purveyed by traditional storytellers and oral remembrancers (*logioi* and *mnemones* in Greek). Such normally ephemeral 'speech genres' for oral performance would comprehend miracle stories (for example, of mysterious superhuman figures who assist in battle, 6. 117); dedication stories (for example, how a particular object came to be dedicated, 1. 50–1); oracular narratives (for example, how a riddling oracle came to be fulfilled, 1. 47–9); and travellers' tales. Such stories are often fantastic and usually partisan (in that they serve and aggrandize the interests of the original local audiences). Because his narrative includes such tales, Herodotos has long been accused of excessive credulity, but as he himself characterizes his method at one point, 'I'm obliged to say the things that are said (*legein ta legomena*), but I'm certainly not obliged to believe them all, and let this formulation hold for the entire account' (7. 152. 3).

Even without this explicit articulation of principle, a careful reading of Herodotos frequently reveals the calculated subversion of one partisan story by its juxtaposition with others that contradict or undermine it. To take just one example, the sequence of stories about the extremely rich, aristocratic Athenian family of the Alkmeonidai in book 6 (121–31) starts from the denial that they could have attempted to betray Athens to the Persians after the Battle of Marathon, insisting that they had always been great 'tyrant-haters' (6. 121. 2). And yet, several of the stories that follow immediately undermine this claim, tracing the sources of the family's fantastic wealth back to the favour of an Asiatic despot (Kroisos, 6. 125) and a Greek tyrant (Kleisthenes of Sikyon, 6. 126–30; for the term 'tyrant', cf. Ch. 2, p. 45).

Another form of oral tale that seems occasionally to impinge on the text of Herodotos is the 'Life of Aesop' tradition. According to late versions of the 'Life' which survive, Aesop (in Greek, Aisopos) was a Thracian, hideously ugly, enslaved to a philosopher on the island of Samos in the sixth century BCE. It is pointless to ask whether there was a 'historical' Aesop: already by the fifth century a whole set of popular stories had grown up around him, describing his cleverness, his constant outwitting of his philosopher master, and especially his use of animal fables for didactic purposes. These tales probably circulated for centuries in oral form before being committed to writing. Herodotos clearly knew the Aesop tradition, since he mentions Aesop himself as the slave of the Samian Iadmon (2. 134), and since, on occasion, he puts Aesopic fables into the mouths of his historical characters (e.g. 1. 141). The inclusion of Aesop's fables and other 'Aesopika' represented a bold generic mixture on Herodotos' part, since prose beast fable occupied the very bottom of the hierarchy of 'literary' genres that culminated in heroic epic. Herodotos' text in fact incorporates the whole gamut of genres, often employed in ironic juxtaposition to one another.

Herodotos is thus a collector of the *logoi* of others who aspires to a comprehensive account, but always maintains a critical distance between himself and the stories he transmits. As Dionysios of Halikarnassos observes, Herodotos' great achievement is his ability to synthesize into a single encyclopaedic whole all the disparate strands that make up his work—disparate strands not only of local histories (Dionysios' focus) but also of the many different genres and traditions, high and low, oral and written, that inform his narrative. Ultimately, it seems that what allows Herodotos his ironic distance on his material is the fact that, first as prose, and then as written record, his narrative is disembedded from a specific ritual or religious performance context. At the same time (and related to this difference in context), Herodotos is free from the pressure to produce simply a celebratory narrative that serves the interests of any single community—in contrast to historical elegy or the tales of *logioi* and oral remembrancers. Instead, Herodotos aims at a comprehensive panhellenic—or even global—account, producing thereby a uniquely capacious and complex text that seems to include the entire world as Herodotos knew it.

It is easy for us to miss the anomalousness of Herodotos' account, which inheres precisely in his generic mixing, ironic detachment, and incorporation of many different, conflicting traditions. In order to appreciate how startling these qualities may have been to ancient readers, we need only consult Plutarch's treatise *On the Malice of Herodotos*. Writing five centuries after Herodotos' composition, Plutarch complains bitterly that Herodotos was a 'barbarian-lover' whose account is filled with 'malice' against the Greeks, since he does not produce a purely celebratory history of the great achievements of the Persian Wars. The first charge (of being a 'barbarian-lover') speaks to Herodotos' even-handed treatment of all concerned—recall that even in his opening sentence, Herodotos promises to memorialize the 'great and marvellous deeds' of Greeks and barbarians *alike*. Plutarch clearly also feels that Herodotos has betrayed the Greeks and sullied their greatest achievements by his inclusion of the many conflicting claims and counter-claims of different Greek states in the Persian Wars proper.

Structure and purpose

What is the structure of the work and what can we infer from this structure about Herodotos' purpose in writing? In the most schematic terms, Herodotos' structure is dictated by the progressive expansion of Eastern empires, first Lydia (1. 5–92), then Persia. As the Persian empire expands, coming into conflict with ever new peoples, Herodotos takes the opportunity to fold into his narrative the histories and ethnographies of various peoples conquered or threatened by Persian expansion. Thus the Lydian ethnography of 1. 93–4 forms the pivot between Lydian and Persian domination of Asia Minor, while book 1 also incorporates the early history of the Medes and the history and ethnography of Babylon and the Massagetai, as the Persian King Kyros encroaches against them. Book 2 is dedicated to the history and ethnography of Egypt, on the occasion of its conquest by Kyros' son Kambyses; book 3 narrates the succession crisis in the Persian monarchy after the death of Kambyses and the eventual establishment of Dareios as Great King; book 4 chronicles Dareios' failed expedition against Scythia, incorporating its history and ethnography along the way; book 5 narrates the events that led up to and precipitated the Ionian Revolt, bringing Greeks and Persians into direct conflict. Books 6–9 then chronicle two successive Persian invasions of mainland Greece, the first of 490 BCE, repulsed at Marathon (book 6), the second, much larger, invasion by Xerxes in 480–479 BCE, in which Greek and Persian forces clashed at Thermopylai and Artemisium (books 7, 8), at Salamis (book 8), and finally at Plataia (book 9). The remainder of the last book narrates the Greeks' taking the initiative and driving east against the Persians, and the combined land and sea battles at Mykale in Ionia. Herodotos' structure thus makes his work a kind of antithesis of the Near Eastern Royal Chronicle, which traditionally records as an unbroken sequence the effortless and divinely sanctioned conquests of the reigning king. Herodotos, by contrast, although he allows imperial expansion to structure his narrative, tends to write from the perspective of those who are threatened or conquered, and shows a particular interest in those peoples who successfully resist royal aggression.

An old theory of Herodotean composition posited that Herodotos began, like Hekataios, as a geographer and ethnographer and only slowly came to realize that his true subject was the great conflict of East and West. According to this theory, much of the first half of the *Histories* represents the relics of Herodotos' original geographic project, awkwardly shoehorned into a frame-narrative of developing East–West conflict (thus, for example, all of book 2, the history and ethnography of Egypt, would be a largely irrelevant digression). More recently, however, a unitarian school of reading Herodotos has marshalled

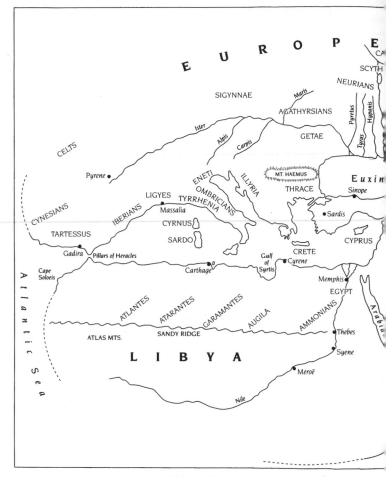

A HERODOTOS-EYE VIEW OF THE WORLD. This modern 'map' attempts to give some
idea of the world as represented in the work of Herodotos in the form of the
kind of map-making which was rapidly developing during the fifth century BCE.

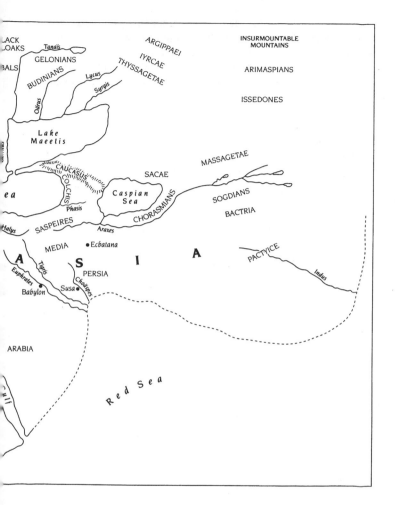

LACK
LOAKS
Tanais
GELONIANS
BALS
BUDINIANS
Oarus
Lycus
Syrgis
THYSSAGETAE
ARGIPPAEI
IYRCAE
INSURMOUNTABLE
MOUNTAINS
ARIMASPIANS
ISSEDONES
Lake
Maeetis
CAUCASUS
COLCHIS
SACAE
MASSAGETAE
Phasis
e a
Caspian
Sea
SOGDIANS
BACTRIA
Halys
SASPEIRES
Araxes
CHORASMIANS
A
S
I
A
PACTYICE
MEDIA
• Ecbatana
Indus
Euphrates
Tigris
PERSIA
Babylon
Susa •
Choaspes
ARABIA
Red Sea
ulf

strong arguments against this theory, demonstrating the integral interconnections between the more ethnographic, wide-ranging first half of Herodotos' *Histories* and the more narrowly focused, historical second half.

Thus one pervasive pattern throughout the *Histories* is the contrast between what we might call 'hard' and 'soft' cultures. Hard cultures tend to inhabit rough countries with a shortage of wealth and means of livelihood; they are under-civilized and usually politically decentralized. Soft cultures enjoy luxurious living, specialization of arts and skills, they are hyper-civilized and are usually ruled by strong centralized monarchies. Paradigmatic hard cultures are the Massagetai (end of book 1) and the Scythians (book 4); paradigmatic soft cultures are the Lydians, the Babylonians (book 1), and the Egyptians (book 2). In war, hard cultures always conquer soft cultures (as the Persians conquer the Lydians and Egyptians), but often themselves become enervated once they are exposed to the cultures they have conquered. Thus the Persians start out as a hard people under Kyros, but become soft from enjoying the fruits of their vast empire, so that a generation later they are no match for the rugged Scythians. Through this pattern, Herodotos elaborates an ethnographic theory of different peoples which also has a historical dimension. For 'hardness' and 'softness' are not dictated simply by geography and climate (as they are in the contemporary Hippokratic medical treatise *Airs, Waters, Places;* cf. p. 129 below), but also by the interaction of peoples and by individual peoples' own deliberate choice through custom and legislation (*nomos*). In the end, this pattern helps account for the 'astonishing' fact that Greek armies could successfully resist much larger invading forces led by Persians in 490 and 480–479. As in the case of the Persian invasion of Scythia (book 4, which reads in many ways like a preview of the Persian War narrative of books 6–9), the Greeks are a 'hard' people who can therefore resist the depredations of the now soft Persians. Thus the expansive sweep of the *Histories'* first half establishes patterns that help us understand the historical events of its second half.

Yet the fact that the Persians in Herodotos' conception could go within two generations from hard to soft suggests that Herodotos' purpose is not merely to explain the past. Many elements in his work (especially in the later books) imply also a didactic purpose that looks to the future: Herodotos' narrative offers a warning to the conquering Greeks not to be seduced in their turn by the lures of luxury and empire. We should remember that Herodotos himself lived through the débâcle of Thourioi (where the panhellenic colony ran into difficulties because of infighting between Dorian and Ionian settlers) and through the great years of the Athenian domination or 'empire' (478–430, Thoukydides' Pentekontaetia or 'fifty years'). Indeed, it is clear that he lived into the first years of the Peloponnesian War at least. Given this context, we can see the didactic element implicit in several vignettes that Herodotos offers in the closing books. There is first the story of the Spartan King Pausanias, the victorious commander at the Battle of Plataia, amazed by the opulence and luxury of the tent of Xerxes captured in the battle. On a whim, he has the Persian king's servants prepare their normal royal meal, which he juxtaposes to the plain fare of the Spartan *sussitia*. He then calls together the other Greek commanders, as he says 'to show them the folly of the Persian, who, when he had such a life-style, came against us to take away our miserable fare' (9. 82). In context, Herodotos' narrative can only be heavily ironic, since, as he tells us discreetly elsewhere, Pausanias would, within a couple of years, be accused of plotting with the Persian king, dazzled by the wealth and luxury he here disdains (Herodotus, 5. 32, 8. 3. 2).

Herodotos' closing vignette of the Athenians is no better. The very last event he narrates in the *Histories* is the Siege of Sestos, commanded by the Athenian Xanthippos (father of Perikles). Xanthippos allows the vengeful Greek populace to crucify the Persian commander Artauktes and to stone his son to death before his eyes (9. 120). These are acts of 'barbarian' savagery comparable to the mutilation of the corpse of Mardonios, which Pausanias had nobly abjured after the Battle of Plataia (9. 78–9). And significantly, this assimilation of Greek behaviour to barbarian norms takes place 'on the shore where Xerxes yoked the Hellespont'. Thus the crucified body of Artauktes marks the crossing-point between Europe and Asia, and ominously foreshadows the ways in which the Athenian empire will come to imitate more and more closely the violent Persian regime it was first formed to oppose. Through these anecdotes, Herodotos shows us implicitly how the Greeks could be corrupted by their success, and how greed and ambition for empire would eventually break down their fragile alliance and lead to the terrible internecine conflicts of the later fifth century.

Between science and rhetoric: Thoukydides

As with Herodotos, we know very little about Thoukydides' life and background beyond what he tells us himself in his *History*. One important bit of information is that his father's name was Oloros; this is a very unusual name, which we know belonged to a late sixth-century Thracian king who gave his daughter in marriage to Miltiades, son of Kimon (who would later be the Athenian commander at the Battle of Marathon). This name strongly suggests that the historian was himself a member of the family of Miltiades and Kimon, one of the wealthiest and most prestigious families in Athens. Thoukydides' wealth and noble birth, as well as his Thracian connections, tend to be confirmed by what he tells us himself: he was elected Commander (*strategos*) in 424/3 (a position that still almost invariably went to prominent aristocrats at this time), and he was in 424 'in possession of the working of the goldmines on the Thracian mainland' opposite the island of Thasos (which implies the acquisition of prodigious wealth from slave-worked mines; Thoukydides, 4. 105. 1). Probably because of his Thracian connections, Thoukydides was dispatched as leader of a campaign force to this area, charged with preventing the defection of Athenian allied cities to the Spartan commander Brasidas. Thoukydides (possibly on his first mission as Commander) miscalculated and arrived just hours too late to prevent the defection of the strategically important city of Amphipolis to Brasidas (Thoukydides, 4. 104–6). Rather than face the wrath of the Athenian people for this crucial military failure, Thoukydides chose voluntary exile for the next twenty years (as he tells us himself, 5. 26. 5). He wrote the history of the Peloponnesian War, starting, as he tells us, when the conflict first began and proceeding by summers and winters down to the twenty-first year of the war (411 BCE), when his account stops abruptly at a semicolon in the middle of a paragraph. We do not know why Thoukydides left his account unfinished; it is usually assumed that his death intervened, but this is not necessarily the case. Calculating back from his stint as Commander, scholars assume that Thoukydides was born in the early 450s; and he certainly survived the end of the War in 404 BCE (again as he tells us himself, 5. 26. 5), perhaps dying in the early 390s. Thoukydides' text reveals to us that he was profoundly influenced by the intellectual developments of his day, especially the Sophistic movement and Hippokratic developments in medicine. The so-called Sophists were performers, writers, and teachers who claimed to be able to impart to students the arts of rhetoric and political governance. Many of them came to Athens in the latter half of the fifth century, drawn by the city's imperial wealth and by the growing need for political and rhetorical training as its system of government came to depend more heavily on public debate and persuasion. The first great generation, including Protagoras of Abdera, Hippias of Elis, Prodikos of Keos, and Gorgias of Leontinoi, were polymaths who systematized many different fields of knowledge (e.g., astronomy, medicine, mathematics, etymology and grammar, ethics), but they seem to have had their most profound impact in the domain of political rhetoric (see Ch. 5, pp. 149–51).

They were the first to teach rhetoric in a systematic way, claiming that there were two opposing arguments (and only two) to be devised on any issue (Protagoras' *dissoi logoi*), while they purveyed distinctive styles of argument, such as the argument from likelihood (*eikos*). Aristotle, in the *Rhetoric*, offers a vivid example of how the argument from likelihood could be used in the lawcourt. Imagine, he says, that a small man beats up a larger man, who brings him up on charges. In court, the accused argues, 'Is it *likely* that I, a small man, would attempt to assault a much bigger man?' The accuser, in turn, argues, 'Is it *likely* that I, a bigger man, would face the shame of this accusation if it were not true?' Thus (notice), the argument from likelihood can be used in the service of the construction of opposing arguments on the same theme (see Ch. 6, pp. 174–5). In like manner, the Sophists popularized a set of conceptual oppositions which could form the basis of opposing arguments: convention vs. nature (*nomos* vs. *phusis*), and the advantageous vs. the just (as Aristotle advises, if your opponent argues from nature, you shift the ground and argue from convention; if, contrariwise, he argues from convention, you argue from nature). The Sophists' rhetorical teaching as well as their other writings reveal them to be pragmatists and relativists, who expressed agnosticism about divine causes but displayed unlimited faith in the power of human reason, ingenuity, and perception. Hence Protagoras' famous dictum, 'Of all things the measure is mankind, of the things that are, that they are; of the things that are not, that they are not'.

Allied with the Sophists in their optimistic faith in progress through the exercise of reason and technique were the Greek medical writers, many of whose treatises have come down to us under the name of the famous fifth-century physician Hippokrates of Kos. The medical writers of the late fifth century had come to reject supernatural causes for illness; instead, they established medicine as a *techne*, a specialized skill and field of knowledge based on close observation and the compilation of many case studies. Thus the Hippokratics engaged in very accurate recording of the empirical facts and symptoms of disease, as a basis for *diagnosis* (distinguishing each illness from every other) and *prognosis* (accurate prediction of the future course of illness). One basic contention of this new medical *techne* was that the combination of past experience and careful observation enabled the practitioner to deduce unseen causes from perceptible symptoms.

Thoukydides' text reveals over and over again the profound influence of these two intellectual movements. The influence of the medical writers is perhaps most obvious in the clinical description of the plague in Athens (2. 47–55), but it informs many other passages of description and analysis as well. For example, in his succinct formulation of the causes of the war: 'I consider the truest cause (*alethestaten prophasin*), though the most invisible in discussion, to be that the Athenians, as they became powerful and provoked fear in the Lakedaimonians, compelled them to fight. But the openly acknowledged grievances on either side were these, which caused them to dissolve the treaties and go to war' (1. 23. 6; Thoukydides then proceeds to narrate the immediate conflicts over Potidaia and Kerkyra). Notice that like the medical writers, Thoukydides rejects any divine cause behind the war, but instead perceives an invisible, underlying motive in Spartan fear of Athenian expansion (*prophasis*, Thoukydides' word for this invisible, underlying cause, was in fact a technical term in Greek medical writing for the visible symptoms of the onset of disease). The form and diction of such passages suggest that Thoukydides regarded the war as a disease that infected the whole of Greece, and took it as his own task to describe its onset and progress.

The Sophistic influence on Thoukydides is even more pervasive, detectable at every level of the text, from his penchant for antithetical expression, to the frequent pairing of opposed speeches in debate, to the speakers' repeated invocation of the argument from advantage and the claim that 'might makes right' (which we can read as a strong form of the nature vs. convention argument). Sophistic models also lie behind many elements of Thoukydides' methodology. For example, immediately after the proem, Thoukydides embarks on a brief survey of early Greek history (1. 1. 3–1. 20). This survey (traditionally called the 'Archaeology') presents a relentlessly materialist analysis, eschewing divine motivation, of human progress through the gradual acquisition of surplus money, defensive walls, and ships. In this account, Thoukydides not only introduces several of his key themes, but also offers a *tour de force* demonstration of his method: deduction from visible evidence (*tekmeria*) and argument from likelihood (*eikos*; see e.g. 1. 9. 4).

In like manner, Thoukydides' well-known statement of his policy with regard to speeches must be understood against a Sophistic background. The historian explains: 'And however many things each of them said in speech before or during the war, it was hard to recall in detail the accuracy of the things said, both for me, of the speeches I myself heard, and for those reporting them back to me from somewhere else, but as it seemed to me that each party would most say the necessary things (*ta deonta*) concerning the things present on every occasion, while I held as nearly as possible to the general idea of the things that truly were said, thus it has been said' (1. 22. 1). A huge amount of ink has been spilled on this statement, debating whether or not Thoukydides gives us an accurate transcription of speeches actually delivered, and what his statement of policy here means. But it is comprehensible as a statement of the Sophistic principle that for each argumentative position (for example, for or against war), there is only one set of things that could or should be said (*ta deonta*).

Given these marked intellectual influences, we must finally ask: did Thoukydides share the Sophistic views articulated by his speakers—making him, as many have thought, the first great advocate of *Realpolitik* and *Machtpolitik*—or was he critical of them? And did he share the optimism, the faith in rationality, of Sophists and medical writers alike? I will return to these questions, but first we need to consider Thoukydides' relation to his written medium.

Writing and textuality: making readers

There was an age gap of at least twenty to twenty-five years between Herodotos and Thoukydides, a gap that perhaps partly accounts for Thoukydides' profoundly different relation to the technology of writing and the constitution of his text. Herodotos, as we saw, on the cusp between orality and literacy, produced a uniquely capacious text, collecting and preserving oral traditions from many different sources. Thoukydides' work, by contrast, is more narrowly focused, both in terms of time and range of subject-matter. In contrast to Herodotos' 220-year sweep, Thoukydides concentrates almost exclusively on contemporary history (the Peloponnesian War, which he himself lived through). More significantly, Thoukydides severely restricts his range of topics to politics and war—men talking and men fighting. He hardly anywhere mentions women or families, social or cultural practices, religion, temples, or sacred space. As such, he is the inventor of political history narrowly construed, a form which seems quite 'natural' to us, but which was at the time (especially in the wake of Herodotos) hardly a self-evident choice.

Thoukydides' self-imposed restrictions are conditioned partly by his methodological assumptions (thus, for example, he seems to think that accuracy can only be attained in the reconstruction of relatively recent events), partly by an uncompromising rationalism—hence his downplaying of religious elements—but also by a greater adaptation to the possibilities and limitations of the written medium than his precursors attained. Thus many passages of Herodotos, in their concreteness and proliferation of contextual detail (for example, descriptions of dedications at Delphi or the layout of battlefields) seem almost to mime the experience of an oral performance in which the audience is itself already well acquainted with (say) Delphi or Plataia. Thoukydides' *History*, by contrast, offers a much sparer, decontextualized account and therefore achieves much greater autonomy as a written text. At the same time, Thoukydides tends to present issues and events in the most general and abstract form possible (as has been noticed, this is a striking feature of the speeches especially). This tendency toward generalization and abstraction further exploits the peculiar strengths of the written medium. Finally, in contrast to Herodotos' constant, multiple citation of sources, Thoukydides almost never cites sources, offering us instead the finished and apparently seamless results of the historian's own laborious enquiries and analysis. Where Herodotos' account attempts to capture in written form the complexities of multiple oral traditions, Thoukydides' text maintains an awesome and severe autonomy, constituting itself as the definitive account of the period.

This contrast in the two historians' deployment of the written medium is clear already in their first sentences: while Herodotos designates his account *histories apodexis hede* ('this display/performance of enquiry'), Thoukydides says simply, 'Thoukydides the Athenian wrote up (*xunegrapse*) the war of the Peloponnesians and the Athenians, how they warred against each other, having begun straightway when the war started and anticipating that it would be great and more worthy of report than all previous events, judging from the fact that both sides were at the peak of their power in all preparation at the time, and seeing that the rest of Greece had aligned itself on either side, part straightaway, the rest also contemplating it.' In contrast to Herodotos' emphasis on performance, Thoukydides chooses the modest verb *xunegrapse*, commonly used of writing up a report or a technical treatise. And yet, the implication of this verb is not so modest after all, since it suggests that the 'facts' to be written up are clear and unambiguous, in need only of recording. It is noteworthy also that, in contrast to both Hekataios and Herodotos, Thoukydides uses no deictic pronoun that might attach his text to a present of performance (not, for example, 'Thoukydides wrote up *this* war', or '*Thus* Thoukydides wrote up the war'). The language of the text makes it completely autonomous. Indeed, when Thoukydides returns to the topic of the greatness of the war at the end of the 'Archaeology', even his authorship has been effaced by the self-evident autonomy of the written text (now fused in perfect adequation with the events it describes): 'And this war ... will make clear to those considering from the events themselves that it was greater than all others' (1. 21. 2).

We must finally ask why Thoukydides chose the medium of writing and why he wrote the way he did, constituting an austere text that comes to be coextensive with—even to replace—the war itself. One answer has been that Thoukydides so completely removes himself from his written text in order to achieve perfect objectivity. But perhaps we have been too quick to construct Thoukydides in the pattern of a modern scientific historian, for the ancient answer was very different. Ancient readers knew Thoukydides as an acknowledged master of *enargeia* ('vividness'), who used that technique (and others) to engage readers' emotions at a visceral level. As Plutarch observed, 'Thoukydides always strives for this vividness in his narrative, and all but makes the reader an actual spectator and listener present at the astounding and dreadful events he describes.' Part of this effect of immediate emotional engagement is achieved by the absence of explicit authorial intervention and commentary, so that events seem to be conjured up directly before the reader without any mediation.

It is, furthermore, telling that Plutarch refers explicitly to 'astounding and *dreadful* events', because at one point Thoukydides himself reveals the centrality of suffering to his historiographic project. In his first sentence, he asserts that the Peloponnesian War was 'greater than all former events and most worthy of recording'; when he returns to the topic of the greatness of the war after the 'Archaeology', he elaborates: 'Of former deeds, the Persian War was the greatest thing accomplished, and this still had a swift resolution through a pair of naval battles and a pair of land battles. But the great length of this war surpassed it, and sufferings (*pathemata*) occurred for Greece during the war such as had no equal in a comparable length of time' (1. 23. 1). Here the measure of the Peloponnesian War's greatness, which inspired Thoukydides to make his historical record, is the unparalleled suffering it caused. This is Thoukydides' real theme, and his seeming authorial objectivity is not the goal, but the means by which he conveys to the reader as immediately and vividly as possible the experience of war. In order to experience the tragic effects of Thoukydides' narrative techniques, the reader need only peruse his description of the first and second ships dispatched to Mytilene (3. 49), the final attempt of the Athenian ships to break out of the Harbour of Syracuse (7. 70–1), or the devastation of Mykalessos by a band of renegade Thracian mercenaries (7. 29).

But these same written techniques have more than just an emotional impact on the attentive reader. Notice, for example, how the deeper meaning of the 'magnitude' of the war only emerges gradually, through the sequential reading of Thoukydides' text. This (small) example offers us a paradigm of how the text works upon the reader, guiding him or her to a richer understanding by subtle shifts and modulations. This pattern is repeated—writ large—for almost every important issue and theme in the *History*, for example, the original causes of the war, or what Thoukydides thought went wrong with the Sicilian Expedition. Traditionally, scholars used to attempt to account for these complex shifts in perspective by positing different layers of composition; after all, if we take Thoukydides at his word in the first sentence, he began writing when the war began and continued for twenty-seven years at least. Surely in that time his thinking changed? And yet, decades of such separatist analysis have produced no consensus on the order of composition or on what Thoukydides' views 'really were', and most scholars have now abandoned this 'Thoukydidean question' as an unproductive line of enquiry. If, however, we shift our focus from production to reception (from the author to the reader), the many minute inconsistencies detected by separatist scholars become evidence for the exact processes by which Thoukydides' text progressively educates its readers. From this perspective it is clear that the text resists easy answers and assumptions at every level and does so in ways that *only* a written text can achieve. Thus, at the level of style, the text consistently fractures conventional antitheses and makes them asymmetrical, while its generalizations are often so deeply embedded in particular situations that they are not extractable. In like manner, juxtaposed speeches and narrative elucidate each other, but in complex and uneven ways that compel the reader constantly to revise his or her understanding.

Thus the text's resistances offer an ongoing intellectual, as well as emotional, challenge to the reader. And here we return to the question of Thoukydides' relation to the Sophists. As we saw, Thoukydides' text is permeated with Sophistic rhetorical techniques and methodology, and the 'Archaeology' (for example) seems to display a characteristically Sophistic confidence in the progressive development of human resources and technology. The first two books also show us on several occasions (especially in the speeches of Perikles) an ideal balance between public deliberation and action. Thus, as Perikles puts it in the Funeral Oration (a model public speech for the Athenian war dead of each campaign, which Thoukydides incorporates into the narrative of book 2), 'In contrast to others, we have also this characteristic: that the same people most of all take risks and also deliberate concerning the things we will attempt, while for others ignorance produces boldness and calculation delay' (2. 40. 3). And yet, as the text continues, we see rhetoric turned more and more to the service not of rationality and reasoned deliberation, but of violence and unrestrained ambition. Thus we can chart a progression from the Mytilenean Debate in book 3—in which the destruction of the rebellious city of Mytilene is narrowly averted—to the Melian Dialogue in book 5 (in which representatives of the neutral state of Melos fail in their argument from honour and traditional values and their entire city is condemned), to the debate on the Sicilian Expedition in book 6—in which Alkibiades inflames the Athenian people with desire for conquest, based on ignorance, misrepresentation, and uncontrollable imperial ambition. Indeed, at one point, Thoukydides even puts into the mouth of Kleon a critique of the damaging effects of competitive rhetorical displays on the Athenian people: 'You yourselves are to blame for stupidly instituting contests of speeches, you who are accustomed to be regular spectators of speeches, but of actions you only hear about them—judging that future actions are possible from those who praise them, but as for the things already done, you do not consider the events you yourselves have witnessed more persuasive than what you hear from those who skilfully reproach you in speech' (3. 38. 4). The fact that Thoukydides consistently portrays Kleon himself as a violent and manipulative demagogue—he is, after all, arguing here for the execution of the entire adult male population of Mytilene (cf. Ch. 6, pp. 176–7)—does not entirely vitiate his denunciation of the Athenians' addiction to rhetorical displays. Here we may have yet another reason for Thoukydides' choice of the written medium and for his peculiar style. His text is defiantly literary; it is deliberately written to be difficult to comprehend when heard, in order to short-circuit the exchange of specious persuasion and public enjoyment that Sophistic rhetoric promotes. Instead, Thoukydides' text forces its audience into isolated—and effortful—private reading.

We have still not yet quite exhausted Thoukydides' critique of Sophistic rhetoric. For it is not just that rhetoric misleads, replacing reasoned deliberation with specious persuasion, but that, in the course of the war, language itself becomes a form of violence. This is perhaps clearest in Thoukydides' devastating description of civil war in Kerkyra, where 'even words were forced to change their meaning in adequation to events', the new terms justifying the most ruthless slaughter (3. 82. 4–5). As *logos* collapses into irrationality and *peitho* (persuasion) into *bie* (force), the *History* offers a scathing indictment of the Sophistic movement and the idiom that forms the text's very fabric.

In like manner, Thoukydides seems simultaneously steeped in the methods of Hippokratic medicine yet ultimately sceptical about their efficacy to change or effect a cure. Thus, at the end of the 'Archaeology' (1. 22. 4), he seems to sound a fairly optimistic note that, human nature being what it is, his careful historical account will serve as a means of diagnosis and prognosis for human upheavals in the future; and, indeed, the statesmen Thoukydides seems most to admire, Themistokles and Perikles, display in his account precisely this extraordinary skill in prognosis (cf. Ch. 5, p. 142). And yet, as his *History* proceeds, it becomes less and less clear that the accurate detailing of symptoms can, in fact, lead to any kind of diagnosis of causes or cure. In the case of the plague at Athens, for example, Thoukydides promises, 'I will discuss what the process was like, and I will clarify those factors from which, if the affliction ever again occurs, one might, by having some advance knowledge, not fail to recognize it' (2. 48. 3), but at the same time, he studiously maintains agnosticism about the cause and acknowledges that there was no successful treatment of the disease: 'Some died in neglect, others died though they were extremely well cared for. As for a remedy, there was nothing—no, not one—that those applying must benefit the sick; for what helped one harmed another' (2. 51. 2).

Analogous to the physical destruction of the plague in Thoukydides' account is the moral and social disintegration of civil war, captured in all its horror by the historian in his 'case study' of Kerkyra (3. 82–5). Here, accurate knowledge of the past and the characteristic trajectory of civil war offers no hope for treatment or improvement, only a clear recognition of the viciousness of human nature:

> And many difficulties fell upon the cities in civil war, the kind that occur and always will occur as long as human nature is the same, but sometimes more mildly and varying in forms, as each set of changes of circumstances arise. For in peace and prosperity, both cities and individuals use higher standards on account of not falling into compulsions against their will; but

war, by taking away the easy satisfaction of day-to-day needs, is a violent teacher and assimilates the passions of most people to their present circumstances. (3. 82. 2)

Thus, in his deeply ambivalent engagement with the optimistic, rationalizing movements of his time, Thoukydides produces a profound critique of 'human nature' under the pressures of war and imperialism. His written text never offers the reader easy answers, but instead guides him or her to probe ever deeper in the process of an exacting private reading.

Postscript: Xenophon and the 'disembodied' reader

It is a truism that all the major historians of the classical period—Herodotos, Thoukydides, and Xenophon—were exiles, and that the status of exile, with its disengagement from embedded political action, was the pre-condition for the writing of history. It is worth acknowledging, though, how exile produced very different effects on the first great practitioners of *historie*. For Herodotos, it was perhaps what inspired the 'global vision' that informs his work, while for Thoukydides, it seems to have enabled the carving-out of a private space for meticulous writing and effortful reading.

The third great classical historian, Xenophon, was also an exile from his native Athens, first by choice and then by necessity, for most of his adult life. A generation younger than Thoukydides, he picked up the narrative of the Peloponnesian War where Thoukydides had left off and completed it, ultimately carrying his *Hellenika* (or 'Greek Things') down to the Battle of Mantinea in 362 BCE. As a young man in 401 BCE, Xenophon had joined an expedition of Greek mercenary soldiers to support the rebellion of Kyros, younger brother of the reigning Persian king. Kyros' army marched from Sardis to Babylon, where Kyros was killed in battle and the Greek commanders were treacherously done away with. Xenophon, who had been largely an observer, helped lead the stranded force of ten thousand Greek mercenaries back to Greek-occupied territory, an expedition he himself recounts in the *Anabasis*, or 'March Up Country'. In 395, Xenophon joined the expedition of the Spartan King Agesilaos to liberate the Greeks in Asia Minor from the Persians. Because of his assistance to Sparta, Athens' enemy, he was at that time officially exiled, though the Spartans rewarded him with an estate near Olympia in the Peloponnese. Late in his life, Xenophon's exile was repealed but we do not know if he ever returned to Athens.

Xenophon's career trajectory looks very different from that of Herodotos or Thoukydides because it was much more shaped and governed by the para-political system of aristocratic guest-friendship: it was guest-friendship (or *xenia*) that motivated his joining the Ten Thousand, and again, joining the expedition of Agesilaos. In this sense, it was not so much that Xenophon chose or was forced to abandon the political engagement of the citizen, but that he spent much of his life participating in an alternative order of networking élites and dynasts, spread over the entire Greek world, Persia, and Thrace. He was thus a throwback to an older kind of aristocratic ideal, as he was in some ways in his writing. For Xenophon was an extremely prolific writer in many genres: in addition to the *Anabasis* and *Hellenika*, he composed treatises on horseman- ship, hunting, and estate-management (all traditional aristocratic pursuits). And since he had been a friend and follower of Sokrates in Athens in his youth, he composed a Defence (*Apology*) of Sokrates, a *Symposium* as a Sokratic Dia- logue (perhaps in part his response to Plato's *Symposium*), and *Memorabilia*, his recollections of Sokrates framed as a defence of his civic 'usefulness'. In these Sokratic treatises Xenophon engages most directly with Athenian politics and civic order, unsurprisingly perhaps given their agenda of defending Sokrates posthumously against the charges on which he was executed by the Athenian state.

But the single topic that engaged Xenophon most in his writings was the leadership of men, and the qualities of the ideal leader. This issue informs his short dialogue *Hieron*, his biographical sketch *Agesilaos*, and his lengthy 'histor- ical novel' *The Education of Kyros*, an idealizing portrait of the education and conquests of Kyros the Great, the founder of the Persian empire. Projected onto the sixth-century struggles for Persian hegemony, Xenophon constructs Kyros as the perfect prince, a canny strategist in war and generous leader in peace, who binds his subjects to him with ties of love and admiration.

In another sense, however, Xenophon diverged markedly from the archaic aristocratic ideal, in that he composed for a disembodied readership. In this respect, we can see Xenophon's writing as the confluence of the developing traditions of history and philosophy. Together, these two traditions bequeathed to the eclectic Xenophon their didactic impulses, their use of exemplarity, their ethnographic fascinations, and perhaps most importantly— by the time of the mid-fourth century, their audience of readers.

5 | Sages, sophists, and philosophers: Greek wisdom literature

ANDREA WILSON NIGHTINGALE

Wise men and the performance of wisdom

The Greek thinkers in the archaic and classical periods performed their wisdom in different ways and in front of different audiences. As a modern audience that encounters these 'philosophers' only in written works, we tend to disconnect their doctrines from their historical and cultural contexts. By focusing on philosophic 'performances' of wisdom—both oral and written—and by examining the audiences addressed by these thinkers, we can better appreciate their lives and activities and, indeed, their different conceptions of the nature of wisdom.

The discipline of Philosophy came properly into existence in the fourth century BCE, when intellectuals laid claim to a distinct mode of wisdom which called for a novel title and an honorary place in Greek society. Philosophy was first defined and legitimized as a specialized discipline by Plato, who appropriated the term *philosophia*—which had previously designated intellectual cultivation in the broadest sense—for his own activities and ideas. How, then, did philosophy evolve as a cultural practice, and what are the links between the fourth-century philosophers and the intellectuals and wise men of the previous centuries? How did these thinkers present their ideas to their fellow Greeks, and what forms of discourse did they use? To attempt an answer to these questions, I will discuss the 'performance' of philosophic wisdom—in speech, in writing, and in action—from the sixth to the fourth centuries BCE; and in particular, the audiences that these thinkers addressed and the contexts in which their ideas were communicated and exchanged.

It is customary to say that Thales of Miletos, who lived in the early sixth century, was the first philosopher. This attribution is due to Aristotle, who (over two hundred years later) was the first to give 'philosophy' a history and a pedigree. Although Aristotle provides precious evidence for the shadowy figures who are counted as early philosophers, we must remember that he was not a historian but himself a philosopher searching for thinkers who adumbrated his own theory of causality. Aristotle's 'history' of philosophy in the first book of his *Metaphysics* is, in fact, a narrative in which philosophy begins as a babbling infant and grows into the mature work of Aristotle. As he says there, 'although all the causes have been spoken of before in one sense, in another they have not been stated at all; for the earliest philosophy spoke about everything in baby-talk, inasmuch as it was new and in its infancy'. Clearly, these early thinkers were not saying exactly what Aristotle wanted them to say. It is for this reason that he accuses them of speaking 'muddily', 'metaphorically', and 'vaguely'. When viewed from Aristotle's perspective, the early Greek thinkers often sound a bit obtuse; thus in chapter 4 Aristotle compares them to 'untrained soldiers who rush around in battle, often striking good blows, but not acting with knowledge; these thinkers do not understand their own statements'.

Resisting Aristotle's revisionary history, I want to examine the early Greek thinkers in their own terms. These men were mature thinkers in their own right, and were not simply paving the way for Aristotle. Rather than locate each individual in his social and political context—there are far too many and they hail from all over the Mediterranean—I will look in more general terms at the activities of these men, both practical and intellectual, and at their intended audiences. By focusing on these issues, we can better understand the kind of wisdom that these 'philosophers' professed.

But let me say right off that I do not believe that we should call the thinkers of the sixth and fifth centuries BCE 'philosophers'. They did not use this term for themselves, nor did others refer to them in this way. The words 'philosophy' and 'philosophize' were very rarely used until the fourth century BCE and, when they were, did not pick out a special and distinct group of thinkers. Rather, the words *sophos* and *sophistes* were the coveted titles: the early thinkers wanted to be ranked among 'the wise'. In this period, wise men came in many forms: poets, prophets, doctors, statesmen, astronomers, and various kinds of inventors and artisans were identified and honoured as '*sophoi*'. Although these different kinds of wise men were clearly seen to be practising distinct activities, there was nonetheless a generalized competition among the different groups for the title of 'wise man'.

To be called wise was to receive a certain kind of 'symbolic capital', a payment in the form of power, status, and honour rather than money or goods. This kind of capital was, of course, a scarce commodity, and had to be won against stiff competition. Thus early historical and 'philosophical' thinkers found it necessary to compete with Homer, Hesiod, and other wise men in order to put themselves on the map as intellectual authorities or 'masters of truth'. We must remember that this was not a culture in which one went to school to get credentials: each thinker had to demonstrate his own authority and expertise to his fellow citizens and Greeks. Since Homer and Hesiod were considered the wisest and most important voices in the tradition, the early Greek thinkers were compelled to work in their wake. In the tenth book of his *Republic*, Plato refers to the 'ancient quarrel between poetry and philosophy'. In fact, the early thinkers did not attack poetry *per se* but rather entered into a competition with a few great poets. In fact, some thinkers such as Xenophanes, Parmenides, and Empedokles rivalled Homer and Hesiod by writing hexameter poetry of their own: they, too, were poets, but with a different theme and message.

The archaic sages

I begin with a brief look, then, at Thales, who is in the peculiar position of being ranked by posterity as both a Sage (one of the élite Seven) and a Philosopher. The fifth-century historian Herodotos offers several short accounts of him in the *Histories*. In book 1, he tells us that Thales predicted an eclipse and that he diverted the river Halys for the benefit of Kroisos and his army (when they were attempting to invade Persian territory); Herodotos also reports that, when the Ionians in Asia Minor were being subdued by the Persians, Thales advised the Ionians to set up a deliberative council on the island of Teos, and to make this the capital of a confederation of city-states. Diogenes Laertius (third century CE), whose *Lives of the Philosophers* is a key source of information about Greek philosophy, relates another story about Thales' 'cunning intelligence': in order to demonstrate how easy it was to get rich, Thales, foreseeing that it would be a good season for olives, rented all the oil-presses and obtained a monopoly on the proceeds (Diogenes Laertius, hereafter DL, 1. 26). These stories about Thales portray a man of many skills. Alongside his astronomical expertise, he demonstrates a great deal of practical wisdom: engineering the diversion of a river, acting as a leader in the political affairs of the day, and exhibiting a keen understanding of agriculture and business.

It comes as a great surprise, then, when fourth-century philosophers such as Plato, Aristotle, and Herakleides of Pontos represent Thales as the prototypical contemplative. In the *Theaetetus*, for example, Plato tell us that Thales fell into a well when he was contemplating the stars; a maidservant mocked him for being so eager to know what was going on in the sky that he did not see what lay at his feet. As Plato goes on to say, this is the lot of all philosophers, who are by definition ignorant of the world of society and politics, having given themselves over to the contemplation of higher truths. In a similar vein, Herakleides of Pontos (a member of Plato's Academy), wrote a dialogue in which Thales claims that he always lived in solitude as a private individual and kept aloof from state affairs (DL 1. 25–6). And Aristotle tells us in his *Nicomachean Ethics* (6. 7. 5) that Thales was 'wise' but not 'prudent' since he did not look to his own interests; Thales possessed a wisdom that was 'rare, marvellous, difficult, and superhuman'—the kind of wisdom that is, Aristotle says, 'useless' (*achreston*) in the practical sphere, since it does not deal with things 'that are good for human beings'. According to Aristotle, Thales is the first known philosopher in so far as he claimed that the world originated from water; his other skills and activities are simply irrelevant. How, then, do we get from the practical, political, polymathic Thales to an other-worldly contemplative—from a performer of wisdom in the social and political arena to a detached spectator of truth?

In order to understand this development, we need to look briefly at the archaic sage and the culture in which he lived. What sort of wisdom made the Seven Sages wise? Although these sages were by no means the only wise men of their day, they were clearly among the most famous and exceptional. To be sure, our evidence for them is scanty and late, and often bears the mark of fictionalized representations; but these at least tell us what counted as wisdom in the archaic period, and this is sufficient for our present task. The extant accounts suggest that the seven sages were a disparate and, to some extent, changeable group of individuals. The most commonly recognized members of the group are Solon of Athens, Thales of Miletos, Pittakos of Mytilene, Bias of Priene (near Miletos), Chilon of Sparta, Kleoboulos of Lindos (on Rhodes), and Periander of Corinth. Many scholars have claimed that what characterized these sages was their poetic and/or political activities. In fact, five of the seven sages were reported to have written poetry, and five to have been involved in politics. But many men of this age were fine poets and politicians, and only a few made it to the ranks of the seven sages. As Richard Martin has recently shown, what distinguished these individuals was their extraordinary 'performances' of wisdom.

The sages could 'perform' their wisdom in different ways. First, by non-verbal actions, as when Thales made a fortune by monopolizing the olive harvest: here, the sage enacted a clever idea and the outcome proved that he had special knowledge. Second, the sage could demonstrate his wisdom by a combination of action and utterance. For example, when Solon wanted to convince his countrymen to renew the war with Megara over Salamis (a proposal that had been declared illegal in Athens), he feigned madness, rushed into the Agora with a garland on his head, and recited a poem that he had written on Salamis which called for war; the Athenians were duly roused to anger, and proceeded to recapture Salamis (DL 1. 46). Here, Solon pretends to madness in order to evince his wisdom and sanity; in addition, his poem is performed in the space of the agora (the civic centre), where discourse is traditionally converted into political praxis.

Both of these examples evince a kind of wisdom that often eludes the modern scholar: what the ancient Greeks called *metis*. *Metis* is a fundamentally practical form of wisdom which is often associated with cunning and clever behaviour. This kind of wisdom does not focus on abstract truths, but rather on the complexities of practical life with all its chancy and changing forces and exigencies. The person who possesses *metis* has a keen eye for the main chance, for what the Greeks called *kairos*—the right thing at the right time. Thus Thales must seize the moment when he perceives that the olive crop will be abundant; Solon must find the right time and the right place to perform his poem (not to mention the demeanour and dress which enables him to get a hearing while breaking a law). An excellent example of an individual with *metis* is Themistokles, who saved the Athenians when they were being attacked by the Persians by convincing them to take refuge in their ships rather than their city. As the historian Thoukydides tells us, Themistokles 'was able to arrive at the most correct idea concerning the future, taking the widest point of view and foreseeing, as far as possible, the hidden advantages and disadvantages in what cannot be seen' (1. 138. 3). Here, *metis* includes an understanding of the larger context of a situation, an intuition of what is hidden in the future, and an unerring sense of what is advantageous at the present moment. *Metis* works with what is at hand, connives with the present: its exquisite sense of timing—of *kairos*—befuddles opponents and brings surprising successes. This kind of wise person does not gaze upon a truth which is detached from the human world; on the contrary, he immerses himself in the tide of events and acts in response to the particularities of the situation. *Metis* is thus a clever form of practical wisdom, and is displayed by men as different as Odysseus and Sokrates.

This notion of the 'performance of wisdom' sheds light on the context if not the content of the wisdom of the archaic and early classical periods. The content of wisdom, in fact, could come in many and various forms: but the contexts of its dissemination were finite. In the most general terms, the wise man operated in a social and political arena in which knowledge was demonstrated by a performer to an audience in a public or a private gathering. When one considers that the technology of writing was only beginning to take hold in the sixth and fifth centuries, it should come as no surprise that wisdom had to be orally or physically enacted; although some individuals did make use of writing, they could have reached only a tiny audience in this period by the circulation of written texts. In the absence of a literate public, a person could be declared wise solely on the basis of the exhibition of exceptional actions or exceptional discourse (be it poetic, political, religious, or intellectual).

Masters of truth

The early sages who later came to be called 'philosophers' formed a small subset of the large group of *sophoi* that populated the culture of this period. Take, first of all, Thales, Anaximines, and Anaximandros, sixth-century thinkers who all lived in Miletos, an Ionian city on the west coast of Asia Minor. Each of these men offered (among other things) a cosmology that explained the operation of the universe by recourse to 'natural' forces rather than individualized divinities struggling for power. These early thinkers initiated a tradition of recording their research (*historie,* cf. p. 135) in prose treatises (some fifth-century representatives of this tradition are Zeno, Anaxagoras, and Demokritos). The use of prose looks like a deliberate rejection of poetic discourse and its popular audiences, since poetry was designed for group pleasure rather than intellectual enquiry. In fact, scholars often ascribe to the early Ionian thinkers the heroic feat of liberating philosophic discourse from the shadowy realms of '*mythos*' (since their 'naturalistic' accounts of the cosmos rejected the poetic accounts that attributed causality to the weddings and wars of the gods). But the many scholarly attempts to trace the movement from poetry to philosophy—'from *mythos* to *logos*'—have foundered on the problem of defining the intrinsic qualities of 'myth' and of 'rational argumentation', and of identifying texts that are either purely mythic or purely analytic. Since the Greek poets were quite capable of constructing arguments, and the 'philosophers' were unable to avoid metaphor and myth, it is difficult to draw a clear distinction between *mythos* and *logos*. To be sure, we see in the Ionians a new way of thinking about the world; but we cannot say that their accounts are devoid of any mythical notions. What we can say is that these thinkers adopted a critical attitude towards received wisdom and were prized for their original speculations.

A very different kind of wisdom was cultivated by Pythagoras, who emigrated from the island of Samos to southern Italy in the second half of the sixth century. Because Pythagoras himself almost certainly did not publish any writings and his society observed a strict code of silence, the sources dealing with early Pythagoreanism offer little reliable evidence about this sage. We do know that he founded a religious society in the city of Kroton. The members of this society, which included women as well as men, lived a life of austerity and discipline, which included a vegetarian diet, the practice of self-examination, obedience to precepts known as *akousmata*, and a vow of silence about Pythagorean doctrine and practice. Pythagoras and his followers, then, were performing an entire way of life; their ideas and doctrines translated directly into daily *praxis* (for example, their belief in the immortality of the soul and its transmigration into animals led them to abstain from meat). In so far as Pythagoreanism offered its members hidden knowledge that could not be divulged, it resembled the mystery religions, which promised to benefit initiates by the revelation of secret wisdom. It is important to emphasize, however, that Pythagoras was fully involved in political life; in fact, he and his followers are said to have taken over the government of Kroton. Like other early sages, Pythagoras' wisdom was practical and political; his access to secret wisdom did not cut him off from the life of the city.

The sixth-century Ionians did not offer their research to large audiences, but rather to small groups of like-minded pupils and associates. And Pythagoras positively prohibited the dissemination of his doctrines to non-initiates. Many early thinkers, however, packaged their ideas so as to reach a broader public. Xenophanes (570–475 BCE) wrote elegiac and hexameter poems; Herakleitos (*fl.* 500 BCE) constructed riddling aphorisms that emulate the discourse of the Delphic oracle; and Parmenides (515—?440) and Empedokles (492–432) opted to rival Homer and Hesiod by writing hexameter poetry. These thinkers set out to compose literary art-works (albeit in different genres) rather than merely to document their ideas in writing. It is worth noting that Xenophanes attacks Homer explicitly, and Herakleitos inveighs not only against the poets Homer, Hesiod, and Archilochos, but also against Hekataios (a proto-historian, cf. p. 117), Xenophanes, and Pythagoras. Such attacks remind us that these thinkers conceived of themselves as rivalling 'wise men' in general rather than the specialized group of intellectuals who were later called philosophers. The fact that Herakleitos' opponents include poets and prose writers, as well as a religious/political guru such as Pythagoras, gives us a good idea of the breadth of 'wisdom' that he himself recognized as authoritative.

What can we say about the dissemination of the works of these thinkers? Unfortunately, the evidence is scanty and, for the most part, derives from the texts themselves. Diogenes Laertius tells us that Xenophanes 'rhapsodised' his own poems (DL 1. 18). This is a bit puzzling, since rhapsodizing generally referred to the performance of Homeric poems (cf. Ch. 1, p. 36). It is nonetheless possible that Xenophanes offered a rhapsodic performance of his hexameter poetry, fragments of which reveal a radical theology attacking the traditional anthropomorphic gods as they are portrayed in Homer and Hesiod. If so, he would have been addressing the same audiences as the Homeric singers. In the case of his elegiac poems, we can infer that these were performed at aristocratic symposia, which were the traditional venue for this kind of verse (cf. Ch. 2, pp. 48–9).

As Diogenes Laertius reports, Herakleitos wrote a book 'On Nature' which he dedicated and placed in the temple of Artemis, deliberately making it more obscure so that only the select few would have access to it (DL 9. 5). Did Herakleitos really opt for the written word as a way of avoiding mass audiences? The mere fact of the survival of his works in ancient times (substantial fragments are still extant) must indicate that this thinker achieved a degree of fame comparable to (at least minor) poets. Many scholars have questioned whether Herakleitos did in fact use writing as a medium for communication, pointing out that the surviving fragments take the form of oral pronouncements put into a pithy, striking, and therefore easily memorizable form. Certainly the fragments resemble oral apophthegms, though this does not mean that Herakleitos did not also commit them to writing. It seems unlikely, however, that the dedication of the book in the temple was designed to keep it hidden from the masses; on the contrary, dedications at temples were generally a form of display. This would have given Herakleitos' book an extraordinary status (hence the legend) and ensured that a fixed text would remain for posterity.

Herakleitos did not simply document his research: he was 'doing things' with his words. Using an oracular form and voice, Herakleitos makes paradoxical and enigmatic pronouncements. He says in fragment 93 that 'the lord whose oracle is in Delphi neither speaks nor conceals, but offers a sign'. Since Herakleitos himself uses language in precisely this way, we may infer that he was deliberately adopting Delphic discourse. He did this, no doubt, because the riddling discourse of the oracle was well suited to conveying his central claim: that unity consists of coexisting opposites. Consider, for example, fragment 10: 'Things taken together are wholes and not wholes, something brought together and brought apart, something in tune and out of tune; from all things one, and from one all things.' Here, the riddling form fits the riddling content.

In adopting this style, Herakleitos also adopts the voice of divine authority that is associated with oracular discourse. Herakleitos speaks from on high to confused mortals:

> Although this account holds forever, men prove to be uncomprehending, both before they have heard it and when once they have heard it. For although all things happen according to this account, men are like those who lack experience, even when they experience such words and deeds as I set forth, distinguishing each thing according to its nature and declaring how it is; but other men fail to notice what they do when awake just as they forget what they do when asleep. (fr. 1)

When encountering such a statement, one may well imagine that Herakleitos is addressing only a few intelligent initiates—after all, the mass of men are far too stupid to get the point. But, at the same time, he claims that the masses have indeed heard the *logos* and experienced his account of the truth. This indicates that his audience is not confined to a few élite associates. Indeed, one could argue that this is a clever piece of rhetoric which invites the ordinary man to remove himself from the common herd by using his reason and tapping into the *logos*. More specifically, it places its audience in the role of the interpreter of an oracle (a not unfamiliar role for ancient Greeks): it exhorts its audience to aspire to wisdom by solving some difficult enigmas. A contradiction arises, then, in that the discourse divulges to the public a knowledge that it proclaims to be unavailable to the majority.

This same paradox is found in Parmenides, whose poem wavers between the discourse of mystery religion and argumentation that is subject to reason and its rules. For Parmenides presents his views about the world in a series of formal arguments using logic that is open for inspection. Yet his poem takes the form of a mystic journey in which wise steeds carry the poet on a chariot escorted by the daughters of the sun. After passing through the gates of the paths of Night and Day, a goddess greets the poet and promises to unveil the truth. 'Come now, and I will tell you—and you shall hearken and carry my word away,' begins the goddess (fr. 2). Parmenides must learn the truth and then convey—'carry'—it to others. This opening recalls the scene in the *Theogony* where the Muses meet Hesiod on Mount Helikon and tell him what to sing (cf. p. 8). But, unlike Hesiod, Parmenides meets his muse in a 'place' that transcends the physical world. The goddess states that there are only two 'routes' of enquiry: the first is the 'path of persuasion' (the 'Way of Truth'), and the second is a track completely closed to enquiry. After expounding the truth of the first track, the goddess turns to a discussion of mortal opinions; here, she gives an account of the very phenomena whose existence is disproved in the first part. Scholars have puzzled over the relation of this (poorly preserved) part of the poem, the 'Way of Seeming', to the first part, the 'Way of Truth'. But its denigration of opinion and 'seeming' is not in doubt: mortals on the path of opinion

> . . . wander, two-headed,
> knowing nothing; for helplessness
> guides the wandering thoughts in their breasts;
> they are carried, deaf and blind at once,
> altogether dazed—hordes devoid of judgement,
> persuaded that to be and not to be are the same yet not the same;
> so the path they all take is backward turning.
>
> (fr. 6).

Like Herakleitos, Parmenides suggests that the 'hordes' of men are ignorant fools. But the audience is nonetheless invited to follow the poet off the beaten track and to enter the realm of Truth. We, too, can be the religious initiates receiving the words of the goddess rather than the blind and deaf hordes who persist in poor reasoning.

As I have suggested, both Herakleitos and Parmenides designed their work for an audience wider than their immediate associates and followers. Each developed a mode of discourse that was poetic and protreptic (from the Greek word *protrepein*, meaning to 'urge on' or 'exhort'). Each used a rhetoric of legitimation that claimed for its author a near-divine authority and conferred on all nay-sayers the status of fools. These thinkers were not only preaching to their converted students but also seeking to make converts (and attract followers) in the wider world. This does not, of course, tell us anything about the size and constituency of their audiences, nor can we be sure of the venues in which these texts were performed.

We know a bit more about Empedokles of Akragas (in Sicily), whose poem the *Purifications* is said to have been performed by a rhapsode at the Olympic games (DL 8. 63). If this is true, then we can say that his work was broadly disseminated by way of oral recitation. Aristotle offers the tantalizing observation that men could recite the verses of Empedokles when drunk, though they are speaking without understanding. This suggests that the work of Empedokles was part of the discursive fare of drinking parties or symposia—a common context for reciting poetry, posing riddles, and performing other intellectual feats. It is worth noting that Aristotle, in a lost dialogue called the *Sophist*, says that Empedokles was himself an accomplished orator who deserves the title of the inventor of rhetoric. Finally, Empedokles' claim that he is a great doctor (which evinces his practical wisdom) is proven by the many references to him in later medical writings. This evidence suggests that Empedokles' poems were widely disseminated, and should warn us against the notion that philosophical ideas were confined to tiny audiences of intellectual élites.

The fragments of Empedokles were originally ascribed to two different works: *On Nature*, a 'naturalist' poem, and *Purifications*, a supernatural story of reincarnation. But some scholars have claimed that the fragments belong to a single poem (a view which is now given strong support by the recent and very exciting discovery of new fragments of Empedokles); as they argue, the separation of the naturalist from the mythical poem is based on the false assumption that true philosophy has no room for the supernatural. The poem begins in the first person, with an address to a man named Pausanias—a gesture that recalls Hesiod's address to his brother in the *Works and Days*. The poet calls on a muse who is a 'much-remembering white armed maiden' to assist him in his narrative, which offers an account of the basic principles of the universe. He claims that two divinities, Love and Strife, act to combine and separate the four 'roots' (earth, air, fire, water), thus bringing the cosmos into different phases or cycles. In this poem, Empedokles responds directly (but not explicitly) to Parmenides, who had deduced that being is changeless, timeless, homogeneous, and unitary. According to Empedokles, the world consists of four distinct elements which everlastingly oscillate between unity (their combination) and plurality (their separation). Here we find a philosophical debate designed for intellectual specialists couched in a poem that reaches out to a wider audience.

Like his predecessors, Empedokles makes use of the topos of the foolish dissenters: 'Fools—for they have no far-reaching thoughts, | who fancy that that which formerly was not can come into being | or that anything can perish and be utterly destroyed' (fr. 11). The audience is encouraged to side with the wise poet rather than join the mass of the ignorant. The poem also contains a pronouncement to the people of Akragas:

> Friends who dwell in the great city of tawny Akragas
> . . . I greet you.
> An immortal god, mortal no more, I go about honoured by all,
> as is fitting, crowned with ribbons and fresh wreaths.
> Whenever I enter the prosperous townships, I am revered by all,
> both men and women; they follow me in countless numbers,
> enquiring where the path to gain lies, some seeking prophecies,
> while others, long pierced by grievous pains, ask to hear
> the word of healing for illnesses of all kinds.
>
> (fr. 112)

In this passage, Empedokles imagines himself adulated as a god and a healer by countless throngs: here is a man who clearly longed for a huge audience! This part of the poem is a visionary account of the story of the soul's exile from happiness, its wandering through many different lives, and its eventual restoration to divine purity. In a number of intriguing fragments, Empedokles describes his own reincarnations, which range from the lowly life of a bush to the lofty heights of godhead. The poem as a whole is unveiled from the divine perspective (how things looked from the point of view of the bush is never, alas, revealed). Even more blatantly than his predecessors, Empedokles lays claim to divine authority.

The work of these remarkable thinkers reveals their need to compete against the most influential 'masters of truth', Homer and Hesiod. Since these were the great educators of Hellas, any wise man offering an intellectual (rather than a practical or technical) product had to match himself against this kind of sage. I am not suggesting that these philosophical poets achieved the kind of popularity enjoyed by more traditional poets: the point is that they exploited traditional forms of poetry in an effort to put themselves on the map. Of course, even as they made use of poetic discourse to gain a hearing, they engaged in a specialized discussion of the nature of the universe, of change, and of reality. Although, at times, the early 'philosophical' thinkers were content to ignore the public and talk primarily to one another, the need to attract followers and to gain authority and (at least local) fame was a basic feature of the life of an intellectual. This can be seen especially clearly in the mid-fifth century, when certain intellectuals decided to make a business out of imparting their ideas and skills.

The variety of professional 'sophists'

The intellectuals in question are those that came to be called the 'sophists'. Although, in the fifth century, the word *sophistes* did not pick out a specific group of intellectuals (until the fourth century, it was often used as a synonym for *sophos*), the term came to designate those men who travelled around the Greek world advertising and selling the products of their wisdom. The most famous 'sophists' of the fifth century are Protagoras of Abdera, Gorgias of Leontinoi, Prodikos of Keos, and Hippias of Elis. The very category 'sophist' has the effect of placing all these individuals in a group, when in fact they did not work in association with one another and did not even purvey the same kind of wisdom. Although they are often bunched together as 'teachers of rhetoric', this categorization conceals the wonderful variety of these thinkers. These men did not form a movement or school; rather, each was a lone ranger, offering a unique product to the growing market.

This is not to deny that many sophists did offer teaching in the 'art' (*techne*) of effective speech and action; certainly there was a wide market for training in the skills that were required for success in the public world. One of the most able masters of rhetorical art was Gorgias, who developed a unique and highly poetic prose style. As he himself claims, poetry is simply 'speech with metre' (fr. B11. 9). In his famous *Encomium of Helen*, he not only demonstrates the power of rhetoric but also offers an explicit analysis of the nature of persuasive speech. The following passage gives a good idea of Gorgianic discourse and ideas:

> Speech is a great lord, which by means of the smallest and most invisible body brings about the most divine deeds: it can stop fear and destroy pain and produce joy and augment pity. . . . What cause prevents the assertion that Helen, similarly, came under the influence of speech against her will,

as if ravished by the force of the mighty? . . . For speech persuading the soul that it persuaded, compelled it both to believe what was said and to approve what was done. . . . For just as different drugs drive out different secretions from the body, and some bring an end to sickness and others to life, so also in the case of speeches, some create pain, others pleasure, some cause fear, others make listeners confident, and some drug and enchant the soul with a certain evil persuasion. (fr. B11. 8–14)

Here, Gorgias persuades us with his musical style even as he discusses the slippery nature of persuasive speech.

As I have suggested, training in rhetoric was only one of many areas of expertise cultivated by the sophists. Consider Hippias, whose expertise included astronomy, geometry, arithmetic, musical theory, orthography, and an astonishing mnemonic art. As Plato reports in the *Lesser Hippias*, when he came to perform at an Olympic festival, Hippias claimed to have made everything he was wearing and carrying himself: a ring, a seal, a strigel, an oil flask, shoes, a cloak, a short tunic, and a woven girdle circling the tunic. This reminds us that Hippias did not confine himself to the higher or 'liberal' arts, but professed a wide variety of manual and technical skills that made him a true polymath.

In what venues did the sophists perform and teach? We know that Gorgias and Hippias reached large audiences by performing their work at the Olympic and Pythian games; these venues offered the sophists a panhellenic platform. Another popular spot was the Athenian agora, the political and economic centre of the city. Since, by the middle of the fifth century BCE, Athens was the bastion of intellectual life in the Greek world, this city was on the itinerary of every major sophist. Although the sophists were held in suspicion by many Athenians, it is clear that they were hugely successful there. Thus we see a large crowd gathering at the Lyceum for two rather minor sophists in Plato's *Euthydemus*, cheering each round of the argument; in Thoukydides, moreover, the politician Kleon chides the men at the Athenian assembly for acting like an audience attending a performance of sophists, seeking diversion rather than serious activity (cf. p. 134). Of course the sophists also performed at private gatherings, where they addressed their hosts and prospective students. In Plato's *Protagoras*, for example, we find the sophists Protagoras, Hippias, and Prodikos living as guests at the house of Kallias, a wealthy Athenian. Here, the sophists are shown addressing smaller groups, though it is noteworthy that Protagoras has brought a flock of foreign followers and a prize pupil along as an entourage (a sort of ready-made audience). Let me add, finally, that the sophists also took advantage of the technology of writing, which was slowly taking hold in the fifth century BCE. Although there are only scanty remains of sophistic texts, we must remember that the sophists were writers and theorists as well as performers, mixing these media to suit their professional needs. Sophistic writings served as performance texts, as exemplary models of rhetorical techniques and, ultimately, as lasting advertisements of the author's wisdom.

The distinction between the sophists and the sages is not hard and fast. Perhaps the most important point of difference is that the sophists were paid professionals: these men were after material as well as symbolic capital. Protagoras is said to have been the first to have taken money for his teaching. We know little about the actual fees, although they seem to have ranged from Hippias' 50 drachma lecture on grammar and language to Protagoras' 10,000 drachma course of study, which was no doubt quite lengthy (a drachma was a qualified worker's daily wage). The fact that Hippias also offered a 1 drachma lecture as an alternative to the 50 drachma lecture suggests that sophists readily adapted themselves to audiences of different sizes and constituencies. Plato compares their activities to that of merchants and salesmen. Like merchants, sophists travelled all around the Greek world, offering their wares to complete strangers. This kind of business transaction was different from those carried out by citizens in their own cities, where exchanges were embedded in a network of social and political relationships. Indeed, the reason why the sophists were held in suspicion in Athens was because they were foreign men who presumed to be telling Athenians how to run their public and personal affairs. They were, then, cosmopolitan intellectuals rather than local sages; not surprisingly, some were strong advocates of panhellenism, urging the Greek cities to put aside their differences and unite against foreign foes.

The medical practitioners of the fifth and fourth centuries resembled the sophists in a number of ways. In addition to treating the sick, Greek physicians offered live performances of their wisdom and expertise. Both Plato and Xenophon provide evidence that doctors performed in public spaces as well as at the bedside; they indicate that physicians addressed the Athenian assembly as experts, and even competed with one another for the office of Public Physician of Athens. Further evidence of the performance of medical wisdom is found in the treatise *On the Nature of Man*, which ridicules those doctors who engage in competitive debates with one another in front of crowded audiences:

> Clearly [these physicians] do not know anything. One can see this especially by attending the debates of these men. For when these men debate with one another in front of the same listeners, the same man never wins three times in a row, but now this man wins, now that one, and then again the man whose tongue is the most fluent in front of the crowd.

The treatise entitled *Precepts*, finally, claims that some doctors wore fancy headgear and exotic perfumes to attract attention, though the author discourages this kind of showy behaviour.

Many medical practitioners also wrote treatises on their own theories and practices. These 'Hippocratic' texts range from technical discussions of medical treatments to more general pieces aimed at a wider public. In these texts, many of which are extant, we can clearly see a group of professionals varying their discourses to suit both specialized and lay audiences. Indeed, many treatises explicitly address the question of how to speak persuasively to the lay public. Like the sophists, the medical practitioners claimed to have an art or skill—a *techne*—which could be taught and put into practice. This kind of wisdom could be systematized and placed in a written package; it was therefore less reliant on *metis*, which was spontaneous and intuitive knowledge that could not be reduced to systems and rules.

Sokrates among the sages

The fifth century also featured the most famous of all Greek wise men: Sokrates the Athenian (469–399 BCE). Although Sokrates did not write anything down and therefore did not contribute directly to the corpus of Greek literature, he has the peculiar distinction of having spawned an entirely new literary genre, the *Sokratikos Logos*, a representation in prose of Sokrates' philosophic conversations. Although there were numerous authors of Sokratic dialogues, all that remains of this vital genre is some few fragments of Aischines and the fourth-century writings of Plato (Greek: Platon) and Xenophon. Unfortunately, Plato and Xenophon offer very different portraits of this elusive figure, and this has led to the problem of identifying the 'true' Sokrates. Already in the fifth century, the comic poet Aristophanes had written a play that featured Sokrates as the protagonist (the *Clouds*). That Sokrates could command this kind of attention suggests that he was very well known in Athens. Interestingly, Aristophanes offers an extremely negative portrayal of Sokrates: he is part scientific quack and part purveyor of shady rhetorical practices. Of course, Aristophanes is trying to raise a laugh, and he can hardly be aiming at verisimilitude. Plato and Xenophon, by contrast, adulate Sokrates, though Xenophon's hero is a pious do-gooder while Plato's is a cagey, complex, and charismatic figure. We must remember that neither of these men was attempting to write a biography of Sokrates; both offered a blend of fact and fiction. If we favour Plato's version, it is because he alone portrays a character who is provocative enough to be put to death at the hands of the Athenians.

Sokrates was put on trial in 399 BCE for corrupting the youth and worshipping deities not recognized by the city. This may not have been the first time that the Athenians put an intellectual on trial; there is some (questionable) evidence that Protagoras and Anaxagoras were indicted for meddling in Athenian affairs. Even if these legends are false, their existence indicates that intellectuals occupied a somewhat dangerous position in democratic Athens. In the case of Sokrates, it appears that the underlying problem was political. Since Sokrates was known to have associated with aristocrats like Alkibiades and Kritias (who had done enormous harm to their city during the Peloponnesian War), he was identified as an enemy of the democracy. He was therefore dragged into court and made to defend himself before a jury of 500. In Plato's *Apology*, Sokrates is represented as delivering a stunning speech challenging the Athenians to take justice and virtue seriously. He claims that he has never been in a lawcourt before, and is unfamiliar with the language of the place. But Sokrates' discourse is a brilliant piece of rhetoric—rhetoric which cries out for an audience of good men. Sokrates' jury voted 280 : 220 against him; his fiery provocations were no doubt insulting to many. Where Sokrates failed, however, Plato succeeded: by writing the *Apology* and other dialogues, Plato ensured that Sokrates found his true audience, albeit after his death.

As a rule, Sokrates did not perform in the political fora of Athens (i.e. the assembly and courts). Instead, he journeyed around the city and its environs striking up conversations wherever he went: in the gymnasia and wrestling schools, in the groves of the Academy and Lyceum (before the famous schools were instituted there), in the agora, at symposia, in the workshops of artisans, and at private houses. He claims in the *Apology* that he deliberately sought out poets, politicians, and craftsmen, since he thought that they might have some wisdom to impart. He is also seen regularly with adolescent boys and young men. Finally, he is portrayed as sparring with many different sophists, sometimes in front of a good-sized crowd.

Although some scholars have argued that his avoidance of political gatherings makes him a 'performer in exile', there is in fact no more embedded and embodied philosopher than Sokrates. Embedded, because he rarely left Athens, and even chose death rather than exile at his trial. To be sure, Sokrates played by his own rules, rejecting traditional social, political, and economic exchanges; but his in-your-face approach to philosophy kept him intimately tied to his fellow Athenians. As he says in the *Apology*, 'I went like a father or an older brother to each of the Athenians' (31b). Sokrates' wisdom was also embodied, for he enacted his wisdom in deeds as well as words: crucial to his performance of wisdom were his extraordinary powers of physical endurance and self-control. He could drink all night without getting drunk, go barefoot in the snow in freezing weather, and had complete control over his sexual appetites (even resisting the beautiful Alkibiades when he stole under the covers with him in a vain attempt at seduction). Sokrates' death, too, is a powerful performance, as he bathes his soon-to-be corpse and drinks up the hemlock in perfect serenity.

Although Sokrates is taken to represent a new turn in Greek philosophy (hence the modern term 'Presocratic Philosophy'), in many ways he is *sui generis*. Here was a thinker who claimed that he did not have knowledge and was not acting as a teacher. Yet he did have some basic principles. For example, his belief that wisdom is necessary and sufficient for virtue (to know the good is to do the good) forms the basis of his philosophy, which centres on the search for knowledge of the essence of the virtues—courage, piety, self-control, justice, etc. In conducting this search, Sokrates adopts a question-and-answer format (now called the 'Socratic method'). He generally plays the role of questioner, though he always insists that he does not himself have the answers. If one focuses on Sokrates' rhetoric and irony as well as his arguments, one can see that he is a master of *metis* (see p. 142); responding to the vagaries of every argument and to the particularities of the characters he interrogates, he always manages to outfox his opponents. Sokrates, in fact, is a consummate performer of wisdom, cut from the same cloth as the early sages. Although some Athenians (like Aristophanes) may have identified him as a sophist, we must remember that Sokrates did not take money, did not travel around Greece as a teacher, did not claim to possess knowledge or any other intellectual product, and in fact never wrote anything down. His performances were very different from those of the sophists: whereas the latter, on many occasions, delivered set pieces that had been composed in writing, Sokrates' discourse was purely oral, formally dialogical, and always *ad hominem*. Moreover, Sokrates' wisdom was not simply intellectual: his practical and physical enactment of the traditional virtues mark him as a sage rather than a sophist.

The 'first philosophers' and their schools

If Sokrates performed his wisdom for all the citizens of Athens ('young and old, rich and poor'), the philosophers of the fourth century focused primarily on writing and private teaching, creating the first official schools of higher education. I say 'philosophers' because Plato and Isokrates were the first intellectuals to appropriate for themselves (and their models) the term 'philosopher' (*philosophos*), a rather rare word which had previously been used to identify anyone pursuing intellectual cultivation. Both Plato and Isokrates offered explicit (and very different) definitions of 'philosophy'; each went to great lengths to defend and legitimize his own brand of wisdom and to debunk that of his rivals. Although we now consider Isokrates a master of rhetoric rather than philosophy, he himself laid claim to the title of 'philosopher'. Given that Philosophy was first constructed as a specialized discipline in the fourth century, we need to pay careful attention to the rhetoric that these intellectuals used in defence of this new cultural practice. These thinkers used the powerful discourse of philosophical protreptic to stake a claim to wisdom, negotiate space, rebuke rivals, and advertise their different styles of pedagogy.

Although Isokrates and Plato were greatly indebted to previous intellectual enterprises, they created brand new fora and forms for promulgating wisdom. Isokrates was the first to found his own school, which was located near the Lyceum (*c.*393 BCE). By creating an educational institution which was permanently settled in one place, Isokrates could offer a lengthy and systematic course of study. Like the sophists, he charged a fee for his teaching (1,000 drachmas for a three- to four-year course of study), but he was neither a traveller nor a performer. In fact, he claimed in a number of speeches that he had a poor voice and lacked the confidence for public speaking. Soon after Isokrates, Plato founded his own school, which was located in the Academy (Greek: *Akademia*), a park just outside north-west Athens dedicated to the hero Hekademos. Plato turned to Pythagoras as a model, creating a *thiasos* or religious brotherhood that was devoted to the cult of the Muses. Plato's school was a legal entity defined by its tutelary deities; the master did not charge fees for his teaching. People from all over the Greek world came to study with Isokrates and Plato, many of whom would have been attracted by the written works of these philosophers. An Arcadian woman named Axiothea, for example, is said to have come to Athens after reading Plato's *Republic* (unlike Isokrates, Plato had female students in his school), and a farmer from Corinth is reported to have joined Plato's school after reading the *Gorgias*.

These institutions of learning conferred on their heads an established position and great prestige in the Greek world. The need for public performances of wisdom was thus reduced if not eliminated. Isokrates' education focused exclusively on rhetoric and its implementation in public and political life, whereas Plato offered a wide array of subjects, including mathematics, astronomy, geometry, logic, metaphysics, epistemology, ethics, and political theory. It is important to emphasize that Plato's school, like that of Isokrates, attracted many influential and powerful students and colleagues (Plutarch lists twelve famous politicians who associated with Plato, and other sources suggest that there were more). Plato's involvement in the political affairs of Sicily, particularly his association with the tyrant Dionysios of Syracuse, is a reminder that he

THE THINKERS. *This mosaic of a group of seven philosophers was made in the first century CE to decorate a villa near Pompeii on the bay of Naples. There has been much discussion whether the figures can be identified with individual philosophers. One theory claims that the figure pointing to the globe with a staff is Plato and the figure on the extreme left is Aristotle. In the background possibly the Akropolis at Athens.*

did not repudiate politics or public life, though he had little involvement in the democratic government of Athens.

Isokrates and Plato, as Athenian intellectuals who belonged to the wealthy élite, would have been expected to participate in the democratic government of Athens. Both opted out, Isokrates because he was unfit for public speaking, and

Plato because he did not approve of Athenian government. By avoiding the political fora of the assembly and lawcourts, they were effectively rejecting the mass audience and its values. Plato was of course far more critical of the democracy than Isokrates was, but both chose to address an audience of élites by way of private teaching and the circulation of written texts. Although literacy was more widespread in the fourth century than in the fifth, only wealthy and educated individuals had the leisure and the money required to buy books and to study them.

Isokrates gives us a good idea of the process of writing and publishing a work in the *Panathenaic Oration* (200–72). He tells us how, after writing the first version of this speech, he 'revised' it in the company of three or four pupils. Upon reviewing the speech, the entire group pronounced it excellent, though it lacked an ending. Isokrates then decided to call upon a former pupil, an admirer of Sparta who himself lived in an oligarchic state, to find out whether anything he said about the Spartans was amiss. This man came and 'read' the speech, and he found fault with Isokrates' critical treatment of the Spartans. Isokrates tells us that he proceeded to deliver a short speech censuring this pupil for his ignorance, a speech which was applauded by the other pupils who were present. A little while later, he 'dictated' this latter speech to his slave, who added it on at the end of the former speech. Several days later, however, as he was 'reading and going over' the speech, Isokrates grew troubled about his handling of the Spartans. He came to the brink of 'blotting out or burning' his text, but opted instead to call in those of his former pupils who lived in Athens and to ask whether the speech should be destroyed or published. When this group comes, the speech is 'read aloud' and (not surprisingly) given a huge applause. Eventually, of course, the students persuade him to publish the speech, 'if he wishes to gratify the worthiest of the Greeks—those who are truly philosophical and not pretenders'.

Both Isokrates and Plato aimed their written work first and foremost at élite and educated men who could read (or listen to another person read) long pieces of prose. But neither was fully confident that his books would find the right readers or evoke the correct response. Isokrates expresses his ambivalence about the written word in *To Philip* 25–7:

> I do not fail to recognize the extent to which spoken speeches are more effective at persuasion than written ones, nor that all assume the former are uttered on important and urgent matters while the latter are written for display and profit. . . . When a speech is deprived of the speaker's reputation, his voice, the variations which are made in the delivery, and of the advantages of timeliness and seriousness about the matter at hand . . . and when someone reads it unpersuasively, without depicting any character, as

though he were reading a list, it is not surprising that it seems to the listeners to be a poor speech.

Here, Isokrates acknowledges that written texts lack the force of embodied discourse, since they must circulate in the absence of the author and his voice. But he argues elsewhere that writing has the advantage over speech in that it offers a fixed document of exactly what one thinks, and does not toady to its audience in the way that oral performers generally do (e.g. *Epistle 1*). In fact, as he claims in the *Antidosis* (*On the Exchange of Property*), a written text can create an 'image' of its author for all time to come; the text is thus 'a monument, after his death, finer than statues of bronze' (7). Indeed, in the *Antidosis* Isokrates goes so far as to include lengthy passages from four of his other speeches. Here, for the first time in literature, we find a writer creating an anthology of his own work—a 'Portable Isokrates' which can 'lay bare the truth' about the life and ideas of its author (140–1).

Plato's view of writing is very different. In a famous passage in the *Phaedrus*, Socrates suggests that

[writing] will introduce forgetfulness into the souls of its learners because they will neglect to exercise their memory; indeed, on account of the faith they place in the written word, they will recall things by way of alien marks external to them, and not from within, on their own. (274e—275a)

As Socrates explains, written texts are neither 'clear' nor 'reliable', since they need the presence of the author to defend them when they are under attack. The disembodied written word can only say the same thing again and again, and it 'doesn't know how to address the right people and to keep silent before the wrong people' (275d—e). Finally, since writing is, as it were, an 'illegitimate brother' of the spoken word, it should not be taken seriously or treated as though it contained real truth. This passage has received a great deal of scholarly attention, since it appears to undermine Plato's own writings. As I see it, Plato is suggesting here that philosophical truth cannot be finalized and placed in a written package, since it demands ongoing argument and enquiry and is simply not suitable for the fixity of writing. Plato demonstrates this principle in most of his texts, refusing to offer final conclusions and pointing towards truths which are beyond the scope of the dialogue. What, then, did Plato intend to accomplish by writing dialogues? First, he wanted to issue an invitation to the philosophical life (and, indirectly, to his own school), offering a sample of the issues and methods involved. And, second, he wanted to entice and perplex the readers, thus pressing them to investigate the issues for themselves. Although Plato placed a much higher value on oral discussions of philosophic issues (which were no doubt the main activity in the Academy), he did not completely reject writing; rather, he tried to create texts that acknowledged their own provisionality.

What can we say about the circulation and reception of these texts in fourth-century Athens? Clearly, a written text could travel the Greek world far more easily than its author. The disembodied word had the advantage of communicating across great distances, and of creating a community of readers that transcended the boundaries of the city-states and their politics. Both Isokrates and Plato attracted pupils from all over the Greek world; this would suggest that their writings were widely disseminated. Although Havelock went too far in claiming that the technology of writing was the cause of a conceptual shift that made philosophic thinking possible, it is clear that writing facilitates the presentation of long and technical arguments and gives readers a chance to study and respond to difficult ideas. By reaching beyond the boundaries of Athens, thinkers like Isokrates and Plato could communicate with like-minded, educated Greeks, thus forming an élite community of cultured intellectuals. In fourth-century Athens, wealth and power were no longer markers of aristocratic superiority, for many members of the 'lower classes' were able to acquire money and political power. The 'liberal' or 'philosophical' education thus emerged as a new marker of élite status. In short, many aristocrats opted for culture and learning rather than power. In theory, of course, the liberal education claimed to prepare young men to be good leaders; but this claim did not always pan out in practice.

Isokrates' philosophic discourse

According to Isokrates, philosophy is a form of practical wisdom. As he says in the *Antidosis*,

> It is not in the nature of man to attain a scientific knowledge (*episteme*) which, once we possess it, enables us to know what to do or to say. I therefore consider those men wise who are able by means of conjecture to hit upon the best course of action; and I give the title of 'philosopher' to men who are engaged in the studies which make them achieve this kind of wisdom most expeditiously. (271)

Here, Isokrates suggests that ethical and political action cannot be turned into a science; because philosophic wisdom must respond to the shifting events of human life, it must be based on conjecture and experience. Isokrates goes on to attack his rivals (including Plato) for cultivating the wrong kind of wisdom:

> They say that the people who pay no heed to things that are necessary but
> enjoy the outlandish discourses of the ancient sophists are philosophers,
> but that the people who are learning and practising the things which
> enable them to manage wisely both their private households and the
> commonwealth of the city are not philosophers. (285)

Isokrates claimed, then, to teach men how to live and govern well. But his actual teaching focused primarily on *logos*, since the mastery of the right kind of rhetoric, he believed, would lead to the proper *praxis*.

Isokrates was an ambitious man: he wanted to influence Athenian politics without speaking in the democratic assembly; he wanted to be seen as an Athenian insider but also to participate in the affairs of other states (including oligarchic and tyrannical regimes). He walked a fine line between these disparate audiences, sometimes incorporating different ideologies into the same speech. The *Areopagitikos* and *On the Peace*, for example, take the form of speeches delivered to the Athenian assembly, and the *Antidosis* takes the form of a court speech in a public trial. In these texts, Isokrates portrays himself as a good democrat and a benefactor to his city, using many of the commonplaces found in Athenian rhetoric. The democratic rhetoric in this and other speeches was not, of course, aimed at the Athenian demos, but rather at an educated readership consisting of orators, politicians, and other influential democrats. Isokrates offers them strong arguments for their own position even as he exhorts them to live up to the early glories of Athens. In the same speeches, however, he inveighs against the ignorance and gullibility of 'the many', and criticizes the sycophants who are infecting the political process. Here, he shows his anti-democratic readers that he is not just a party hack. By skilfully tapping into different ideologies, Isokrates appeals to a disparate audience of literate and leisured Greeks, some of whom favoured democracy, others oligarchy, and yet others monarchy.

Although Isokrates made an impact on Greek politics by educating various princes and leaders, he also wanted to wield power by means of his writings, many of which discuss political issues and urge specific courses of action. In short, he wanted his speeches to be speech-acts: words that make or remake the world. In several of his late speeches, Isokrates openly admits that his written texts had little effect on political decision-making. He says more than once that his *Panegyric Oration* created an enormous stir and brought him great fame, yet he bitterly complains that no one took the advice he gave there. His texts, as it seems, were admired but not obeyed. Because he refused to declaim his discourses, he was unable to convert his *logos* into praxis; in this period, a written text simply could not compete with oral performances. In addition, Isokrates' musical and verbose rhetoric produces a smooth elegance that does not have the power demanded of political speeches. Even when his writings take the form of forensic and political speeches, he uses an artful style associated more with display and entertainment than with power politics.

In the *Antidosis*, Isokrates expresses his astonishment that the Athenian people voted against him at a trial concerning the payment of a liturgy (an expensive civic service that was compulsory for the richest Athenians). Here, he portrays himself as a great benefactor to the city of Athens: he admits that he has not participated in the public discourse of the assembly and courts, but claims that his wisdom has brought immense glory to the city. His speeches and his school, he asserts, have done an extraordinary service to Athens, and should be seen as a new kind of liturgy. In addition, since Athenians are known to be 'the best educated in thought and speech' of all the Greeks (294), Isokrates' intellectual activities render him the quintessential Athenian. Thus he suggests that his disembodied voice (i.e. the written speeches) can and should be embedded in Athenian social and political discourse. This is a novel and fascinating endeavour, even if it did not produce the desired results.

Plato and philosophic performance

Plato developed a quite different relation to the city and culture of Athens, one that evolved and changed as he matured. Plato's works are generally divided into three periods: the early, which include the *Apology, Crito, Euthyphro, Protagoras*, and *Gorgias*; the middle, which include the *Symposium, Phaedo, Republic*, and *Phaedrus*; and the late, including the *Sophist, Statesman, Timaeus*, and *Laws*. In his early dialogues, Plato focuses on Socratic discussions of ethical and political concepts. Sokrates, of course, was no aristocrat, and his language reflects the class of artisans from which he came; indeed, he is 'always speaking about pack asses, or blacksmiths, or cobblers, or tanners' (*Symposium* 221e), exploring the difference between the technical knowledge of the craftsman and the ethical wisdom of the sage. This kind of language clearly annoyed Athenian aristocrats; in the *Gorgias*, for example, Sokrates positively revels in this low language in his encounter with Kallikles (an aristocratic snob):

SOCRATES: What about cloaks? Perhaps the best weaver should have the biggest cloak, and the most cloaks, and go around in the prettiest cloaks.

KALLIKLES: Cloaks indeed!

SOCRATES: Well, clearly shoes then. He who is the best and wisest expert in shoes should have the lion's share of them. The cobbler, I suppose, should have the biggest shoes and the most numerous shoes in which to walk around. . . .

KALLIKLES: By god, you never stop talking about cobblers and fullers and cooks and doctors, as though our argument were about them.

SOCKRATES: Then please say what things the stronger and wiser man should get more of, when he justly overreaches and takes more than his share.

(*Gorgias* 490d—491a)

Plato's use of common and lowbrow discourse in a prose text is a bold new venture in Greek literature; since his readership consisted of wealthy and educated men, this serio-comic uncrowning of 'high art' is even more remarkable.

Although Sokrates' dialogues take place in the presence of relatively small groups of people, the political context and ramifications of these conversations are often underscored. In many texts, Plato creates a historical or political frame for the discussion that is to come. At the opening of the *Charmides*, for example, Sokrates explains that he has just returned from a battle in Potidaia—an event that illuminates the dialogue's discussion of virtue and self-control. In the *Euthyphro*, the protagonist encounters Sokrates just before he goes to trial on a charge of impiety; their dialogue, not surprisingly, focuses on the nature of piety. The *Apology* re-enacts Sokrates' trial and indictment, an event that occurred five years after the disastrous end of the Peloponnesian War. In this speech, Sokrates turns the tables and puts Athens on trial for impiety and injustice; he openly criticizes the democracy and claims that he would have been put to death long ago if he had engaged in Athenian politics. In these and other early dialogues, Plato portrays Sokrates as a sage whose intellectual and physical activities are performed in a specific cultural context. This context serves as a reminder that an individual's ideas and values have momentous consequences: true knowledge, as Sokrates conceives it, necessarily produces good and virtuous action (and, correlatively, ignorance produces vicious action). In Plato's early 'dramas', then, we see how *logos* affects *praxis*, how ideas affect deeds. He thus encourages his readers to pursue a brand of wisdom which is fundamentally practical and civic in orientation.

In the middle dialogues, Plato introduces a new kind of philosopher, a sage who is not at home in Athens or any other Greek city, and is not even really at home in his own body. In the *Symposium*, for example, we are told that, as he was walking to the drinking party, Sokrates wandered off to a nearby porch to enjoy a period of silent contemplation (174d—175a). Later in the dialogue, Alkibiades tells a story about Sokrates when they were on a campaign together:

One day, at dawn, he started thinking about some problem or other, and stood there lost in thought, and when the answer didn't come he still stood there thinking, refusing to give up. By midday, many soldiers had seen him and, quite surprised, they told each other that Sokrates had been standing there thinking ever since dawn. He was still there when evening came, and after dinner some Ionians brought their bedding outside (this was in the summer) partly because it was cooler and more comfortable and partly to see whether he was going to stay out there all night. Well, he stood on that very spot until dawn, and then he said his prayers to the sun and went away. (220c—d)

Here, Sokrates plays a novel role—that of a contemplative philosopher, lost to the world as he labours in thought. We find no trace of this kind of activity in the early dialogues. Plato offers here a new conception of the 'true' philosopher: this new sage is most at home when he is engaging in *theoria* (contemplation). In the *Republic*, Plato will insist that the philosopher who has found a happy contemplative life outside the cave must journey back into the darkness to educate and—ideally—rule over the ignorant masses (514a—518b). He has certainly not given up on politics or *praxis* (his two most monumental works, after all, are the *Republic* and *Laws*), but he has created a philosopher who, by nature, belongs in a higher world.

Plato's new philosopher is not embedded in the (non-ideal) city and its affairs, and is only tenuously attached to his own body. As he says in the *Theaetetus*, the true philosopher does not know the way to the market-place or lawcourts or council chamber; does not know whether people are upper or lower class; and never takes part in popular entertainment. Indeed,

> he is not even aware that he is ignorant, for he holds aloof not for reputation's sake, but because it is really only his body that resides and is at home in the city, while his thought, considering all such things petty and worthless, disdains them and takes wing . . . studying the plains by means of geometry and investigating the heavens though astronomy, seeking the true nature of all that exists . . . and never lowering itself to what lies close at hand. (173d—e).

To be sure, this portrait is somewhat exaggerated; Plato himself would not have met these criteria. But since, for him, human souls are immortal and can dwell outside the body, it is the task of the philosopher to 'practise death' by separating his soul and mind from his body as much as possible during this present incarnate life (see esp. *Phaedo*). In the middle dialogues, Plato erects a new metaphysical system which calls for a new kind of philosopher. It also calls for a new kind of literature—a mode of discourse which can investigate and reveal an incorporeal world that exists beyond the borders of earthly life. To communicate this new vision, Plato availed himself of a huge variety of styles, often mixing high language with low, and austere philosophic analysis with myths, allegories, and ornate rhetorical speeches. This unique style is designed to engage readers both intellectually and emotionally—to make them understand that their very lives are on the line.

Most of Plato's middle and late dialogues are devoted to the analysis and defence of the many facets of this new metaphysical system. Whereas in the early dialogues he dealt exclusively with ethical and political issues, in the middle and late dialogues he tackles a wide range of topics, including epistemology, ontology, psychology, logic, and cosmology as well as ethics and political theory. Although some of the middle and late texts are more conclusive than the open-ended dialogues of the first period, he never abandoned the dialogue form. In addition, by refusing to speak in his own person in any dialogue, Plato avoids setting himself up as an authority. Rather, he invites his readers to enter into a dialogue with the text—to investigate the philosophical issues for themselves rather than accepting the author's own views. For Plato, dialogue is the only way to 'do' philosophy; his choice of the dialogue form thus directly reflects his philosophical methodology.

In addition to developing the vocabulary and argumentation to suit his metaphysical system, Plato also creates a new kind of rhetoric—a rhetoric of conversion—which spirits the reader into the 'real world' existing above and beyond the material realm. The famous 'allegory of the cave' at the opening of book 7 of the *Republic* offers an excellent example of this kind of rhetoric: we humans are shackled in a cave (Sokrates tells us) watching the shadow-play reflected on its back wall; but if we are released from these bonds by a philosophic guide, we can journey into the real and radiant world existing outside the cavern. Consider, too, this passage from the eschatology at the end of the *Phaedo*:

> Next, said Sokrates, I believe that the earth is vast in size, and that we who dwell between the river Phasis and the Pillars of Herakles inhabit only a tiny portion of it—we live around the sea like ants or frogs around a pond—and there are many other peoples inhabiting similar regions. There are many hollow places everywhere in the earth, places of every shape and size, in which water and mist and air have collected. . . . We do not perceive that we are dwelling in its hollows, but think that we are living on the earth's surface. . . . But if someone could reach the summit, or take wing and fly aloft, when he put up his head he would see the world above . . . and he would know that this is the true heaven and the true light and the true earth. (*Phaedo* 109a—e)

This kind of rhetoric says to the reader: you know not where you are. It exhorts

THOUGHT IN WRITING. This fragment from Plato's dialogue Gorgias, written in the second century CE, is typical of the pieces of papyrus excavated from the sands of Egypt in the last 100 years in that the writing is very well preserved but the papyrus survives only in small pieces. A classical Greek text was normally written in columns (without word divisions) along the length of one side of a long roll of papyrus. The lettering of a literary text was usually as here neat and easy to read.

the audience to make a heroic journey beyond the body and outside the city and its puny affairs.

Plato's decision to write dramatic dialogues—complete with heroes and villains—reminds us of the debt he owes to Attic tragedy and comedy: he deliberately borrows from both these genres. It is easy to see the comic spectacle in a dialogue like the *Protagoras* (which makes fun of the sophists) and the tragic undercurrent in texts like the *Gorgias* and *Phaedo* (which deal with the death of Sokrates). Plato also exploits the device of dramatic irony, where the readers know more than the characters in the drama. Whereas Sokrates' irony centred on his disavowals of knowledge, Plato's irony is more wide-ranging, sometimes affecting the entire structure of a dialogue. In the *Menexenos*, for example, Sokrates demonstrates to Menexenos how easy it is to give a successful funeral oration; but Plato indicates to his readers that this kind of discourse is hollow and, indeed, harmful. Consider also the passage in the *Phaedrus* which discusses the technology of writing: here we find Sokrates, who did not write anything down, offering a critique of writing in a dialogue written by Plato.

In spite of his borrowings from tragedy and comedy, Plato announces in *Republic* that there is an 'ancient quarrel' between philosophy and poetry, especially tragic poetry. In books 2 and 3, he offers a lengthy critique of the treatment of gods and heroes in epic and tragic texts. Here, he draws a formal distinction between tragedy and epic: the former consists entirely of 'imitation' or dramatic impersonation, whereas the latter includes long narrative portions and is therefore less reliant on impersonation. Plato makes it clear that he prefers the form of epic, yet he himself is writing in the dramatic or 'imitative' mode. In book 10, he takes his critique even further by banishing all poetry from the ideal city (except for hymns to gods and encomia of good men). In particular, he claims that the poets do not possess knowledge and thus end up infecting the viewers' minds and 'feeding' their appetites and emotions.

As Plato says in the *Laws*, Athens has shifted from a 'rule by the best' to 'rule by the audience' (a 'theatrocracy'). This is, in part, the fault of poetry, which has fostered the irrational and unruly elements in the souls of the spectators. Once again, however, Plato's own writings are implicated: for his dialogues do not simply appeal to reason, but also play on our emotions and desires. The dialogues, after all, contain a good deal of myth and rhetoric; this kind of discourse is designed to evoke a passion for truth, shame for living in ignorance, and fear of its painful consequences. Plato uses this discourse because he wants to convert his audience—to turn his readers into lovers of truth. Like many of his predecessors, he incites his readers by claiming that only a few élite individuals can achieve wisdom. By making the ordinary world look dark and strange, and offering his readers a home in the 'real' world, Plato attempts to make a new kind of man.

I have suggested that Plato in his middle dialogues portrays the philosopher as a man who revels in *theoria*, even though the truth that he contemplates contains an injunction to virtuous deeds and actions. But note that, even as Plato privileges *theoria* over *praxis*, he conceives of contemplation as something that is performed: Sokrates stands contemplating for all to see on a stranger's porch, or he gets lost in a trance in front of the entire Greek army. The contemplative philosopher described in *Republic* 5–6 and the *Theaetetus* is said, moreover, to appear foolish and ridiculous to the common man. This philosopher is on view, performing a new kind of wisdom that consists in contemplation; *theoria* becomes a sort of heroic feat in the eyes of intelligent people. So Plato's dramas manifest an interesting tension. On the one hand, they create a philosopher who is neither fully embodied nor embedded, since his mind dwells elsewhere and his activities are detached from civic life. At the same time, however, he enacts a bodily performance of *theoria* for the benefit of his fellow citizens (though most men will see him as useless rather than beneficial). In spite of the move towards detached contemplation, then, Plato's philosopher is still a performer of wisdom. As Sokrates says in *Republic* 5, the philosopher is the most useful man in the city, but people do not know how to put him to use. The contemplative philosopher performs a new kind of wisdom, and thus appears to the many as a comic fool. It is perhaps for this reason that Plato prefers oral or 'living' discourse to the disembodied voice of the written text: unlike Isokrates, he believes that wisdom must be performed by an active soul in a human body.

From performer to spectator: Aristotle

Aristotle (Greek: Aristoteles) came from Macedonia to Athens in 367 BCE and spent twenty years in Athens as a pupil of Plato. After Plato's death in 348, he left Athens for twelve years, during which time he travelled in Asia Minor and Macedonia, and served as the teacher of Alexander of Macedon (then in his teens). In the 330s, Aristotle returned to Athens and established his own philosophical circle in the Lyceum (Greek: Lykeion), a grove sacred to Apollo located just outside of Athens. Initially the Lyceum, as this school was called, was housed in public buildings, but Theophrastos (Aristotle's successor as the head of the Lyceum) bought property near the grove and created a permanent place for the school. A very wide variety of subjects was studied in the Lyceum (also known as the Peripatos), including biology, zoology, cosmology, logic, ethics, politics, metaphysics, history, and literature.

As a metic or resident alien in Athens, Aristotle was barred from political life. His orientation to the civic affairs of Athens was therefore very different from that of Isokrates and Plato. During his residency in Athens Aristotle could not participate in political *praxis*, so it is perhaps in keeping with this that he completely separated practical and theoretical reasoning, privileging the latter over the former. As he argues, the man who leads a contemplative life will not spend much time on practical or political affairs, since his gaze is fixed on the 'eternal and unchanging' rather than on the vagaries of human life. Although the philosopher will need to engage in some kinds of *praxis* in order to sustain a contemplative life, he will keep these to a minimum, since they can 'obstruct' philosophic activity (*Nicomachean Ethics* 1178b). Correlatively, the man who perfects his practical reasoning and chooses a life of politics will not have the leisure to engage in contemplation. Aristotle makes it clear that the contemplative life is superior to the political life, though both are considered good lives.

Aristotle composed two kinds of written works: those he called '*logoi exoterikoi*', which were aimed at intellectuals outside of his school, and those called '*logoi kata philosophian*', which were technical treatises designed for his philosophical colleagues and pupils. Unfortunately, the 'exoteric' works are no longer extant; only the technical treatises have survived. These latter texts, often referred to as 'lecture notes', are written in a terse, economical style, and are not works of literature in the full sense. Although they have been edited by later writers, they give us a good idea of Aristotle's style as a lecturer and teacher. His 'exoteric' works, which survive only in fragments, were literary treatises and dialogues comparable to Plato's written works. As the fragments attest, these texts contained a good deal of protreptic discourse; they were clearly designed to reach the educated élite in the Greek world. Unlike Plato, however, Aristotle chose to cast himself as a character in these dialogues, thus creating a very different effect. For these texts tell us exactly where Aristotle stands, offering the fixed conclusions that Plato took such pains to avoid.

One of Aristotle's technical treatises must be mentioned in a discussion of literature, since it deals explicitly with literary discourse: the *Poetics*, one of the most influential works of literary criticism ever written. In the *Poetics*, Aristotle rescues tragedy from the clutches of Plato: 'the standard of what is correct in the art of poetry is not the same as in the art of politics or any other art' (1460b). Contrary to Plato, who focuses on the effects that the performance of poetry has on the polis, Aristotle claims that the performed 'spectacle' (*opsis*) of tragedy can be ignored, since the 'art' inheres in the structure of the drama. Aristotle offers a formalist interpretation of tragedy, paying no attention to the socio-political context in which the plays were performed. He does, however, discuss the effect that a good tragedy has on the soul of the reader or viewer: by arousing 'pity and fear', tragedy brings about a '*katharsis* of these emotions' (1449b). There are many different interpretations of the concept of *katharsis*; all of them agree, however, that it somehow involves a purgation of the soul that is beneficial and pleasurable. The *Poetics*, then, uses an analytical discussion to defend the art of poetry. For Aristotle, there is no 'quarrel' between tragic poetry and philosophy, since the two modes of discourse are completely distinct and offer different kinds of instruction and pleasure.

A brief look at Aristotle's *Protrepticus* (now fragmentary) exemplifies the rhetoric and discourse he used in his 'exoteric' works. Like Plato, he wants to make philosophers out of his readers. The following passage sketches out his conception of the true philosopher:

> It is not surprising, then, if wisdom is not useful or advantageous; for we say that it is not advantageous but good, and it should be chosen not for the sake of any other thing, but for itself. For just as we travel to Olympia for the sake of the spectacle, even if we got nothing more out of it (for the spectacle is more valuable than a large sum of money), and just as we are spectators at the Festival of Dionysus not so that we will gain anything from the actors (in fact we spend money on them), and just as there are many other spectacles that we would choose over a large sum of money, so too the contemplation of the spectacle of the universe must be honoured above all things that are considered to be useful. For it is not right that we should take such pains to go and see men imitating women and slaves, or to see men battling and running, but not think it right to contemplate the nature of reality and truth without any reward or payment (fr. B44)

Here, Aristotle suggests that true wisdom consists in viewing the spectacle (*theoria*) of reality, which produces nothing beyond itself but is chosen entirely for its own sake. This conception of wisdom as 'useless' and non-productive is quite new. For the Greeks had always expected their sages to be useful; even Plato insists that philosophers are beneficial to society. For Aristotle, the wisest man is a spectator rather than a performer, casting his gaze on that which is eternal and unchanging.

We find this same notion outlined in the last book of the *Nicomachean Ethics* (one of his technical treatises, given the title *Nicomachean* to distinguish it from another work on Ethics, known as *Eudemian*). Although Aristotle spends most of the first nine books analysing practical wisdom, he turns in book 10 to a form of wisdom which is far superior—the divine activity of contemplation (*theoria*). This book is considered by some scholars to contradict the arguments in the rest of the treatise, since it celebrates a quite different kind of life: the impractical life of the contemplative. Consider the following passage from book 10:

> The generous man will need wealth in order to perform generous actions, and the just man will need it in order to pay his debts (since mere intentions are invisible and even unjust men pretend that they wish to act justly). And the courageous man will need strength if he is to perform any brave actions, and the temperate man will need opportunities for intemperance. For how can he or any other man be visibly virtuous? . . . But the contemplator (*theoron*) needs none of these externals to engage in his activity; in fact, these things are generally a hindrance to contemplation. (1178a–b)

Here, Aristotle elevates the life of *theoria* over that of ethical *praxis*. Interestingly, the practical life is identified by its 'visible' performance, whereas *theoria* is the activity of the invisible power of the mind (*nous*). As Aristotle indicates at 1178a22, *nous* may exist 'separately' from the body, whereas practical virtue is performed by the 'composite' of body and soul. The contemplative man, in short, is not a performer but a disembodied spectator; he does not perform *theoria* (as Plato's philosophers do) but rather engages in the divine activity of 'thought thinking itself'.

I have emphasized the emergence of an ideology that privileges contemplation over practical reasoning because this both reflects and legitimizes the detachment of the philosopher from the political life of his city. It should be emphasized that the ideology of detachment was not always put into practice. Indeed, the fourth-century philosophers I have discussed all engaged in politics at some point in their lives (not to mention their ventures into political science). But these philosophers did not take part in the political gatherings of democratic Athens, and thus avoided the demotic audience. Opting instead for written discourses, these philosophers invited their readers to adopt a new cultural practice designed only for the select few. Rousing their readers with complex arguments and powerful protreptics, the great philosophers of the fourth century created new forms of literature.

Epilogue: The Hellenistic period

From the reign of Alexander the Great onwards, the Greek city-states were no longer politically autonomous. Beginning in this period, the Greek world was divided into larger political units whose rulers lived at great distances from most of their subjects. This political shift diminished the local loyalties of the city-states and encouraged a more cosmopolitan culture. After Alexander died

(323 BCE), there followed a period of wars and dynastic struggles throughout the Mediterranean. A new bastion of Greek culture was established in the city of Alexandria; although Alexandria replaced Athens as the centre of arts and sciences, Athens remained pre-eminent in philosophy.

In a world of rapidly changing cultural and ethnic boundaries, traditional notions of personal and political identity were being called into question. Responding to the breakdown of social, political, and cultural cohesion, the philosophers developed new systems of thought and specific styles of life that were grounded in these systems. In fact, many of the philosophers of this period were consummate performers, since each set out to model a unique 'art of living'. Though their philosophies differed in many crucial ways, both Epikouros (familiar Latin spelling Epicurus) and the Stoics advertised and enacted a life of supreme tranquillity, free from anxiety and psychic turmoil.

It is a great misfortune that so few philosophical texts from this period survive. There is no complete text from the early Stoics (Zeno, Kleanthes, and Chrysippos), little early evidence of either Pyrrhonian or Academic scepticism, and only scanty remains of Epikouros' voluminous writings. We do know that these schools attempted to attract followers from a wider social group than did Plato or Aristotle, and a brief look at the Stoics and Epicureans will give some sense of the audiences addressed by the Hellenistic philosophers. Both 'Schools' set out to popularize their teaching, attempting to gain followers from all walks of life. In his *Letter to Herodotos*, Epikouros says that he has prepared an epitome of his philosophy for those unable to study his technical writings. He also compiled a set of simple ethical maxims, explicitly designed to be learned by heart. The Stoics, on their part, composed pieces they called 'suasions and dissuasions'; these offered moral advice that was easily accessible to the ordinary reader.

Epikouros came to Athens from the island of Samos, establishing his school there in c.307/6 BCE. Diogenes Laertius says that Epikouros' writings ran to 300 rolls. Among his most important works were *On Nature* (thirty-seven books), *On the Criterion*, and a collection of ethical texts including *On Lives, On the Goal, On Choice and Avoidance*. His school—known as 'The Garden'—was a closed community, located just outside the city; its members were allowed to bring women and children into the group, and they had few reasons to be in contact with their former associates in their native countries. In his will, Epikouros speaks of the membership in the community as a commitment 'to spend one's time there continuously, in accordance with philosophy' (DL 10. 17); pupils were explicitly instructed not to engage in political life. Epicureanism, in short, offered personal salvation and group solidarity.

Epikouros' ethical philosophy focused on the proper approach to pain and pleasure and the avoidance of anxiety and fear (especially the fear of death); its ultimate goal was tranquillity (*ataraxia*). His natural philosophy, based on the thesis that the universe is composed of atoms and void, offered a scientific grounding for his ethics. As he says in the *Principal Doctrines*: 'If we were not troubled by alarms at celestial phenomena, nor by the worry that death somehow affects us, nor by a failure to understand the limits of pains and desires, we would have no need to study the science of nature' (11). The Epicurean, then, engages in *theoria* for the purpose of *praxis*. Thus, Epicurean wisdom is fully embodied, since its adherents must perform an entire way of living. This philosophy is not, however, embedded, for the full Epicurean must be detached from his or her city of origin and of all its social and political affairs. Indeed, it is precisely this detachment that enables the Epicurean to achieve happiness and tranquillity. Not surprisingly, Epikouros communicated his philosophy to the Greek world by way of the written word. He confined his personal performances to the (relatively) small and select audience of men and women who left their cities to come and live in the Garden.

In 301/300 BCE, Zeno of Kition (in Cyprus) began to philosophize in the Painted Colonnade (Stoa) in Athens, thus founding the Stoic school (DL 7. 5). The Stoa was located alongside the agora, in the very centre of town. Zeno takes his place in a succession of philosophers moving from Sokrates and his follower Antisthenes to the Cynics Diogenes and Krates (who was Zeno's teacher). Like these predecessors, Zeno performed his philosophy in the public eye. To be sure, Zeno was not as extreme as his Cynic forerunners; Diogenes, after all, was wont to masturbate, urinate, and fart in public—'to use any place for any purpose' (DL 6. 22). More in keeping with Sokrates, Zeno was austere and frugal, and apparently impervious to cold, rain, heat, and disease; when he did take part in parties and festivities, he was completely unaffected (DL 7. 26–7). Zeno made a point of performing a life of poverty, even begging for money from bystanders in the Stoa (DL 7. 13–14). Since Stoicism was a way of life as much as a system of thought, the masters of this school had to enact what they taught. It is noteworthy that Zeno's public performances commanded the attention of a man as powerful as Antigonos Gonatas (a king of Macedon), who frequented his lectures and even invited him to attend a party. Having elicited this royal invitation, Zeno proceeded to steal away from the festivities, thus exhibiting a Stoic indifference to the trappings of power (DL 13). Zeno played to a public audience that ranged from the ordinary person to rich potentates. At the same time, his written works reached a huge audience of readers all over the Greek world.

Zeno is reported to have written treatises such as *Life According to Nature*, *Emotions*, *That which is appropriate*, *Universals*, *Disputatious Arguments*, and *Homeric Problems* (DL 7. 4). Of his immediate successors, the most important are

Kleanthes (300–232 BCE) and Chrysippos (281–201 BCE). Of the writings of the early Stoics, only fragments survive. Later sources indicate that the Stoics constructed a philosophy in which ethics, physics, and logic formed a completely coherent and systematic whole. The Stoics represented this system by portraying philosophy as a fertile field in which logic corresponds to the surrounding wall, ethics to the fruit and harvest, and physics to the soil or vegetation. According to this philosophy, the universe is fully accessible to human reason, since it is itself a rationally organized structure; reason (*logos*), which enables humans to think and speak, is embodied in the physical universe. In contrast to dualistic philosophies that denigrated nature and the body, the Stoics developed a monistic theory that identified rationality with the physical universe. Thus when the Stoics encouraged their followers to live a 'life in accordance with nature', they were referring to a natural world that was providentially guided by a rational cosmic principle. Since humans are akin to the universe in so far as they possess reason, all men are therefore citizens of the world. Only the wise man, however, can offer the perfect embodiment of Stoic philosophy, since he alone understands the universal *logos*.

Stoicism was a philosophy that addressed, at least in principle, the entire human race; this forced the Stoics to develop many different kinds of teaching and writing. Take, for example, Kleanthes' *Hymn to Zeus*, a hexameter poem that dealt explicitly with Stoic principles:

> Nothing occurs on the earth apart from you, god,
> nor in the divine vault of heaven nor on the sea,
> except what bad men do in their foolishness.
> But you know how to make the odd even,
> and to order things that are disorderly;
> to you the things that are alien are akin.
> And so you have blended all things into one, the good with the bad,
> so that there arises a single everlasting *logos* of all things,
> which all bad men shun and neglect,
> unhappy wretches, always longing for the possession of good things
> they neither see nor hear the universal law of god,
> obeying which they would have a good life accompanied by reason.
>
> (ll. 15–25)

Like the Epicureans, the Stoics offered their followers a happy and tranquil life; but this was not to be achieved by abandoning one's city or community. On the contrary, the Stoics claimed that the wise man should take part in politics and attempt, so far as possible, to create a just and humane society. The serious Stoic was therefore embedded in his own society at the same time as he took his place in the cosmic community.

6 | Observers of speeches and hearers of action: The Athenian orators

CHRIS CAREY

From art to science

Oratory was always part of Greek public or semi-public expression. It already plays a major role in the fictive society of Homeric epic. The education of the Homeric hero (exemplified in the case of Achilles) was designed to make him 'a speaker of words and a doer of deeds' (*Iliad* 9. 443). When Odysseus and Menelaos visited Troy to argue for the return of Helen, they found an audience which could appreciate their oratory (*Iliad* 3. 204–24). The three envoys sent to Achilles in the ninth book of the *Iliad* each deliver a speech to him in turn, to receive a speech in reply. If we jump three and a half centuries from Homer's Greece to the fourth century BCE, we find ourselves struck more by the continuity than by any radical change. When Athens began peace negotiations with Philip of Macedon in 346, they sent ten ambassadors to open negotiations. We have an account of the meeting with Philip from one of the participants, the Athenian politician Aischines (Aischines, 2. 25–38). Like those sent to Achilles, each of the ambassadors in turn delivered a speech (some evidently long) to Philip and his circle. After a brief recess, Philip gave an extended response, dealing in turn with each Athenian speaker's arguments. For Greeks of all periods past and present alike were characterized by extended spoken discourse as a means of persuasion.

It would be a mistake, however, to suppose that nothing had changed in the interval between Homer and the age of Demosthenes. The sixth and fifth centuries saw a remarkable effervescence of intellectual activity, in physical science, medicine, geography, and ethnography, historiography (see Chs. 3 and 4). This is an age when the world is subjected to a set of rules. The fifth century in particular sees the rise of the *techne*, the technical manual. Within this intellectual trend it is not surprising that oratory too was gradually systematized. The basic structures of the speech were mapped out and lines of argumentation developed. Particularly important for the future of oratory was the identification of argument from probability as a staple tool for the process of persuasion. Argument from probability gave a speaker the means to capitalize on any facts which might support his own case and undermine his opponent's case by arguing from general patterns of human conduct to particular instances, instead of relying entirely on traditional sources of proof such as witnesses, oaths, and laws. To illuminate the new-found awareness of the susceptibility of fact to manipulation by argument from probability, I have taken an illustration from two speeches in the first of the *Tetralogies* (a collection of speeches offering matching prosecution and defence in a series of fictitious trials) of the late fifth-century politician and speech-writer Antiphon. The fictive situation is that a man has been murdered. The accused, an enemy of the dead man and therefore an obvious suspect, needs to offer alternative scenarios for the killing, while the prosecution needs to anticipate and counter the defence arguments:

> [PROSECUTION] ⟨It is unlikely that the murder was committed by robbers.⟩ Nobody would have exposed his life to the most extreme danger and then abandoned the profit which had been acquired and achieved; for the victims were found with their clothing.
> [DEFENCE] It is not improbable (as my opponents maintain) but probable that he was killed for his clothes while wandering late at night. The fact that he was not stripped is no indication. If they didn't have time to strip him but left him on being frightened off by some people approaching, they showed good sense and were not crazy in valuing safety over profit.
>
> (Antiphon, *Tetralogy* 1)

The development of argument from probability is very much of a piece with the other rationalizing advances of the period, since it is based on the underlying assumption (found also in Thoukydides' history) that human nature too is subject to rules and that a given set of circumstances will in general prompt a predictable mode of behaviour. The genesis of rhetorical theory thus belongs as much in the realm of behavioural psychology as in that of verbal artistry. The same (tacit) element of behavioural psychology is also present in the underlying assumption that audience response too is predictable and that a knowledge of modes of argumentation enables a speaker to steer the audience towards a favourable decision.

Tradition (and there is no obvious reason to doubt our sources) associates the beginning of this process with Sicily, specifically with the democracy which followed the overthrow of the ruling house of Syracuse in the 460s. It is no coincidence that decades later the new skills found a favourable climate in one of the other great democratic cities of the period, Athens. Although we have ample evidence that oratorical skill could be deployed to good effect in non-democratic states, the connection between oratory and democracy is made repeatedly by our ancient sources when they explore the ethical problems raised either by rhetoric or by democracy. It is made for instance by the Argive herald who engages in political debate with the Athenian king Theseus in Euripides' *Suppliants*. Though he is clearly an unsympathetic character, his speech illustrates the connection between unscrupulous oratory and democracy in one strand of fifth-century political debate:

> The city from which I come
> Is controlled by one man, not by the mass.
> Nor is there anyone who deluding it with words (*logois*)
> Turns it this way and that for private gain,
> And by ingratiating and giving much pleasure for the moment
> Harms it later, and then with fresh slanders
> Conceals his former failures and escapes justice.
>
> (Euripides, *Suppliants* 410–16)

Democracy offered more occasions and larger audiences to be manipulated by effective public speaking. The political context, combined with the cultural prominence of Athens in the fifth century, attracted visits from the sophists, whose course offerings included the art of speaking, for which they found a ready market in Athens (cf. pp. 149–50). The pupils of the sophists were able to exploit their technical expertise in the political arena or to earn substantial sums by hiring their services to write speeches for the lawsuits heard by the jury panels of classical Athens.

Though many of the broad effects, and some specific devices, of classical oratory are prefigured in earlier poetry, and must have played a role in pre-rhetorical oratory, the new focus on rhetoric as technique gave the art of speaking the impact of a new medium of communication for Greeks of the fifth century; like all new media, it raised prospects which were simultaneously exciting and disturbing. The excitement generated by the new perception of the power of the word is vividly captured by the fifth-century sophist Gorgias, a native of Leontinoi in Sicily, in his *Helen*, a fictitious defence speech for Helen of Troy which simultaneously advertises (through its argument and opulent style) and celebrates the power of speech, *logos*. In the extract quoted on pp. 49–50, Gorgias attributes to persuasive speech an almost magical power over the mind of the hearer, an idea in earlier generations associated with the poet.

Both the notion of words as magic and the use of the language of power (*logos* is a *dynastes*, 'master', 'ruler' it has *dynamis*, 'power') present speech as a means of control, with the skilled speaker as the manipulator and the audience as passive objects. Though one has to view with caution the professional rhetorician's claims for the product of his training, Gorgias' own career is itself testimony to the intoxicating effect of verbal skill in the fifth century, for according to our ancient sources the Athenians were captivated by his oratory when he came to Athens on a diplomatic mission in the 420s. Not only did this win pupils for his lectures on rhetoric, his highly artificial style had a profound effect on subsequent prose writers. It is important for the modern reader, in an age of entrenched divisions between high and low culture, to bear in mind that, although the customers of Gorgias and the other sophists were drawn from the propertied classes, the admiration for rhetorical skill was not confined to the wealthy. The audience which was captivated by Gorgias was not an élite group but the popular assembly. The historian Thoukydides puts into the mouth of the fifth-century Athenian politician Kleon a diatribe against the Athenian fondness for bravura oratory:

> You're the ones to blame for this with your mismanagement of these contests. Your habit is to be observers of speeches and hearers of action, assessing the possibility of future events from good speakers. But as for things which have already happened, you don't take what's been done as more plausible because you've seen it than what you've heard, under the influence of people who produce a clever verbal critique.... Each of you wants ideally to be the most able speaker, and failing that you compete with such speakers by seeming not to be slow-witted in following them . . . (Thoukydides, 3. 38. 4)

As always with oratory, nothing here is straightforward. The criticism is disingenuous, since the style in which it is expressed is itself highly artificial, and the speaker is deliberately adopting the posture of a blunt and simple man. More than this, we cannot be certain how far the wording and even the content of Kleon's speech (as with all speeches in Thoukydides) is the invention of the historian. But the overall picture the speech gives of a popular audience which took genuine pleasure in carefully crafted oratory is confirmed by the pronounced influence of formal oratory on Athenian tragedy, another art-form performed for a mass audience.

The response to the growth of rhetoric was not unambiguously positive. Passages in both comedy and tragedy indicate that the appreciation of skilled oratory coexisted with a profound suspicion of an art which threatened to substitute illusion for truth. This anxiety has its roots in the same conception of the audience as under the control of the speaker which we find in Gorgias. This suspicion persisted and is manifested most clearly in courtroom contexts where speakers either directly or indirectly lay claim to lack of experience in public speaking. The following is one of many examples: 'I could have wished, gentlemen, that my powers of speaking and experience of affairs were equal to my misfortune and the evils which have befallen me. As it is I have more experience of the latter than is fair, while in the former I am more deficient than is safe.' (Antiphon, 5. 1)

Unfortunately we have little oratory from the late fifth century BCE. Apart from the surviving pieces of Gorgias, our earliest texts, from the politician and speech-writer Antiphon, date to the period between 420 and his death after the short-lived political coup of 411 which briefly replaced the democracy with a narrow oligarchy. Some of these were written for the courts; others (the *Tetralogies* cited above) were composed for fictitious legal cases, as a means both of exemplifying and advertising the rhetorician's art. We also have the speech composed by the politician Andokides some time after 410 (*On his Return*) pleading for permission to return to Athens from exile. Otherwise our most important source for fifth-century Athenian oratory are the speeches which Thoukydides puts into the mouths of the characters in his history.

Oratory in context(s)

In his *Rhetoric* the fourth-century philosopher Aristotle divides oratory into three categories, symbouleutic, dikanic, and epideictic. The primary basis for the definitions (as for almost all archaic and classical literature) is the performative occasion. The first kind (symbouleutic) is aimed towards deliberative bodies and is the ancient equivalent to the parliamentary speech. In the Athenian context this means primarily speeches delivered before the Assembly (*ekklesia*). Athenian democracy, unlike most systems known to us, was a direct democracy; policy was decided not by a small cohesive group ('the government') with an advertised political programme but by the popular Assembly. Although attendance figures for the Assembly are controversial, and there must always have been a preponderance of city-dwellers and those living near the city at Assembly meetings, there was evidently little difficulty in enticing several thousand Athenian citizens, and at least for some occasions as many as six thousand, to attend public meetings which devoured a substantial portion of the day and to listen to extended speeches on major policy issues. The Athenian populace was by any standards an unusually politicized group. Though all adult male citizens were entitled to participate in the decision-making, in reality policy was driven by individuals, often organized into loose and shifting groups, who had the private means to devote their time to politics. And they achieved and maintained influence through the spoken word. The Assembly met regularly and its business ranged from major issues of peace and war and legislation (though from the fourth century the actual drafting of law was devolved to legislative panels) through to honorary decrees for public bene-factors. It also included control of the magistrates. There were regular opportunities for the Assembly to vote its officials out of office if their conduct was perceived as unsatisfactory. We know from a number of sources that addressing the Assembly was no easy task. A passage in Plato gives some flavour of an Assembly meeting:

> 'Why, when,' I said, 'a large crowd are seated together in assemblies or in court-rooms or theatres or camps or any other mass public gathering, and with loud uproar express disapproval of some of the things that are said and done and approve others, both in excess, with loud clamour and clap-ping of hands, and beyond this the rocks and the region round about re-echoing redouble the din of the criticism and the praise.' (Plato, *Republic* 492b—c)

Although Plato, no lover of Athenian democracy, presents us with a scene of indiscipline, what it really demonstrates to the unjaundiced reader is the lively engagement of ordinary assembly-goers with the issues addressed, and the absence of a culture of automatic deference to influence and authority.

The second type of oratory is directed towards the lawcourt. Though the legal system was based on a principle of trial by a panel of ordinary citizens, Athenian lawcourts were quite unlike anything experienced in the modern world. The jury panels themselves were massive by our standards. For the least significant private cases the minimum panel size was 200, while for public cases (which for the Athenians meant not only overtly political cases but also trials for offences which were felt to affect society at large) the panels would begin at 500 and increase in size by multiples of 500, on occasion reaching a scale in the thousands. The distinction between the juries and the Assembly must not be pressed too hard: the lawcourts were an accepted arena for fight-ing political feuds. In this respect the courts were an extension of the Assembly and the audiences must have overlapped to some (unquantifi-able) degree. Addressing the jury panels required no small measure of nerve. Athenian juries did not comport themselves with the sober silence expected of modern juries. The testimony of Plato about the behaviour of the juries (quoted above) is amply confirmed by many places in the orators where the speaker tries to anticipate a hostile (and vocal) response from the jurors. This passage from a fourth-century speech may exaggerate, but presumably it is

SPACE FOR DEMOCRACY. The Assembly (ekklesia) in classical Athens was open to all citizens and was held on the hill of the Pnyx to the west of the Akropolis and the agora. This view of the space where the Assembly listened to their orators looks towards the south.

based on a shared perception of just how difficult an audience an Athenian jury might be:

> He read out this and told all the other lies he thought useful, and he put the jurors in such a frame of mind that they refused to hear a single utterance from us. (Demosthenes, 45. 6)

In a memorable debate in *Wasps*, produced in 422, a play devoted to the legal system (cf. pp. 102–3), the comic playwright Aristophanes presents the jurors as vindictive, self-indulgent old men who like to be flattered and feared and who revel in the irresponsible and capricious exercise of power. On the basis of this and other evidence it is sometimes supposed that the courts are no more than another area of élite competition in which the rights and wrongs are ultimately of secondary importance. But with comedy, as with oratory, caution is needed in interpreting the evidence. Although our perception is distorted by the fact

VOTING BEFORE ATHENA. The myth narrated how the leaders of the Greeks at Troy voted after a debate between Odysseus and Ajax for the award of the great armour of Achilles. On this cup painted in Athens (c.470s BCE) the votes can be seen accumulating on the low plinth, under the supervision of Athena.

that surviving lawcourt speeches are the work either of politicians or of professional speech-writers writing for moneyed clients, with the result that we lack any direct evidence for smaller cases involving more humble characters, it is an inescapable fact that the courts were in fact an arena for competition among men of property. And the susceptibility of the jurors to flattery is amply demonstrated in surviving oratory. Furthermore, the feeling of power over the wealthy which Aristophanes describes must have been a real psychological bonus for the jurors, as well as confirming on a daily basis the principle of equality which underpinned the ideology of democracy. At the same time, a cursory reading of the orators reveals the pains taken by speakers to argue the case on its merits, however much (like litigants at all periods) they may digress, distort, and obfuscate. The jurors were considerably more shrewd, and a more intellectually demanding audience, than their critics suppose. It is important to bear in mind that Aristophanes in *Wasps* is particularly concerned with the political role of the courts. It was much easier to engage in systematic evasion in political trials, where the specific issues came wrapped in larger questions of public policy, than in private cases.

But one important point which does emerge from Aristophanes' lampoon of the legal system is the entertainment value of the courts. We should not imagine that the jurors were motivated solely by a desire to do their civic duty or even to collect the pay for service (about half the labourer's daily wage in the late fifth century, about a third in the fourth century when inflation had lowered the purchasing power of the drachma). Other people's lives are endlessly fascinating and the courts offered a spectacle comparable in certain ways with the grander dramas played out on the tragic stage.

The third kind (epideictic) is intended for public occasions where no formal outcome is sought. In essence it is oratory of display, *epideixis*, though the English word trivializes what for the Greeks was a serious activity. The term also ignores the overlap between *epideixis* and civic ideology, the importance of the speaker's status, and the tendency of epideictic speakers to take an explicitly competitive stance towards their predecessors and to utilize devices which identify them as in some sense the advocate of those they praise or exculpate. Epideictic oratory is exemplified especially (though not exclusively) by the speeches composed for delivery at the mass civic funerals which Athens held at the end of each year in times of war to honour the war dead. The historian Thucydides tells us that it was the custom for a distinguished public figure to speak in praise of the dead. These funerals offered an opportunity for the assembled citizen body to celebrate the achievements of the dead and the greatness of the city and constitution in whose name they fought and died. Like all ritual, they are as much about the shared identity of the audience as about the overt religious activity.

This tripartite division is not rigid. The boundaries are permeable. Even a cursory reading of lawcourt oratory reveals that in public cases at least there is room for a pronounced epideictic element. Politicians involved in trials not infrequently draw on the motifs (praise of ancestors, references to the great events of the past) which are the raw material of the public funeral orations. Deliberative oratory often has a pronounced adversarial element to it, inevitably given the nature of political competition in democratic Athens. It may be useful simply to draw attention to a single example. In 330 the politician Aischines brought to trial a minor political figure, Ktesiphon, for his proposal to give a crown of honour to Aischines' political enemy Demosthenes for conspicuous merit in the service of the city. A decade earlier Aischines had been a major player in Athenian politics and had been influential in negotiating peace between Athens and Philip of Macedon. By the date of Ktesiphon's trial, however, the peace had failed and Aischines was a spent force in Athenian politics. His sense of himself as an outsider is reflected in the way he presents the dominant political group (3. 250–1):

> Or don't you think it monstrous that the Council chamber and the
> Assembly are ignored, while the letters and embassies come to private

houses, not from people of no consequence but from the leading men of Asia and Europe? . . . And the people are discouraged by their experiences, like someone senile or out of his mind; they preserve only the name of democracy, while they have surrendered the real thing to others. Then when you go home from Assembly meetings you have not decided policy but like men coming from a picnic you have been given a share of the scraps.

The politicians get the benefits, the people get the leftovers. There is, however, nothing new in all this. The themes are encountered for the first time in surviving literature almost 100 years earlier in Aristophanes' *Wasps*, where the character Bdelykleon argues his father out of his passion for jury service by showing that the jurors are the dupes of the politicians:

> PHILOKLEON: So where does the rest of the money go?
> BDELYKLEON: To these 'I-shall-not betray-the-Athenian-rabble but-will-fight-for-the-masses-forever' types.
>
> .   .   .   .
>
> BDELYKLEON: Just look how, when you and everyone else could be rich,
> you've been circled about without realizing by the perpetual 'people' people,
> you who rule the most cities from the Black Sea to Sardis
> and get no benefit but this small wage. And this they always drip
> into you with wool like oil by drops to keep you alive.
> They want to keep you poor, and I'll tell you why:
> so you'll know your keeper, and then when with a whistle
> this man urges you on against an enemy, you leap on them savagely.
>
> (Aristophanes, *Wasps* 665–7, 698–705)

More significantly for our purposes, this presentation has a marked affinity to a description of the leading group by Demosthenes in 349/8 in his *Third Olynthiac*, almost twenty years before Aischines' speech, when Demosthenes had yet to become a major political force:

> Now the reverse is the case; the politicians control the benefits and everything is done through their agency, while you the people, hamstrung and stripped of money, allies, have been reduced to the position of servant and appendage, content if these men give you a share of the theoric money or hold the Boedromia, and—the most manly thing of all!—you're even grateful to get what belongs to you. (Demosthenes, 3. 31)

Demosthenes' account occurs in a deliberative speech, Aischines' in a lawcourt speech, but the theme and stance are the same. On occasion epideictic oratory adopts the stance of other forms. But for all the dangers of restrictive application, Aristotle's categories are not to be dismissed. Each category is directed towards a different context and that context has a profound impact on its form and content. Although there is a constant transmigration of motifs, the motifs are often deployed to different ends. When the great deeds of the past are used in epideictic contexts, the aim is straightforward praise of the dead and, through the pride and shared origin enacted in the narrative, a ritualized celebration of group identity which unites speaker and audience. When they appear in forensic oratory the pride engendered by the epideictic motifs serves an ulterior purpose.

Often, it is utilized as a means of isolating the opponent; pride is a means to stimulate other emotions, as when the late fifth-/early fourth-century speech-writer Lysias briefly slips into epideictic mode during the prosecution of Nikomachos early in the fourth century for alleged misconduct in his office as drafter of the revised lawcode. Nikomachos (himself probably a man of servile extraction) is placed on one side of the balance, the ancestors who built the fifth-century empire on the other, and the audience is invited to express a preference:

> I gather he claims that I am guilty of impiety in putting an end to the sacrifices. Personally, I would think that Nikomachos could make this sort of statement about me if I were making laws. As it is, I am asking him to obey the shared and established laws. I am surprised that he does not reflect that, when he alleges that I am behaving impiously in saying that we must sacrifice according to the *kyrbeis* [the early lawcode] and the columns according to the drafts, he is also accusing the city. For this is what you decreed. And if you think this is intolerable, you must surely suppose that those men did wrong, who only carried out the sacrifices on the *kyrbeis*. And yet, judges, one should not learn piety from Nikomachos but reflect on the basis of past events. Our ancestors while carrying out the sacrifices on the *kyrbeis* handed on the city as the greatest and most successful in Greece, and so it is right that you make the same sacrifices as those men because of the good fortune which resulted from those offerings, if for no other reason. (Lysias, 30. 17–18)

For Aristotle (*Rhetoric* I. 3. 5) the particular goal of deliberative oratory is the expedient; that is the speaker must persuade his audience that a policy or course of action is to their advantage or disadvantage. In fact, appeals to the interests of the judges play a significant role in lawcourt oratory, though as a means to an end (it is to the advantage of the judges or the city to convict/acquit) not as an end, as for instance in the following passage from a speech written by Demosthenes for the prosecution of a man named Konon for an alleged assault:

But Konon will beg and weep. Now consider: who deserves more pity, the man who suffers what I have suffered at his hands, if I leave the court as a victim of further outrage, deprived of justice, or Konon, if he is punished? Is it more advantageous for each of you that people should be free to commit assault and outrage or not? I think not. Now if you acquit, there will be more of these people, but if you convict, there will be less. (Demosthenes, 54. 43)

The goals of each oratorical category are not exclusive to that category; they are merely the final goals to which all other considerations are subordinated.

The means of persuasion

Aristotle in the *Rhetoric* recognizes two kinds of means of persuasion, the *entechnos pistis*, that is the means which derives from *techne*, art, technique, and the *atechnos pistis*, 'artless/inartificial means of persuasion. I shall return to inartificial means of persuasion later. For now I shall concentrate on 'technical' proof. Aristotle lists three kinds of technical proof. The first, character (*ethos*), is not personality but moral character, that is the impression created through the speech that the speaker possesses qualities which invite trust and belief. The second, emotion (*pathos*), is the emotional effect created in the audience by the speech. The third, argumentation (*logos*), is the most obvious for us. It is for Aristotle also the most important of the proofs; but because the rhetorician must operate in the real, not an ideal, world, Aristotle accepts the importance of the other two types.

Character (in the sense of the character of the speaker) is equally at home in all oratory. To induce the audience to share his view of the political situation and support his political stance, the speaker in the Assembly must establish his authority; so too must the litigant in court or the speaker over the war dead or at the panhellenic festival. There is however a difference. The speaker in the Assembly comes with a past, since he is located in a particular set of affiliations and brings with him an implied context; the audience brings with it both its knowledge of this larger context and a set of (often conflicting) prejudices. The speaker of declamatory oratory is likewise a man with a past, particularly in the case of the funeral oration, where he owes his selection to his public credentials. This would of course also apply to politicians in court. But in the case of the ordinary Athenian in court, plaintiff or defendant, character is indeterminate until he begins to speak. This is sometimes forgotten in discussions of *ethopoiia* (character delineation) in the orators; some modern writers suppose that the speech-writer fits the speech to the (real) character of the speaker. But in the case of obscure individuals only a minority of judges (if any) would know anything of them in advance. Rather, the character of the speaker in such cases is generated by rhetorical need. All self-presentation is to some degree fictive; that is, it involves the adoption of roles dictated by the expectations of the audience as much as by any desire for self-revelation. What distinguishes law-court oratory is the thoroughness of the fiction, or at the least the clear space free for fiction, which is not delimited by any previous experience of the hearer. The speaker's character is a blank page to be filled in by the speech-writer according to his needs. There is another way in which lawcourt oratory has more room in character portrayal: the character of the opponent. It is not true that speakers in the Assembly do not resort to character assassination, but it is obviously more difficult to disguise this as relevant to the subject at issue. In contrast, in the courts theoretically any personal information can be offered as relevant. The loose Athenian conception of relevance in legal contexts means that there are few slanders which cannot be uttered against one's opponent. The absence of firm rules on relevance in most Athenian courts makes such considerations germane to the discussion. The following example, taken from a relatively insignificant speech written for an inheritance case by Isaios (who specialized in such cases), shows how readily the Athenians resorted to quite serious allegations:

> For my opponent, when he was living here, was first of all arrested in the act as a thief and taken to prison. Then after being released by the Eleven along with some others, all of whom you publicly condemned to death, he was later denounced to the Council as a felon; he slipped away and failed to appear, and from that time he did not return to Athens for seventeen years, until the death of Nikostratos. He has never in your service served in the army or paid any levy, except since he laid claim to Nikostratos' property, nor performed any other public service. (Isaios, 4. 28–9)

Emotion too is at home in every kind of oratory. Long before the age of technical rhetoric Greek speakers realized that the emotional response of the hearer is as much a part of the decision-making process (and therefore as much a part of the speaker's task) as the intellectual engagement with ideas and arguments. The use of emotion differs according to oratorical type. In general, the range of emotions generated by the most common form of epideictic oratory, the funeral oration, is quite narrow. A sense of loss may be created, though emotion of this kind is limited; more common is the feeling of awe at and pride in achievement, as for instance:

> But indeed I do not know what need there is to lament this way. For we were well aware that we are mortal. So what need is there to complain now

over a fate we long since were expecting to suffer, or to grieve so heavily at natural misfortunes? For we know that death is the common lot both for the basest and for the best. He does not spurn the wicked or admire the good but offers himself equally to all. If it were possible for those who escape death in war to be immortal for the rest of time, it would be proper for the living to lament the dead for all time. As it is, our nature is subject to disease and age, and the power that has control of our destiny is inexorable. So it is right to consider those men most happy who ended their lives by facing danger for the greatest and most honourable of causes, who did not trust their fate to the arbitration of chance or wait for that death which comes in its normal course but chose the most noble one. (Lysias, 2. 77–9)

The range of emotions in deliberative and forensic oratory is much wider, as the situations arising are more varied. It is, however, in forensic oratory in particular that emotions tangential to the case (in particular gratitude for service to the state) are utilized as a means of persuasion. Though, as the passage from Demosthenes' *Third Olynthiac* quoted above demonstrates, speakers addressing the Assembly try to generate hostility against their rivals, the Assembly is not asked explicitly to vote out of goodwill for the politician or hostility or distrust for his rivals. Though arguably that is a significant part of the whole deliberative process, it is implicit at most. In court the audience is invited explicitly to show its gratitude to the speaker. It is also asked explicitly to hate the opponent and to register this hatred when casting the vote. This, taken from Ariston's prosecution of Konon for assault, is not untypical:

So I urge you, judges, now that I proved my case in full justice, and have given you a pledge in addition, that just as each of you would personally hate the perpetrator if he had suffered this, he should feel the same anger against Konon here on my behalf, and not regard as a private matter any such thing which might perhaps befall anyone. Whoever it befalls, you should give aid and grant justice, and hate people who in the face of their crimes are bold and impetuous and when put on trial are shameless and wicked and care nothing for custom or anything else in their efforts to escape punishment. (Demosthenes, 54. 42)

The third of the rhetorical means of persuasion, *logos*, is more difficult to accommodate, simply because it would require a book-length discussion to determine the differences between different rhetorical modes. Here we are largely confined to forensic and deliberative contexts, since the largely descriptive thrust of the funeral oration leaves little scope (or need) for logical argument. It would be interesting to examine logic in forensic and deliberative contexts to see whether there is any significant difference. In general, however, a cursory survey suggests that there is no difference between the two categories so far as the quality of the argument is concerned. Just as the logical means (essentially argument from probability) are the same, so the logical strength is not a function of genre but of situation and writer. But equally my impression is that forensic oratory differs from deliberative oratory in that in many cases its approach to argument is accretive, that is, there is often a tendency in the courts to pile up arguments in order to hit the target from as many directions as possible, to survey arguments in rapid succession where deliberative oratory tends to maintain its themes for longer. There is greater diversity and less sustained argument in the courts. This is not necessarily a strength, since in some writers (particularly Lysias and Aischines) the result can be a rather loose concatenation of arguments. In the following passage an anonymous client of Lysias, charged with destroying the stump of one of the sacred olives scattered about Athenian territory, moves rapidly from argument to argument, as he presents his case before the Council of the Areopagus, which had jurisdiction in many religious matters:

> And was it more in my interest, Council, to break the law under the democracy or in the time of the Thirty? [the ruthless junta which ruled Athens briefly at the end of the fifth century] I say this not because I had influence then or because I'm suspected now but because it was much more open for anyone to do wrong then than now. You will find that I committed no crime of this sort nor any other in that period. How, unless I was my own worst enemy, when you take such care, could I have attempted to eradicate a sacred olive from my farm, when there is not a single tree in it but a single olive stump (so my opponent says), and the road surrounds it on all sides and neighbours live on both sides, and the farm is unfenced and visible from every direction. (Lysias, 7. 27–8)

Shaping the speech

The function and context of oratory also impacts on structure. The most significant difference is in the role of narrative. For Aristotle narrative is an essential part *only* of the courtroom speech, but the case is overstated (in fact his language indicates that the reality is rather more complex); one has only to think of the pronounced narrative element in the Athenian funeral oration to realize this. But the narrative in the funeral oration is itself merely a variant on narratives shared by the city. That is, the speaker praising the war dead may reshape collective history or city myth but the raw material remains broadly familiar and indeed the same themes often recur. Marathon, one of the defining moments of Athenian history, is a regular theme in praises of the city, as in this extract from a funeral speech ascribed to Lysias:

> Ashamed that the barbarians were in their country, they did not wait for their allies to hear of it or aid them, and they did not feel that they should be grateful to others for their rescue but that the other Greeks should be grateful to themselves. With this shared resolve they met them, few against many. They thought that to die was a fate they shared with all mankind to die but to show courage was a fate they shared with few ... No wonder then that though these deeds were performed long since their courage is admired now still by all mankind as though the deeds were fresh. (Lysias, 2. 23–6)

Within the sphere of political oratory, indirect evidence suggests that there was more room for narrative in ambassadorial oratory than within purely internal political debate. But even ordinary political debate allows room for narrative, as can be seen from Andokides' speech *On the Peace*, composed in the late 390s. Andokides had served as one of the Athenian delegates at a peace congress held at Sparta, and the speech was delivered on his return. In an attempt to persuade the Athenians to conclude peace with Sparta he surveys Athenian history and demonstrates (by a rather cavalier use of the evidence) that peace has always been beneficial, while war has been ruinous. But again this is a variation (however distorted) on shared narrative, while the narrative in court is not shared but individual. The juror looks to the litigants for basic information as well as opinion and argument to a degree found in no other context. When the speaker of Lysias 1, a man on trial for homicide who defends himself on the ground that he found the dead man in adultery with his wife, presents his case, he is our sole authority for the events he narrates and his case to a large extent stands or falls on his ability to impose his version on the jurors. This passage presents his account of his wife's duplicity after she was seduced:

> After a time, gentlemen, I came home unexpectedly from the country. After dinner the baby cried and howled; he was being tormented by the maid on purpose to make him, because the man was in the house— afterwards I discovered all of this. And I told my wife to go off and give the baby the breast to stop him crying. To start with she refused, as if she were pleased to see me back after a long absence. When I grew angry and told her to go she said: "Oh yes, so that you can have a go at the serving girl here! You've groped her before too when you were drunk!" I for my part laughed, while she stood up, went out and closed the door, pretending she was joking, and then turned the key. And I thought nothing of all this and suspected nothing, but went to sleep gladly, having come from the

country. When it was almost daylight, she came and opened the door. When I asked why the doors banged in the night, she said that the lamp by the baby had gone out and so she had got a light from the neighbours. I said nothing, and believed that this was true. But I thought, gentlemen, that she was wearing make-up, though her brother was not yet dead thirty days. Still, even so I said nothing about the matter but went off without a word. (Lysias, 1. 11–14)

The pronounced narrative component in courtroom speeches brings more to the text than diverse material. There is a difference of manner. The narrative voice is usually distinct to some degree from the voice of argument. The narrative section provides ostensible fact either alone or interspersed with judgement. The argument section usually brings a marked change of presentational mode, from 'fact' to overt argument and opinion, generally a series of arguments from probability. This difference can best be appreciated if we compare the narrative in Lysias 1 with the speaker's arguments later in the speech. These two passages deal with events leading up to the killing of the wife's lover:

But first of all I want to give you an account of what took place on the last day. I had a close friend, Sostratos, whom I met on his way from the country after sunset. I knew that having arrived so late he would find nothing he needed at home, and so I invited him to dinner. We reached my house and went upstairs and dined. When he had eaten his fill, he went off while I went to sleep. Eratosthenes, gentlemen, came in, and the serving girl woke me at once and told me that he was in the house. Telling her to watch the door, I went downstairs in silence and left the house. I called on one man after another; some I didn't catch at home, while others, I found, were not even in town. (Lysias, 1. 22–3)

As I said before, gentlemen, my close friend Sostratos met me on his way from the country around sunset and dined with me, and when he had eaten his fill he went off. Yet consider first of all, gentlemen, whether, if I was plotting against Eratosthenes that night it was better for me to dine elsewhere myself or to bring a dinner guest home. For in the latter case Eratosthenes would have been less likely to venture into the house. Then again, do you think I would have let my dinner guest go and leave me alone and unsupported, or ask him to stay, so that he could join me in taking revenge on the seducer? Furthermore, gentlemen, don't you think I would have sent word to my associates during the day and instructed them to gather in the nearest of my friends' houses, instead of running around during the night as soon as I found out, without knowing whom I would find at home and who would be out? (Lysias, 1. 39–41)

In this case the difference of manner is so great that the modern reader, with time to reread and interrogate the text at leisure, is struck by the marked difference between the innocent transparency of the character presented by the narrative and the sharp and skilful arguments built on the foundation of the earlier 'factual' narrative. It is almost as though there were two speakers. But the formal difference within the speech is an illusion. The role of the narrative is to induce the hearer to accept a particular version of events as reliable, not to provide the audience with transparent fact. A good narrator deploys a whole variety of narrative devices to shape the audience's response without explicit comment.

Controlling the agenda

A related difference between the three categories of oratory is the question of agenda. The audience of the epideictic speech have come to listen to a declamation on a set theme. There are no competing voices and the only surprises in content consist in variations on set themes. The deliberative speech starts with an agenda which is essentially predetermined. Again the audience brings with it a shared knowledge and a shared set of expectations. There is always scope in debate to spring surprises; but the terms of the debate have been significantly delimited in advance, since the context of discussion is shared by all participants. Peace or war, alliance or not, military intervention or not, the broad issues are a given, and the broad issues bring with them both in general and in the individual context a set of arguments which the audience can predict to some degree.

The same is true, though to a lesser extent, of those forensic debates which arise from political rivalry. The prosecution of Ktesiphon by Aischines in 330 for his proposal to honour Aischines' enemy Demosthenes was clearly intended by Aischines as the final showdown in a political feud which had raged for a decade and a half. When the jurors sat down to enjoy this magnificent grudge match, they could predict the broad tenor of the opposing cases with reasonable confidence. But the element of predictability dwindles in direct proportion to the public visibility of the participants. It has been maintained that all trials in classical Athens are potentially political, since the litigants are almost always drawn from the moneyed classes and this is the sector of Athenian society which engaged in politics at the crucial level of initiative (as distinct from attendance at the Assembly). The socio-economic point is correct: as was observed above, financial litigation, often on a substantial scale, is prominent in surviving oratory, while the cases that bulk large in our system, what we would call 'criminal' cases, are conspicuously few. But the conclusion is suspect. Most surviving speeches which are not directed towards political issues are apolitical in the further sense that they avoid reference to questions of policy or influence. Where the case turns on non-political issues (or involves people who are not prominent in public life) the agenda is not a given. By agenda I mean the facts of the case, the identity, personality, and general conduct of the litigants. The agenda is a vacuum, and it becomes the duty of the speech-writer to fill this vacuum for the audience with a sustainable version of the events and participants. There is far more room for manœuvre in court.

The need to control the agenda is increased by the nature of the judicial process. The politician facing Assembly or Council is usually operating within a set of broader goals. The individual moment is important, but there is always the possibility that defeat can be reversed either in later meetings of the Assembly or through the medium of political trials, as for instance the eventual reversal in the power ratio between the proponents and opponents of peace with Macedonia, which was both advanced and signalled by the political prosecutions of the late 340s. Defeat in court is not entirely irreversible—for one thing there is always the prospect of attacking the opposition witnesses for perjury. But there is no appeal on the main action and, even where collateral actions are possible, the loser starts at a disadvantage, since a previous jury had found for his opponent. This means that everything must be subordinated to a single goal, immediate victory.

Despite all this, there is one respect in which lawcourt oratory is more circumscribed than other forms. In Aristotle's discussion of the means of persuasion, it is noteworthy that, although the artificial means of persuasion (character, emotion, argument) are applicable to all modes of oratory, the artless proofs (*atechnoi pisteis*)—that is the proofs which do not depend on the rhetorician's art—are all peculiar to forensic oratory. Aristotle lists (*Rhetoric* I. 15) laws, witnesses, contracts, tortures, oaths. This means that unlike other oratorical forms, forensic rhetoric must engage directly with external material. Epideictic oratory is free to select as it chooses from the topics available. Deliberative oratory, though it cannot escape its external context, is free to reshape that context through argument. Forensic oratory has a problem in that in order to command belief it must include external proof to substantiate the speaker's statements. We do on occasion find courtroom speeches which make no use of documentary evidence; and although some of these are supporting speeches (in which case the leading speaker may well have provided a substantial body of evidence), some certainly represent the only speech delivered for this side in court. But the rarity of such speeches indicates that this is a strategy avoided by litigants wherever possible. Which in turn means that the audience were reluctant to trust a litigant who could not bring some element of independent evidence to bear. So the speaker has to include a body of alien material. These external voices must be mastered and brought under the control of the speaker. In fact Athenian litigants make use wherever possible of friendly witnesses. But even so the witness is outside the speaker's control to the extent that he does not simply say whatever the litigant wants him to say, unless of course he is unusually obliging, foolhardy, or unscrupulous; there was always the possibility of prosecution for false evidence and our texts indicate that the Athenians were ready to use this tool against their opponent's witnesses. From about 380 BCE written testimony was used; this was read out by the clerk and the witness simply confirmed the text he heard. The text itself, where we have evidence for the drafting, was the work of the litigant, but the witness still had to verify the statement and so the litigant cannot simply invent. It becomes the litigant's task to shape the deposition in such a way as to obtain maximum support from the witness.

Another important voice in oratory is the law. Not only do speakers speak about law, they also cite laws (that is, the law itself is read out in court in the clerk's voice). And again the law needs on occasion to be massaged. An example from Aischines' speech for the prosecution of a rival politician, Timarchos, for (alleged) homosexual prostitution in 346/5 may clarify. The clerk is about to quote the law dealing with the law banning prostitution by citizens. But Aischines himself quotes it, mixes it up with pejorative details relating to Timarchos (here presented in italics), and so at one and the same time associates the law with Timarchos, puts a negative complexion on Timarchos' public life, and wraps the law in an emotional haze:

> But once he is entered in the deme register and knows the city's laws and is now able to determine right and wrong, the legislator from now on addresses nobody else but at this point the individual himself, Timarchos. And what does he say? If any Athenian (he says) prostitutes himself, he is not to have the right to serve as one of the nine archons (*the reason being, I think, that these officials wear a sacred wreath*), nor to undertake any priesthood, *since his body is quite unclean*; and let him not serve (he says) as advocate for the state or hold any office ever, whether at home or abroad, whether selected by lot or elected by a vote; let him not serve as herald, nor as envoy (*nor let him bring to trial people that have served as envoys, nor let him bring malicious prosecutions for pay*), nor let him voice any opinion in the Council or the Assembly (*not even if he is the cleverest speaker in Athens*). If anyone acts against these provisions, he has allowed for indictments for prostitution and imposed the most severe penalties. Read this law out to them as well, to make you aware of the noble and decent character of the established laws, against which Timarchos has dared to address the Assembly, a man whose way of life is known to you all. (Aischines, 1. 18–20)

I have so far presented this external material as somehow threatening, though it can also be an enormous help for the speaker in need of support. The law is not always relevant to the case. Sometimes it represents a rather desperate attempt to establish a case by analogy, as in Hypereides 3, where the speaker tries to fill what looks like a gap in the law of sale by building up a set of tendentious parallels. His opponent has sold him a perfumery run by a slave who has run up some massive debts for which the speaker now finds himself liable. It looks as though Athenian law made no specific provision for this and so the speaker has to argue at length from comparable legislation. In [Demosthenes] 46 the speaker quotes law after law irrespective of its immediate relevance, evidently as a means of browbeating the jurors into seeing things the speaker's way. It would be easy to see this as evidence for a cavalier attitude to law in Athenian society. But the reverse is true. The law speaks with authority and the litigant is exploiting the voice of the law (as authoritative text) to strengthen his case.

It remains a distinguishing feature of forensic oratory that the speaker must absorb alien material in its raw form within the speech, neutralize it where necessary, enhance its support where possible. And while making this material subservient to his will, the speaker must maintain the authority which comes from the seeming independence of the support he cites. Unlike the other forms of oratory, forensic oratory presents a seeming multiplicity of voices, with its move between argument and narrative and its need to draw in external support. The multiplicity is however illusion, impersonation, for ultimately the voices are reducible to one, the speaker's, and that voice is devoted to the single task of persuasion.

Style and context

Aristotle notes that the three categories of oratory differ in style. A detailed account of the style of Athenian oratory is beyond the scope of this discussion; but the different occasions do create different audience expectations and these in turn determine stylistic tendencies. The most cautious branch of oratory in this respect is courtroom oratory. Even here, however, some speeches were written for delivery in court by active politicians while others were delivered by ordinary citizens, and as was noted, the writers for the courts tend to fit their speeches as far as possible to the person of the speaker. This extends to style as well as statements explicitly or implicitly characterizing the litigant. So speeches for private citizens tend to be less grand in language, with a general avoidance of extended simile or metaphor. This is not true of the earliest period of professional speech-writing; the disclaimer of experience in speaking made by the young man who delivered Antiphon 5 (quoted above p. 178) uses an elaborate style which is at odds with the claim made, and it is difficult to believe that the audience would fail to detect the professional speech-writer behind the litigant. Any stylistic effect which creates a rift between the avowed personality and the mode of expression risks creating a simultaneous rift between speaker and audience; the audience must feel that the speaker can be trusted. Accordingly Antiphon's successors as forensic speech-writers were more cautious. Lawcourt speeches delivered by politicians are not subject to the same restraint. The jurors expect politicians to sound like experienced speakers and so such speeches are closer in style to deliberative oratory, which more readily admits grand effects.

The following two passages from Demosthenes' *Third Olynthiac* (a delibera-tive speech of 348 in which Demosthenes argues for the redeployment of state hand-outs to fund Athenian intervention to protect the city of Olynthos from the expansionist ambitions of Philip of Macedonia) and his speech *On the Crown* (written for the trial of Ktesiphon in 330, when Demosthenes acted as supporting speaker for Ktesiphon) show the convergence between political speeches in court and in the Assembly:

> If even now at last you were to abandon these habits and agree to serve as soldiers and behave in a manner worthy of yourselves and use this surplus domestic revenue as a basis to achieve external benefit, perhaps, just perhaps, men of Athens, you could gain some complete advantage and be rid of hand-outs of this sort, which are like the food given by doctors to the sick. For the latter neither provide strength nor allow the patient to die. Likewise, what you receive now is not sufficient to provide any substantial assistance nor does it allow you to give it up and do some-thing else; no, this is what increases the sluggishness of each one of you. (Demosthenes, 3 [*Third Olynthiac*]. 33)

> [To Aischines] You talk to us now about the past? You are like a doctor who when he visits his patients while they are sick gives not a word or an indication about the means by which they will escape their illness, but once one of them dies and his funeral rites are being performed goes with the procession to the tomb and holds forth: 'if this man had done this or that, he would not have died'. (Demosthenes, 18 [*On the Crown*]. 243).

During the mid- to late fourth century at least, the grand manner becomes even more overt, as politicians make free use of passages from classic poetry and drama to achieve emotional effects and to enhance their authority, as for instance with this passage from the speech written by Aischines for the prosecution of Ktesiphon of 330:

> The poet Hesiod expresses himself well on situations like this. He says at one point, as he seeks to educate the masses and advise the cities, that they should not tolerate corrupt demagogues. I shall pronounce the verses; the reason I think we learn by heart the poets' thoughts as children is to make use of them when we are men.
>
> > Often enough the whole city has paid for an evil man
> > who does wrong and devises deeds of wickedness.
> > Upon them from heaven Cronus' son brings great woe,
> > famine and plague together, and the people perish.
> > He may destroy their vast army or their walls
> > or take vengeance on their ships at sea, far-seeing Zeus.
>
> If you remove the rhythm and examine the poet's sentiments, I think you will see that they are not Hesiod's poetry but an oracle directed at Demosthenes' political career. For indeed army and fleet and whole cities have been obliterated as a result of his policies. (Aischines, 3. 134–6, quoting Hesiod, *Works and Days* 240–5)

Similar effects are achieved in the political-forensic speeches of his enemy Demosthenes and the one complete surviving speech (*Against Leokrates*) by their contemporary, the distinguished politician Lykourgos.

Lawcourt speeches for politicians and deliberative oratory form an intermediate stylistic class between forensic speeches for private citizens at the more sober end of the scale and epideictic speeches at the grandiose end of the scale. The audience for oratory of display has come to participate in a great public occasion, with the full expectation that the speech will be appropriate to that occasion, both as sentiment and as performance. The speech written for declamation wears its verbal craftsmanship with pride, indulging in musical and rhythmical effects which would be avoided, or used less flamboyantly or liberally, in other oratorical types, as this passage from the funeral oration attributed to Lysias illustrates the point:

> It is not easy for one man to narrate the dangers faced by many nor to declare in a single day deeds performed through all time. For what speech or time or speaker could be sufficient to tell the courage of the men who lie here? With the greatest toils and the most illustrious trials and the noblest dangers they set Greece free . . . (Lysias, 2. 54–5)

From audience to reader

We encounter the Athenian orators as written text. But in most cases their status as literary texts is either accidental or secondary. These speeches were first and foremost performed works. It is important to bear in mind when reading the orators that what we have no more reflects the full experience of the work for its first audience than do the texts of tragic and comic plays. We have ample evidence that some of the more controversial political orators in the late fifth century adopted a flamboyant mode of delivery; and although both contemporary comic playwrights and later sources tend to present this as a striking departure from tradition, probably we are dealing with a difference of degree rather than of kind.

In the fourth century we know that the politician Aischines, who had worked as an actor, had a very impressive speaking voice, which must have more than compensated for features of his speeches which are often perceived as flaws by students of rhetoric. In the fifth and early fourth century it was by no means inevitable that a speech would ever reach the status of text. Early in the fourth century we still find Gorgias' pupil Alkidamas (in his essay *On the Authors of Written Speeches*) praising the flexibility of the unwritten, extemporized, speech over the rigidity of the written speech. But the practice not only of writing down but also of publishing speeches had already begun in the fifth century. There was a book trade in Athens in the late fifth century and the fictitious speeches of teachers like Gorgias, even if they began their lives as performed exemplars designed to illustrate the potential of specific effects, were clearly also available in book form. The same is presumably true of the *Tetralogies* of Antiphon.

The practice of publishing lawcourt speeches had also begun by the end of the fifth century. The speeches of Antiphon written for real trials show a degree of polish which suggests that they were at least prepared for publication during the author's lifetime. Although the market for such speeches probably consisted largely of people interested in acquiring speaking skills, the embedded Greek appreciation of good oratory—attested in particular by the frequency in tragedy of speeches displaying the influence of formal rhetoric—suggests that even at this stage there must have been an aesthetic as well as a practical interest in the speeches. In political oratory the practice of publishing speeches did not begin until the fourth century. Apart from the aesthetic and practical appeal of such texts in a society dependent on speech-making in most public contexts, the publication of political speeches allowed them to achieve a second life as pamphlets in continuing political debate both before a contemporary audience and ultimately before the audience of future generations. In the case of the speeches written by Demosthenes and Aischines for their showcase political contests in the lawcourts we have ample evidence that changes were made to the speech during the process of revision for publication. As a result we can never be entirely sure how far our written text deviates from the oral-aural text of the first performance. During the fourth century, as we can see from the sheer volume of surviving speeches, there was a substantial market for published oratory of all kinds and this market continued into the Hellenistic period and beyond. The scholars of the Ptolemaic library at Alexandria edited and commented on the Athenian orators, and the texts continued to play a major role in the education of both Greeks and Romans.

7 | Sophisticates and solecisms: Greek literature after the classical period

JANE L. LIGHTFOOT

Hellenistic, post-classical—the old world's spiral into decline? The mainland Greek states continued their old squabbles for supremacy after the Peloponnesian War; but a new power was rising, and within a couple of generations it produced a figure who, in thirty-two years of life, would change the whole political geography of the world for good. The power was Macedon, and the figure was Alexander, soon known as the Great. He swept across Greece, Asia Minor, and Persia, obliterating the last Persian king; and, that done, stampeded over the central Asian steppe, only to be brought up short in the Punjab by a mutiny. But he had shown them regions no Greek had ever seen, and monarchy on a scale yet undreamed of; and when he died, in Babylon in 323 BCE, he had also irrevocably altered the Greeks' cultural horizons.

Inevitably, the successors of this neo-Homeric hero were lesser men, who immediately started wrangling over his legacy. They carved out domains for themselves and hacked away at each other for years before any sort of steady state emerged; but by the time the dust cleared, there were immigrant Greeks resident in new, royal foundations in kingdoms in Egypt, Asia Minor, Syria, Mesopotamia, Central Asia—all the way to modern Afghanistan and India. It is against this background that we have to measure the literature of the Hellenistic period, many of its producers and consumers no longer the classical city-states of mainland Greece, but residents of the new world, further east.

The new foundations had constitutions that looked like those back home; but they were under the thumb of the king; and the looming presence of the Hellenistic monarchs is vital when we come to consider what became in our period of the literary genres of archaic and classical Greece. So is the newness of the terrain: Greeks were now resident where no Greek had ever lived before. The old view, now rather threadbare, would portray them in their new communities as restless, uprooted, trying to defend their Greekness against the natives of threatening, unfamiliar territory. But it is an exciting period, precisely because of this newness of terrain, because of the possibility of testing responses to conditions the Greeks had never before encountered, because of the new sorts of literature which resulted from their dislocation from their old homes and ways.

It is also probably the first period of Greek literature in which we have a substantial body of direct information about audiences and readers as well as authors, about the consumers of literature as well as its producers. It was in the Hellenistic period that there first developed a para-literary industry: scholars and interpreters for the first time gathered and edited and commented on literary texts. We even know something of the sorts of scrutiny to which they subjected them and ways in which they read them. We owe much to the sands of Egypt, where numerous sites have yielded a wealth of texts on papyri which, though mostly documentary in character, also include a substantial body of literary material. Information from these sources can tell us what was being read, in what form (for example, it can indicate the state of a particular author's text at any one time), and occasionally even *how* and *by whom*. Find-contexts can—though all too rarely—tell us a little about the owners, while marginal annotations may tell us a little about the concerns of readers and of the sorts of questions asked of texts. Meanwhile a different sort of evidence for readers and audiences in the Hellenistic period comes from epigraphy—inscriptions mainly from mainland Greece, the Aegean islands, and Anatolia. Being for the most part public inscriptions these record different sorts of activity, and form a necessary and important counterbalance to the Egyptian papyri with their evidence for mostly private reading. The inscriptions concern festivals and recitations, performances and displays which took place in theatres and concerthalls in Greek cities, and remind us that in a world of increasing textuality the traditional enunciative, performative aspect of Greek culture was not on the wane.

Players and plays

To begin with drama, the great public genres which the Greek world inherited from classical, democratic Athens, is to emphasize the continuity of this aspect of Greek culture—and, indeed, its massive success and influence in the Hellenistic period. Drama was Athens' most enduring literary legacy, for it came to be seen as a necessary constituent of urban life: to have a theatre was to be Greek. We are only now coming to understand the pace at which theatres were established all over the Greek world, right from the end of the fifth century onwards—in mainland Greece, in southern Italy in the Hellenized area known (in Latin) as Magna Graecia, and then, after Alexander's conquests, in the new foundations where Greek immigrants settled. Particularly famous is the site of Ai Khanum on the northern limit of modern Afghanistan: a theatre, a gymnasium, and a library were three indispensable elements of Greek culture that not even so remote a colony could do without.

There was a rash of new festivals, founded for a myriad of reasons: to honour a king (or 'liberator'); to commemorate an accession, or a victory, or the repulse of an enemy (the Soteria are famous, marking the defeat of the Gauls who had descended on Delphi in 279); or because someone, invariably with some ulterior motive, had declared that the local deity had appeared and ordained it so (a famous example is the Leukophryena, founded at the end of the third century in Magnesia on the Maeander following an epiphany of the local equivalent of Artemis). Or there were Dionysia in the time-honoured way—but not quite like the classical festivals, for the god's range of powers was now extended to include all the performing arts, music and singing as well as theatre. Athletic events too had a place in these great occasions. Dionysos was also the special god of the new Macedonian rulers of Egypt, the Ptolemies (named after their founder, the general Ptolemaios), who also loved pageantry. So it is not surprising to find them as assiduous patrons of festivals, an interest reflected in many epigrams and other works by contemporary poets. Theokritos (of whom more anon), praising King Ptolemy II, claimed that 'No man who knows how to sing a clear melody has come to the sacred contests of Dionysos without receiving a gift worthy of his skill'.

Yet, transplanted from the city in which it grew, Hellenistic drama has often been supposed to have been in a parlous state. Allegedly, the Hellenistic monarchies rode roughshod over the cities' freedom, leaving their political institutions worn out and exiguous: there was no longer any forum for what is seen as drama's main function in the classical polis—the assertion and/or interrogation of civic culture and values (cf. pp. 99–104). Allied to this is the loss of most Hellenistic drama: isn't it obvious that it didn't survive because it was no good? On the other hand, evidence for the widespread revival of classical plays begins in the Hellenistic period. This is all of a piece with the crystallization in this period of notions of 'the classics'; but has also been held to point to the drying-up of creativity. It is difficult to redress this situation, since virtually all Hellenistic tragedy and satyr drama is sadly lost, and much the same is true of comedy, although here at least we have Menander at the very beginnings of our period (see below). But we do have much valuable evidence of other kinds—including the excavations of theatres—and a great deal of documentation about the performance of drama. Using what we have will enable us to make some interesting and useful observations about what concerns us most here—the public.

It is true that the performance of drama slipped from the hands of ordinary citizens, but specialization in the obviously skilled business of the theatre is detectable from very early in its history. Already in the middle of the fifth century in Athens we hear of prizes awarded to principal actors; by the middle of the fourth, Aristotle in his *Rhetoric* could pronounce that actors had become more important than the poets themselves. The fourth century saw the rise of the star—men like Aristodemos and Neoptolemos, Theodoros and Polos, whose boast was that they could have whole audiences in tears. Theodoros, apparently, succeeded in so moving the hard-hearted tyrant Alexander of Pherai that he had to leave the theatre lest he be seen to weep. Despite the elaborate gear they had to wear—masks and increasingly high-soled boots—their acting is praised in terms of emotional realism, as when Polos is supposed to have made uniquely affecting his portrayal of Elektra's grief for the dead Orestes, by carrying in his hands the urn containing the ashes of his own dead son.

By Aristotle's day there were probably also professional or semi-professional members of choruses; and we hear also of troupes of actors touring the countryside. They prided themselves on their *techne*, or artistry (or better still, craftsmanship); and it is hardly surprising to find that by the 280s they are orchestrated into large professional bodies calling themselves 'Artists' or, better, 'Artisans' or 'Craftsmen', of Dionysos. They comprised not only actors but others associated with the theatre—chorus-trainers and costumiers; and they admitted not only those musicians who supplied the accompaniment for drama, but instrumentalists and singers of all kinds.

Inscriptions tell us a lot about these groups. The big three in the Hellenistic period were those at Athens, at Isthmia and Nemea, and in the Ionia and Hellespont region. There was another in Alexandria, and groups and leagues of poets were present in Rome by the early second century BCE. There was strength in numbers: it was a little like belonging to an actors' union able to secure for its members contracts, privileges, and often extremely good wages; and able, furthermore, to ensure safe conduct over the long journeys which participants in the festival circuit then had to travel. Internal organization was elaborate, as the guildsmen constituted themselves into miniature cities-within-cities, conducting negotiations on equal terms with the cities who contracted for their services. They were often associated with the royal house (as at Pergamon), and contributed to royal shows and pageants; and they had a liking for ceremony, presenting themselves and their activities with a distinctly religious cast. According to their ideology, the performance of drama was the discharge of a sort of civic piety—a religious duty, even at this late stage in drama's evolution.

Hellenistic performing artists were a highly skilled, articulate, vain, noisy, self-protecting group—and at the higher end of the profession extremely well-off. They were perhaps a little like the star operatic singers of the eighteenth century.

Hand-in-hand with the growing specialization of performing artists went changes both in theatre staging and in the internal structure of plays. From the early third century onwards, theatres began to be built with a high raised stage. This consisted of a portico whose 'roof', raised two or three metres above ground level, was in fact a place for reciting or declaiming. The clearest consequence was that chorus and actors could no longer interact as they had done in classical drama. Indeed, the chorus dwindled and was relegated to musical interludes, transferable from one play to another: Aristotle associates this change with a tragic poet, Agathon, active at the end of the fifth century. Delphic inscriptions record choruses of no more than fifteen for a lyric genre, dithyramb, where fifty had been the classical norm; and seven or eight for comedy. Tragedy probably had a similar number, though inscriptions do not make this explicit. On the other hand, the actors themselves started to sing lyrical set-pieces of exhibitionist emotionality called 'monodies': again, the beginnings are discoverable already in Euripides. A group of progressives at the end of the fifth century had started employing music very much more elaborate than the traditional 'modes' associated with tragedy, with different sorts of scales, virtuosic ornamentation, and 'bends' (cf. pp. 67–8): it all sounded very strange and degenerate to traditionalists when first introduced, but by the Hellenistic period had won the day. The case of the traditionalists has hijacked our attention because it is stated on the formidable authority of Plato and Aristotle; but what the Hellenistic public wanted to hear were the sophisticated new works of the modern virtuosi. When drama was reperformed, it was not always in its original form: actors made their own additions, deletions, and 'improvements' (which have sometimes found their way into the preserved texts of drama, creating headaches for modern editors); and its original music was replaced by something more modish. Often reperformance took the form of the recital of highlights: to illustrate this we have a third-century BCE papyrus which contains lyrical excerpts from Euripides' *Iphigeneia in Aulis*, equipped with music. These trends continued so that, by the imperial centuries, even the iambic passages of dialogue were set to music—which no classical dramatist would ever have dreamed of doing. The recognition that these were the 'classics' did not stop their being drastically revamped: most unlike the modern fashion for authenticity.

Less is known of audiences. Material evidence allows us to say that theatres were often built to accommodate a very large proportion of a town's population; the theatre of the Egyptian provincial capital, Oxyrhynchos, could hold 11,000 of a total population probably of around 30,000. But further details are more elusive. Since so much information about Hellenistic drama derives from public inscriptions, it uses honorific language which tells us much about group ideology but little about the composition of the audience—let alone public response. We depend for that on anecdotal evidence, which presents (as we might expect) colourful, dramatic episodes, on whose reliability there is little check. If an audience disliked an actor, we hear, they might throw things at him, or hiss, or physically eject the object of their displeasure from the stage. On the other hand, supporters might mobilize claques to orchestrate applause— it all sounds quite familiar. What we read of the emotionality of audiences ties in with the reports of performance style: stories of tearfulness abound. Flattery of the audience's taste and discrimination are counterbalanced by reports of actors and poets lowering themselves to suit the tastes of a base, depraved public: every statement has to be scrutinized in its context. We should dearly like to know what expectations, indeed what knowledge the various sections of the public brought with them when they went to the theatre. Aristotle in his *Poetics* famously states that even the best-known stories are only known to a few. But knowledge of plots would increase as circulation of texts increased; the Hellenistic period saw many educators, and even one or two quite well-known scholars, turn their hands to writing plot-summaries and mythographical handbooks and comparative studies of the myths in tragedy. The greater the availability of texts, perhaps, the more likely the audience was to have a base-line from which to scrutinize the play—old or new, traditional or adapted—on stage before its eyes.

The new kind of comedy

Of the surviving literature, we are served best by the remains of comedy. By the end of the fourth century, Old, Aristophanic, comedy had given way to New. And we return, once more, to Athens, where the genre's main practitioners were residents or natives. It was at the traditional Attic drama festivals of the Dionysia and Lenaia (cf. pp. 78–83) that these playwrights first staged their works, but the style was so popular that it was quickly exported all over the Greek world, wherever theatre companies took it. It was carried to Egypt, where papyri have allowed the rediscovery of very sizeable portions; to the Greek-speaking areas of southern Italy, and thence to Rome. And it is Rome that provides our other major source of evidence for New Comedy, since the Greek New Comedy, adapted to Italian dress—the so-called *comoedia palliata*—

flourished there between about 240 and 160 BCE. Indeed, the fates of New Comedy in the two halves of the Mediterranean world are in curious contrast. Our papyri of its most celebrated Greek practitioner, Menander, fail after 500 or so, and apart from transmitting quotations from him in anthologies, the Byzantines had no interest in him. Plautus and Terence, on the other hand, never fell from favour, and Terence, in particular, remained the second most widely read Latin poet after Virgil throughout the Middle Ages; his influence on the Western tradition of comic drama has been profound.

The most famous poet of New Comedy was Menander (in Greek, *Menandros*), c.342–290 BCE. His career was much shorter than that of Alexis, whom an ancient source claims as his uncle, and both shorter and less successful in terms of recorded victories than that of another contemporary, Philemon. But Menander it was whom later antiquity remembered as the classic exponent of the genre. Of his hundred known plays we have one virtually complete—the *Dyskolos*, or *Misanthrope*—and substantial portions of another six. In them we encounter a world very different from the one we left with Aristophanes (see pp. 81–3, 102–4). Anarchic fantasy has been replaced by something more rule-governed: stock character-types have crystallized, many of them drawn from Old Comedy, but now constrained in a bourgeois world revolving round a limited number of themes. The political awareness of Old Comedy (cf. p. 103) has all but vanished; up-to-dateness and topicality have been replaced by a homogenized sort of universalism, of which the most obvious sign is the disappearance of the episode where the chorus would come forward to harangue the audience on matters of contemporary concern, the *parabasis*. In fact the chorus has almost entirely disappeared: the papyri divide the plays into five acts separated by a direction to the chorus to perform its song, but this was a separable adjunct and bore no relation to the matter in hand. Another salient formal feature is the drastic reduction and simplification of metre: Menander uses only two, the basic iambic trimeter which came closest to everyday speech, and a livelier, racier metre, the trochaic tetrameter. But contrasts of other kinds—of pace and intensity and individual speech-styles—can still be used to vary the dramatic texture.

The plays are mostly set in Attica, but local detail is of little importance (and ironed out still further in Latin adaptations). The absence of interest in politics seems eloquent about the level of contemporary political consciousness in Athens—or at least about the fora in which politics could be discussed. Part of what may have happened is a change in the demographics of the audience: in the classical theatre a *theoric* (or viewers') fund subsidized theatre attendance for the less well-off, and by some point in the fourth century this fund had ceased to operate. Scholars have pointed to 322/1 as a plausible date, since lower limits were then placed on the property-holdings of those eligible to take part in political life. The plays can be seen, amongst other things, as entertainment for this relatively moneyed, urban constituency. Interestingly, satyr drama in the Hellenistic period seems to have taken a parallel path: an epigram praises a poet, Sositheus, for restoring it to its rightful, traditional context—away from the city, and back in the wilds; this implies that in most other playwrights, satyr play had become a fundamentally civil affair, shorn (perhaps) of its wilder Dionysiac excesses.

In the third quarter of the fourth century in Athens, the theatre was rebuilt with a permanent stone auditorium and stage building. This represented a set of dwellings and their entrances: a city street is the most usual (but by no means the only) setting for New Comedy, which is peopled with bourgeois types and their concerns. The marital affairs of well-born Athenians are its stock-in-trade. An amorous young man is thwarted by a father who controls the purse-strings; a greedy uncle plots to marry his niece, an heiress; a slave-girl prostitute schemes to restore an exposed child to its rightful parents; doubts raised by an impossibly early pregnancy are dispelled when it transpires that the husband himself raped his wife before their marriage. The basic unit is neither the polis, nor the individual, but the family. The plays seem deeply conservative in this respect: they are preoccupied with socially appropriate and procedurally correct unions 'for the harvesting of lawful children', as the traditional Athenian formula of betrothal had it. Indeed, they seem to speak of an audience so preoccupied with the legitimacy of their offspring that even a violent rape can be a plot-device to bring about the desired happy ending. Often a mass of detail about the characters' circumstances is presented at great speed, suggesting an audience both alert and with a taste for the complicated intricacies of family relationships. With due allowance made for the fictionality of drama, the plays provide good evidence about Athenian marriage law and the status of women. The reluctance to show unmarried free women on stage reflects Athenian unwillingness for them to appear in public in all but ritual or ceremonial contexts. With further allowance made for fictionality, and for the dramatic context in which each statement is made, the plays also provide evidence for male attitudes towards women. All the dramatists, and most if not all audiences, were male, and if there were any women present in his audience, Menander could afford to overlook them when, at the end of the *Misanthrope*, he appealed for applause to 'youths, boys, and men'. On the whole it is not a very cheering picture: demands for women's liberation are made by those so disenfranchised as to make them sound absurd. Yet when a male character is over-hasty in

COMIC MUSIC. *This fine mosaic was made for a villa at Pompeii in about 100 BCE. The stage and the masks show clearly that it is a scene from New Comedy. The plays of Menander provided favourite subject-matter for paintings and mosaics; and it is likely that this scene of musicians playing outside a door is drawn from his play* Theophoroumene (The Possessed).

misjudging or condemning a woman, the plot will sometimes gratifyingly prove him wrong.

Menander is extremely inventive in devising complex domestic imbroglios from which his characters have to extricate themselves. Although the gallery of characters is not unlimited, it can be enriched by variations on familiar types. It is some of the minor figures who are most familiar—the parasite, or hanger-on, who boards with the well-to-do in return for services rendered; the boastful soldier; the complaining chef, forever feuding with the waiter; the put-upon slave. The plays have a certain rhetoric of *noblesse oblige,* but these are platitudes addressed to the well-off, not serious calls for reform, and take their place among other bland pietism and moralizing. As Gorgias says to the hero in the *Misanthrope*:

> You've approached this business without disguising your character,
> Straightforwardly, and you've been prepared to do anything for the sake
> Of this marriage. Though loving luxury, you took a mattock, and dug and
> Were ready to sweat. A man of your class shows himself best when he's prepared,
> Though rich, to level himself with the pauper. This kind of man will bear up best
> To changing Fortune.

> (ll. 764–70)

Fortune, or Tyche, is one of the most important deities, reflecting the more general rise to power of this personified abstraction in the Hellenistic period. She could stand for Fortune in a good or bad sense, but the 'theology' of New Comedy is less one of shifting, capricious chance than one of confidence that ultimately all will get their due. She wears her more capricious aspect with regard to wealth, for wealth is easily lost; but the more important message is that virtue, finally, will prevail.

New kinds of tragedy?

In the case of tragedy, very much less survives. What we do have, and in its entirety, is a work which is, if not a tragedy, at least in the form of a tragic messenger's speech; but it is so untypical, so monstrous, and so rebarbative, that it is difficult to use it to say very much at all about the wider context of Hellenistic drama. It was written in Alexandria by the early third-century poet Lykophron of Chalkis in Euboia, who had come to Egypt's new capital to work on the texts of drama. The *Alexandra,* his only surviving work, has the distinction of being quite the most repellent poem to survive from antiquity (some claim this distinction for Nonnos, but I do not believe them: cf. pp. 264–6). It purports to be a prophecy some 1,500 lines long by Kassandra (the Alexandra of the title), spelling out in lugubrious tones the doom of the Greeks returning from Troy. Lykophron's hyper-riddling verse goes on like this for pages:

> Alas, poor nurse, who formerly was burned
> By trouble-breeding warships built of pine—

THE POWER OF FORTUNE. *The goddess Tyche or Fortune was a favourite figure for Hellenistic sculptors. This marble statuette dating from the second century CE was first published in 1994. It represents her, as often, wearing a crown of towers, symbolizing her power over a city (or cities) as well as individuals.*

—The lion of three evening's, who was once
Devoured by Triton's hound with jagged teeth.

(ll. 31–4)

(Who would have guessed the reference is to Herakles' sack of Troy?) The poem also has something to say about the rosy future of the Roman descendants of the Trojans—the theme of Virgil's *Aeneid*. Indeed, certain sections on the rise of the Romans look as if they were written much later than Lykophron, and one recent hypothesis is that the problem passages are later interpolations with an Italian audience in mind, made when the play was adapted for performance by travelling groups of actors. The Craftsmen of Dionysos often performed excerpts, so that similarly styled additions may have been made to Lykophron's poem for performance in a southern Italian programme in (probably) the late second century BCE. If this is right, then there were sections of the public with a very high tolerance of learned mythological poetry and with very strong stomachs. Perhaps the reciter made frequent pauses and waited until his audience guessed the riddles.

More interesting, and untypical of Hellenistic drama in quite a different way, is a sizeable fragment by an Alexandrian Jew called Ezekiel, dramatizing at length the first fifteen chapters of the Septuagint version of *Exodus*. It is important evidence for the way Hellenized élites borrowed the clothes of Greek literary high culture to represent themselves to each other, and also to Greeks. As an illustration of the translation of the Jewish mode into the Greek one, consider first, the biblical version of the episode in which God transforms Moses' rod into a snake and back again:

> And the Lord said unto him, What is that in thine hand?' And he said, A rod. And he said, Cast it on the ground. And he cast it on the ground, and it became a serpent; and Moses fled from before it. And the Lord said unto Moses, Put forth thine hand, and take it by the tail. And he put forth his hand, and caught it, and it became a rod in his hand. (Exodus 4: 2–4)

And now Ezekiel:

> GOD: What is this in your hand? Say now!
> MOSES: A rod, to punish four-foot beasts and men.
> GOD: Now hurl it to the floor and rush away.
>   A frightful snake, a marvel, shall appear.
> MOSES: Lo, I have cast it down. Be gracious, Lord.
>   Oh, frightful, monstrous: mercy on me, Lord!
>   I shudder at the sight, my limbs all quake.
> GOD: Fear not, stretch out your hand and take its tail,
>   And, as before, it will become a rod.

(ll. 120–8)

Here Ezekiel hits off tragic stichomythia with stop-gap sentence-fillers, and its explicit enactment of emotional and physical responses which are only implicit in the Hebrew. Other features of Greek tragic idiom—the narrative prologue, the messenger-speech—are present elsewhere. Unfortunately we know nothing about the performance context of this fascinating hybrid but—if indeed it was written with performance in mind—it would interestingly imply that, whatever later rabbis may have had to say on the subject, at least some Jews in Alexandria at this time went to the theatre.

Other great classical public genres lived on—adapted to new circumstances, and formally much simpler, but still important vehicles for public display and sentiment. The dithyramb, for example, sung by massed forces in honour of Dionysos (cf. pp. 63–4, 89), continued to be performed—though with reduced, professional choirs—in festivals on Delos, and in Athens until the second century CE. Very little of these is left; but we do possess two Hymns to Apollo performed by the Athenian guild of the Craftsmen of Dionysos during one of the Athenians' periodic mass pilgrimages to Delphi (127 BCE). Propaganda, pageantry, and piety combine in these great display pieces. These are fascinating and unique texts, since we know, not only the occasion on which they were performed, but also something of what they sounded like, for they are accompanied by musical notation.

Another important type of hymn is the Paean in honour of a human ruler or military leader. These could be performed both in festivals and on other occasions. They have been taken to demonstrate the servility that set in with that notorious new departure in Hellenistic religion, ruler-cult, and simultaneously to testify to the decline of traditional religious feeling. The one that usually gets quoted was performed by the Athenians with choirs and dancers in honour of Demetrios Poliorketes in 291, and includes the lines: 'For other gods are a long way away, or have no ears, or do not exist, or pay not a jot of attention to us: but we see you before us, not in wood or stone, but in the flesh.' To the ancient author who quotes it, no less than to us, this sounded like flattery, but before we start announcing the twilight of the gods, we have to set this statement in a wider context. It is an extreme specimen of the hyperbole used as cities struggled to come to terms with the new phenomenon of their super-powerful foreign leaders. And its language is henotheistic rather than monotheistic: this means that it pays special homage to one god, without denying the existence of others.

Mime: Mini-sketches

Closely related to comedy from the beginnings of its history was the 'mime'. This, in its origins, was a sub-literary form, in which punchy, robust sketches, often from low life, were performed by a single actor or a troupe. Narrative was less important than the vigorous evocation of personality and scene. Mime exploited situations and character-types which it shared with comedy, both because of direct borrowings (and parodies), but also because of common origins and parallel development. Comedy's ancient relations lived on healthily in the Hellenistic period. A second- or third-century CE text preserves vivid and tantalizing details about the many sorts of popular entertainer familiar to the Hellenistic public. We hear, for example, of *hilarodoi*, 'joyful singers', who dressed in white robes, boots, and a golden crown to parody tragedy to the accompaniment of a harpist: one or two papyrus fragments, including a free-wheeling farce based on Euripides' *Iphigenia among the Taurians* show the sort of thing they may have got up to. The *magodoi* or *lysiodoi*, meanwhile, took their parts from comedy, cross-dressed, and noisily took the parts of whores, pimps, and drunkards. The *Ionikistes*, also known as a 'shameful singer', specialized in lavatorial humour and abuse. Yet this genre had some surprisingly distinguished exponents, including Sotades, who worked in Alexandria and was known to Kallimachos. On one occasion he addressed a notorious remark to the king, Ptolemy II, about his incestuous marriage to his sister Arsinoe, claiming that the king was 'thrusting his prick into an unholy hole'. His indiscretions finally sank him—quite literally—for he was shut in a lead container and dropped in the sea.

Surviving mime from the Hellenistic period is represented mainly by two poets—and in true Hellenistic fashion, it has been made complex, fused with other forms. The mimes of Herodas are known as 'Mimiambi', a cross between the subject-matter of mime, usually in prose, and the metrical form of iambus, used by the archaic poets for realistic subjects—sex, food, vituperation (cf. pp. 50, 51–4). They are vignettes of about a hundred lines each: characters from New Comedy people them, along with other urban grotesqueries—an old procuress, a brothel-keeper, a delinquent schoolboy, women having affairs with their slaves, or enthusiastically discussing dildoes purchased from a man who purports to be a shoe-maker:

> He works at home and sells in secret—
> Every door now trembles at the tax-man.
> But his work—what work it is! You'd think
> You were looking at Athene's handiwork,
> Not Kedron's. When I saw them—you see, Metro,
> He came with two—my eyes popped out at the sight.
> Men don't make phalloi (we're on our own) so straight.
> And not just this: they're soft as sleep, and their little straps
> Are wool, not straps.
>
> *(Mimiamboi 6. 63–73)*

Recent work on these texts emphasizes the sophistication of their form, rather than the crudity of their subject, which is mimesis of urban low life. This makes it all the more desirable to know something of their public, a matter on which the texts themselves are silent. Probably they were performed, but whether by a single actor or whole troupe is unclear. Their content may look undemanding, but their language, which imitates the Ionic of the sixth-century Hipponax, is incompatible with the idea that they were intended for an unlettered public.

The other author is Theokritos of Syracuse. What he is best known for is a collection of thirty poems (a few spurious), most of which are in hexameters. The shortest is effectively an epigram, the longest over two hundred lines long. Antiquity called them *Eidyllia*, 'Idylls', which just means 'Poems in different styles'. They are indeed very different, but the largest group among them consists of mimes, understood in the same sense as poems which present a piquant or evocative mini-drama. They also include other species: a few short mythological narratives; poems in which the speaker addresses, or admonishes, a young (male) beloved; poems which praise a monarch, appeal for patronage, or accompany a gift. The praise-poetry and the appeals for patronage are important documents for the literary history of the period and the contexts in which poets operated; but it is the mimetic poems for which Theokritos is best known.

The majority of these are set in a fictive and idealized countryside that is peopled with herdsmen and shepherdesses. They show off, quarrel, compete in song, exchange gifts—and above all lament unrequited love, all in a curious high-flown poetic version of the Doric dialect, mainly of Theokritos' own devising. Yet there are also echoes, however distant, of traditional rural songs, refrains, and amoebean (antiphonal) singing, all refracted through the extreme refinement of the epic hexameter. The effect is perfectly calculated, and derives not least from a three-way incongruity between the speakers and subject-matter, linguistic register, and literary form:

> I go to serenade Amaryllis, while my goats graze
> On the mountainside, and Tityrus drives them on.
> Tityrus, my well-loved friend, please graze my goats,
> And drive them to the spring. The billy-goat—
> The yellow Libyan—watch out for him, in case he butts.
> —O lovely Amaryllis, why no more
> Do you peep from yonder cave and call me in,
> Your sweetheart? Do you hate me? Do you think
> Me snub-nosed, nymph, and bearded, when close by?
> You'll drive me to the rope. But see, I bring
> Ten apples, from the place you told me, and
> Tomorrow I'll bring you another ten!
>
> (Theokritos, *Idylls* 3. 1–11)

This is obviously sophisticated urban entertainment, and no one for a minute would have been misled by these underemployed languishing rustics. The very fact that they could be represented like this is eloquent testimony to the distance that the poet and his readers had moved away from the reality of the countryside and its traditions. Theokritos is not the first poet to have written about the countryside, but he is the first known to have cultivated this bizarre, nostalgic, anti-realist form, and antiquity remembered him principally as its first pastoral poet.

The other two who wrote in Greek were Bion and Moschos. The following extract (falsely attributed to Moschos) illustrates another aspect of bucolic poetry—not its frivolous or mannerist side, but a capacity for poignant reflection on human mortality that is reflected in the tradition of the bucolic lament:

> Alas, for the mallows, which die in the garden,
> Or the green parsley, or thick bushy dill,
> Again come to life and another year flourish;
> Yet we men, so tall and so strong and so wise,
> When once we die, then in hollow earth heedless
> We sleep the long sleep with no end and no dawn
> ([Moschos], *Lament for Bion* 99–104)

But Theokritos' non-bucolic *œuvre* is equally interesting, and until recently comparatively neglected. The fourteenth *Idyll* exploits the tension between country and town, between unreality and contemporary life, when the main speaker announces his intention of giving up rustic frivolities and going to enlist as a mercenary under Ptolemy. Virgil's *Eclogues* would take this disjunction much further. And with the very celebrated fifteenth poem we enter the world of contemporary Alexandria itself. Two Syracusan housewives, Gorgo and Praxinoa, are on their way to the palace to see a display put on by Queen Arsinoe as part of the annual festival of Adonis. The poem begins with a domestic scene showing their gossip; it accompanies them as they push through the streets to the palace; and then it describes what they see when they get there—a magnificent tableau with tapestries and figures of the goddess and youth disposed on a couch. It concludes with a hymn sung by a professional female reciter, in an elevated and quite different style from the rest of the poem. What makes the poem particularly interesting, for our purposes, is that it dramatizes a public response to a work of art. Firstly, the women marvel at the embroidered tapestries in the tableau: their only criterion of excellence is realism. 'The figures stand and turn so naturally they're alive, not woven.' Then they marvel at the singer's knowledge: 'Praxinoa, the woman is cleverness itself. Happy to know so much, happy above all to have so sweet a voice.' And then the mundane and bathetic: 'Still, it's time to go home. Diokleidas hasn't had his dinner.'

The women have often been considered 'vulgar'—not just because their critical vocabulary is so limited, but because of their very obvious characterization throughout the poem as prattling urban housewives incapable of thinking an original thought. But how are *we* supposed to respond to the hymn, in the light of their response to it? Their terms of praise seem misplaced: the singer has not really displayed out-of-the-way mythological erudition. Equally, though, it is not at all clear that we are supposed to take the composition merely as a tawdry crowd-pleaser. Is it that Gorgo and Praxinoa can still appreciate a display of virtuosity that they don't fully understand? To move away from Arsinoe's palace altogether, might a broadly common value-system allow quite large sections of the public to appreciate fairly demanding·material—not to understand it in every single detail and nuance, but to be familiar enough with its background and conventions to be able to enjoy it? Might the enormous popularity of (say) tragedy also be framed in this way? While we should not split the public into the lettered few and the unlettered many, it remains the problem to try to define more precisely the constituency of each literary genre and each type of performance.

The Mouseion and Alexandria

And so to the literature of Alexandria itself. This dominates the high Hellenistic period, and raises some of the most important and controversial questions about literature and the public in this chapter of literary history. 'Alexandrian literature' is a phrase often used as if it is synonymous with 'Hellenistic literature', the geographical term coterminous with the chronological one. This is, strictly, incorrect; but it is easy to see how the usage came about.

In Alexandria, at the mouth of the Nile—originally Alexander's foundation—the first Ptolemies established a sort of research centre, following in the footsteps of Aristotle, some of whose pupils and followers oversaw its founding. This centre comprised the famous Library and Museum, which lay within the palace quarter. The Museum derived its name from the older Greek *Mouseion*, originally a sanctuary of the Muses, but now with primarily literary and cultural connotations. These were places that supported philosophy and the arts. Literary studies, then, were but one of the many specialisms in Alexandria, which acted as an international magnet to scholars attracted by the promise of a well-paid collegiate life with magnificent resources at hand, all of which of course redounded to the glory of the Ptolemies. Alexandria and later similar institutions, for example at Antioch, and, later, Pergamon on the west coast of Asia Minor, were among the most concentrated centres of literary activity in the Hellenistic period, as they were of intellectual excellence in general. But before coming to the creative literary activity that went on in them, we need to consider their treatment of the literature of the past, which they carefully husbanded and reappraised, and to which they devoted scholarly attention on a scale hitherto unknown in Greece. Some of the best-known and most characteristic poets of the Hellenistic period are the so-called scholar poets, whose philology informed their creative activity.

The Ptolemies were egregious book collectors, and formed the astonishingly completist ambition to secure for their library a copy of every book in existence (their holdings have been estimated at about 500,000 rolls of papyrus). In this they were probably inspired by the ideals of Aristotle and his school, the Peripatetics, who collected information with the ultimate aim of explaining all things. The Ptolemies impounded books which arrived on ships in the harbour, and acquired others in the famous book-markets of Rhodes and Athens. They did not restrict their ambitions to works written in Greek, for the ancient Zoroastrian scriptures were also translated and filed away in their new library, while a priest from the holy city of Heliopolis, Manetho, wrote a Greek reinterpretation of ancient Egyptian history. The Greek translation of the Jewish scriptures known as the Septuagint has been attributed to royal impetus, but it is more likely to be due to private initiative, and to the need to render the scriptures comprehensible to Greek-speaking Jews within the synagogues themselves. The scholars who came to work on this huge body of assembled material ordered and classified it, and set about its textual criticism and elucidation. The works which attracted their attention were, in the first place, the classic works of epic and drama: only later was scholarly attention given to prose (beginning with Herodotos' *Histories*) and works by contemporary writers. These early scholars established the basic genres of literary scholarship still practised today—editions, commentaries, specialist studies, and monographs. One should not expect their work to have had much impact beyond the walls of their academies, yet in at least one famous instance it did: the Alexandrian scholars succeeded, within a very short space of time, in standardizing the very divergent texts of Homer in public circulation. This is the more remarkable when one considers the ancient method of producing and distributing books: with each text copied out by hand, and with no possibilities for mass production, there was no way for an author to impose a standard text or format on the market.

Scholarly sifting led in turn to the grouping of texts into literary genres—in the case of poetry mostly by metre and/or setting, in the case of prose mostly by purpose of composition or occasion of delivery. But this was done in a pragmatic and untheorized way. Thence came the drawing-up of canons of the approved authors (classics, not moderns) in each genre, a set of choices sanctioned by time and tradition and in part by popular taste: Homer and Hesiod inevitably topped the list of epic poets, while the contention for pre-eminence in tragedy, satirized in Aristophanes' *Frogs*, was settled by the Hellenistic canons which grouped the top three dramatists in each genre. This process of sifting has been considered symptomatic of an age which now acknowledged its discontinuity with, and inferiority to, the past; only now, it is claimed, had the Greeks acquired a sufficient sense of distance from classical literature, work on which had now become a labour of imaginative reconstruction no longer linked by living participation. But it is very doubtful how far we can go down this path: a sense of 'belatedness', of coming at the end of a tradition, had already been expressed in some famous lines by Choirilos of Samos at the end of the fifth century (quoted above p. 39).

The elements of Alexandrian philological method emerged well before the Alexandrians; so too, in certain genres, did the notion of a classic. The scholars' lists were not in themselves prescriptive. Our papyri do not indicate that they inhibited the reading of non-canonical authors in the world at large; but they formalized tastes and preferences which were probably not so very different from those among the educated public. When classical tragedy was revived, it was usually Sophokles or Euripides, while with dithyramb it was Timotheos, whose statue was also one of those that adorned the library at Pergamon.

So too with the alleged 'two publics' of the Hellenistic period, the lettered and the unlettered. A central theme of this chapter is that even the most learned members of Hellenistic society can nonetheless be seen as representing the extreme end of a very wide spectrum whose members shared a broadly common value-system held in place by the very conservative nature of Greek literary education. The scope for learnedness was very much increased, at least in well-off areas: beside the royal libraries we hear of a growing number of public libraries, mostly in the old, wealthy cities of mainland Greece, Asia Minor, and southern Italy and Sicily. In a few tantalizing cases we even have hand-lists of some of their books. There was also a change in the pattern of the education of young men, which came to embrace at least a smattering of literary culture in addition to athletic training: beauty of body *and* mind was now the ideal, the cultivatedness or *paideia* which the Greeks prized so highly. Yet the state never made much provision for primary education, which was left to the generosity of private benefactors and probably cost money which many people could ill afford. In many rural areas there is likely to have been little or no education available at all, except at home. When we talk about the 'public' or even the 'publics' of Hellenistic literature, we have to bear in mind that although resources improved in many areas in the Hellenistic period, the numbers of those who could read and had access to education, books, and libraries were probably still relatively small. In this respect, therefore, distinguishing between an 'élite' and a 'popular' readership is not very helpful.

As for the ancient scholars, what is most interesting about them are their methods, wherever discoverable, and their ways of reading. To deal with a work of literature was to set its text in order, to understand it on a lexical level—whence the compilation of lists of rare or dialectal words or *glossai*—and to elicit information about topics arising from it. The plot of a drama could be summarized and compared with other forms of the myth, genealogies could be given, antiquarian information of all kinds could be accumulated to shed light on the matter in hand. Aesthetic or literary-critical judgements could be formulated too, as we know from Homeric commentaries—which, while often banal, are still capable of insight or sophistication which is impressive even by modern standards. There are also papyri containing commentaries that seem to emanate from the private study or the schoolroom. Here, too, the text is subjected to paraphrase, gloss, and factual scrutiny. In general, we would do well to remember the ways in which ancient readers approached their texts, and the concerns they brought to bear on them—above all, that Homer should be elevated and edifying; the growing sophistication of their analytical technical vocabulary; the very fact-based, antiquarian drive to amass supporting detail. It is salutary to recall the apparent gulf between what texts seem to *us* to be saying and what ancient readers seem to have made of them, though we should also acknowledge that the bald and barely adequate marginal annotations can hardly be expected to tell the full story of ancient readers' responses to texts in all their complexity and richness.

Alexandrian poets: Kallimachos

The most creative century of the Hellenistic period, in literary terms, was the third, especially its first half; and many (but by no means all) of its most famous names were associated with the new royal capitals. Those associated specifically with the royal libraries—Alexandria, principally, but also Pella in Macedon, and Antioch in Syria—are the representatives of that notorious Hellenistic hybrid, the 'scholar poet'. He is variously regarded as a perfect blend of poetry and scholarship that prefigured the best aspects of Renaissance humanism, or, less romantically, as a token of the degeneracy of the Hellenistic age, which could produce only learned, trivial footnotes to the golden-age classics. Actually we should keep in mind the great mass of Hellenistic poets whose *œuvre* is all but lost, who are barely names to us, and who never set foot in the royal capitals in their lives. But the most famous poets of the age are undoubtedly those who worked in Alexandria. In the first generation there was the elegiac master Philitas of Kos, who came as tutor to the young Ptolemy II, then after him Kallimachos and Eratosthenes, both, in their different ways, polymaths; there was also Apollonios, born in Alexandria but with a Rhodian connection. The tragedians Lykophron of Chalkis (see above, pp. 208–9) and Alexandros of Aitolia worked in both Alexandria and Pella, while Aratos, who came from Soloi in Kilikia, divided his time between the Syrian and Macedonian capitals but has no known connection with Alexandria. Theokritos was certainly resident at some point in Alexandria, but we do not know that he had any connection with the Library.

The most famous of all was Kallimachos. A Cyrenean by birth, he was in Alexandria at the latest by the time the second Ptolemy came to the throne, in 283, and perhaps before that. Kallimachos was never Librarian, but he was the library's tireless bibliographer, and he devised a cataloguing system for it on tablets called *Pinakes*; he also wrote copious treatises on antiquarian, literary-historical, and literary-critical subjects. But his main fame is for his poetry, whose versatility and multiformity owed much to the diversity of the material at his command. Of his huge output, only six Hymns have come down to us through the manuscript tradition, as well as those epigrams of his preserved in the big Hellenistic and post-Hellenistic anthologies. The hymns are all in hexameters, except the fifth, and divide into three which purport to re-create the occasion of performance (2, 5, 6) and three which do not (1, 3, 4). Orthodoxy, never quite unassailable, is that the first group seeks no more than to create the illusion of performance:

> How Apollo's laurel branch is shaking,
> How the whole shrine moves! All sinners, flee!
> Apollo's handsome foot already beats
> The doorway: don't you see? The Delian palm
> Has given a sudden pleasing nod, and in the sky
> The swan sings sweetly. Bolts, be now drawn back;
> Be now withdrawn, you bars: the god is near.
> Young men, strike up the song, prepare to dance
> *(Hymn 2. 1–8)*

They are extremely subtle compositions, traditional in so far as they invoke the god through his or her epithets, enumerate powers, and lay special emphasis on the birth or the coming-to-power of the deity; untraditional in their occasional political agenda (1 hails king Ptolemy), their mixing-up of dialects and metres never mixed before, and their wry self-consciousness and wit.

What else we have derives from papyri and citations in other works, and neither sort of source is very conducive to the fluent reading or easy comprehension of this accomplished but formidably difficult poet. Papyri may be badly copied, scrappy, or incomplete, while excerpts are chosen for citation precisely on account of their difficulty. Kallimachos' other major works of poetry are his four-book elegiac poem *Causes* (in Greek, *Aitia*), which ferrets out the origins of festivals and rituals, statues and cities; and the *Hekale*, a new and conspicuously unheroic sort of epic poem on a much-reduced scale, which told the story of an elderly lady who once entertained Theseus on his way to slay the Marathonian bull. His thirteen *Iambi* are as thematically varied as they are (in fact) metrically diverse; now purveying wisdom through fables, now vituperating, now on the defensive, now recounting yet more stories of origins, Kallimachos ranges much wider than the sixth-century Hipponax (cf. pp. 51–2) whom he claims as his model. He also wrote a large number of occasional poems: victory poems to celebrate success in competitions, for example, or a marriage-poem for the queen, Arsinoe.

Kallimachos' is the most individualistic voice among all the Hellenistic poets. He is staggeringly erudite, and does not wear his learning lightly; and there are times in his *Causes* when self-advertisement carries over into self-parody. There is a banquet and heavy drinking going on all around, but Kallimachos, not one to waste an opportunity to add to his store of recherché knowledge, is busily quizzing his neighbour, who hails from Ikos: 'Do answer my question: why *is* it your ancestral custom to worship Peleus the king of the Myrmidons?' He rounds off the famous narrative of the love of Akontios and Kydippe by versifying the names of his historical sources, as if a love-story needs footnoting; elsewhere he proclaims, 'I sing nothing that is unattested'. He loves attitudinizing, and finds especially congenial the pose of the aloof and fastidious aristocrat which he took especially from Pindar, poet of aristocrats (cf. pp. 64–6). 'Tread the paths that carriages do not follow,' Apollo is supposed to have told him: 'do not drive your chariot in the common tracks of others.' 'Let another man bray like the long-eared beast,' he continues in his own voice a little later on in the same passage; '*I* am the refined one, the winged one.' Returning to the authoritative Apollo, at the end of the *Hymn* to this god, he makes him contrast the large and filthy river Euphrates with a small, pristine freshwater spring—metaphors for undiscriminatingly copious poetry and his own choice verse. He loves to portray himself as embattled, bedevilled by ignorant critics: he knows they mutter malice against him, carping because his poems are too short, or unheroic, or too generically miscellaneous. Yet his songs are 'more powerful than malignity', mightier than Envy, whom Apollo, his spokesman, spurns with his foot.

Until very recently, Kallimachos was (rather oddly) taken at his word. He has been seen as the hypersensitive aesthete in whom he would have us believe, favouring a sort of small-scale, exquisite poetry, a highly wrought artefact that would stand minute scrutiny and was the product of profound erudition. He affects a psychotic aversion to the vulgar mob: 'I detest everything public' is one of his more notorious *dicta*. And the tastes of these vulgarians have been reconstructed in minute detail on the basis of the way he himself characterizes them. His enemies complained that he did not churn out 'continuous poems' in 'thousands of lines', while they themselves wrote about 'kings and heroes'— from which it is inferred that they continued to write epic pastiche in the old style. Popular taste, therefore, was for tired, dead literary forms. But if it is mistaken to infer biographical details from an author's work in any over-simple way, it can be no less so to try to reconstruct his milieu from his own heavily loaded account of it. Recent work has sought to modify the traditional account of the literary wars Kallimachos portrays himself as waging, to redraw the battle-lines. Each of his polemical statements has a particular literary context and background: they should not all be bundled up together and turned into a manifesto or dogma. For example, there is no evidence that he laid down a ban on imitating Homer; and little indeed that he was surrounded by a horde of semi-literate third-rate epic pastichists. The portrayal of his opponents should be recognized for what it is, tendentious caricature.

Kallimachos can teach us the dangers of making *a priori* assumptions about the public. Since his own verse is so difficult, it has been inferred that it *must* have been written for coteries of intellectuals: he is viewed as the archetypal ivory-tower poet, and his *Causes* are the quintessence of this aesthetic. His polemic is read as academic in-fighting, and squabbles have been reconstructed (such as a notorious feud with Apollonios of Rhodes) for which good evidence is seriously lacking. Perhaps a more serious error still is to oppose his poetry to what lay outside the ivory tower, as if there were murky areas of popular culture out there to which the Kallimachean spirit was deeply alien. Because he is lexically difficult, allusive, recondite in his subject-matter, it is presumed that only scholars could read and appreciate him. But papyri are coming to light which indicate that he was popular outside the élite circles of Alexandria.

Here perhaps we should introduce a distinction between the envisaged and actual readership, for an ancient author had no control over the circulation of his works once they were in the public domain. Ancient poets would make their works public in the first place through recitals, only afterwards circulating them in book form—presumably primarily among friends. But whatever circles Kallimachos originally wrote his poetry for, it appears that they soon reached readers elsewhere who were able to identify with the devious sinuosities of Egypt's most accomplished poet. Our prize exhibit is the Lille papyrus, recovered from the bandages of a mummy of the late third century BC—only a generation or so after the poet's death—which came from the Fayûm, a large oasis area on the west bank of the Nile which was a favoured site for Greco-Macedonian colonization. The very substantial fragments of Kallimachos it preserves come from the beginning of the third book of the *Causes*, and tell the story of the origin of the Nemean games, at which the Egyptian Queen Berenike had won a chariot-race. They are interspersed with a commentary that is obviously not pitched at a very high level: it might, for example, be the work of a local schoolmaster. The notorious 'I detest everything public' apparently did not prevent his being enjoyed by the sort of public who had to have their mythological allusions spelled out to them, and even the relations of their royal family underscored.

At first sight it seems easier to find a 'how' than a 'why' to Kallimachos' popularity: Greek education was so conservative, and so privileged 'the classics', that it might seem strange to have a modern author canonized so quickly. Yet traditional hermeneutic methods could easily be applied to him. If he was lexically demanding, so was Homer himself; and he could be glossed and paraphrased and his adaptations of (for example) the vocabulary of epic or Attic drama could be noted by diligent schoolboys. If he was allusive, then the classical texts to which he made allusion could be identified. Above all, if he sought out innumerable recondite myths and dwelt lovingly on the minutiae of local tradition, it was quite within the competence of ancient readers to deal with them. They had been taught to ask about sources, variants, the mythographical and historiographical backgrounds to their texts. We have papyri of Kallimachos—albeit from the second century CE and later—which well exemplify the way ancient readers approached a text: they explain difficult words and provide background for allusions; they summarize the story, and cite ancient authorities. The total number of papyri of his work which contain marginal annotations is higher than that of any other Hellenistic author, showing that ancient readers rose to the challenge of interpreting this interesting and complex poet.

In respect at least of its concern with foundation legends and aetiologies (the search for origins), Kallimachos' *Causes* was typical of its age. In his very individual way, and as a poet rather than as an antiquarian, he was treating the same sorts of themes with which the Greeks habitually constructed their political identities, wrote their histories, and talked about their religion. The Greeks' extraordinary taste for heroic genealogies in the archaic period is seen as a way of structuring their own history, and of viewing and manipulating the relationships between different ethnic groups. We should perhaps understand the interest in local traditions in a similar way: not, or not only, as antiquarianism, but as a sort of universally understood currency. Local antiquities—foundation myths, details of ritual and cult practice—were the topic of many recitals at local festivals (including at Alexandria). They were an expression of local patriotism and pride. They were also a way to bring cities geographically or culturally on the margins within the pale of Greek civilization: the inhabitants of Kanobos on the Nile delta could relate to other Greeks, and vice versa, if they claimed it was founded in memory of Menelaos' steersman (for example). Traditions might also be used as diplomatic counters and had international bargaining power, as when ambassadors arrived in a foreign city and prefaced their requests to that city with claims to kinship extending back into the heroic period. They might even use poetry to support their case, as when a couple of diplomats sent out from Teos in about 170 BCE to several cities in Crete in order to secure a grant of immunity for a local temple. They presented their request before several cities, but for some reason the citizens of Knossos and Priansos got special treatment—a diatribe about those cities' origins, including a cithara recital of excerpts from the dithyrambic poets Timotheos and Polyidos and others, and a whole cycle of myth synthesized from poets and historiographers on Crete and its native gods and heroes.

The varieties of epic: Apollonios

There is some evidence for epic poems written about particular races or regions, but for the most part we know little more about them than their names: thus, we hear of the works on Aitolia, Oita, Thebes, and perhaps Boiotia by one of the Nicanders, and an epic in sixteen or more books by Rhianos, who also wrote an epic on one of the wars fought by archaic Sparta with her Peloponnesian neighbours. There is, however, surprisingly little evidence for the sort of epic which has long been postulated as the most popular and characteristic of the Hellenistic period—multi-book historical epic, of the kind certainly written by Roman writers for encomiastic purposes. The one full-length epic which we possess from the Hellenistic period is in fact on a mythological theme—the *Argonautika* of Kallimachos' contemporary, Apollonios of Rhodes. And few texts reflect the age's abiding interest in aetiology, in charter-myths of cults and cities, and in religious topography, more clearly than this one. Apollonios also wrote a number of foundation poems about cities of Egypt, Asia Minor, and the Aegean—Alexandria and Naukratis, Kaunos, Rhodes, and Knidos—which evidently had a similar bent, but only fragments of them survive. But it is the four-book *Argonautika* which best illustrates his concern to ground contemporary practices, especially religious practices, in heroic antiquity. Formally it might seem to be heir to a hundred earlier poems on the same theme. In fact it is a curious mixture of the traditional and the (very) modern—though it is hard to say how experimental it is, because of the loss of other material with which to contextualize it.

Jason leaves Thessaly for Kolchis to fetch back the golden fleece from the Kolchian tyrant, Aietes. Once there, he is helped in the superhuman trial of strength imposed as a condition of the fleece's recovery by Aietes' daughter, who has fallen in love with him. Medeia is a sorceress, and enables Jason both to overcome fire-breathing bulls and sow a field with dragon's teeth, and to rescue the fleece from the formidable serpent which keeps guard over the tree where the fleece is kept. She then escapes her father's fury by fleeing back to Greece with Jason. The story is familiar, the tale-type (that of the youth who leaves home to prove his manhood) traditional. The literary form is conservative, and the narrator's obviously intimate knowledge of the Homeric poems—which inform the poem on every level, from set-piece episodes to similes, characterization, and divine machinery—might even suggest that this was some sort of throw-back to cyclic epic. But nothing would be further from the truth. Here are literary textures, narrative complexity, and authorial self-consciousness like nothing ever seen in Homer.

First is Jason himself: by turns lacking in initiative, despondent, bungling, and very much less than competent in battle, he is anything but heroic. Here, for example, is his reaction to Aietes' challenge:

> Thus spoke Aietes; Jason fixed his eyes
> Down on the ground in silence, and sat nonplussed
> By this disaster. Long he turned the matter
> This way and that, but found no brave device
> To undertake a task that seemed so huge.
>
> (*Argonautika* 3. 422–5)

Yet his advocacy of speech and strategy is as double-edged as was Odysseus', and his duplicity is shown to far worse effect in the shocking scene of the murder of Medeia's brother, Apsyrtos (4. 464–81). Jason is at the centre of a love-intrigue with the Kolchian king's daughter, and the romantic interest is a large part of the poem's attraction for modern readers. Consider the sensitivity of the following simile and observation:

> . . . And her whole soul grew warm inside
> And melted, as when dew on roses melts
> When warmed by light of dawn. Now shyly both
> Fixed eyes upon the ground, and now again
> Upon each other they would cast their gaze,
> With tender smiles beneath their radiant brows.
>
> (*Argonautika* 3. 1019–24)

Yet the relationship shows severe signs of fraying already in the course of the poem, and anyone who has read Euripides knows its calamitous sequel: it is therefore extremely hard to see Jason as a romantic hero either. The love-theme looks very new in epic, but has to be set beside a certain amount of earlier mythographic evidence about the Argonautic legend, and above all beside the great escalation in erotic themes across the field of Hellenistic poetry. The prominence of the female domain in general, the close interest in the psycho-pathology of female passion look back to Euripides (of course); so, uncomfortably, does the story of Medeia in particular, whose characterization as the archetypal Greek 'other', woman and barbarian, becomes increasingly menacing as the poem progresses.

The *Argonautika* is laden with aetiology. In the first and second books we have an account of the outward journey of the Argonauts; and in the fourth, of their return. We read of the various stops made by the Argo's crew, a journey made in mythological time but in real space, and of customs, rites, and land-marks instituted by them, which the poet claims are 'still in existence to this very day'. A good example is the story of Kleite, a young queen of Kyzikos on the Black Sea coast who kills herself for grief on the death of her husband. This story becomes in typically Hellenistic fashion the origin of both a local spring and a custom at a modern festival, as the private and pathetic story broadens out to encompass timeless features of the landscape and the contemporary festival calendar:

> The woodland nymphs themselves bewailed her death;
> And from the tears which rolled down from their eyes,
> The goddesses wrought a spring called Kleite still,
> The famous name of that unhappy girl.
> Most grievous dawned that day for all the folk,
> Women and men, of the Doliones; for none
> Could bear to eat, and long throughout their grief
> They took no thought for grinding meal, but lived
> Just as they were, eating the uncooked food. And even now,
> When Kyzicene Ionians year by year
> Pour offerings to the dead, the common mill
> Is where they grind the corn to make their meal
> (Argonautika 1. 1065–77)

The attitude to past, present, and future is profoundly different from Homer's. In the *Iliad*, the only explicit and detailed forward-reference to an event outside the framework of the poem is to the obliteration of the Greek wall in a deluge, that is, to an act of destruction; the Hellenistic writer, on the other hand, char-acteristically binds mythological past and present together in a continuum in which real-life detail is constantly explained by its reference to the past. The tragic vision which keeps the heroic world at an insurmountable remove is completely absent.

Apollonios studs his poem with other sorts of detail that point to the present: recent discoveries in Alexandrian science spill over into it, as when, famously, Medeia's overwrought state is described in terms of the nervous system which doctors had recently discovered, or as when Eros, the Hellenistic putto, is cajoled into action with the lure of a sphere representing state-of-the-art astronomy. The poem dramatizes the confrontation of Hellenes with barbarians, exhibiting some of the cultural over-confidence typical of the Greeks in their encounters with non-Greek culture, though Apollonios' heroes emerge by no means uniformly well. Interestingly, the Kolchians were believed to be descended from the Egyptians, but Apollonios has chosen not to highlight this, let alone reflect ethnic confrontation in the Egypt of his day. The ultimate superiority assumed for Greek culture and the elevated epic genre have flattened out the contours of any serious attempt to individualize the portrayal of the Greek–barbarian opposition.

Who read the *Argonautika*? As with Kallimachos, there are papyri of the poem—about half as many as there are of Kallimachos, but still enough to bear ample witness to its popularity; they date from about the first century BCE to the fifth CE. Some note textual variants, gloss the more difficult words, and explain other points of interest in marginal scholia. Internal evidence from the poem itself can tell us little enough about the contexts in which it was read. Obviously it no longer belonged even distantly to any oral tradition (cf. pp. 12–15); nor would its length be amenable to its complete performance viva voce at festivals. Yet the ancient biography of Apollonios which tells the story (myth?) of the failure of the poem's first edition speaks of Apollonios 'reciting' the poem, as if this is at least plausible, whether or not it actually took place. Neither the work's inherent complexity, nor the fact that its literary language was both archaic and extremely artificial, are themselves factors that would prevent the public recitation of at least selections from the poem.

Our information about the poem's readers, however, comes mainly from its adaptation by other poets. There is certainly contact between the *Argonautika* and Kallimachos' *Causes*, but if it is the case, as seems likely from the placement and content of the passages at issue, that it is Apollonios who is the borrower, then we are deprived of evidence for Kallimachos' treatment of this epic. The same may be true of the two episodes Apollonios has in common with Theokritos, the story of Hylas and the fight of Amykos and Polydeukes. The *Argonautika* was enjoyed in late Republican Rome, where a translation was made by Varro of Atax, and his poem provides framework and context for

Catullus' celebrated sixty-fourth poem. Here Catullus tells how Peleus and Thetis met during the *Argo*'s outward voyage, an event absent from Apollonios, who speaks only of their separation towards the end of his poem; both poets give different sorts of intimation about the couple's terrifying offspring, Achilles, and create different sorts of foreboding about the story's aftermath. But Apollonios' most sensitive ancient reader by far was Virgil in the fourth book of the *Aeneid*.

The other famous mythological epic from the Hellenistic period was *Hekale*, by Kallimachos himself—but modern terminology often refers to it by the diminutive term 'epyllion'. Since it is only known from fragments, we do not know exactly how long it was, but it has been put at at least a thousand lines—perhaps, therefore, approaching the length of one of Apollonios' shorter books. The term 'epyllion' was invented by early modern scholars to embrace a category including various narrative hexameter poems shorter than a traditional epic. But their dissimilarity with one another—their lengths varying from under a hundred to perhaps sixteen hundred lines, their style and manner varying just as much—should make us think twice before using the term to imply anything like a cohesive set. *Hekale* was one of Kallimachos' most popular poems—every bit as popular as the *Causes*. Its subject-matter resembles that of the *Argonautika* in being the story of a young man's coming to manhood; but its treatment is also similar to the extent that the centre of interest is elsewhere than on the hero's prowess. It is named after an old woman who had fallen on hard times and was living in poverty in Attica, and who gave shelter to Theseus when he was coming from Troizen, place of his upbringing, to rid Attica of the menace of the Marathonian bull. After Theseus has killed the bull, there is a sizeable digression presenting a conversation between two birds: the crow seems to be reciting stories whose moral is that bringers of bad news are unpopular. And indeed, when Theseus returns in triumph to Hekale's hut he finds her lying on her funeral pyre. In her honour he sets up a precinct to Zeus Hekaleios, and institutes the Attic deme named after her. So it is yet another Hellenistic foundation myth.

The basic elements of this story are epic—the hero on a quest, his kindly host who lives in noble poverty; the story counts as a single, discrete action with beginning, middle, and end, so corresponds to Aristotle's requirements for an epic. What is non-traditional is the emphasis: it is as if a short epic were to be written in which Odysseus and Eumaeus, or Odysseus and Eurykleia, featured as the two main characters. The poet's use of local colour lets him show off his erudition: there is loving detail about Attic myth and topography, and among the great wealth of glosses that enrich Kallimachos' vocabulary are many from Attic Old Comedy. The poem was particularly admired for its use of the hospitality theme: the imitations, both Greek and Roman, tend to linger over the details of the humble meal that seems obligatory fare on such occasions, just as Kallimachos had dwelt with loving botanical accuracy and lexicographical precision on the species of Attic olive which a kind old lady had served up to her guest:

> Olives which grew ripe on the tree, and wild olives, and the autumn ones
> Which she had set aside to soak in brine while still light green.
>
> (fr. 36, Hollis)

Ethical pleasure in the old lady's nobility is matched by the aesthetic piquancy of describing her humble surroundings in high literary vein. The famous and fantastic episode of the garrulous crow was also influential. Unexpected twists like this are characteristic of Hellenistic narrative, as if poets shunned linear sequence; another way of doing it was to include a set-piece descriptive passage or *ekphrasis* which could also be a literary and rhetorical *tour de force*. An example is a poem by the second-century Moschos about the rape of Europa, an important document, for it is one of the very few surviving poems from the second century which is not epigram. This includes a description of the mythological scenes on Europa's basket—in fact pointedly relevant to her own situation. Of Catullus' sixty-fourth poem, over half is formally a descriptive digression, the *Lamento di Arianna*. Ekphrases occur throughout Hellenistic and imperial literature, based ultimately on epic sequences such as the shield of Achilles in *Iliad* 18; and we have already met an important Hellenistic example, Theokritos' *Adoniazousai*, which also dramatizes the response of the viewer to the art-work.

Impractical didactic

The other major sort of epic written in the Hellenistic period was didactic, and followed the precedent, not of Homer, but of Hesiod (cf. pp. 8–12). Of these works unquestionably the most immediately and enduringly popular was the *Phainomena* of Aratos. Kallimachos knew how to praise it when he wrote that

> The song and manner are Hesiod's. Not the poet
> To the very hilt, but, one might say, the sweetest
> Of his verses has the man of Soloi creamed off. Hail, subtle verses,
> Product of Aratos' wakefulness
>
> (*Palatine Anthology* 9. 507)

The man of Soloi here is Aratos: Soloi was a city of Kilikia, and Aratos exemplifies a common pattern for Hellenistic intellectuals in that he gravitated to a major centre of culture from obscure origins, in his case in a city that was not even fully Greek. (Even its Greek speakers spoke Greek so badly that the term 'solecism' (*soloikismos*) was coined after them.) In adult life he spent time in the courts of Macedonia and Syria, and was not employed in Alexandria even though Kallimachos knew his work. The *Phainomena* is a hexameter work in 1,150 lines on the subject of the night sky and weather lore. Its conception is piously Stoic (cf. pp. 172–3): Zeus is the Providence that presides over all aspects of the world, and ordained that the stars should order times and seasons and that the sky should also furnish weather-signs for humans to interpret.

In fact the larger part of the text versifies a treatise about the heavenly bodies by the astronomer Eudoxos of Knidos. In the event, it was not very accurate. No matter: its popularity was guaranteed long before anyone ever bothered to point out its mistakes. It describes the placement of the constellations, its content much more neutrally descriptive than mythological or aetiological, though there is a famous description of the embodiment of Justice, Astraia, leaving the earth in disgust at humanity's growing wickedness to become the constellation Virgo:

> But when her people thronged the hilly heights,
> She warned them and chastised their evil ways,
> Refusing to attend them in their plight:
> 'How inferior was the race your fathers left
> After the Golden Age! Yet worse shall be
> Your own. For wars, and unrelenting strife
> Await mankind, and bitter sorrow's load.'
> And with these words she sought the hills, and left
> The folk behind, gazing towards her still.
> Yet when they too were dead, and in their place
> The Bronze Age came, and men more vicious yet—
> The first to forge the highwayman's dark blade,
> And first to taste the ploughing oxen's flesh—
> Then did Justice hate that race, and fly
> Up to the heavens. And she made her home
> There, where the Maiden still appears by night
> To mankind, near to Bootes the far-seen
> *(Phainomena* 120–36)

The career of this poem in Rome is well known: Cicero translated it as did Varro of Atax, Germanicus, and Avienus, and Virgil was influenced by the section on weather lore in his *Georgics*. The story told less often is that of the poem's career in Greece itself—apart from its ringing endorsement by Kallimachos. Its reception outside learned circles is both informative and neglected. Astronomy was taught in gymnasia and formed one of the subjects lectured on by itinerant sophists and rhetors who, not unlike their classical forebears (see pp. 167–70), travelled the centres of Greek culture and gave talks to paying audiences. The text of Aratos was at the centre of their curriculum. It offered an ideal field for grammatical, mythological, and technical scholarship: among decrees and epigrams that commemorate educators of astronomy is one mentioning a man who was both Homeric commentator, astronomer, and geometer. This combination of expertise—polite learning, the modest polymathy offered by Hellenistic education—evokes an important context in which Aratos' work could be read and enjoyed. Perhaps the subject-matter appealed to an age increasingly interested in astrology; but astrology is absent from the text itself, and the section on weather-signs is different again, imparting rural lore whose juxtaposition with the modern treatise is actually very representative of ancient science in general. Virgil's adaptation emphasizes still further the dislocation between sophisticated form and quaint, archaizing content; this was not a manual that anyone would seriously think of using. But readers could enjoy the narrator's pious traditionalism and Stoic stance, his conception of a Zeus who had ordained the universe for mankind's benefit. And they could appreciate Aratos' use of the didactic form, used neither with Hesiodic rambling nor Virgilian complexity, but to impart information with quiet authority and the characteristic Kallimachos had diagnosed in it all along, 'refinement'.

There are two other didactic epics which survive from the Hellenistic period, the *Theriaka* and *Alexipharmaka*, both by Nikandros of Kolophon on the improbable subject of poisonous animals and the remedies for their bites. The extant poems and fragments make reference to the cult of Apollo in Klaros just outside Kolophon, where the author is said to have been hereditary priest. This is an important datum. Kolophon was one of the ancient Ionian cities of Asia Minor, and had strong poetic traditions that reached back to the archaic period. Not only did it lay claim to Homer (along with dozens of other cities) and Mimnermos, but was also home in successive centuries to the rationalist Xenophanes; the scholarly Antimachos, sometimes seen as a Hellenistic poet *avant la lettre*, whose best-known work *Lyde* was the topic of lively debate in Kallimachos' Alexandria; and the elegist Hermesianax. We also have the funerary epigram of one Gorgos, another priest of Klarian Apollo, dating from the late Hellenistic period. It describes him as a priest, a poet, and a polymath—a bibliophile, a lover of *sophia* (poetic wisdom), an 'elder' among bards who culled the fruits of the written page (a semi-coherent but telling mixture of poetic terminology, ancient and modern). Gorgos' poems are entirely lost, but he very probably wrote hymns (and oracles) for the shrine of Klarian Apollo. He suddenly brings into focus for us the numbers of Hellenistic poets no longer known even by name, but who continued to thrive outside Alexandria and the grand new royal courts in the traditional centres of Hellenic culture. It is most suggestive that his mourners praised his poetry in terms of the very same aesthetic—erudition—usually seen as the hallmark of the poets of the Library.

No one could say that Nikandros is not erudite. He is—obsessively, wearisomely so. Like Aratos, he borrows his erudition from a prose treatise; but both subject and manner of presentation are far more esoteric, and though Nikandros claims that his work will be useful to the ploughman, herdsman, or woodcutter who finds himself in need of a remedy, this is impossibly unlikely. No one suffering from a snake- or scorpion-bite would dream of consulting an epic poem which describes its menagerie of poisonous animals in heroic terms, the wounds they inflict in gory but unscientific detail, and their herbal remedies either in impenetrably specialist vocabulary—or often not at all:

> . . . As for the sufferer,
> Sometimes his throat is parched with a dry thirst,
> Often he freezes to his fingers ends
> And surging wintry blight invades his limbs.
> Often he vomits up a load of bile,
> All jaundiced, and a clammy sweat more chill
> Than falling snow pervades his limbs. Sometimes
> Like gloomy lead his complexion will seem,
> Or murky, or like metal particles
>
> (*Theriaka* 249–57)

(The poem might, on the other hand, be of interest to those interested in ancient taxonomies of animal species, though this is poetry not science.) It belongs to a mini-genre of baroque snake-bite descriptions, attested also in Apollonios' *Argonautika*, and later and most famously by Lucan. Nikandros exemplifies the virtuosic handling of poetically intractable material, and whether it ever found a wider readership than some of the Latin poets of the late Republic is difficult to judge.

The golden age of epigram

Hexameters have dominated our survey of Hellenistic poetry because they dominate the surviving material. But what needs emphasis is the great success in this period of the elegiac metre as well. In the long term what had happened was that the diverse lyric metres of the archaic and classical periods had died out, or lived on in a few etiolated and radically simplified forms, and elegiacs moved in to colonize much of the ground they had forsaken. (An example of a lyricist still active in the Hellenistic period is Korinna, a Boiotian poetess who specialized in lyric narratives, at least one apparently performed by a choir of local women: her style is plain-spoken and direct, her metres simple, her interests patriotic and mythological.) But there was also a loosening of the general categories of applicability of metre to subject-matter. This means that Kallimachos (for example) could write victory odes in elegiacs, that hymns were beginning to appear in elegiacs, that Nikandros could turn even his uniquely baneful didactic genius to elegiacs. That elegiacs could be used for longer narratives was already the case in the archaic period (cf. pp. 55–6), and was even more clearly asserted by the *Lyde* of Antimachos (*c*.400 BCE), which perhaps used the death of the poet's wife or mistress to frame long sections of mythology and stretched to at least two books. The controversy surrounding this 'thick and unclear' poem in Alexandria should highlight rather than obscure its great influence on the Hellenistic elegists. Philitas of Kos, long famous as an elegiac master, is mostly an unknown quantity because only scraps of his work survive—a particularly cruel loss. Kallimachos, of course, was a grand master; and the great Eratosthenes in the next generation wrote an admired elegy on the Attic heroine Erigone (perhaps an opportunity for an excursus on the origins of Attic tragedy). But the lesser figures who accompany these men should also be allowed to enter the picture—Hermesianax of Kolophon, Phanokles, Alexandros of Aitolia, all of whom survive only in fragments, though in a few cases quite long ones. What they delighted in was catalogues of various kinds; their frequent predilection for erotic subject-matter was not necessarily incompatible with, let us say, a robust sense of irony:

> And even the bard, by divine fate ordained
> Of all Muses' servants sweetest soul—
> Godlike Homer himself—for wise Penelope
> Set lowly Ithaka to verse, for love.
> For her he suffered much, and left his broad
> Country behind for a mean island home.
> Ikarios' race, Amyklos' folk, he famed;
> And Sparta, all in keeping with his woes
> (Hermesianax, fr. 7. 27–34, trans. Powell)

Who read them? Hard to say, but at least the numbers of authors writing in this mode show that it was modish. And with the elegiac metre there was at least the theoretical possibility of performance. But it is interesting and perhaps surprising that, whereas the inscriptions which mention events in musical and poetic festivals refer to prizes for 'epic' (i.e. hexameter) poets, they do not do the same for elegists.

It is another curious fact that elegy of any length disappears after the end of the third century. What continues is epigram, which indeed dominates the field until a renaissance of third-century genres came about in late Republican Rome with Parthenios of Nikaia. An epigram is literally an 'inscription', a poem written on something, and as such it had already been practised in Greece for centuries—in epitaphs, dedications on objects, sometimes inscribed on victory monuments to record success in a competition. It was mainly, but not exclusively, written in elegiacs (the very earliest were in hexameters), and its characteristics were directness and simplicity.

It was early in the third century that it was expanded from its original context and raised into a literary form. Of its early practitioners, Leonidas of Taras and Anyte of Tegea represented a Doric tradition, further developing the epigram in its existing contexts of grave-inscriptions and dedications. Anyte wrote dignified epitaphs, among them several for animals, while Leonidas developed a distinctively convoluted, dithyrambic style and had a keen eye for the working lives of those who lived off the land. The following example is by Nossis, a poetess from South Italy, and is an epitaph for a writer of farces or *phlyakes* in the southern Italian and Sicilian tradition:

> Pass by with a loud laugh and a kindly word
> For me: Rhinthon of Syracuse am I,
> The Muses' little nightingale; and yet
> For tragic farce I plucked an ivy wreath
> (*Anthologia Palatina* 7. 414)

On the other hand, epigrams increasingly came to borrow from the traditional subject-matter of archaic and classical elegy, as performed at symposia—love, wine, and song (cf. pp. 54–5). For such subjects we look, not to the Doric tradition, but to Asklepiades of Samos, who moved in the same circles as Kallimachos (and is supposed to have been one of his literary enemies) and Theokritos, whose seventh *Idyll* refers to him as a master poet. He handled the epitaph genre as well, but it was Asklepiades who first turned his hand to writing of mistresses and revels, bittersweet love and sorrows drowned in wine, in the form of epigram:

> Imbibe, Asclepiades. Why woe and tears?
> Not you alone has Kypris victimised,
> Not you alone have felt the smart of Love's
> Arrows and bow. Why, living, lie in dust?
> Let's drink Bakchos' pure drink. The day's a thread.

Shall we await the lamp that bids us sleep?
Let's drink, sad lover. The time is not far away,
Sad wretch, when we must sleep the long-drawn night
(*Anthologia Palatina* 12. 50)

Kallimachos, Aratos, Theokritos, and Poseidippos took the genre still further. Kallimachos whimsically reflects on all the subjects in epigram's domain—love, death, and dedications—and many more besides: Aratos' newly published *Phainomena*; the pitfalls and exigencies of producing drama; family history, and anecdote. It was certainly the Hellenistic period's growth genre, and its first practitioners were also great metrical experimenters. It could be turned to political lampoons, to the description of natural marvels, and apparently even to metamorphosis stories. But we sometimes have to reckon with looseness of terminology and borderline cases, and situations in which it can be hard to distinguish between short elegy and long epigram. What is most characteristic of Hellenistic literary epigram is not innovation, but elegant or witty or otherwise pointed retractation. One poet caps another, surpassing him in wit. Or it can remain true to its archaic character and the traditions of monumental epigraphy, which required ideas to be expressed in the simplest and most straightforward way—which was often the most poignant, too.

Poseidippos' is an interesting case, because in addition to the twenty epigrams assigned him by our main source for the genre, a huge Byzantine compilation known as the Palatine Anthology, we are also awaiting publication of a papyrus roll, now in Milan, containing another hundred of his epigrams, subdivided into broad classes. This roll dates from the second half of the third century, and is much our largest ancient collection of epigrams on papyrus, though it is not alone. Poets do seem to have published collections of poems which they wrote, presumably, as occasional pieces, and anthologies of different authors were also compiled from quite an early date.

The first anthology to have had a big impact is Meleagros' *Garland*, published in about 100 BCE. Meleagros was a Syrian from Gadara—home not only of Gadarene swine, but also of Philodemos, a philosopher whose controversial view that we should not pretend that poetry is of any ethical benefit whatsoever is presumably reflected in his own extant raunchy epigrams. Meleagros claims to be trilingual in Greek, Phoenician, and Syrian, and inhabits a world in which Greek erotic epigram can be written about a love-triangle involving a Jew for whom 'love burns hot even on cold Sabbaths' (*Anthologia Palatina* 5. 160). This infiltration of Greek literary idiom into Semitic territory is as fascinating as the case of Ezekiel (above, p. 210). Prefacing his collection with an introduction assigning every named poet a flower (whence the collective name

Anthology, or Garland), Meleagros arranged his poems by alternations of author and thematic links. It made an immediate impact in Rome when it was published there: aristocratic poetasters turned their hand to imitating Greek conceits. At the same time, however, and across the Greek world, we have to bear in mind the continuing production of epigrams for their traditional purpose—on tombs, and on votive objects. The impact on these of their more literary cousins is an untold story. Once or twice, in relatively out-of-the-way places, we find that a local stone-carver has inscribed a poem in bombastic vocabulary, or in a curious or pretentious metre, and we wonder what gave him the impetus to do it.

Hellenistic prose

Why so little mention of prose, in all of this? Principally because so little of it survives. After the fourth century there is very little Greek prose substantially extant until Polybios in the middle of the second century (cf. pp. 236–7, 245), and after him a number of historiographers whose date brings them within the scope of the next chapter. Yet we have enough fragments, and testimonia, and references, to have some idea of the size of the wreck, and of the character and range of what is lost. More material was committed to writing than ever before, a lot of it of a specialist nature; yet the age's wealth of historiographical, rhetorical, philosophical, scholarly, scientific, technical and non-technical writings, compendious and brief, educative and diverting, are mostly just names to us, their loss due to accident, or to their ephemeral nature, or to the fact that they were later superseded and forgotten. In a survey like this, we must skim over writings which barely classify as literature—the mathematical treatises of Archimedes and Apollonios of Perge, the work of the mathematical astronomers (all but vanished because superseded by Ptolemaios), the fragments of medical writers, great though their discoveries were.

The works of the philosophers also survive, where they survive at all, mostly in paraphrases in later commentators, critics, and excerptors. Just about the only treatises to survive in their original wording are the letters of Epikouros (familiar Latin spelling, Epicurus), of which the longest fascinatingly expound the master's physical and ethical system in atrocious prose (Epikouros didn't care for style), and the treatises of his later disciple Philodemos, preserved in a charred and crumpled state in the library of a villa in Herculaneum. Their interest is even greater but their style is, if anything, worse still. Yet the availability of written treatises may be just one factor in the unprecedented popularity and influence of the philosophical schools in the Hellenistic period.

When the Roman rhetorician Quintilian came to survey the historio-graphical achievement of the Greeks, his list jumped from the historians of Alexander the Great to the Augustan Timagenes (*Institutiones* 10. 1. 73–5). This reflects the belief that history had hit a low point in the Hellenistic period, which in turn is at least partly a reflection of the fact that it was not on the curriculum of schools (unlike its close cousin, rhetoric). The papyri show the popularity of Herodotos, Thoukydides, and Xenophon, but Hellenistic histori-ography does not seem to have been subject to canon-formation and judge-ments about what constituted a classic.

Yet the period did produce several very influential figures. Ephoros of Kyme and Theopompos of Chios are both reputedly connected with Isokrates (cf. pp. 154–9), and are the two main Hellenistic exponents of rhetorical histori-ography. This means that their work employs rhetorical figures, speeches, character-assessments, and moralizing in accordance with history's perceived ethical purpose. Theopompos (mid-fourth century) had in fact worked as an orator. He continued Thoukydides' history down to the year 394, but his main work was a history of Philip of Macedon in fifty-eight books, in fact a history in the Herodotean tradition of the 'deeds of Greeks and barbarians' with Philip's career as its organizing principle. When he produced a prose epitome of Hero-dotos, he became the first known exponent of a genre with a great future—the boiled-down, user-friendly, easy-to-take-in summary. Ephoros wrote thirty books of *Histories*, known above all from the substantially extant history of Diodoros of Sicily, who uses him (not always straightforwardly). They covered the post-mythological era from the return of the Heraclids until the year 340. With a wide scope, lively interests, and an organization in which individual books seem to have been concerned with particular areas, Ephoros was con-sidered by Polybios to have been the first universal historian. At the same time, the local histories continued to flourish, both within works of a larger compass (Ephoros was particularly interested in city foundations), and in more special-ist, independent chronicles: the Atthidographers who specialized in the history of Attica are the outstanding examples here.

Our longest extant text of any Hellenistic historian is Polybios, who was concerned with the rise to power of Rome—a subject no historian after 200 BCE could ignore, and therefore really a topic for the next chapter (cf. p. 245). His informative discussions of method distinguish histories dealing with city foundations and kinship, genealogies, and political history. He would have us believe that he was one of the select few to opt to write the last kind, but of course his self-advertising suggestion that he stands magnificently alone is over-simple. He also attacks the writers of so-called 'tragic history', purveyors of sensationalism and purple prose, whose ringleader is Phylarchos. This might seem in tune with the emotionality in vogue in other genres, but his polemic may well distort or mislead, because it obscures the prevalence of emotive writing throughout the genre—even in the Master, Thoukydides.

The sophistication of Hellenistic literature, its allusiveness and awareness of place in a tradition, the burgeoning literature in prose, and the greater availability than ever before of written material all tend to give the impression that the public were now above all readers. Despite the fact that much ancient reading was done aloud, the tendency for written matter to create a sort of private mental world for its reader has somehow fed into a much broader myth that the Hellenistic period was characterized by 'alienation', the distancing of people from the traditional social structures and supports of the classical city. The individual was now, it is claimed, alone. But as far as concerns reading versus performance, the traditional performative element in Greek culture was still demonstrably alive and well, and still adaptable. We have encountered festivals, competitions, and recitals of new poetry—tragedy, comedy, and dithyramb, hexameter verse and lyric; and revivals of the literary classics. The Homeric epics were still performed, though in excerpts. Athenaios speaks of rhapsodes and 'Homeristai', and their introduction into theatres first in the Hellenistic period; he talks, too, of the 'chanting' of Homer, Hesiod, Archilochos, Mimnermos, and Phocylides, implying that they were set to new music, and he also mentions the comic 'acting' of Semonides of Amorgos, Homer and Hesiod, as if these poets were mauled about for popular entertainment.

But it would be wrong to identify popular culture solely with performance, and élite culture solely with books. Virtually any sort of composition could be performed and has plausible contexts for performance. Many scholars suspect that certain poems in the Theokritean corpus (for example 16, 24) were written for particular competitions, though in the absence of independent evidence it is difficult to be sure. While we cannot rule out the possibility that poets sometimes fictionalize performance-contexts in their poetry rather than evoke real ones, we know also that histories were read aloud. In fact, most of our evidence for the recital of history comes from the Hellenistic period; and we even hear from time to time of the performance of learned, scholarly, or antiquarian material. One man even seems to have recited historical notes or *hypomnemata* at Delphi.

Many of the questions we most want to ask about the Hellenistic public are unanswerable (as indeed they are about any period). Nevertheless, we must ask them. Who *was* the public for Hellenistic literature, in all its variety? To what audience would each literary genre have appealed, and with what overlap?

Would any of the audience who enjoyed the antics of the magodes also have enjoyed Menander—and if Menander, then also Euripides? How many were literate, and to what level? How many went to school, or beyond school to the gymnasium? A recent book has suggested that the high point of Greek literacy occurred in certain Hellenistic cities, but even then reached only 20–30 per cent. But that figure seems a little arbitrary. In any case how does literacy or illiteracy affect the appreciation of literature in performance? And to what extent was there regional variation?

We are in the best position to assess élite culture, which leaves behind most traces; what we can see of it gives the impression of homogeneity. The educational system was conservative, and pressed the same texts into service wherever it spread. Canonical pieces of wisdom were disseminated—for example the maxims of the Seven Delphic Sages written on a wall at Ai Khanum, or epigrams and inscriptions which purvey standardized, prepackaged information: names of islands, rivers, poetesses, the Seven Wonders of the World. The Greek dialects gradually died out during the Hellenistic period, to be replaced by a species of international Greek known as *koine*, the common tongue. Did those who had been through a Greek education therefore come out knowing, speaking, thinking the same? Against the homogeneity thesis stands the wealth of local customs and traditions in each and every area that came within the orbit of Greek civilization, which could affect those of Greek descent as well as Hellenized non-Greeks; against it, too, the different forms Hellenism took when cross-bred with the pre-Greek civilizations of Egypt, Anatolia, Syria, Iran, or further still. Even with so much material before us, there is still so much that we do not and cannot know about this fascinating period.

8 | Romanized Greeks and Hellenized Romans: Later Greek literature

JANE L. LIGHTFOOT

The fact of Roman rule

Kallimachos knew a story about Gaius the Roman, which he included in his *Causes*. Gaius was the hero of a battle against the Peucetii, who were besieging the city of Rome. But he was wounded in the battle, and the wound gave him a limp. His mother was as unsympathetic as Roman matrons of the old school always were. She just told him to stop complaining (fr. 107 Pfeiffer).

Not very informative perhaps, but typical. Like a Greek, Kallimachos only names Gaius by his praenomen, and we have hardly any idea who he was. The main point, though, is that Kallimachos has already reproduced a Roman story exactly in accordance with the ideology that created it. The Greeks had had long experience of this insistently militaristic nation through their dealings with southern Italy and Sicily. It was in 229 BCE that Roman military might first obtruded itself on the Greek mainland—a petty enough action against Illyrian pirates, but within not many decades a succession of military campaigns took advantage of the irresolution of the Hellenistic monarchies to bring what the historian Polybios called 'the whole inhabited world' under Roman sway. Mainland Greece became the Roman province of Macedonia when Lucius Mummius defeated Corinth and razed it to the ground in 146 BCE. (The Roman historian Tacitus thought that this was when theatrical performances were first imported into Rome: in fact they had existed long before, but the causal connection is quite a revealing mistake.) Imposts, taxes, and racketeering by officials led to the reduction of Greece to a state of miserable poverty and depopulation, so that by the first century one of Cicero's correspondents could point to the desolation of some of its most famous sites and cities—Aigina, Megara, Peiraieus, Corinth—to draw philosophical solace about the mutability of human affairs (*Ad familiares* 4. 5. 4).

But this was not the end of the matter: the fortunes of Greece and the Greek

East were to improve. The senatorial historians may have hated the Emperor Nero, but Nero was also one of the more extreme manifestations of Roman love of Greek culture; and he even briefly gave the Greeks their freedom. Under successive regimes Greek provincial aristocrats were admitted to the Roman senate, while philhellene emperors, especially Hadrian, bestowed benefactions which in the earlier Empire, no matter how well disposed their rulers had been to the Greeks, had somehow failed to materialize. In the second and third centuries CE Greek culture reached such heights of prestige, and educated Greeks had been so successful at brokering it to the Romans, that the Greek East actually enjoyed a prosperity such as it had never enjoyed before. These centuries have left some of antiquity's most splendid monuments. In mainland Greece, think of Herodes of Attica's beautification of Athens; and in Asia Minor, think of Ephesos. And there were no costly wars to dissipate the wealth gained by imperial patronage, nor to destroy the public monuments erected by rich benefactors eager to flaunt their goodwill. The age was no less abundant in its production of works of literature. This state of felicity was disrupted in the middle of the third century, with several decades of misrule; the period thereafter is conventionally labelled the Low or Late Empire, Christianized under Constantine (d. 337 CE). Yet many areas still enjoyed prosperity; barbarian invasions were more successfully repelled by the East than the West, while Christianity countered pagan religion and culture more successfully by borrowing its vocabulary than by warring against it. As the Roman Empire fell apart, literary education nevertheless managed to hold its own for quite a while in the eastern empire, though one by one the schools eventually closed. A symbolic date sometimes chosen for the final collapse of pagan culture is 529 CE, when Justinian closed the philosophical schools at Athens—though even then it was not altogether final.

Within a chronological and geographical framework as broad as this, generalizations are the best we can do. It is clear, though, just as with the Hellenistic period, that literary culture—high culture—was only available to relatively few. The state still did not bother with provision for elementary schools, for the assumption was that elementary education was to be had privately. Typically, though, the state *was* concerned to provide the prestigious high-profile resources enjoyed by the élite, as emperors founded 'professorships' of rhetoric and grammar in the big cities, and towns provided funding for middle- and high-level teachers. Libraries are more widely attested: the remains of the magnificent library of Celsus in Ephesos, for example, are among our most glamorous witnesses to the privately funded building projects in the second-century renaissance of the Greek East. But Ephesos was one of the chief centres of literary culture in Asia Minor: such privileged resources are still hardly

SHOWPIECE LIBRARY. When Celsus, the distinguished citizen of Ephesos in Asia Minor who had become a Roman consul, died c.120 CE, his heirs built a magnificent monument over his mausoleum. This was a library which hoped to rival (in architecture at least) those of Pergamon and Alexandria.

common. Oxyrhynchos in Egypt, whose life we now know so intimately from the contents of its ancient rubbish-dumps, must serve to illuminate the sorts of literature that might be available in a middle-ranking town (though we have no check on how typical it was). It is pleasing to find here, not only the inevitable Homer and Euripides and Menander, but also a good deal of exotica. Book-production, as ever, was subject to chance and circumstance, as scriptoria in which books could be produced and distributed *en masse* were still lacking. The normal method for a poet to publicize his works was still to give a reading and then distribute a copy among friends afterwards.

Greek literary culture is still strongly stamped with its traditional performative character. The performing arts, tragedy and comedy, are still attested (though nothing composed in this period survives), at least until local festivals peter out in the third and fourth centuries. So is dithyramb, the art of singing to the cithara, and other sorts of virtuoso recitals that took place in theatres. A genre which had a tremendous vogue was the art of the mime or pantomime— mimetic dancers who assumed roles from tragedy, myth, and romance, and acted them out to musical accompaniment. A series of inscriptions from the Greek East refers to these 'actors of rhythmic tragic movement', in honorific language as courteous as that employed for any performing artist, and show us that they were eventually allowed to take part in competitions in the traditional Greek festivals. We even possess a treatise enumerating their various roles, claiming they share their subject-matter with tragedy (Lucian, *On the Dance* 31). Its detractors might sneer at it, as at mere 'popular entertainment' (a typical piece of cultural snobbery), while its admirers rallied to its defence by alleging its kinship with tragedy, and (less plausibly) its educative and morally uplifting nature.

A great deal of Greek literature—in fact the bulk of what we possess—survives from the imperial period, but it does not come from such circles. Most was written by well-educated Greeks from the cities of old Greece or Asia Minor, which regained their old primacy in literary culture against the cities founded by the Hellenistic princes: even Alexandria was no longer the leading light. To well-educated Greeks careers were now open in the imperial administration, and much of our literature is written by those at, or with access to, the centres of political power. They, or their offspring, could become senators, or hold lucrative administrative posts, or, at the very highest level, provincial governorships and consulates. Those who achieved such heights tended to come from families which had held, and continued to hold, provincial dignities— priesthoods, magistracies, and important local offices. They and the philhellene Romans could understand each other because they aspired to a similar cultural ideal, that of polite learning or *paideia*. It was achieved by progressing through the stages of an élite education which the Greeks called *enkuklios paideia* and the Romans the *liberales artes*, conventional in subject-matter and predominantly rhetorical in approach, which was supposed to equip its beneficiaries for a laudable and suitably ill-defined goal—to receive 'virtue'. Our imperial Greek literature is mostly a literature of privilege, produced and received by the possessors of this polite culture.

The ideals of *paideia* and its largely homogenizing effects on those who possessed or sought it are illustrated on page after page. One of the most characteristic products of the age is the *Deipnosophistai*, or *Sophists at Table*, of Athenaios, a learned writer from Naukratis in Egypt who was active at the end of the second century CE. It documents, as do several other imperial treatises including Plutarch's *Questions of the Banqueters*, the longevity of the symposium in élite circles. Originally in thirty books but now in fifteen, it describes the course of a banquet, extending over several days, at which the learned guests include professors of literature, orators, jurists, philosophers, doctors, and a musician. Greeks and Romans all (it is hard to tell them apart when Greeks might carry Roman names through their acquisition of citizenship, and provincial Greeks might be descendants of Italian settlers), they are gathered in the house of a wealthy Roman bibliophile who is praised for his antiquarian learning in legal and religious history. He has been impelled to make his researches independently 'because of the decay of popular taste' (the ostentatious separatism is characteristic). The topics of the diners are as wide-ranging as their professions: law, music, literature, medicine, philosophy, food, and above all the conventions of the symposium itself. None is presented with any degree of originality, and indeed to require originality would be to miss the point. These learned gentlemen show off their knowledge using literary tags, and their refinement is demonstrated by their degree of intimacy with Greece's literary and cultural past. The epiphany of each new dish on the table is accompanied by quotations from a whole encyclopaedia of Greek authors (the work is far more often treated as a treasure-trove of excerpts from lost works than for its own sake), and it is characteristic of the age that knowledge itself is treated as a delicacy to be enjoyed by connoisseurs: 'the plan of the discourse reflects the rich bounty of a feast, and the arrangement of the book the courses of the dinner' (1b). 'Polymathy' is a term of the highest praise, and it is clear that it connotes genteel amateurism in a wide variety of pursuits. The first thing we hear of the great jurist Ulpian himself is his insistence on correct linguistic usage as attested in works of literature, an obsession he carries with him in public streets, avenues, bookshops, and baths.

Here is another important point: usage. From the middle of the first century BCE onwards, a literary movement had been gathering momentum, whose goal was the restoration of the linguistic usages—syntax and vocabulary—of fourth-century BCE Athens, which had now been canonized as the golden age of Greek prose. This Atticist movement obviously had different realizations and goals as times changed and the living language moved ever further away from the original Attic; different authors also exhibited very different degrees of commitment to the ideal. Nevertheless it was in principle an archaizing, purist movement whose adherents demonstrated their level of culture by classicism. At the end of the first century BCE the orator Dionysios of Halikarnassos recommended a range of ancient authors whose style might profitably be imitated; by the second century CE prescriptive lexica were in existence (the *Onomastikon* of Pollux, the *Ekloge* of Phrynichos) which labelled words 'Attic' or 'Hellenic' (that is, contemporary), or, worse still, 'common', to be avoided.

They had less to say about the contexts in which Atticism was to be put into practice, and the situation is complex because the living language itself had an educated form which might be preferred in some contexts for the sake of precision of meaning or conciseness of expression. Nonetheless the significant point is that now the issue had been raised, the language of literary prose could be as artificial as the literary language of poetry. Furthermore, the pursuit of Atticism was a mark of status, since no attempt was ever made to prescribe the linguistic usages of the non-élite. Galen (see p. 254), no lover of Atticism, makes this absolutely explicit by associating it with professional people and the well-to-do, or the merely ambitious; this was something to which the mob could not aspire.

What underlay such backward-looking classicism? According to some, it had come about precisely because the Greeks were now, effectively, politically impotent: it was a form of nostalgia for the days of the city-state. This needs nuancing: Greeks could rise to the highest positions of state albeit within the *Roman* administration, and the passion for classicism affected their political masters, the Romans, as well. In certain moods the Romans, no less than the Greeks, missed—or affected to miss—the cut and thrust of political rhetoric in the turbulent days when things were really happening, and expressed anxiety about their present state of well-fed inertia. Nevertheless the basic point remains: for the Greeks the question underlying this whole, huge, period, a key theme in the present chapter is, how does one respond to the realities of Roman rule?

The historiography of Empire

The genre that best illustrates the shifting responses to this question, and the changing contexts in which it was posed, is historiography. The first to consider is Polybios, born around 200 BCE in Achaia, but taken to Rome in 167 as one of a thousand political detainees who were held there, indefinitely, without charge. His *Histories* were originally intended to cover the period from 220 to 167, but he explains in a preface that he extended his former design by a further ten books, so as to cover the years up to the destructions of Carthage and Corinth in the year 146. Of the forty books of the entire work, the first five are intact, and most of the remainder survives in abridgements and excerpts. For Polybios, the sudden irruption of Roman power needed explanation, and though he refers several times to a Roman readership (and an élite readership at that), it is more likely that the majority of his readers would be Greeks, as bemused by Rome's sudden ascendancy as he. Not that Polybios' brand of hard-headed *Realpolitik*—'pragmatic history' is what he calls it—tells his readers what to think. In dispassionate Thucydidean tones he tells them that, while it would be reasonable to expect Greeks to help other Greeks out in time of trial, 'by defending them, masking their errors, or deprecating the wrath of the ruling power', nevertheless history's sole aim should be to tell the truth (38. 4. 7–8), and it will help them avoid similar mistakes in the future. Polybios is more specific than Thucydides about history's value as prophylaxis.

Writing a century after Polybios, Poseidonios of Apamea no longer needed to come to terms with the upstart newcomer: Roman rule was a fact of life. His work began where Polybios' left off and took the story up to the 80s, or perhaps the 60s, BCE. Although it was an extensive work, in fifty-two books, history was not by any means the speciality of its author, a Stoic philosopher and leading intellectual. But since it survives only in fragments, the reconstruction of its attitudes is fraught with difficulty.

In the Augustan period a trio of writers emerges—Diodoros of Sicily, Nikolaos of Damaskos, and Dionysios of Halikarnassos. Two are writers of 'universal history'—in theory, the history of all peoples in the known inhabited world: it is no accident that this efflorescence of universal writings coincides with Roman universal dominion (the universal geographer Strabon, discussed on pp. 254–5 below, was also in the same circles of patronage as Dionysios). Nikolaos (born *c*.64 BCE) was court historian of Herod the Great, and wrote on wonders and marvels in the genre of 'paradoxography', also an autobiography, and a panegyric of Augustus. But of his 144-book universal history, the only surviving excerpts come from books 1–7, dealing with early history up to the time of the Achaemenids, and 123–4, on the reign of Herod the Great. The situation is very different with Diodoros, of whose forty-book universal history to the year 60 BCE, books 1–5 and 11–20 survive in their entirety, the rest in excerpts. This is a substantial amount of text. Diodoros' primary interest is in Greece and his native Sicily until his sources for Roman history begin to fill out at the start of the First Punic War. And then there is Dionysios, whose *Roman Antiquities* in twenty books cover the entire period from Rome's foundation to the end of the First Punic War. We still have the first eleven books, and excerpts of the rest. Diodoros and Dionysios were both immigrants to Rome, a move typical of the demographics of first-century BCE intellectual life. But their responses to the ruling culture are in great contrast. While Diodoros' relations to the Romans seem to have been somewhere between distant and hostile—we hear of no links with Romans of influence—the well-connected Dionysios threw himself energetically into the task of elaborating the old Greek myth of the Romans' Trojan descent—a story Diodoros actually denied. It was a traditional Greek mechanism for dealing with a non-Greek people to make them their kinsmen by mythical descent; Dionysios goes further by emphasizing connections with Greece throughout every stage of Rome's cultural infancy.

He explains his procedure in his preface. Many Greeks labour under a misapprehension about the Romans, considering them vagabonds whom Fortune has unjustly brought to power: he, therefore, will demonstrate the truth of the matter (1. 4. 2–3). He will instil his message into minds willing to hear the truth about the Romans, so that they cease to feel indignant at Fortune: the superior inevitably rule the inferior (1. 5. 2). Early Roman history, moreover, abounds in virtuous deeds and doings which hitherto have lacked their historian, so that the Greeks have been unaware of them: and he, Dionysios, will step into the breach. This apparently targets Greeks as the audience. Yet things are not quite so simple. Whereas one suspects that a Greek readership may in fact underlie Polybios' references to Roman readers, in Dionysios it is evident that his references to Greeks in fact imply Roman addressees. For a little later, he adds his hope that the descendants of these early Roman heroes will be fired by ambition on hearing the tales of their ancestors (1. 6. 4). He means to map their conduct onto that of modern-day Romans, so it is they who are targeted by his encomia. He thus presents the Romans with an idealized model, of which the subject nation naturally hopes its rulers will be worthy. His cleverly devised work is worthy of his profession as an orator, and his other special claim on our interest is that we possess several of his works of literary criticism—studies of Thoukýdides and of individual orators, and works on imitation and prose style, where he unsurprisingly emerges in the van of the Atticist movement. He associates the triumph of Atticism with the triumph of Roman civilization and rationality, a happy union of the stylistic and the political. With Dionysios we see principles put into practice in rhetorical historiography.

After the Augustans no Greek historian seems to have cared to write a synoptic history of Rome until the middle of the second century, with the twenty-four-book *Roman History* of Appian of Alexandria. Appian enjoyed imperial patronage, at a modest level. He chose a novel format for his work—not the annalistic one covering events year by year, but treating each people separately in order as they fell under Roman domination. This means he was able to present Rome's rise to power from the provincial viewpoint, and he makes no attempt to whitewash the Romans. Of his great work, the portions that survive deal with Rome's civil wars, and wars with the Celts, Spain, Hannibal, Carthage, Illyria, Syria, and Mithridates. Lost are the books on the regal period, Egypt (a particularly unfortunate loss), Dacia, and Arabia, and on the conquest of Greece. He is entirely dependent on his sources, though he has good taste in choosing them.

Appian's contemporary Arrian (born 85–90 CE) was the first known Greek senator from Bithynia. His contemporaries knew him best as a philosopher, and he published a record of the teachings of the Stoic Epiktetos whom he had heard in Nikopolis in north-western Greece in the 120s. But he was also, like many others, exercised by Greece's famous past. His *Anabasis* told of a journey which easily rivalled Xenophon's in his work of the same title (cf. p. 136)—the history of Alexander the Great. Other works are adjuncts to this: a virtuoso piece of Indian ethnography in the Ionic dialect, and a lost continuation of the Alexander history. Persistent loyalty to a native land he had left behind can be seen in his *Bithynian History*, while devotion to the Trajanic regime can be surmised in the *Parthian History* and its Roman set-up. These twin focuses of loyalty are typical of Greek intellectuals of his age. Most imperial historiography, whether in Greek or in Latin, was written by senatorial historians, following a principle first exemplified by Thoukydides, whereby the historian was also a man of affairs. This remained true even in times whose political uneventfulness led to complaints that historiography, real historiography, had lost its bite. By the time the last full history of Rome was written by the reactionary senator Cassius Dio in the first half of the third century, the author had identified so completely with Rome that he did not feel the need to eulogize or even to discuss her at all.

The second era of 'Sophists'

Rhetorical historiography, with its speechifying, *exempla*, floridity, and high moral tone, was a typical product of its age. For all types of formal and public language had now become rhetoricized. The Attic orators (cf. Ch. 6) were the objects of greatest admiration. Indeed, the contexts in which public speeches had been made in classical times were still occasions for rhetoric, but a great many more now joined to them. One would make formal speeches on deputations to an emperor, or provincial governor, or to welcome a dignitary into one's own city. There were speeches of praise, invitation, thanks, pleading, and condolence; speeches to mark arrivals and departures; epideictic or display-rhetoric on public occasions, and private speeches at weddings and funerals.

Not the most distinguished, but among the most characteristic, works of the period are the two treatises which date from the third or fourth centuries and go under the name of Menander Rhetor—a *rhetor* is an exponent of the art of public speaking, which became a distinctive profession in these days of display and showmanship. They codify the typical motifs, tropes, or *topoi*, of the various genres of speeches as we see them exemplified in literature—not, of course, as mechanically as this, but still creatively deployed within a very conventionalized framework. The first treatise begins with the general theory of epideictic oratory, and concentrates mainly on encomia of countries and cities. The second work gives detailed rules about speeches on miscellaneous public and private occasions, and even lays down a framework for a type of talk whose purpose is to give a semblance of spontaneity, the *lalia*. They both point out appropriate classical, and some 'modern', stylistic models for use in particular contexts—Plato for a rapt, visionary tone, Xenophon for graceful language, Isokrates and Demosthenes for their handling of particular genres of forensic or epideictic rhetoric. Stilted, platitudinous, even laughable they may be (witness the *kateunastikos logos* or 'bedroom speech', an earnest sermon delivered to the bridegroom outside the bridal chamber); nevertheless they are eloquent about the sorts of rhetoric which public and private occasions required and expected. Displays requiring bravura handling of conventional material were ways in which the age demonstrated its *politesse* and its continuity with the past.

There was a period from the end of the first century to the middle of the third when the declamation was the most highly regarded of all literary activities, and the most celebrated professional orators enjoyed unparalleled influence and privilege. This age was called the 'Second Sophistic' by the man who wrote it up and gathered *Lives* of its foremost exponents, Philostratos, writing at the beginning of the third century. Philostratos distinguished the Second Sophistic, which took historical themes or personality-types as its subject-matter, from the 'First Sophistic', spearheaded by the classical sophist Gorgias (cf. pp. 149–50). Oddly, Philostratos specified that Aischines was founder of the Second Sophistic movement, though he was unable to name more than a very few continuators of his alleged school before the imperial centuries. But in so far as the imperial rhetors did not spring from nowhere, he was right. They were the descendants of the Hellenistic orators who acted as international diplomats, of the prize speakers in inscriptions documenting performances at festivals, and of the literary gentlemen of the Greek East who came on embassies to Rome from their beleaguered homelands at the end of the Republic and beginning of the Empire. It had always been their literary culture that had given them the right to speak and be heard by their political overlords, and in our period they attained a prestige which peace, prosperity, and the possibilities of advancement available to Greeks could translate into real political and economic power.

Some of the biggest names among this new type of sophist include Herodes of Attica, Adrianos of Tyre, and Favorinus the anomaly from Gaul (who, to make matters worse, was supposed to be a eunuch). Most of their works are lost: Herodes' gorgeous embellishments to the city of Athens have survived, while his literary monuments, save one extant in Arabic translation, have not. Of the authors mentioned in Philostratos' *Lives*, the only ones whose work survives in bulk are Dion of Prousa (eighty treatises attributed to him) and Aelius Aristeides (over forty surviving works). Yet both men's status as sophists is questionable. Dion is part-rhetor, part-philosopher (the two professions are in theory distinct and not infrequently hostile, yet have a wide overlap), while Aristeides called himself a 'rhetor' yet never 'sophist', would not declaim extemporaneously, and spent much energy trying to extricate himself from the expensive public duties or 'liturgies' which a prominent public figure would be expected to undertake.

Sophists sometimes declaimed on forensic themes, taking improbable scenarios whose rights and wrongs they elaborated with gusto. But more often they preferred the historical topics mentioned by Philostratos as characteristic of their repertoire. Invariably these pertained to the golden age of classical Greece, the orators, or Alexander's conquests. Innumerable episodes are on record as declamation topics from the Peloponnesian War, the career of Demosthenes, or the meeting of Dareios and Alexander (cf. e.g. Aristeides, 5, *On Sending Reinforcements to those in Sicily*, and 6, *The Opposite Argument*). Aristeides shadow-boxed with Plato on the worth of rhetoric. Philostratos also understands elegant trifles—unserious encomia, such as Dion's *Encomium of a Parrot*, or Lucian's *Encomium of a Fly*—as fit matter for sophistic rhetoric. But his definition barely allows for the political speeches made by sophists—encomia of cities (for example, praises of Rome, Athens, Kyzikos, all by Aristeides, and sounding suspiciously alike), speeches of advice to cities and emperors (Dion's four *Discourses on Kingship*, all probably addressed to Trajan), tonics for civic discord (Aristeides, 24, *To The Rhodians: Concerning Concord*), praise of gods (Aristeides' prose hymns to Athene, Asklepios, Dionysos, Herakles, Zeus), fundraising appeals for cities (e.g. Aristeides, 17–21, the series of orations concerning Smyrna, which had been devastated by an earthquake and sought imperial funds to restore it). The ceremonial function of these speeches was far more important than the pragmatic value of what was said. One of Dion's most famous and constantly imitated speeches or *Orations* was the Euboian discourse, in fact a misty-eyed evocation of the life of virtuous Euboian peasants, followed by a profoundly unrealistic programme of urban social reform (*Orations* 7). By far his longest speech, the Rhodian Discourse (*Orations* 31), fears for the Rhodians' international reputation as a result of their practice of rededicating statues; *Orations* 33 lengthily rebukes the Tarsians for an obscure national vice usually translated as 'snorting'. Matters of great international moment these were not; they were the pastimes and amusements of the affluent in well-off cities.

It was more than this, of course. It was power and prestige for its practitioners, wealth for the cities who hosted the events, and above all, advertisements by all who took part that they possessed Hellenic *paideia*. In his twelfth Oration, held at the still-great panhellenic centre of Olympia, Dion evoked the crowd's pleasure in the 'formidable rhetors, delightful writers of verse and prose, sophists with their followers, lifted up as if on the wings of their reputation like peacocks'. It was, for him and for them, a great pageant. The great sophists performed with such theatricality that their techniques were sometimes referred to as a *skene*, the word for the backdrop of a theatre. Philostratos describes the performances of Polemon thus:

> He would come forward to declaim with a relaxed and confident face . . .
> He would consider the proposed subject, not in public, but withdrawing
> briefly from the crowd. His voice was clear and true, and there was a mar-
> vellous ringing quality in his delivery. Herodes says that he even leapt from
> his chair at high-points in his argument, so great had his impetus become,
> and when he rounded off a period he would pronounce the final phrase
> with a smile on his face as if to demonstrate the ease with which he said it;
> at certain points in his arguments he would stamp his feet just like the
> horse in Homer. (*Vitae Sophistarum* 537)

No matter that the content of the sophists' speeches was mostly trite and commonplace: it was sheer artistry. Audiences would cheer to hear the masters round off their beautifully turned, effortless periods.

Sophists tended to come from mainland Greece—Athens, to be more precise—and the old cities of Asia Minor, especially Ephesos and Smyrna. And they usually came from wealthy backgrounds, since their training and professional activities entailed the outlay of large amounts of money, for fees, travelling expenses, and above all for the benefactions expected of prominent individuals and office-holders. When Lucian (Greek Loukianos) was a young man, as he later told the story, he was first apprenticed to a stonemason, deterred from the further pursuit of *paideia* by its expense. He returned to education as a result of his unhappy experiences as an apprentice and after a dream in which Paideia herself made him grandiose promises—fame and illustrious friends—and showed him a vision of all the lands where he could reap eloquence's rewards.

Lucian was a native of Samosata, a former provincial capital of Roman Syria. He refers several times to himself as a Syrian, wearing Syrian costume in his youth and speaking, not Greek, but Aramaic. His Greek culture was a secondary acquisition, a fact which may explain his touchiness about his Greek, and he never became a star sophist; Lucian himself distinguishes his 'popular rhetoric' (*rhetorike demosia*) from that of the sophists (*Apology* 15). He describes his own activity in several passages: he travelled the cities giving lectures (*epideixeis* and *akroaseis*), not always in the most prestigious locations (Philippopolis, modern Plovdiv, was not the big time for a sophist), in some places more than once, and at least once returning to his home town. The talks, prepared in advance, were sometimes preceded by a prologue or *prolalia*, some of which are extant. He says more than once that the crowd found his talks strange and novel; but he professes to *want* to be praised, not for novelty, which matters nothing in itself, but for the virtues the age admires most: good, Atticist vocabulary; conformity to the ancient canon; keenness of mind; and good construction.

But what was the novelty? About eighty works by Lucian survive, and include a few sophistic pieces of the types noted above. Many are harangues or essays delivered in the first person, but his main novelty lay in the genre perhaps most characteristic of him, the dialogue. Not the Aristotelian dialogue, given over as it was to lengthy exposés in essay form, but a racy version of the Platonic dialogue dedicated to Lucian's favourite subject, the relentless exposure of pretension, folly, and vice in all its species. As he himself views the matter, his dialogues have married the philosophic dialogue, comedy, the sort of popular harangue or diatribe associated with the Cynic school, and a type of social satire combining prose and verse and known as 'Menippean' after Menippos of Gadara. Here, for example, is Lucian's take on the rhetorical circuit in which he lived and the crowds which it drew, in the form of pseudo-advice to a would-be rhetor:

> So they admire the copiousness of your speeches, begin with the *Iliad* or the wedding of Deukalion and Pyrrha, or whatever takes your fancy, and take the story as far as the present day. There'll be few who will understand you, and they'll mostly keep silent out of courtesy anyway. And even if they do say anything they'll be thought to do it out of envy. Most people will marvel at your get-up, voice, gait, bearing, sing-song delivery, high-heeled shoes and affected diction; and when they see you sweat and pant

they won't be able to stop themselves believing you a formidable opponent in debates. Anyway, your extempore skill will make up for a lot and will make the crowd admire you. Be sure never to write anything down or come forward prepared, as that is sure to show you up. (*Rhetorum Praeceptor* 20)

This does not make for comfortable reading, but beyond what he tells us we hardly know how people reacted to him. His great subsequent popularity as a hard-hitting and witty cynic tells us nothing about ancient responses. Only one contemporary, Galen, mentions him, and that is to tell a story about how he forged a treatise in the style of Herakleitos: a philosopher wrote a learned commentary on the work, and Lucian enjoyed his discomfiture when he revealed the work as a fake. It would be typical, if true. It takes a Lucian to show us the counter-side of all those refined gentlemen discussing sympotic culture in Rome—an ignorant Syrian book-collector who amasses books out of the proceeds of a legacy merely in order to show off. Instead of the internationally famous sophists, he shows us meretricious attention-seekers, with nothing to recommend them but loud voices and lubricious manners. And instead of professors of philology, pedants.

The varieties of learning

The connections between rhetoric and philosophy are illuminated by many other authors besides Lucian. They might lie at the level of literary form: Lucian borrowed the clothes of the dialogue and diatribe. Or they might consist in the use of rhetorical techniques of delivery. What qualified representatives of very different professions to be dubbed 'sophists' by Athenaios was skill at expounding their various subjects (they include a lawyer, a musician, and a doctor). But the connection subsisted especially at the level of content. Dion's treatises are replete with commonplaces from the dominant philosophical sect of imperial times, Stoicism. Philosophy and rhetoric reached their happiest union, however, in Plutarch (Greek Ploutarchos) of Chaironeia (born before 50 CE, died after 120). 'Philosopher', if anything, is what he should be called. But he was also a scholar, either with access to an extremely well-stocked library of his own, or gifted with a prodigious memory—and probably both. And for the last thirty years of his life he was a priest at Delphi, combining faith in traditional religion and expertise on cultic antiquities with a more intellectualized, philosophic piety. The following passage is taken from Plutarch's account of the Egyptian deities Isis and Osiris. Far from trying to anathematize them as tainted 'oriental' monstrosities, he claims that they stand for things common to all mankind. It is typical of Plutarch, presupposing readers who share his sort of benign universalism, and a framework in which potential tensions between competing races and religions can be smoothed out by calm rationality:

> Nor do we think that different people have different gods, barbarian and Greek, south and north. But just as the sun and moon, ocean and land and sea, are common to all, though called by different names among different peoples, in the same way for the one Reason that ordains all and for the one Providence that governs them, and for the assistant powers appointed over all things, there are different conventional names and prerogatives among different peoples. They sanction the use of symbols, some of which are obscure and others clear, which direct the intellect towards the divine.
> (*Isis and Osiris* 67)

The seventy-eight surviving treatises which together constitute his so-called 'Moral Essays', or *Moralia*, represent about a third of his original output in this field: Plutarch was fluent, relaxed, and discursive. As a philosopher he has little claim to originality, nor is it easy to trace much development in his thought. He too uses the dialogue form, but this time in the Aristotelian rather than Platonic mould, with long speeches of exegesis—not, however, entirely at the expense of characterization. He writes mainly on themes of popular moral philosophy, emphasizing ties of private affection, devotion to the gods, and acquiescence in Roman rule. He seems to have been only on the fringes of sophistic culture: no true sophist would have stayed in a backwater like Chaironeia, and Plutarch claims his residence was in order to stop the place becoming smaller still. It is the dedications of his treatises that give us the clearest idea of his audience (not that they need imply any degree of intimacy with their dedicatees): they include Greek notables, literary men (Dion among them), but also those involved in imperial administration. His biographies—to which we shall return—are dedicated to Q. Sosius Senecio, twice consul (99 and 107 CE). Yet the treatises are also peopled by locals and by those Plutarch had known in his student days in Athens: doctors, philosophers, literary men. 'Plutarch's aim was to convey the essence of Hellenistic *paideia* to his pupils, to his powerful contemporaries, and to posterity', in the words of his most distinguished recent commentator.

Medicine, at this period, is also closely allied with philosophy. Rhetoric could do little more than influence the style of its presentation; yet medicine might lend itself to display and *epideixis*. Dion scathingly describes public displays put on by doctors, who 'sit themselves down in our midst and run through all the linkages of joints and articulations of bones and their juxtapositions and that sort of thing, pores and respirations and filtrations. And the crowd are all agog and more spellbound than children.' But it was doubtless a course of lectures of a very different kind that helped bring Galen, Greek Galenos (born 129 CE), recognition in Rome; Galen is not to be connected with the sophists. Perhaps the most prolific writer of the entire imperial period, and certainly its most formidable polymath, his writings fill over twenty volumes in the standard nineteenth-century edition. Here I cannot even begin to sketch his achievements in anatomy and physiology, pathology and psychology, his scholarly labours on the writings of the Hippocratic school, nor his influence on contemporaries and posterity. Yet we cannot overlook a man who exercised his talents in so many fields—including grammar and philology and the philosophy of language. Born in Pergamon to wealthy parents, Galen had pursued the normal school curriculum for a boy of his class, and though he had little time for either literary connoisseurship among Greeks or for philhellenic posturing among Romans, he never lost his concern for language as a tool for precise self-expression, nor his flair for rhetorical self-promotion.

Another subject allied to philosophy was geography. There are two important imperial treatises on geography: the *Geography* of Strabon and the *Periegesis* of Pausanias. Strabon, writing in the reigns of Augustus and Tiberius, was the author of the first universal geography in seventeen books. An essentially descriptive and mostly practical account, it works slowly from west to east, stretching from Spain to Iran, Arabia and Egypt; Strabon himself is located in Rome, the political centre. He is a priceless source for ancient geography, topography, ethnography, social and political history, and for Augustan intellectual culture in general. The broad sweep of the first two books, which discuss theoretical matters, the philosophy of geography, his predecessors, and the geographer's proper attitude towards Homer (an unavoidable question), is complemented by the rich, empiricist detail of the remaining fifteen. He emphasizes the need for wide learning, *polymatheia*, in order to write geography. But his addressees are men of affairs, not theoreticians, and can be relied on to have a basic level of technical competence, beyond which they need only the general attainments of *paideia* in order to be able to follow the book. He stresses his subject's practical utility, especially for rulers, statesmen, and generals, those 'who bring together cities and peoples into a single empire and political management', and he claims that its uses are in the domains of politics and the public weal; his work is explicitly intended for 'those in high office' (1. 1. 23). Yet his true critics, those most fit to judge his work are those acquainted with 'virtue and reflection and the studies that pertain to them' (1. 1. 22): in other words, his addressees, the ruling élite, are the gentlemen amateurs. He writes from Rome, addresses Romans, and is an apologist for Roman rule. Yet he shows his greatest degree of personal involvement when discussing Greek intellectual culture of Asia Minor, his political and cultural horizons somewhat out of focus in a way which also emerges in the writings of Galen and other Greek intellectuals. Greeks could also read his work, and there is some limited evidence that they did; and Strabon's representation of Greeks and Romans to each other looks both backwards and forwards to other historians and orators.

Pausanias' work is very different in character. Written in the middle of the second century CE, it is essentially a study of the monuments of old, mainland Greece; Pausanias takes little note of anything later than Hellenistic. 'Periegesis' is literally a 'leading around', and the work, in ten books, conducts its reader through an ambitiously large, but still delimited space, concentrating on cults and temples, votive monuments and other works of art, myth, history, and the grey area in between. He appears to have witnessed most of them for himself, and he is a demonstrably accurate guide. There is no programmatic introduction, no theoretical preface: Pausanias launches straight in with 'On the Greek mainland opposite the Kyklades islands and the Aegean sea, the promontory of Sounion projects from the Attic land', beginning, as only appropriate, with Attica.

He himself seems to have come from Magnesia-on-Sipylos in Lydia, and his references to persons are, yet again, predominantly to the Greek intellectuals of Asia Minor. We are left to infer his readership from the work itself. The itineraries are planned so that real travellers could follow them, but there is also matter for the armchair tourist. The combination is perhaps not very practical in either context, but Pausanias' envisaged audience is anyone who wanted to know about Greek antiquities. In theory it could be Greeks or Romans, in practice it was perhaps slightly likelier to be Greeks, but in actuality there is no evidence about any ancient readership until he came to be excerpted by the late imperial grammarian Stephanos of Byzantion, who rather missed the point, being interested only in geographical names and their ethnic adjectives.

Perhaps the most famous episode from Pausanias is an anecdote eloquent about the international culture of its day and the intellectual *koine* shared by Greek-speakers from all over the Empire (7. 23. 7–8). He recalls meeting a Phoenician from Sidon in an Achaian sanctuary of Asklepios. The Phoenician, strikingly silent about the traditional Sidonian identification of their patron deity as Asklepios, instead launches into a philosophic discourse in which he asserts that Phoenician notions are superior to the Greek: Asklepios is really the fresh, healthy air. Nonsense, interjects Pausanias: this is a Greek idea just as much as a Phoenician one. To such an extent had these banal rationalizations become common currency that both cultures, Greek and Phoenician, could wrangle over them and claim them as their own.

Fiction

Greek fictional writing seems to answer many of our own requirements: to revalue the canon, to engage with what could be seen as antiquity's most postmodern genre, to elicit evidence about evolving ancient attitudes to the relation of the sexes, in which the novels are so rich. But the novel in antiquity is an amorphous category embracing different types of narrative under a single umbrella, defined, of course, in modern terms. We need to distinguish several types of narrative. 'Ideal' romances are concerned with the trials of a boy and a girl who, in the standard plot, fall in love at the outset, are then separated and suffer such slings and arrows as abduction by pirates, slavery, mock-sacrifice, and, worst of all, the predatory advances of would-be seducers, but who are eventually reunited with their fidelity more or less intact to consummate their love-match. This category extends from relatively simple narratives, such as the anonymous romances of Ninos and of Parthenope and Metiochos, to fully fledged novels. Of these Chariton and Xenophon of Ephesos are relatively plain, while at the other end of the scale are the three 'sophistic' novels by Heliodoros, Achilles Tatius, and Longus, so-called because they exhibit the literary, linguistic, and rhetorical sophistications of the age of the sophists. Goethe liked Longus' novel about the loves of the innocent rustics Daphnis and Chloe so much that he recommended yearly rereading. It dramatizes their loss of innocence against the background of the changing seasons. Here is the moment when Chloe first falls in love with Daphnis, which illustrates the *faux-naïf* tone which is sustained throughout the whole:

> She persuaded him to have another bath, and watched him bathe, and as she watched, touched him, and went away praising him, and her praise was the beginning of love. The young country-bred girl had no idea what had happened to her, never having even heard the name of love. Her soul was in distress; she was not mistress of where her eyes wandered; and she kept babbling Daphnis' name. She forgot to eat, stayed awake at night, ignored her flock. Now she would smile, now cry; now she slept, now started up. Her complexion was pallid, but suddenly burned with a flaming blush. Never was cow more tormented by a gadfly.

Such tender and—mostly—chaste loves are very different from the salacious romps we find in another class of narrative—the tales of innocence lost in squalor and knockabout bawdry in works such as Petronius' *Satyricon* in Latin, and, in Greek Lollianus' *Phoenician Tales* or the Iolaos story (both preserved on papyrus). Then there are novels of travel and wanderings: Antonius Diogenes' *Wonders Beyond Thule*, or Philostratos' own *Life* of Apollonios of Tyana, or the send-up of such writings in Lucian's *True Story*, a Swiftian broadside against travellers' humbug, and indeed a great influence on *Gulliver's Travels*. And there are also novelistic elaborations of the deeds of historical kings: most influentially, the Alexander Romance, but also tales of the Pharaoh Sesonchosis (Herodotos' Sesostris) which may go back to narratives with which the Egyptians trumped their arrogant Persian overlords. A classical prefiguration of this genre is Xenophon's pious romanticization of the childhood of Cyrus, the *Cyropaedia*. Pseudo-historical backgrounds confer a patina of historiographical authenticity on other works, too: the court of Polykrates of Samos is the setting for the romance of Parthenope and Metiochos, while the heroine of Chariton's novel was supposedly the daughter of the statesmen who led Syracusan opposition to imperialist classical Athens. Another sort of narrative is the Troy romance, with surviving specimens in both Latin and Greek. Characteristically, these are apocryphal chronicles purportedly written by participants in the conflict, and set out to elaborate on the accounts of the Trojan War in the epic cycle. Finally, via embroideries on the lives of national heroes, romantic motifs find their way into apocryphal religious literature: such are the novellas of Joseph and Asenath, or of St Paul and Thecla.

Our earliest specimen of narrative fiction is a papyrus romance about the Assyrian king Ninos, the handwriting datable to some time between 50 BCE and 50 CE. The latest may be the *Ethiopian Story* of Heliodoros, conventionally of the late fourth century, though an influential new view would place it towards the middle of the third century, also the date of Philostratos' *Life* of Apollonios (cf. p. 261). As for place, it seems that a, or the, major area from which the novel's influence radiated was the west coast of Asia Minor. For this is a focus of interest for several novels, and the purported homeland of maný novelists. It is also the notional setting of a species of seedy narrative called 'Milesian Tales' which influenced episodes in some of the extant novels. On the face of it, some of our works of fiction could be products of the long-established Greek communities of the eastern Aegean and Anatolia, where high levels of culture were available for élites in the cities. Chariton, author of one of the less complex ideal romances, claims to come from Aphrodisias in Caria.

The question of the origins of the novel is now seen as something of a dead-end. We cannot hope to separate out the ingredients of so complex a confection, nor assign clear-cut genealogies to so inveterate a hybrid. The novel is grand panjandrum appropriating, as it needs them, elements of historiography, epic, tragedy, comedy (especially New Comedy), plot-devices lifted from myths and folk-stories, facts and fantasies from travel literature, and topoi scavenged from suitable earlier material. On the other hand, it is well worth debating the question of readership. It is true that we have very little evidence indeed outside the texts themselves, so that we are as unlikely to reach a definitive answer. Nevertheless, the questions are real, and need to be asked.

One view of the matter is based on anachronistic assumptions. Like modern pulp fiction, the novels were written for mass consumption, and since their subject-matter—love, in the case of the ideal romances—is trivial, the readership was mainly female, or juvenile. The alternative would be to believe that adult males in the senescence of Greek civilization had sunk to reading such rubbish. The women-and-children thesis is now quite out of favour, recognized as a mostly modern projection, unsupported by probability that very many women or juveniles had the requisite literacy levels, and uncorroborated by the fragments discovered on papyrus. On the one hand, the physical form of these is not different from that of other literary fragments; on the other, they are conspicuously few in number, far fewer than those of the favoured prose authors. And both sophistic novels and the more 'popular' works are represented. So this was no mass-produced plebeian genre: antiquity had no such thing as pulp fiction. Papyri inform us that some inhabitants of the middle-ranking towns of Roman Egypt read fiction ranging from Lollianus to Achilles Tatius, but other data is harder to find. Mosaics of Ninos and Metiochos in a second-century villa in Antioch were not necessarily inspired by novels rather than mimes. And while we can certainly find scattered allusions to various novels in imperial literature, literary sources almost by definition are records of élites. So we cannot conclude either that the novels in question were *meant* primarily for a readership of that level, or that they even *reached* mainly those readers.

Deductions drawn from the novels themselves are no less slippery. The narrative technique of the earlier ones tends to be simpler—but need this imply a 'simpler' audience? And if, on the other hand, the narrative technique of the sophistic novels is more complex, need this imply a more sophisticated readership? The sophistic novels use Atticizing Greek, while others are linguistically much less polished (Lollianus, for example). But would it really be fair to conclude either that a classically educated gentleman had little time for Lollianus, or that *none* but the classically educated gentleman can have enjoyed Achilles Tatius? Yet allusiveness is, in many novelists, at such a premium that an advanced education must have been an advantage, if not a requirement. Chariton (not even among the sophistic novelists) draws on a formidable array of archaic, classic, and Hellenistic works from the canonical authors in many genres. It seems reasonably likely that the educated who knew and relished the domestic complications of Menander, the emotionality of a Euripidean tirade, and the courtroom rhetoric of Demosthenes, would be the novel's optimal readers. A further point to note is the novel's intertextuality, not only with other genres, but with itself. The sophistic novels seem to presuppose the readers' familiarity with the conventions of the genre, while even the most *outré* of the novels, exhibiting the bawdries of Lollianus, Diogenes, or the Greek original of Apuleius' *Golden Ass*, gain in richness if they are seen as pointed travesties of the 'ideal' romance. The genre is self-referential and potentially self-parodic even in its early manifestations.

There are also richer veins to be tapped on the subject of their milieux. One view has been that novels play out the spiritual isolation of rootless Hellenistic and post-Hellenistic man; the other side of this coin, equally suspect, is that the novels are in fact designed to guide initiates by means of coded messages to personal salvation in mystery religions. The novel has become the playground for social, even intellectual, historians, seeking to recover reflections and refractions of society's changing attitudes to love, sex, marriage, the city, the gods. Their emphasis on highly eroticized chastity *for males* as a prelude to marriage seems unlike anything in the classical period. Does this new emphasis (which Christians could exploit in novellae about the virgin brides of Christ) reflect a change in sexual morality, or is it not quite so simple?

Above all, the ideal novels bring married love to the fore and endow mutual passion with a positive value not hitherto seen. Women could perhaps identify with this, though it is still far from proving that they *did* read these works—and it is further still from genuine sexual equality.

And so to a genre which, in certain incarnations, can be a species of prose fiction, biography. Yet it is important to stress that with biography, we are not speaking of a single category at all, but rather, of a body of writing loosely defined in modern terms by its subject-matter, which in ancient texts can manifest itself in writings of enormously different types. And in the imperial period there was a huge effloresence of many types of biography, some in the old style—lives of generals and statesmen and philosophers—and many more in new forms, such as the life of the holy man or saint or Christian martyr. The reasons lie in complex political, social, intellectual, and spiritual developments whose momentum effected other types of change throughout society. There are two things to keep in mind. First, through all the complex ramifications involved in a discussion of the ancient concept of 'character', it is to be remembered that throughout antiquity there remained a basic notion that man was an objectifiable unit in a rational, fundamentally knowable universe. Secondly, biography reflects just as much on its writer as on its subject.

The culmination of the classical tradition of biography is Plutarch. In total we possess forty-eight of his biographies, of which forty-four belong to a series of *Comparative Lives* of Greeks and Romans. The scheme was not his invention, but he wrought it to its most elaborate form. The life of a Greek is juxtaposed with that of a Roman who pursued a similar career, and the two are followed by a comparison or *synkrisis* which follows the method of the rhetorical schools (and does not show Plutarch at his best). The best lies in the ambitiousness of the overall design and its amassing of rich and evocative and sympathetic detail. Essentially what he gives are vignettes bridged by link-passages, rather than continuous narrative, each of which is underpinned by the question, 'What sort of a man was he?' These heroes are all knowable and fundamentally static.

The design is thought-provoking: is it an assertion of cultural parity? Did Plutarch intend it as a demonstration to both Greeks and Romans of each other's capacities? Did he even, as has sometimes been suggested, intend to show Romans that Greeks were generals as good as they, and Greeks that Romans were just as civilized? There may be something in this, for one of Plutarch's other treatises, *The Glory of Athens*, presents a similar argument about the Greeks, which may have been topical at a time when Greeks were being newly admitted to the Senate. Yet in the *Lives* themselves, Plutarch only ever speaks of an ethical purpose. He tells us in the preface to the *Timoleon* that he began the work 'for the sake of others', to teach and improve them. Hearing of virtue and nobility immediately generates an imitative zeal in the listener. Plutarch is the culmination of a tradition of biographical writing which holds its subject up for judgement, and presents him as a potential model for action.

It was not the only way to go about it, of course. Biography could be there to monumentalize a subject wholly unreachable by emulation, like the Alexander of the countless Alexander histories. Alternatively, monumentalizing and holding up for emulation could go together, as they did in those most curious productions of all antiquity, the Christian Gospels, which certainly have a place in *a* biographical tradition, even if it is not necessarily a Greek one (Jewish historiography surely has a bigger role in their genesis). One of the most important functions of the great body of ancient biography is to present models or anti-models of behaviour according to which its audience should regulate its own—that is, it is normative. This is a powerful motive in the lives of Christian martyrs, monks, and other holy men which are produced towards the end of our period in vast numbers. Some of them are explicitly written for emulation.

Pagans and Christians

Another bizarre production of late paganism which may well have been written under the influence of these Christian lives of holy men and quite transmutes its pagan inheritance is a *Life* of Apollonios of Tyana, a holy man from Cappadocia in the second half of the first century CE. His biographer, Philostratos, is the same man as the author of the *Lives* of the sophists, but here shows himself in very different guise, narrating an eight-book story of an ascetic pagan saint who 'wooed wisdom and soared above tyrants', discoursed with mages and Brahmins and Egyptian divines, foresaw the future, raised the dead, and quite confuted everyone with his esoteric wisdom culled from the traditions of Pythagoras. Paganism appears in this text as defiant, perhaps embattled, asserting itself against the upstart Christians. At one point, Apollonios is brought to trial before the Emperor Domitian, suspicious of a man who claims to be a god. Apollonios takes an option apparently unavailable to Christ in a similar position before Pontius Pilate: confounding his captors he simply vanishes into thin air. Pagan biography has here become fantastic wish-fulfilment—an assertion of unanswerable superiority before tyrannical Rome on the one hand, and the galloping blight of Christianity on the other.

So what was it about this strange Jewish heresy which meant that it eventually won out, not just over poor Apollonios, but over all of classical paganism? How did it, within just three centuries, become the religion of Constantine, and thence of the Roman Empire? Adaptability, opportunism, cunning, argumentativeness, infuriating persistence, and sheer good fortune all had a part. But above all, Christians proved extremely articulate communicators, with a whole armoury of rhetorical techniques and literary genres at their disposal. They used letters and homilies, biographies and dialogues to get their message across. And since the appeal of their religion was universal from the outset, their literature potentially addressed itself to everyone. This is in total contrast to the situation which prevailed with all the pagan literature considered hitherto, produced by and for an élite.

One of the most important of the early churches was at Corinth, established by St Paul in about 50 CE. Some of the converts were Jews, but more still were Gentiles; many belonged to the poorer classes, among them slaves (which is not necessarily incompatible with their being well educated). In addressing himself to them, Paul uses a language which is apparently classless and universal:

> Unto the church of God which is at Corinth, to them that are sanctified in Christ Jesus, called to be saints, with all that in every place call upon the name of Jesus Christ our Lord, both theirs and ours. (I Corinthians 1: 2)

A little later his words, while hinting at the low social status of some of the community, exalt this lack of status in a new and subversive Christian value-system:

For ye see your calling, brethren, how that not many wise men after the flesh, not many mighty, not many noble, are called: But God hath chosen the foolish things of the world to confound the wise; and God hath chosen the weak things of the world to confound the things which are mighty; And base things of the world, and things which are despised, hath God chosen, yea, and things which are not, to bring to nought things that are. (I Corinthians 1: 26–8)

Women were also an important part of the community, and Christianity and its literature makes them visible in a way that pagan literature does not—albeit sometimes by accident. They are recipients of letters (some of the letters of the New Testament address them), or dedicatees of treatises and meditations. They are the subject of saints' lives which hold them up for emulation. Sometimes they can do better and leave behind writings of their own—a letter, the record of a pilgrimage, occasionally something more; in one exceptional case, a *cento*, or patchwork, made up of lines rearranged from Homer to spell out a Christian message. Is the situation really this rosy? Hardly. It is still relatively unusual for women to be addressed, especially in genres—like the letter—whose main aim is to get something practical done (for which women were of less use than men), and it is all too clear, when they are addressed at all, that the space Christianity has made available for them is one that maps onto them simple faith and unprovocative chastity, denying them the wider cultural references available to their male counterparts.

As it spread and came into conflict with paganism, one of Christianity's initial strategies was to insert itself within an existing literature of opposition, protest, and defiance. Thus a small body of Alexandrian nationalist literature dating from the second and third centuries CE documents various showdowns between city-leaders and the emperor. The consequences for the former are predictably fatal—but the unassailable moral high ground gained by martyrdom is the whole point, as it was also for those Roman Stoics who stood out against the emperor's tyranny and left behind accounts of their suicides in the Roman historiographers. It was the Christians, though, who best understood this genre. They knew how to die, and how to write about it, to maximum effect, and their martyrologies were as much acts of self-advertisement as testimonies to bitter or ingrained antagonism with the Roman state.

The next extract is from one of the most famous texts, narrating the martyrdom of Polycarp, bishop of Smyrna. It uses unembellished, occasionally colloquial, prose, and is very concerned to authenticate itself as an accurate transcript of what went on. The immediate addressees are the members of a neighbouring Church, but they are asked to pass on the testimony 'to our more distant brothers', so that its outreach is potentially to 'all the communities of the holy Catholic Church everywhere'. Despite, or rather because of, its harrowing content, the reader is constantly spurred on to emulative zeal, for this is an example which 'everyone desires to imitate':

> When he had said his Amen and rounded off his prayer, the men in charge of the pyre kindled it. As a great flame blazed out, those of us privileged to see it beheld a great miracle, which we have preserved so as to relate the events to others. The flame made the shape of an arch like the sail of a ship bellying out in the wind, and encircled the martyr's body as if by a wall. And in the middle it was not like burning flesh, but baking bread, or gold and silver being smelted in a furnace. And we perceived such fragrance as if from gales of incense or some other costly perfume. (*The Martyrdom of St. Polycarp*, § 15)

For all their high profile, however, persecutions of Christians were not all that frequent: most of the time pagans could afford to let Christians be. But while the pagan world-view could usually, with certain constraints, tolerate monotheism, the converse was not the case. Literary evidence takes us beyond competing ideologies and shows how the oriental newcomer borrowed and was parasitic on the classical culture made available to it. For in the long term, the appropriation of pagan genres and methods of argumentation was more effective than head-on collision. Indeed, it was inevitable that Christians should use the language and literature of the society in which they lived, the culture in which they had been educated—what else was there? The twist, though, was the appropriation of the arguments of classical philosophy to attack classical philosophy, rhetoric against rhetoric, meaning against meaning. The techniques are already in place in Paul himself. If (for example) we return to his first letter to the Corinthians, we find him protesting that when he came to visit them,

> My speech and my preaching was not with enticing words of man's wisdom, but in demonstration of the Spirit and of power. (2: 4)

He opposes persuasive words of wisdom to practical demonstration. 'The Greeks seek after wisdom', he has said, but his own 'demonstration' is definitive and final: it is of the power of God. Yet the terms of both halves of the antithesis—persuasion and demonstration—are already familiar from classical analyses of rhetorical technique. So in a way, Paul has trumped pagan rhetoric too.

As Christianity took hold of the upper classes, we encounter such figures as the dazzlingly well-educated Gregory of Nazianzus (in Cappadocia), a fourth-century bishop whose speeches and letters are steeped in classical rhetoric, whose verse is studded with allusions to the authors on the school curriculum (and a good many others encountered in Gregory's wider reading). The audience is no longer the urban poor of Corinth, but, potentially, those who have received the most privileged of educations. Conversely, we also encounter a pagan culture transformed by its encounter with the newcomer and coming increasingly to have to stand its ground against it. Above all the pagan offensive was led by the Emperor Julian (d. 363), himself an apostate from Christianity, so knowing well how to turn Christian polemic back on the Christians—which he did, venomously. And it is perhaps in this context that we ought to introduce one of antiquity's most extraordinary productions.

The imperial period is not a great one for Greek poetry, so it is all the more notable that it has produced the longest surviving poem to survive from all antiquity, the forty-eight-book *Dionysiaka* of Nonnos of Panopolis in Egypt (*fl.* mid-fifth century CE). Often this epic about the career of the late-antique Dionysos is written off as unpalatable, turgid, monotonous, for Nonnos uses very strict metrical principles with predictable patterns of stress, a uniformly lush, many would say overwrought, style, and strives after effects of blood-and-thunder Baroque monstrosity. Yet I must put in a defence of this wonderful, misunderstood—and significant—poem. Nonnos is formidably learned, and one way of approaching him is as a cross between an archaeological site and a treasury whence relics of antiquity's lost poetry can often be recovered. His use of his predecessors is sometimes heavy-handed but often intelligent. But he is also a priceless document about the tastes and spirit of his age. His account of Dionysos' entire earthly career, and his construction of its chronology, involves the melding of traditions drawn from epic and mythography and Alexander histories with the extraordinary imperial literature of phoney Dionysiac mysticism attributed to Orpheus, all overlaid with the age's abiding passion for astrology.

The poem traces the birth of three successive incarnations of Dionysos, each as a result of a divine rape. This extract comes from Zeus' rape of Semele, and illustrates some important aspects of Nonnos' poetry—Dionysiac excess, grotesqueness, and an unflinching and uninhibited range of voyeuristic detail:

> A writhing snake crept over her, and licked
> The rosy neck of that affrighted bride
> With gentle lips, then mounting on her chest
> Encircled her firm breasts' circumference,
> Hissing a wedding-song, and pouring forth
> A swarming bee's sweet honey, not the gall
> Of deadly vipers. Zeus prolonged the match,

And as beside a wine-press, cried 'Euhoi'
Engendering the son who'd love that cry.
And love-mad mouth to mouth he pressed, and gushed
Intoxicating nectar for his bride,
So that her son would be the harvest's prince
(*Dionysiaka* 7. 328–38)

The result is a Dionysos who is now the Euripidean god of brute irruptive force, now a new Alexander, conqueror of India, now a prancing insouciant adolescent—and yet also a great saviour divinity who undergoes a passion out of love for humankind for all the world like a pagan riposte (yet another one) to Christ. 'Lord Bakchos wept tears, that he might allay mankind's sorrows.' Some said that Nonnos became a Christian bishop. The fact that he appears to have written a paraphrase of St John's gospel in exactly the same overblown style as the *Dionysiaka* is immensely eloquent about the relationship between paganism and Christianity in Nonnos' Egypt. However limited our data about the *Dionysiaka*'s immediate readership—for papyri do not serve us well, and the 'Nonnian style' in fact seems to have got underway rather before Nonnos himself—the insights to be gleaned from Nonnos about the spiritual culture of late antiquity are priceless. He reflects, not only an intensely lettered yet still adaptable paganism, but also a Christianity which seems to have been happy to dress up in paganism's gaudiest clothes. For the sting in the tail is that it looks increasingly as if the *Dionysiaka* was written *after* the paraphrase, that is, after Nonnos became a Christian. What does that tell us about the relationship of Christian and pagan culture?

Imperial Greek literature, like most classical literature, is mainly the record of the winners. We possess little not written by the élites. One of the few non-prestige genres of which anything survives is that of the fable, traditional parables of homespun wisdom. But even this could please refined palates with its arch simplicity and traditionalist morality, and indeed parables were often used in high literary genres. If imperial literature is the story of the winners, it is set against a complex background in which the Greek élites were increasingly Romanized into the political culture of their overlords, yet Romans were increasingly Hellenized into the more prestigious intellectual culture of Greeks.

The ideal Roman, from the Greeks' point of view, was Larensis, the Roman host of Athenaios' Greek sophists who makes them feel that 'Rome is their native land', and does this by being bilingual and having antiquarian interests, learning, well-stocked conversation—in short, gallons of *paideia*. How many Romans lived up to Greek fantasy is another matter altogether. Imperial Greek literature shows us various stages in this process of accommodation: first, assigning the Romans a place in a still Hellenocentric universe (some even claimed Latin as a dialect of Greek); then with various uneasy assertions of parity, or admissions of weakness which could be tempered by harking back to a glorious past. Yet, on the part of many, there was a publicly unproblematic identification with Rome, for Strabon already uses 'we' of Rome. And eventually Greeks, enfranchised as Roman citizens along with the rest of the Empire in 212 CE, became Romans, *Romaioi*.

Further Reading

1. HOMER AND RELATED POETRY

W. Burkert, 'The Making of Homer in the 6th Century BC: Rhapsodes versus Stesichorus', in *Papers on the Amasis Painter and his World* (J. Paul Getty Museum, Malibu, 1987), 43–62.

D. Cairns (ed.), *Oxford Readings in Homer's Iliad* (Oxford, forthcoming).

A. Dalby, 'The "Iliad", the "Odyssey" and their Audiences', in *Classical Quarterly*, 45 (1995), 268–79.

M. W. Edwards, *Homer: Poet of the Iliad* (Baltimore, 1987).

R. Janko, 'The Homeric Poems and Oral Dictated Texts', in *Classical Quarterly*, 48 (1998), 1–13.

J. Latacz, *Homer, His Art and His World* (1985, English trans., Ann Arbor, 1996).

C. W. Macleod, *Homer Iliad Book XXIV* (Cambridge, 1982).

I. Morris, 'The Use and Abuse of Homer', in *Classical Antiquity*, 5 (1986), 81–138.

G. Nagy, *Homeric Questions* (Texas, 1996).

R. Osborne, *Greece in the Making 1200–479 BC* (London, 1996).

R. B. Rutherford, *Homer*, Greece and Rome new surveys in the Classics, 26 (Oxford, 1996).

S. Schein (ed.), *Reading the Odyssey* (Princeton, 1996).

E. Stehle, *Performance and Gender in Ancient Greece* (Princeton, 1997).

W. M. Thalmann, *Conventions of Form and Thought in early Greek Epic Poetry* (Baltimore, 1984).

Translations

Homer

Homer: Iliad, trans. R. Lattimore (Chicago, 1951).

Homer: Iliad, trans. R. Fitzgerald (New York, 1974; Oxford World's Classics: Oxford, 1984).

Homer: Iliad, trans. R. Fagles (New York, 1990).

Homer: Iliad, trans. M. Hammond (in prose, Penguin: London, 1987).

Homer: Odyssey, trans. R. Lattimore (New York, 1965).

Homer: Odyssey, trans. R. Fitzgerald (New York, 1961).

Homer: Odyssey, trans. R. Fagles (Penguin: London, 1996).

Homer: Odyssey, trans. W. Shewring (in prose, Oxford World's Classics: Oxford, 1980).

Homer in English, ed. G. Steiner (Penguin: London, 1996).

Hesiod

Hesiod, trans. M. L. West (Oxford World's Classics: Oxford, 1988).

Homeric hymns

Homeric Hymns, trans. T. Sargent (New York, 1973).

Hymn to Demeter, trans. H. Foley (Princeton, 1993).

2. ARCHAIC GREEK POETRY

Important general discussions

E. L. Bowie, 'Early Greek Elegy, Symposium and Public Festival', *Journal of Hellenic Studies*, 106 (1986), 13–35.

C. Calame, *Choruses of Young Women in Ancient Greece* (London, 1997).

A. Carson, *Eros the Bittersweet* (Princeton, 1986).

K. J. Dover, 'The Poetry of Archilochos', in *Archiloque*. Fondation Hardt pour l'étude de l'antiquité classique. Entretiens 10 (Geneva, 1964), 183–212; repr. in K. J. Dover, *Greek and the Greeks: Collected Papers I* (Oxford, 1987), 97–121.

T. Figueira and G. Nagy (eds.), *Theognis of Megara: Poetry and the Polis* (Baltimore, 1985).

B. Gentili, *Poetry and its Public in Ancient Greece from Homer to the Fifth Century* (Baltimore, 1988).

M. Griffith, 'Personality in Hesiod', *Classical Antiquity*, 2 (1983), 37–65.

C. J. Herington, *Poetry into Drama: Early Tragedy and the Greek Poetic Tradition* (Berkeley and Los Angeles, 1985).

L. Kurke, *The Traffic in Praise: Pindar and the Poetics of Social Economy* (Ithaca, NY, 1991).

I. Morris, 'The Strong Principle of Equality and the Archaic Origins of Greek Democracy', in J. Ober and C. Hedrick (eds.), *Dêmokratia: A Conversation on Democracies, Ancient and Modern* (Princeton, 1996), 19–48.

G. Nagy, *The Best of the Achaeans* (Baltimore, 1979).

—— *Pindar's Homer* (Baltimore, 1990).

E. Stehle, *Performance and Gender in Ancient Greece* (Princeton, 1997).

M. L. West, *Studies in Greek Elegy and Iambus* (Berlin, 1974).

J. J. Winkler, 'Double Consciousness in Sappho's Lyrics', in *The Constraints of Desire: The Anthropology of Sex and Gender in Ancient Greece* (New York, 1990), 162–87.

Studies of the symposium

F. Lissarrague, *The Aesthetics of the Greek Banquet: Images of Wine and Ritual*, trans. A. Szegedy-Maszak (Princeton, 1990).

O. Murray (ed.), *Sympotica: A Symposium on the Symposion* (Oxford, 1990).

R. Neer, *Communicating Vessels: Style and Politics in Athenian Vase Painting, ca. 520–470 B.C.E.* (Cambridge, 2000).

W. J. Slater (ed.), *Dining in a Classical Context* (Ann Arbor, 1991).

Translations

Greek Lyric Poetry, trans. M. L. West (Oxford, 1993), provides verse translations of all archaic poetry down to 450 BCE, excluding Pindar and Bakchylides.

Greek Lyric, ed. D. A. Campbell, 5 vols. (Loeb Classical Library: Cambridge, Mass., 1982–93) offers prose translations and includes Bakchylides.

For Pindar, the most readable translation is F. J. Nisetich, *Pindar's Victory Songs* (Baltimore, 1980).

3. THE GREAT AGE OF DRAMA

P. Cartledge, *Aristophanes and his Theatre of the Absurd* (Bristol, 1990).

E. Csapo and W. Slater, *The Context of Ancient Drama* (Ann Arbor, 1995), an accessible and comprehensive collection of the ancient evidence (with all texts in translation) for the theatre in its social and historical context.

P. Easterling (ed.), *The Cambridge Companion to Greek Tragedy* (Cambridge, 1997).

S. Goldhill, *Reading Greek Tragedy* (Cambridge, 1986).

E. Hall, *Inventing the Barbarian: Greek Self-Definition through Tragedy* (Oxford, 1989).

J. Herington, *Poetry Into Drama: Early Tragedy and the Greek Poetic Tradition* (Berkeley and London, 1985).

R. Seaford, *Reciprocity and Ritual: Homer and Tragedy in the Developing City-State* (Oxford, 1994).

J.-P. Vernant and P. Vidal-Naquet, *Myth and Tragedy in Ancient Greece* (New York, 1988).

J. Winkler and F. Zeitlin (eds.), *Nothing to do with Dionysos?: Athenian Drama in its Social Context,* (Princeton, 1990).

For contrasting views on the specific issue of women in the audience:

S. Goldhill, 'Representing Democracy: Women at the Great Dionysia', in

R. Osborne and S. Hornblower (eds.), *Ritual, Finance, Politics: Athenian Democratic Accounts Presented to David Lewis* (Oxford, 1994), 347–69.

J. Henderson, 'Women and the Athenian Dramatic Festivals', *Transactions and Proceedings of the American Philological Association*, 121 (1991), 133–47.

Translations

The Complete Greek Tragedies, ed. D. Grene and R. Lattimore (Chicago), various translators: this is a generally reliable and sometimes excellent edition, though some of the translations date from the mid-century.

Other recommendations

Aeschylus, 'The Oresteia', ed. and trans. M. Ewans (Everyman: London, 1995).

Sophocles: Antigone, Oedipus the King, Electra, trans. H. Kitto, ed. with introduction and notes by E. Hall (Oxford World's Classics: Oxford, 1994).

Two new translations of Aristophanes

Aristophanes: Birds, Lysistrata, Assembly-Women, Wealth, trans. with introduction and notes by S. Halliwell (Oxford World's Classics: Oxford, 1998);

Loeb Classical Library edition and translation by J. Henderson, in production.

4. HERODOTOS AND THOUKYDIDES

On Herodotos, his contemporaries, and his oral background

C. Dewald, 'Narrative Surface and Authorial Voice in Herodotus' *Histories'*, *Arethusa*, 20 (1987), 141–70 (plus other essays in this special issue on *Herodotus and the Invention of History*).

J. A. S. Evans, *Herodotus, Explorer of the Past: Three Essays* (Princeton, 1991).

R. L. Fowler, 'Herodotos and his Contemporaries', *Journal of Hellenic Studies*, 116 (1996), 62–87.

J. Gould, *Herodotus* (London, 1989).

F. Hartog, *The Mirror of Herodotus: The Representation of the Other in the Writing of History*, trans. J. Lloyd (Berkeley and Los Angeles, 1988).

J. M. Redfield, 'Herodotus the Tourist', *Classical Philology*, 80 (1985), 97–118.

R. Thomas, *Oral Tradition and Written Record in Classical Athens* (Cambridge, 1989).

On Thoukydides

W. R. Connor, *Thucydides* (Princeton, 1984).

G. Crane, *The Blinded Eye: Thucydides and the New Written Word* (London, 1996).

S. Hornblower, 'Narratology and Narrative Techniques in Thucydides', in S. Hornblower (ed.), *Greek Historiography* (Oxford, 1994), 131–66 (as well as the other essays in this volume).

J. Ober, *Political Dissent in Democratic Athens* (Princeton, 1998).

On Xenophon

J. K. Anderson, *Xenophon* (London, 1974).

S. Johnstone, 'Virtuous Toil, Vicious Work: Xenophon on Aristocratic Style', *Classical Philology*, 89 (1994), 221–52.

S. Murnaghan, 'How a Woman Can be More Like a Man: The Dialogue Between Ischomachus and his Wife in Xenophon's *Oeconomicus*', *Helios*, 15 (1988), 9–22.

J. Tatum, *Xenophon's Imperial Fiction* (Princeton, 1989).

On Aesop

For English Translations of the 'Life of Aesop' and Aesop's fables, see L. W. Daly, *Aesop without Morals* (New York and London, 1961).

W. Hansen (ed.), *Anthology of Ancient Greek Popular Literature* (Indianapolis, 1998).

Translations

Herodotus, trans. R. Waterfield, with Introduction and Notes by C. Dewald (World's Classics Series: Oxford, 1998).

Thucydides: History of the Peloponnesian War, trans. R. Warner, with Introduction and Notes by M. I. Finley (Penguin: London and New York, 1972).

Xenophon: A History of my Times, trans. R. Warner, Introduction and Notes by G. Cawkwell (Penguin: London and New York, 1979).

5. GREEK WISDOM LITERATURE

J. Barnes, *Aristotle* (Oxford, 1982).

M. Detienne, *The Masters of Truth in Archaic Greece*, trans. J. Lloyd (New York, 1996).

P. Friedländer, *Plato*, trans. Hans Meyerhoff, 3 vols. (Princeton, 1958–65).

W. K. C. Guthrie, *A History of Greek Philosophy*, 6 vols. (Cambridge, 1962–81).

E. A. Havelock, *A Preface to Plato* (Cambridge, Mass., 1963).

G. A. Kennedy, *The Art of Persuasion in Greece* (Princeton, 1963).

G. B. Kerferd, *The Sophistic Movement* (repr. Cambridge 1984).

G. E. R. Lloyd, *The Revolutions of Wisdom. Studies in the Claims and Practice of Ancient Greek Science* (Berkeley, 1987).

A. A. Long, *Hellenistic Philosophy: Stoics, Epicureans, Sceptics* (2nd edn., Berkeley, 1986).

A. A. Long (ed.), *The Cambridge Companion to Early Greek Philosophy* (Cambridge, 1999).

R. Martin, 'The Seven Sages as Performers of Wisdom', in C. Dougherty and L. Kurke (eds.), *Cultural Poetics in Archaic Greece* (Cambridge, 1993).

A. Nehamas, *The Art of Living. Socratic Reflections from Plato to Foucault* (Berkeley, 1998).

M. C. Nussbaum, *The Fragility of Goodness: Luck and Ethics in Greek Tragedy and Philosophy* (Princeton, 1998).

K. Robb (ed.), *Language and Thought in Early Greek Philosophy* (La Salle, Ill., 1983)

G. Vlastos, *Sokrates, Ironist and Moral Philosopher* (Ithaca, NY, 1981).

Translations

Presocratics
The Presocratic Philosophers, trans. G. S. Kirk, J. E. Raven, and M. Schofield (2nd edn., Cambridge, 1983).

Sophists
The Older Sophists: A Complete Translation, R. K. Sprague (Columbia, SC, 1972).

Socrates and Plato
The Dialogues of Plato, vol. i: *Apology, Euthyphro, Crito, Meno, Gorgias, and Menexenus*, trans. R. E. Allen (New Haven, 1984).

Plato: Complete Works, ed. with introduction and notes J. M. Cooper, associate ed. D. S. Hutchinson (Indianapolis, 1997).

The Collected Dialogues of Plato, trans. E. Hamilton and H. Cairns (Princeton, 1961).

Xenophon: Conversations of Socrates, trans. H. Tredennick and R. Waterfield (London, 1990).

Aristotle
The Complete Works of Aristotle, 2 vols., trans. J. Barnes (Princeton, 1984).

The Poetics of Aristotle, trans. and commentary S. Halliwell (Chapel Hill, NC, 1987).

Aristotle: On Rhetoric, trans. G. A. Kennedy (Oxford, 1991).

Isocrates
Isocrates, vols. i and ii, trans. G. Norlin (Loeb Classical Library: Cambridge, Mass., 1928–9).

Isocrates, vol. iii, trans. L. Van Hook (Loeb Classical Library: Cambridge, Mass., 1945).

Hellenistic Philosophy
Hellenistic Philosophy: Introductory Readings, trans. with introduction and notes B. Inwood, L. P. Gerson (Oxford, 1991).

The Hellenistic Philosophers, vol. i: translations of the principal sources with philosophical commentary by A. A. Long and D. N. Sedley (Cambridge, 1987).

6. THE ATHENIAN ORATORS

R. G. A. Buxton, *Persuasion in Greek Tragedy: A Study of Peitho* (Cambridge, 1982).

T. Cole, *The Origin of Rhetoric in Classical Greece* (Baltimore, 1991).

M. Edwards, *The Attic Orators* (Bristol, 1994).

E. M. Hall, 'Lawcourt Dramas: The Power of Performance in Greek Forensic Oratory', *Bulletin of the Institute of Classical Studies*, 40 (1995), 39–58.

G. Kennedy, *The Art of Persuasion in Greece* (Princeton, 1963).

D. M. MacDowell, *The Law in Classical Athens* (London, 1978).

I. Worthington (ed.), *Persuasion: Greek Rhetoric in Action* (London and New York, 1994).

Translations

C. Carey, *Trials from Classical Athens* (London and New York, 1997), contains a selection of translations of speeches from the classical orators, with brief interpretations.

The Loeb Classical Library contains a full set of translations of the orators, with separate volumes on the major writers and a two-volume collection of *Minor Attic Orators*, trans. K. J. Maidment.

A complete collection of translations is in preparation by the University of Texas Press. The following are available to date:

Antiphon and Andokides, trans. D. MacDowell and M. Gagarin (Austin, 1997).

Lysias, trans. S. C. Todd (Austin, 2000).

Aischines, trans. C. Carey (Austin, 2000).

7. GREEK LITERATURE AFTER THE CLASSICAL PERIOD

A. Cameron *Callimachus and his Critics* (Princeton, 1995) (for wider social and intellectual context).

—— *The Greek Anthology: From Meleager to Planudes* (Oxford, 1993).

L. Canfora, *The Vanished Library* (London, 1989).

P. M. Fraser, *Ptolemaic Alexandria*, 3 vols. (Oxford, 1972) (on Alexandria itself).

A. S. F. Gow and D. L. Page, *Hellenistic Epigram* (Cambridge, 1965).

—— *The Garland of Philip* (Cambridge, 1968).

—— *Theokritos*, 2 vols. (Cambridge, 1950).

W. V. Harris, *Ancient Literacy* (London, 1989), see esp. pp. 116–46.

A. S. Hollis, *Callimachus' Hecale* (Oxford, 1990).

R. L. Hunter, *The New Comedy of Greece and Rome* (Cambridge, 1983).

—— *The* Argonautica *of Apollonius: Literary Studies* (Cambridge, 1993).

—— *Theocritus and the Archaeology of Greek Poetry* (Cambridge, 1996).

R. Pfeiffer, *Kallimachos*, 2 vols. (Oxford, 1949–53, repr. 1998).

G. Sifakis, *Studies in the History of Hellenistic Drama* (London, 1967).

Translations

Jason and the Golden Fleece (the Argonautika), trans. R. Hunter (Oxford World's
   Classics: Oxford, 1998).
Callimachus: Hymns, Epigrams, Select Fragments, trans. with introduction and
   notes S. Lombardo and D. Rayor (Baltimore, 1988).
Theocritus: The Idylls, trans. R. Wells (Penguin Books: London, 1989).
Where no other translation is specified, the reader is referred to that given in the
   Loeb Classical Library. W. G. Arnott's translations of the plays of Menander in
   this series are particularly highly recommended.

8. LATER GREEK LITERATURE

G. Bowersock, *Greek Sophists in the Roman Empire* (Oxford, 1969).
K. J. Clarke, *Between Geography and History: Hellenistic Constructions of the Roman
   World* (Oxford, 1999).
E. Gabba, *Dionysius and the History of Archaic Rome* (Bari, 1996).
M. Gleason, *Making Men: Sophists and Self-Presentation in Ancient Rome* (Princeton,
   1995).
W. V. Harris, *Ancient Literacy* (Cambridge, Mass., 1989), see esp. pp.175–284.
F. Millar, *A Study of Cassius Dio* (Oxford, 1964).
J. R. Morgan and R. Stoneman (edd.), *Greek Fiction: The Greek Novel in Context*
   (London, 1994).
G. L. Schmeling (ed.), *The Novel in the Ancient World* (Leiden, 1996).
S. Swain, *Hellenism and Empire: Language, Classicism, and Power in the Greek World
   AD 50–250* (Oxford, 1996).
—— 'Biography and Biographic', in M. J. Edwards and S. Swain (eds.), *Portraits:
   Biographical Representation in the Greek and Latin Literature of the Roman Empire*
   (Oxford, 1997), 1–37.
J. Tatum (ed.), *The Search for the Ancient Novel* (Baltimore, 1994).

Translations

Menander Rhetor, ed. with trans. and commentary by D. A. Russell and N. G.
   Wilson (Oxford, 1981).
Galen: Selected Works, trans. P. I. Singer (Oxford World's Classics: Oxford, 1997).
Plutarch: Greek Lives, trans. R. Waterfield (Oxford World's Classics: Oxford, 1998).
Plutarch: Selected Essays and Dialogues, trans. D. A. Russell (Oxford World's
   Classics: Oxford, 1993).
Appian's 'Civil Wars', trans. C. J. Mackenzie (Penguin: London, 1996).
Collected Ancient Greek Novels, trans. B. P. Reardon (Berkeley, 1989).
Where no other translation of a cited work is specified, the reader is again
   referred to the translation in the Loeb Classical Library.

Chronology

This chronology was compiled for *Literature in the Greek and Roman Worlds*, which includes the material in this edition.

Date	Historical Events	Literary and Related Developments
BCE	Traditional date of first Olympic Games (776) Traditional date of foundation of Rome (753) Age of Greek settlement in Italy, Sicily, and East	Development and dissemination of Greek alphabet on Phoenician model (800–750)
750	Development of heavy 'hoplite' armour and emergence of polis society	
700	Spartan expansion (from *c*.730)	Homer and Hesiod active about now Archilochos active as poet (675–640)
650	Greeks begin to penetrate Egypt	Terpander, Kallinos, Semonides, Tyrtaios, Mimnermos, Alkman active as poets
600	Earliest Greek coins minted (*c*.595) Solon archon at Athens: social and political reforms (594) Greek mercenaries carve their names on the Abu Simbel inscription (591)	Sappho and Alkaios active as poets (610–575) Solon active as poet (600–560)
575	Age of 'Tyrants' in major Greek states other than Sparta	Thales predicts eclipse of the sun (585) Rise of panhellenic festivals (Pythia 582, Isthmia 581, Nemea 573) Anaximander active as philosopher (570–550) (570–475) lifetime of Xenophanes (philosopher-poet)
550	Croesus king of Lydia (560–546) Cyrus the Great founds Persian empire (559–530) Cyrus' conquest of Lydia and Ionian Greeks— *'The year the Mede arrived'* (546) Carthaginians and Etruscans check Greek expansion in western Mediterranean	Stesichoros, Theognis, Hipponax, and Ibykos active as poets Anaximenes active as philosopher

Date	Historical Events	Literary and Related Developments
525	Darius seizes the Persian throne (521)	Anakreon active as poet (535–490) City Dionysia festival established at Athens (by 534) Pythagoras active as philosopher Simonides active as poet
500	Foundation of Roman Republic (traditional date) (509) 'Democratic' reforms of Kleisthenes at Athens (508) Ionian Revolt against Persian rule (499, defeated with Battle of Lade and sack of Miletos 494) First Persian expedition to mainland Greece: Battle of Marathon (490) Persian and Carthaginian invasions of Greece and Sicily: Battles of Artemision, Thermopylai, Salamis (480); Plataia, Mykale (479); Himera (480)	Alkmaion (doctor), Hekataios (historian), Herakleitos, Parmenides (philosophers) active Earliest surviving poem of Pindar (498) Phrynichos prosecuted for his play *The sack of Miletos* (494) First comedy performed at the City Dionysia at Athens (480s) Bakchylides active as poet First victory of Aischylos (active 499–456)
475	Foundation of Delian league against Persia under leadership of Athens (478) Battle of Eurymedon effectively ends Persian threat (467) Radical reforms and murder of Ephialtes at Athens Perikles' supremacy begins (461–429)	First victory of Sophokles (active 468–406) Anaxagoras (philosopher) arrives in Athens
450	Athenian expedition to Egypt ends in disaster Treasury of Delian League moved from Delos to Athens—regarded as beginning of 'Athenian empire' (454) 'Peace of Kallias' ends hostilities between Athens and Persia (449)	First production by Euripides (active 455–406) Zeno and Empedokles active as philosophers Work begins on Parthenon in Athens Herodotos active as historian (445–426) Publication of the Laws of the Twelve Tables at Rome
425	Peloponnesian War between Athenian and Spartan alliances (431–404) First Athenian expedition to Sicily 427 'Peace of Nikias' between Athens and Sparta and their allies (421) Disastrous Athenian expedition to Sicily (415–413)	Thoukydides begins his *History* (431–404) Demokritos (atomist philosopher), Hippokrates (doctor), Sokrates and Protagoras (philosophers), Hellanikos (historian) active

Date	Historical Events	Literary and Related Developments
425 *cont.*		Embassy of Gorgias to Athens also begins the formal art of rhetoric *Acharnians* of Aristophanes (active 420s–380s) Hippias (antiquarian and polymath) active
400	Oligarchic coup of 'the 400' at Athens (411) Democracy restored at Athens (410) Spartans destroy Athenian fleet at Battle of Aigospotamoi; Siege of Athens (405) Capitulation of Athens; installation of regime of 'the Thirty' (404) Fall of 'the Thirty'; democracy restored at Athens (403) Sack of Rome by the Gauls	Andokides and Lysias active as speech-writers (410–387) Antisthenes (cynic), Aristippos (hedonist), and Euklides, pupils of Sokrates, active (400–360) Trial and execution of Sokrates (399) Isokrates (writer and educator) active (397–338) Plato (philosopher) active (396–347); founds the Academy (387) Antimachos, epic poet, active Xenophon (historian and essayist) active (390–354)
375	Following Corinthian War (395–386), Peace of Antalkidas ('King's Peace') imposes Persian-backed control by Sparta on Greece (386) Thebes destroys Spartan power at Battle of Leuktra (371) Domination of Greek world by Thebes under Pelopidas and Epaminondas (371–362)	Diogenes (cynic philosopher) active (360–323)
350	Philip II becomes king of Macedon (359) Phokians seize Delphi and provoke Sacred War, bringing Philip into central Greece against them (356–352) Philip defeats Athens and Thebes at Chaironeia: end of Greek independence (338)	Theatre at Epidauros built Literary and political careers of Demosthenes (d. 322) and Aischines (left Athens 330) begin Theopompos (historian) active (350–320) End of *History* of Ephoros (340)
325	Death of Philip: accession of Alexander (336) Alexander crosses into Asia: Battle of Granikos and conquest of Asia Minor (334) Foundation of Alexandria in Egypt (331) Conquest as far as Punjab (327) Death of Alexander, aged 32; regency of Perdiccas (323) and period of 'the successors'	Aristotle begins teaching at Athens and founds the Lykeion (Peripatetic school) (335) Pyrrho (sceptic) active as philosopher Career of Menander (321–289); *Dyskolos* performed 317

Date	Historical Events	Literary and Related Developments
300	Peace between the successors recognizes in effect the division Antigonos (Asia), Cassandros (Macedon/Greece), Lysimachos (Thrace), Ptolemy (Egypt), and by omission Seleukos (the Eastern domains) (311) Battle of Ipsos: destruction of power of Antigonos and Demetrios; Antigonos killed (301)	Klearchos (Peripatetic philosopher) visits Ai Khanum in Afghanistan (310) Zeno of Kition establishes Stoic school in *Stoa Poikile* at Athens (310) Philitas of Kos (scholar and founder of Alexandrian poetry) appointed tutor to future Ptolemy II Epikouros establishes his philosophical school at Athens (307) Ptolemy I founds Mouseion of Alexandria Zenodotos royal tutor and first head of the Library Euclid (mathematician) active
275	Pyrrhos of Epeiros crosses into south Italy to aid the Greek cities: is defeated by the Romans (280–275) Earliest Roman coinage Antigonos Gonatas, son of Demetrios, defeats Gauls; becomes king of Macedon, founding Macedonian dynasty (276) Ptolemy unsuccessfully supports Greek independence from Macedon (267–262)	Douris of Samos (leading exponent of 'tragic history') active
250	First Punic War between Rome and Carthage, ending in Roman victory (264–241) Eumenes I founds independent power at Pergamon (263–241) Diodotos establishes independent Greek kingdom in Bactria (239–130)	Kallimachos, Theokritos, Lykophron, Aratos, Poseidippos active as poets Manetho (historian and Egyptian priest) lays foundations of Egyptian history Hieronymos of Kardia (historian of the Successors) dies aged 104; Timaios of Tauromenion (historian of the West) dies aged 96 (260) Apollonios of Rhodes writes the *Argonautika* Herodas (author of Mimes) active
225		Livius Andronikos (earliest Roman poet and playwright) active (240–207) First play of Naevius produced (236) Chrysippos succeeds Kleanthos as head of Stoic school (232)

Date	Historical Events	Literary and Related Developments
200	Second Punic ('Hannibalic') War—Hannibal invades Italy (218–201) First war between Rome and Macedon (214–205) Scipio Africanus defeats Hasdrubal in Spain: Spain divided into two provinces (211–206) Scipio defeats Hannibal at Battle of Zama; Carthage becomes a dependent of Rome Roman conquest of Cisalpine Gaul (202–191) Second Macedonian (200–197)	Career of Plautus (204–184); *Miles Gloriosus* performed (204) Ennius active at Rome as poet and teacher (204–169) Q. Fabius Pictor writes first prose history of Rome, in Greek (202)
175	Battle of Pydna: end of Antigonid kingdom of Macedon; Rome divides territory into 4 republics (167)	Polybios the historian arrives in Rome (167) Plays of Terence produced (166–159)
150	Macedonia becomes a Roman province (149–148) Carthage destroyed by Romans; Africa becomes Roman province (149–146) Achaian War: sack of Corinth (146)	Karneades (head of the Academy) comes to Rome on an embassy (155) Publication of Cato's *Origines* or history of Rome Panaitios (Stoic philosopher, *c*.185–109) arrives in Rome (144)
125	Attalos of Pergamon bequeaths his kingdom to Rome (133) War against Jugurtha in Numidia (122–106)	Calpurnius Piso (Roman historian) consul Lucilius (Roman satirist) active
100	Gaius Marius consul for first of six times; he reforms the army (107) Social War in Italy over citizenship (91–88)	Meleagros of Gadara (poet and collector of earliest epigrams in *The Greek Anthology*) active Aristeides of Miletos' 'Milesian Tales' translated into Latin by Sisenna
75	Sulla appointed dictator of Rome: Sullan reforms (87) Slave Revolt of Spartacus (73–71) Pompey's reorganization of East: end of Seleucid monarchy, and of independent kingdom of Judaea; Bithynia, Cilicia, Syria, Crete, organized into provinces; client kingdoms established elsewhere (66–64)	Poseidonios (philosopher, historian, polymath) active at Rhodes (87–51) Cicero's earliest extant speech (81) Philodemos (poet, Epicurean philosopher) active at Rome (75–35)

Date	Historical Events	Literary and Related Developments
50	Caesar campaigns in Gaul (58–49) Civil War between Caesar and Pompey (49) Dictatorship of Caesar (47–44; murdered 15 March 44) Octavian seizes consulate (43) Defeat of Republicans at Philippi by Octavian and Mark Antony	Diodoros of Sicily, Dionysios of Halikarnassos (historical writers) active Sallust (historian and moralist) active Catullus active as poet (59–54) Caesar writes his account of the *Gallic Wars* (58–52) Death of Lucretius: posthumous publication of his poem *On the Nature of the Universe* (55) M. Terentius Varro (antiquarian) active (49–27) Virgil's *Eclogues* published (38) Horace's *Satires* written (37–30)
25	Octavian defeats Antony and Kleopatra at Actium: annexation of Egypt by Rome (31–30) 'The Republic Restored'—first constitutional settlement; Octavian takes name 'Augustus' (27)	Strabon (geographer and historian) active (44–21 CE) Propertius' *Elegies I* published (29) Vitruvius' *On Architecture* (28–23) Ovid begins his *Amores* Death of Tibullus and of Virgil (19)
1CE	Final dynastic settlement: Tiberius given tribunician power (2–4)	End of Livy's history of Rome (9 BCE) Death of Horace and of Maecenas (8 BCE) Ovid banished to the Black Sea (8 CE)
25	**The Julio-Claudians**: reign of Tiberius (14–37) Reign of Gaius Caligula (37–41)	Philo (Jewish writer) active Death of Elder Seneca (writer on oratory) (37)
50	Reign of Claudius (41–54) Reign of Nero (54–68) Pisonian conspiracy against Nero (65) Jewish Revolt (66–73)	St Paul's *Letter to the Corinthians* (58) Younger Seneca's *Letters* (62) Lucan (epic poet) and Persius (satirist) active Suicides of Seneca and Lucan (65) Josephus, rebel leader in Judaea and future author, deserts to the Romans (67) Chariton, Heliodoros, Achilles Tatius, Longus (Greek novelists) active (precise dates uncertain)

Date	Historical Events	Literary and Related Developments
75	'The Year of the Four Emperors': Galba, Otho, Vitellius, Vespasian struggle for power (69) **The Flavians**: reign of Vespasian (69–79) Reign of Titus (79–81) Eruption of Vesuvius: destruction of Pompeii and Herculaneum (79) Reign of Domitian (81–96) Campaigns of Agricola in Britain	Frontinus (administrator and technical writer) active Death of Elder Pliny (administrator, naturalist, and encyclopedist) investigating eruption (79) Statius, Silius Italicus, Martial (poets), and Quintilian (writer on rhetoric) active
100	**The Antonines**: reign of Nerva (96–8) Reign of Trajan (98–117): under him, Roman Empire reaches its greatest geographical extent Trajan conquers Dacia; annexes Armenia and Mesopotamia (101–17) Jewish Revolt (115–17)	Dio Chysostom (Greek orator), Epiktetos (moralist), and Plutarch (essayist and biographer) active in Greek literature Pliny the Younger (orator and letter-writer) consul and governor of Bithynia (100–11) Tacitus writes *Histories* and *Annals*
125	Reign of Hadrian (117–38) Hadrian's visit to Britain; Hadrian's Wall from Tyne to Solway (122–7) Final dispersal of Jews following Bar Kochba's revolt (132–5)	Appian (historian), Arrian (philosopher and historian), Lucian (satirist), and Ptolemy (astronomer) active in Greek literature; Suetonius (biographer) and Juvenal (poet) in Latin
150	Reign of Antonius Pius (138–61)	Pausanias writes his description of Greece Herodes Atticus (Greek orator) and Fronto (Latin orator) active Aelius Aristides, Dion (orators) active Apuleius (poet) and Galen (doctor and polymath) active
175	Reign of Marcus Aurelius (161–80) Reign of Commodus (180–92)	*Meditations* of Marcus Aurelius (174–80) Athenaios writes *Deipnosophistai*
200	**The Severans**: reign of Septimius Severus (193–211) Severus campaigns in Britain and dies at York (208–11) Reign of Caracalla (212–17) *Constitutio Antoniniana* grants citizenship to all inhabitants of the Empire (212) Reign of Elagabalus (218–22)	Philostratos (literary biographer), Herodian (historian), Marius Maximus (biographer), Sextus Empiricus (Sceptic philosopher), Alexander of Aphrodisias (commentator on Aristotle), Tertullian, Clement, and Origen (Christian writers) active

Date	Historical Events	Literary and Related Developments
225	Reign of Alexander Severus (222–35)	Cassius Dio (historian), Plotinos (Neoplatonist philosopher), Nemesianus (Latin poet), Minucius Felix (philosophical writer) active
250	Period of military anarchy, with almost twenty emperors, problems on frontiers and with bureaucracy and economy (235–84)	
275	**The Late Empire**: Diocletian re-establishes central power and founds the Tetrarchy (284–306) Roman Empire partitioned into Eastern and Western portions	
300	Career of Constantine the Great (306–37) Christianity declared official state religion at Rome (312) Constantine reunites Empire Last persecution of Christians in Rome (303–11) Edict of Milan: Constantine establishes toleration of Christianity (313)	
325	Foundation of Constantinople (324) Seat of Empire moved to Constantinople	
350	Rome splits into two Empires again under sons of Constantine (340) Reign of Julian the Apostate (360–3)	Gregory of Nazianzus (Bishop and letter-writer) active Ausonius (teacher of rhetoric, poet) active (c.310–94)
375	Reign of Theodosius the Great (378–95) Roman legions begin to evacuate Britain Visigoths cause trouble on eastern frontiers Theodosius reunites the Empire for the last time (392–5)	Ambrose (bishop) active Ammianus Marcellinus (Latin historian) active Symmachus (letter-writer) active Prudentius (composer of hymns) active
400	Division of Empire between sons of Theodosius Sack of Rome by Alaric the Visigoth (410)	Saint Augustine's *City of God*, following sack of Rome (411) Jerome (Christian writer) active (c.347–420) Paulinus (bishop, poet) active (c.353–431) Claudian (poet and panegyrist) active

Date	Historical Events	Literary and Related Developments
425	Barbarians settle in Roman provinces – Vandals in southern Spain, Huns in Pannonia, Ostrogoths in Dalmatia, Visigoths and Suevi in Portugal and northern Spain	*Digest* of Roman law is compiled (439) (?)Macrobios (Intellectual writer) active
450	Vandals sack Rome (455)	Proklos (neoplatonist philosopher), Nonnos (Greek poet), Sidonius Apollinaris (Gallic prelate and Latin writer) active
475	End of Roman Empire in the West: German Odovacar deposes the derisively titled Emperor Romulus Augustulus and is proclaimed king of Italy (476)	
500	Clovis, king of the Franks, founds Merovingian power; is converted to Christianity Conquest of Italy by Theodoric the Goth: he founds the Ostrogoth kingdom of Italy (493)	Boethius (scholar, philosopher, theologian) active Stobaios' *Anthology of Greek literature*
525	Justinian, Eastern emperor, seeks to reconquer Italy and Africa (527–65)	Justinian orders the closure of the Academy at Athens (529)

Acknowledgements

National Archaeological Museum, Athens	p. 25
National Archaeological Museum, Athens. Photo: Hirmer Fotoarchiv, Munich	p. 29
Museo Nazionale di Villa Giulia, Rome. Photo: Soprintendenza Archeologica per l'Etruria Meridionale	p. 30
© British Museum	p. 34
The J. Paul Getty Museum, Malibu, California	p. 47
© British Museum	p. 49
Staatliche Antikensammlungen und Glyptothek, Munich	p. 58
Piraeus Archaeological Museum, Port of Athens	p. 73
Based on a drawing by Peter Connolly	p. 80
The J. Paul Getty Museum, Malibu, California	p. 85
National Museum, Naples. Photo: Archivi Alinari	p. 156
The Bodleian Library, University of Oxford, Shelfmark MS. Gr. Class. c. 54(P)V	p. 165
Alison Frantz Collection, American School of Classsical Studies at Athens	p. 180
Kunsthistorisches Museum, Vienna	p. 181
National Museum, Naples. Photo: Archivi Alinari	p. 207
The J. Paul Getty Museum, Malibu, California	p. 209
Photo: Henry Stierlin, Geneva	p. 241
Abegg-Stiftung, Riggisberg, Berne	p. 265

Index

Archilochos of Paros, 40, 46, 51, 120, 144, 237; Cologne papyrus, 52–3; persona, 43, 45

Archimedes, 235

Argonauts, 37, 39, *see also* Apollonios Rhodios

Arion, 120

aristocracy: Greek, 136–7, 153, 161–2, 220, (archaic era) 4–5, 18–23, 55, 57, 61

Aristodemos (actor), 202

Aristophanes, 81; *Acharnians*, 76, 82–3, 102, 103, 104–5; *Birds*, 88; *Clouds*, 69, 152, 154; *Frogs*, 84, 88, 93, 94, 108, 217; *Knights*, 98; *Lysistrate*, 81–2, 111–12; *Peace*, 79, 109–10; *Wasps*, 84, 98, 102–3, 180–1, 183; *Wealth*, 76 *Women at the Thesmophoria*, 110; *Women in Assembly*, 76, 91, 93, 98

Aristotle, *156*, 167–70; on Archilochos, 43 on early philosophers, 138–9, 141, 147; on New Music, 68; and politics, 168, 170; school, Peripatos, 167–8, 216; on Solon, 53; and writing, 170 WORKS: *Metaphysics*, 138–9; *Nicomachean Ethics*, 141, 168, 169–70; *Poetics*, 37, 168–9, 227; *Protrepticus*, 169; *Rhetoric*, 128–9, 178–85, 192, 202; *Sophist*, 147

Arrian, 247

Asia, 199

Asklepiades of Samos, 233–4

astrology, 264

astronomy, 140, 226, 235, *see also* Aratos

Astydamas (tragic poet), 89

Athenaios of Naukratis, 69, 237, 243, 266

Athenis (sculptor), 52

Athens: Academy, 153, 155, 171; agora, 150, 153; Areopagos, 100–1, 188; Assembly, 177, 178–9, *180*; book trade, 197, 216; citizenship, 104–6, 112; Dionysos, precinct of, *80*, 84, 206; Hellenistic culture, 171, 211; Homer refers to, 22; empire, 77, 86–7; festivals, 71, 81–3, 88–9, 211, (*see also* Dionysia; Lenaia; Panathenaia); funeral orations, 109, 134, 182; Lyceum, 150, 153, 155, 167–8; and Macedonia, 174, 192, 211; in Peloponnesian War, 77, 83, 129, 135;

philosophical schools, 171, 172, 240, (*see also* Academy *and* Lyceum *above*); Pnyx, hill of, *180*; Public Physician, 151; social change, 5th century, 99; sophists, 128, 150, 250; Stoa, 172; theatres, *80*, 84, 206; tyrants, 33, 36, 45, 71; *see also* courts; metics; *and under* comedy; democracy; drama; pottery; tragedy

athletic competitions, 24, 43, 48, 201

Atthidographers, 236

Atticist movement, 243–4, 246, 251, 258

audience: Christian, 261; élite Roman, 240; emotional response, 175, 186; Hellenistic era, 171, 200, 203–4, 217, 237–8, (poets), 214–15, 221–3, 232–3; involvement in drama, 75–6, 84, 90, 94–5, 97–9; Theokritos dramatizes response, 214–15, 228; *see also under major genres and authors*

Augustan era, 245–6

Augustus, Emperor (Gaius Iulius Caesar Octavianus): panegyric of, 245

aulos, 40, *47*, 50, 63, 74, 75

authority: and authorship, 44–5; divine, 145–6, 147, 148

Avienus, 229

Axiothea (student of Plato), 155

Bakchylides, 41, 45, 46, 63–4, 65, 66, 89

barbarians, 106, 225, 226; invasions, 240

basileus (pl. *basilees*, 'lords'), 8–9, 11–12, 20, 30, 31

Battle of the Gods and Titans (epic), 38

Bentley, Richard, 4, 5, 15

Bias of Priene, 120, 141

biography: Christian, 259, 260, 261, 262; Greek, 137, 259–60

Bion (pastoral poet), 214

blame poetry, Greek, 51

books: Greek trade, 197, 216; production methods, 216; *see also* libraries

Boupalos (sculptor), 52

bucolic poetry, *see* pastoral poetry

Burkert, Walter, 33–4, 35

calendars; *see also* festivals

canons, literary, 216, 238, 251

Cassius Dio, 247

Catalogue of Women (*Ehoiai*, anon. hexameter poem), 38

catalogue of Alexandrian Library, 219

Catullus, Gaius Valerius: poem, 64, Peleus and Thetis, 226–7, 228

character, 185–6, 259

Chariton, 256, 257, 258

Charon of Lampsakos, 117

Chilon of Sparta, 120, 141

Chios, 23, 32, 35, 36

Choirilos of Samos, 39, 217

choral lyric, Greek, 46, 50, 58, 61–6, 69

choregia, choregoi, 84, *85*, 86

chorus, dramatic, 84, 87, 202, 203; in comedy, 103–4, 203, 205; in dithyramb, 203, 211; and music, 73–5; in tragedy, 87, 96–7, 202, 203

Christianity, 240, 260–6; audience for literature, 261; biography, 259, 260, 261, 262–3; and classical literature, 240, 261, 263–6; dialogues, 261; Greek literature, 260–6; political status, 264

Chrysippos (Stoic), 171, 173

Cicero, Marcus Tullius: letters, 239; translates Aratos, 229

civic culture and society: emergence, 30–1, 43, 55, 61; local patriotism, 116, 249; and public performances, 43, 49, 86, 104–6, 200, 201

colonies: Greek *apoikiai*, 31, 65–6

comedy

OLD (Athenian political), audience, 98–9, 103–4, 104–11; chorus, 103–4; costumes, 92, 93; debate forms in, 102–3; at Dionysia, 71, 89, 104; at Lenaia, 81–83; and oratory, 177, 197; origins, 72, 79, 211; *parabasis*, 103–4, 205; and Plato, 166; poets other than Aristophanes, 89; political role, 69, 76, 78, 102–4, 205–6; time span, 76; women portrayed in, 111–12; *see also* Aristophanes

NEW, 204–8, 238, 257, 258, apolitical nature, 76, 205–6; audience, 205–6; performance, 203, 237

commentaries: Hellenistic textual, 218, 222

competitions, literary, 36, 71, 88–9, 237, (at funeral games), 10, 11, 24

Constantine I, Emperor, 240

Constitution of the Athenians, The, 78

Coptic art, *265*

Corinth, 45, 239, 261–2, 263

costume, theatrical, 70, 92–4, 109

courts: Athenian, 76–7, 100–1, 179–82, 186

craftsmen: of Dionysos, actors, 202, 209, 211; poets as, 11, 45; Sokrates and, 153, 161

cross-dressing in drama, 94, 109

Cycle, epic, 37–8

Cynics, 172, 251

dactylic rhythms, 50 *see also* hexameter

dedications: of book in temple, 145; Greek epigrams, 233, 235

Delos, festivals on, 23–8, 48–9, 211

Delphi, 24, 31, 211, 252; festivals, 24, 150, 201, 203, 237

Demeter, cult at Eleusis, 38

Demetrios I Poliorketes of Macedon, 211

democracy: Athenian, 76–7, 78, 104, 153, 175, 178–9, 182–3; and oratory, 99, 175–6; Syracusan, 175

Demodokos (poet in *Odyssey*), 17, 35

Demokritos, 143

Demosthenes, 180, 183, 184–5, 187, 194, 198; later reading of, 248, 258; style, 195, 196, 248

dialects, Greek, 218, 219, 238; mixed, in poetry, 13, 23, 31, 219

dialogue form: Christian use, 261; Lucianic, 251; philosophical, 152, 154, 166

didactic poetry: Hellenistic, 39, 228–31

Dio Cassius, 247

Diodoros of Sicily, 236, 245–6

Diogenes the Cynic, 172

Diogenes Laertius, 140, 144, 145, 171

Dion of Prousa, 249, 250, 252, 253–4

Dionysia: Athenian City, 71, 79, 83, 84–91, 104, 204; Attic Rural, 79, 81; Hellenistic, 201

Dionysios of Halikarnassos, 117–18, 122, 244, 245, 246

Dionysios II of Syracuse, 155–6
Dionysos, 47–8, 72–3, 75; Athenian precinct of, *80*, 84, 206; Christianization, *265*; Craftsmen of, 202, 209, 211; and drama, 72–3, 75, *80*, 89, 201
dirges, see *threnoi*
dithyramb, 43, 61, 63–4, 67, 71, 242; Bakchylides, 63–4, 89; Hellenistic, 203, 211, 223, 237; Timotheos, 67, 217, 223
Doric dialect, 46, 50, 213, 233
drama, 70–114; audience, 75–6, 84, 87–8, 90, 91–9, 104–11, 205–6; and Dionysos, 72; freedom of speech, 75–8; Greek influence in Rome, 239; Hellenistic, 200–15; music, 72–5, 203; one-off and repeat performances, 81; origins, 62, 70–5; performance context, 70–1, 78–83, (*see also* Dionysia); political role, 77–8, 79, 99–104, 200, 201; stage technology, 91, 92; and women, 109–14; *see also* actors; *choregia*; chorus; comedy; costume; dithyramb; masks; mime; satyr-plays; tragedy
dynastic reinforcement, 21–3

education: Greece, late, 5th-century change, 68–9; Hellenistic era, 204, 217, 236, 238; in philosophy, 155, 159, 167–8, (*see also* Athens (philosophical schools)); school books and exercises, 37, 218, 222; social and cultural, through performance, 42–3, 68–9, 104; sophistic, 68–9, 151, 176, 230; *see also* literacy; *paideia*
Egypt, 123, 126, *265*; Hellenistic era, 199, 204, (*see also* Alexandria; papyri; Ptolemaic dynasty)
Ehoiai (hexameter poem), 38
eikos (likelihood), 128–9, 130, 175
ekphrasis, 228
elegiac metre, 50, 231–3
elegy: Greek, 46, 50, 54–7, 69, 116–17, 144; Hellenistic, 231–3
embassies, 174, 248, 223; oratory, 177, 189

emotion, 94, 112, 237; in oratory, 185, 186–7
Empedokles, 140, 144, 147–8
enargeia ('vividness'), 132
ephebes (young men), 85–6, 105, 153
Ephesos, 240, *241*, 250
Ephoros of Kyme, 236
epic poetry, 4–39; ancient scholars on, 216, 227; competitive recitations, 36; didactic, 39, 228–31, (*see also* Hesiod); on gods, 8, 9, 11, 17, 38; Hellenistic, 39, 220, 223–31; Herodotos and, 9, 119, 120; *kleos*, 11, 12, 16, 17; *Kyklos*, 37–8; language, 13, 23, 31; and lyric poetry, 41–2, 43; oral tradition, 5–6, 12–13, 14, 19, 27, 32; other than Homer and Hesiod, 34, 37–9; papyri, 37, 38; patrons, 19, 21–3; performance context, *see under* Homer; Roman period, 264–5; self-reference, 5, 8, 9–10, 10–11, 16; school exercises on, 37; socio-historical context, 28–32; visual arts represent, *34*, 34–5, 37; and writing, 13–15, (*see also* Apollonios Rhodios; Hesiod; Homer)
Epicurus and Epicureanism, 171–2, 235
epigram, 219, 233–5
Epikouros, *see* Epicurus
Epiktetos, 247
epinikia, 43, 64–6, 67, 69, 91, 220
epistles, *see* letters
epitaphs, 233, 235
epithalamia, *see* wedding songs
epitomes, historical, 236
epodes, 50
Eratosthenes, 219, 232
ethnography, 117, 123, 126, 247, 254
ethos, 'character', 185–6
Euboulos, 47–8
Eudoxos of Knidos, 229,
Eumelos (Corinthian poet), 39
Eupolis, 89
Euripides: costumes, 92–3; Hellenistic interest, 212, 217, 242, 258; monody, 203; reception in lifetime, 83; at Rural Dionysia, 79, 81; Sophists' influence, 102

WORKS: *Bakchai*, 72–3, 94; *Erechtheus*, 111; *Hekabe*, 112; *Helen*, 93; *Hippolytos*, 99, 105, 108, 112; *Ion*, 111, 112; *Iphigeneia in Aulis*, 203; *Medeia*, 88, 106, 112; *Orestes*, 88; *Rhesos*, 76; *Suppliant Women*, 106, 112, 176; *Trojan Women*, 87, 101–2, 112

eye-cups, 48, *49*

Ezekiel; dramatization of *Exodus*, 210, 234

fables, animal, 266; Aesopic, 121–2; in Greek lyric poetry, 51, 54, 220; Phaedrus',

Favorinus, 249

festivals, 10, 11, 23–4, 31, 71, 88–9; Hellenistic, 200, 201, 211, 237; inter-communal, 23–8, 31, 65–6; literary competitions, 36, 71, 88–9, 237; lyric performances, 46, 48–9, 55–6; in Roman period, 242; *see also* Dionysia; Lenaia; Panathenaia

fiction, prose, 256–60; *see also* Apuleius

Fortune as goddess, 208, *209*

foundation literature, 223, 227

funerals, *29*, 50, 248; epigram, 230–1; games, 10, 11, 24, *25*; orations at public, 182, 185, 186–7, 188–9, 196; see also, *threnoi*

Galen of Pergamon, 244, 252, 254

games: Greek athletic competitions, 24, 43, 48, 201

genealogy, 117, 218, 222

geography, 117, 123, 254–5

glossai, Hellenistic, 218

gods, 166, 249; Archaic view, 8, 9, 11, 17, 38

Goethe, Johann Wolfgang von, 256

Gorgias of Leontini, 128, 149–50, 176–7, 197

Gospels, Christian, 260, 265–6

graffiti: on Greek pottery, 13–14, *14*

grammatical tradition, 254

Greek culture in Roman era, 239–66; Atticist movement, 243–4, 246, 251, 258; biography, 259–60; Christian literature, 260–6; chronological background, 239–40; education, see *paideia*; fiction, 256–60; geography, 254–5; historiography, 244–7; learning and science, 252–5; philosophy, 252–3; rhetoricization of language, 247; Roman assimilation, 240, 266; Second Sophistic, 247–52

Greek world, 1–266; Archaic period, 4–69; Classical period, 70–198; *see also individual genres and authors and* Greek culture in Roman era; Hellenistic era

Gregory of Nazianzus, 263–4

guest-friendship (*xenia*), 136–7

guilds, actors' and poets', 202, 209, 211

Hadrian, Emperor, 240

Hegelochos (actor), 88

Hekataios of Miletos, 117, 118–19, 120, 123, 144

Helikon, Mount, 8, 10–11

Heliodoros; *Ethiopian Story*, 256, 257

Hellanikos of Lesbos, 117

Hellenism, 31, 66; *see also* Greek culture; panhellenism

Hellenistic era, 199–238; canon, setting of literary, 238; historical background, 170–1, 199–200, 200–1; performative culture, 200, 237; *see also individual authors*, Alexandria, *and under individual genres and* audience; education; festivals; metrics; monarchy

Herakleides (travel writer), 78

Herakleides of Pontos, 140–1

Herakleitos, 35, 117, 144, 145–6

Hermesianax of Kolophon, 230, 232

Herod the Great, king of Judaea, 245

Herodas; 'Mimiambi', 212–13

Herodes of Attica, 240, 249

Herodotos, 115–16, 117–27; and epic, 9, 119, 120; epitome, 236; life, 115–16; and oral/written cultures, 116, 118–22, 131, 132; structure and purpose, 117, 123, 126–7; on Thales, 140; on tragedy, 97–8; world view, *124–5* heroes, 31, 65, 166; Homeric, 6–7, 15, 20, 174

Hesiod, 8–12, 24; Aischines quotes, 196; canonical status, 139–40, 148–9, 216; in Hellenistic era, 228, 237; Herakleitos attacks, 144; and Muses, 8, 10–11, 146; and oral tradition, 12–13; self-presentation, 8, 9–10, 11; socio-historical context, 8–9, 11–12, 28–32; *Theogony*, 8, 9, 10–11, 11–12, 16, 38, 146; *Works and Days*, 8–9, 9–10, 11, 37; and writing, 14–15

hetairoi, hetaireiai, 47, 48, 57

hexameter poetry: in dithyramb, 68; Greek philosophical, 140, 144, 173; Hellenistic, 219, 237

Hieron, tyrant of Syracuse, 65, 66

hilarodoi, 211–12

Hipparchos, son of Peisistratos, 71

Hippias, tyrant of Athens, 71

Hippias of Elis, 119, 128, 149, 150, 151

Hippokratic corpus, 152, 254; *Airs, Waters, Places*, 126; *On the Nature of Man*, 151; *Precepts*, 151–2; *see also* medicine (Hippokratic)

Hippokrene, spring of, 10

Hipponax of Ephesos, 45, 46, 51–52; influence, 212, 220,

historical narrative, Greek elegiac, 46, 50, 55–6, 116–17

historie ('research, enquiry'), 117, 143

historiography: early narrative elegy, 69, 116; classical prose, 69, 115–37; epitomes, 236, Hellenistic, 235, 236–7; local, 117; and novels, 257; performance, 119–20, 237; Roman period, 244–7, 257

Homer, 4–39; aetiology, 21–2; archaic survivals in, 13; and aristocracy, 4–5, 18–23; biographical myth, 9, 23, 35, 230; canonical status, 32–7, 71, 139–40, 148–9; Classical treatment, 32–7; dictation theory, 14, 19, 32; epithets, 6; first references to, 33–5, *34*; formulae, 12; geography, 254; and Herodotos, 9, 119; heroes, 6–7, 20; identity, 5–7, 9, 23, 35; *Iliad* and *Odyssey* as complementary, 6–7; language, 12, 13, 23, 31; later epic

and, 224; localizations absent, 21–3, 31; lyric performances embedded in, 42, 43; narrative structure, 7, 12; and oral tradition, 5–6, 12–13, 14, 32; and pan-Hellenism, 23, 71, 90; papyri, 32; and patrons, 21–3; performance context, 4–5, 6, 14, (accounts of performances in poems), 15–18, ('*Delos* model' (inter-communal)), 23–8, ('*Odyssey* model' (aristocratic)), 18–23; performance history, 36, 237; Plato on, 36–7; poetic diction, 12, 13; similes, 27–8; socio-historical context, 20, 28–32; textual transmission, 32–3, 216; and war, 6, 7, 11, 15–16; and writing, 13–14, 15, 32–3

Homeric Hymns, 38–9; *Hymn to Apollo*, 25–6, 27, 35, 38–9, 48–9

Homeridai, 23, 32, 33, 36

Homeristai, Hellenistic, 237

honour, see *time*

hoplite warfare, 30, *30*

hymns, 64, 232; Hellenistic, 211, 219, 220; see also *Homeric Hymns*

Hypereides (orator), 194

iambic poetry, 46, 50, 51–4; (in drama), 68, 74, 203, 205

Ibykos of Rhegion, 45, 46, 57, 60

immortality conferred by poetry, 11, 17

India, 24, 199, 247

inscriptions: Athens, Parian Marble, 63; on drama, 200, 203, 204; Herodotos' wording resembling, 120; laws, early, 30–1

inter-communal gatherings, Greek, 31; poetic performances, 23–8, 48–9

Iolaos story, 256

Ion of Chios, 89

Ionian philosophers, 9, 35, 117, 138–40, 143–9, 173

Ionic dialect, 46, 50, 117, 212, 247

Ionikistes, 212

Iophon, son of Sophokles, 89

Isaios, 186

Isokrates, 154–9, 159–61, 236, 248

Italy, Greek cities of southern, 201, 239; epinikia, 65; New Comedy, 204;

social function, 42–3, 49, 55, 62, 68–9; symposium poetry, 46–8, *47*, 50, 54–5, 57–61, 69; and tragedy, 64, 67; and writing, 42

Lysias, 184, 186–7, 188–9, 189–91, 196

lysiodoi, 212

Macedon, 8–9, 192, 199, 218; *see also* Alexander III; Philip II

maenads, 72

Magnesia on the Maeander, 201

magodoi, 212, 238

maiden songs, see *partheneia*

Manetho, 216

marriage: laws, 206–7; *see also* wedding songs

martyrology, 262–3,

masks, 48, *49*, 70, 72, *73*, 91, 202

mathematics, 235

medicine: Greek, in Roman period, 253–4; Hellenistic, 226, 235; Hippokratic, 126, 128, 129–30, 135–6, 151–2, 254

Megara, 45, 72, 239

Meleagros; *Garland*, 234–5

melic, *see under* lyric poetry

Menander, 76, 205, 238, 258; Roman interest, 242; *Theophoroumene*, *207*

Menander Rhetor, 248

metics, Athenian, 85, 106–7, 168

metis, *see* wisdom (practical)

metrics: comedy, 205; epigrams, 234; Hellenistic variation, 219, 220, 232

Milesian Tales, 257

militarism: Greek exhortations, 46, 50, 56–7

Mill, John Stuart, 42

mime, 211–15, 242, 258; *see also* pantomime

Mimnermos, 46, 54, 55, 116, 230, 237

mnemones (oral remembrancers), 121

mobility, 11, 31, 45

monarchy: Hellenistic, 199, 202; Homer and, 20; *see also* tyrants

monody, Greek, 46, 50, 57–61, 69, 203

mosaics, *156*, *207*, 258

Moschos, 214, 228

mourning songs (*threnoi*), 42, 43, 74

Muses, 8, 10–11, 146

music: accompaniment to epic, 18; competitive festivals, 48, 56, 71; in drama, 72–5, 203; emotional impact, 74, 75; Hellenistic, 201, 203, 211, 237; New Music, 67–8, 203

Mycenean Age, 13

Mykale: cult of Helikonian Poseidon, 24

mystery religions, 38, 144, 146

myth: in choral poetry, 61; Hellenistic handbooks, 204; Ionic prose works, 117; Stesichoros' narratives, 62–3

mythos and *logos*, 143

Mytilene, 45, 57

narrative structure: Homer, 7, 12; oratory, 188–91

nature vs convention, 130

Naukratis; Apollonios' foundation poem, 223

Neoptolemos (actor), 202

Nero, Emperor, literary and artistic interests, 240

New Poets, *see* neoterics

Nietzsche, Friedrich Wilhelm, 99

Nikandros of Kolophon, 230–1, 232

Nikolaos of Damaskos, 245

Ninos, romance of, 256, 257, 258

nomes, kitharodic, 67

nomos (law, custom), 99, 100, 129, 130

Nonnos of Panopolis, 264–6

Nossis, 233

novels, 256–9, *see also* Apuleius

Old Oligarch, 78

Olympia and Olympic games, 23–4, 31, 119, 147, 150

On Music (Greek text), 46, 55–6

On the Nature of Man (Hippokratic text), 151

oracle, Delphic, 31

oracular discourse, 121, 144, 145–6

orality, 12–13; and drama, 70; Herodotos and, 116, 118–22, 131, 132; Homer, 5–6, 12–13, 14, 32; lyric poetry, 42; modern instances, 19, 27; philosophy, 138, 142, 154, 167; *see also* performance

oratory, 174–98; Aristotle on, 169, 178,

185; 'Asiatic' style, Christian, 261,
264; control of agenda, 191–4;
disclaimers of experience in speaking,
177–8, 195; deliberative/
symbouleutic, 177, 178–9, 185,
187–8, 191, 192, 195–6, 197–8; and
democracy, 175–6; and drama, 69,
100–1, 177, 182–3, 195–6, 197;
embassies, 177, 189; epideictic/
declamatory, 99, 178, 182–3, 184,
185, 186–7, 191, 192, 196; (in Roman
period), 248, 251, 253; forensic/
dikanic, 176, 177–8, 179–82, 187–8,
191–4, 249, (political), 177, 179, 181,
182–3, 184, 189, 191–2, 195–6,
(private), 185–6, 189–91, 192–4,
194–5, 248; external proof (*atechnoi
pisteis*), 192–4; on historical topics,
249; in literature, 174; performance,
197, (contexts), 178–85; poetry
quoted in, 195–6; publication, 197–8;
scholarship on, 198; sophists and,
128–9, 134–5, 149–50, 175, 176–7;
structure, 188–91; style and context,
194–6; systematization, 5th-century,
174–5; 'technical' proof, *entechnos
pistis*, 175, 185–8; *see also* funerals
(orations)
Orphic literature, 264
ostracism, 104
Oxyrrhynchos, 204, 240, 242

paian, 42, 43, 63, 64, 211
paideia (polite learning), 242–3, 250, 251,
253, 266
painting, *see* scene-painting; wall-
painting
Palatine Anthology, 233–4
pamphlets, political, 197
Panathenaia, 36, 56, 71, 107
panegyric, 245
panhellenism, 23, 31, 71, 122, 150,
151
pantomime, 242
Panyassis (poet, relation of Herodotos),
39, 115, 116
papyri, literary, 200, 240, 242;
Apollonios, 226; Archilochos,
Cologne papyrus, 52–3; hexameter

poems, 32, 37, 38; Kallimachos,
219–20, 221–2; lyric poetry, Greek,
41, 58, 61, 64, 69; New Comedy, 204,
205; Plato, *165*; Poseidippos, 234;
Timotheos of Miletos, 67–8
parabasis, 103–4, 205
parables, 266
paradoxography, 245
Parian Marble, 63
Parmenides of Elis, 140, 144, 146–7, 148
parody: encomia, Second Sophistic, 249;
in Greek fiction, 259
parrhesia (free speech), 78
Parry, Milman, 12
partheneia (maiden songs), 41, 43, 61–2,
64
Parthenios of Nikaia, 233
Parthenope and Metiochos romance, 256,
257, 258
pastoral poetry, 213–14
pathos, emotion, 185, 186–7
patronage: and epic poets, 19, 21–3;
Greek lyric poetry, 21, 45, 64, 65;
choregia, 84, *85*; of Greek culture in
Roman period, 245; Ptolemies and,
201; Theokritos of Syracuse appeals
for, 213
Paul, St, 261–2, 263
Paul and Thecla, Acts of, 257
Pausanias (geographer), 14, 254, 255
pay, public, 182
pederasty, 60
Peiraieus, 81, 239
Peisistratos, tyrant of Athens, 33, 36, 71
Pella, 218, 219, 229
Peloponnesian War, 77, 104–5, 127–36,
153
performance: context, *see* audience;
festivals; *and under individual genres
and* Homer; emotional effect of
visual, 94; Hellenistic culture, 200,
237; medicine, 151–2; social purpose
of Greek lyric, 42–3, 49, 55, 62, 68–9;
sophists, 150, 250; *see also*
recitations; wisdom (performance
of); *and under individual genres*
Pergamon, 202, 215, 217
Periandros of Corinth, 120, 141
Peripatos, 167–8, 216

popular genres, 211–12
Poseidippos, 234
Poseidon, Helikonian, 24
Poseidonios of Apamea, 245
pottery: Athenian, *25, 29, 47, 49, 58, 181*; Corinthian, 29, *30*; early verse graffito, 13–14, *14*; eye-cups, 48, *49*; geometric style, 29, *29*; Homeric scenes, *25, 34,* 34–5, *181*; Rhodian, 13–14, *14, 34,* 34–5; Tarentine, *85*
Precepts (Hippokratic text), 151–2
probability, argument from, 128–9, 130, 175
processions, Athenian, 85–6, 107
Prodikos of Keos, 128, 149, 150
professionalization: music, 68
prognosis, 129, 135
prose: development, 116, 117, 161–2; *see also individual genres*
Protagoras of Abdera, 128, 129, 149, 150, 151, 153
protreptic, philosophical, 147, 155, 168
psychology, behavioural, 175
Ptolemaic dynasty, 201, 215
Ptolemy II of Egypt, 201, 212, 218, 219
public sphere, *see* politics
puns, Aristophanes', 82
Pyrrhon of Elis, 171
Pythagoras and Pythagoreanism, 143–4, 155, 261

Quintilian (Marcus Fabius Quintilianus), 236

readership, *see* audience
reading, private, 135, 222
recitations, 14, 36, 71, 237
remembrancers, oral, 121
rhabdouchoi (theatre 'police'), 98
rhapsodes, 36, 147, 237
rhetoric, *see* oratory
rhetoricization of language, 247
Rhianos, 223
Rhodes, 216, 223; pottery, 14, *14, 34,* 34–5
riddles, Lykophron of Chalkis', 208–10
Roman world: imperial period, 245–6; Late Empire, *see also* Greek culture in

Roman era *and individual authors and topics throughout index*
romances, Greek, 256, 258

sages (*sophoi*), 139, 140–3, 151; Seven, 120, 141–3, 238; Sokrates as, 152–4
Salamis; Battle of, 67, 123; tombstone, *73*
Samos, 45, 60, 115
Sappho, 45, 46, 57–60, *58,* 120
satyr-plays, 89–90, 206
scene-painting, 91
Scepticism, 171
scholarship: Hellenistic, 41, 198, 200, 215–18, 219, 222; scholar poets, 216, 218
science, 226
Second Sophistic, 247–52
self-consciousness and self-reference: Alkman, 62; development after Homeric period, 39; Greek fiction, 259; Hellenistic, 219, 224; Hesiod, 8, 9–10, 10–11; Homer, 5, 16, 39
Semonides of Amorgos, 46, 51, 237
senate, Roman: Greeks in, 242; historians in, 247
Septuagint, 210, 216
Shield (Greek hexameter poem), 38
shields in epic, 15, 38, 228
Sicily: Athenian expedition, 83; Greek settlements, 45, 65, 72, 217; Plato in, 155–6; and Rome, 239
Sikyon, 22–3, 45
similes, 27–8, 59–60
Simonides of Keos, 45, 54, 63, 64, 120; Elegy on the Battle of Plataia, 41, 46, 56, 116
Skylax of Karyanda, 120
slaves and slavery: Christian, 261; educated, 157; at dramatic performances, 107–8; Solon and, 53–4
Smyrna, 23, 55, 249, 250
snake-bite descriptions, genre of, 230–1
social order: and drama, 99, 107, 108; and lyric poetry, 42–3, 62, 68–9
Sokrates, 68, 81, 142, 152–4, 161–2; performance of wisdom, 153–4, 162, 167, 172

Dionysia, 71, 79, 81, 84, 87, 89–90; and Dionysos, 72–3, 75; distance from audience's world, 97, 105–6, 111; emotional effect, 74, 75, 94; Hellenistic, 200–4, 208–11, 217, 237; *katharsis*, 96, 97, 169; and lyric poetry, 64, 67; music, 72–5, 203; and oratory, 177; origins, 70–5, 79; political role, 76, 77–8, 99–102; public/private conflict in, 112–14; recital at symposia, 83; Roman world, (adaptation of Greek), 180–1, (Greek-language), 203, 239, 242; time span of Athenian, 69, 76; violence in, 95; visual impact, 94–6, 168; women portrayed in, 111, 112–14; *see also individual tragedians*

Trajan, Emperor, 247, 249

transmission of classical texts, 32–3, *see also* papyri *and under individual authors*

travel literature, 121, 256–7

tripods, bronze, 10, 22

trochaic metres, 50, 205

Troy romance, 257

Tyche (Fortune), 208, *209*

tyrants, Greek, 45, 65, 71, 115

Tyrtaios, 44, 45, 54, 55, 64, 116; military exhortation, 46, 56–7

Ulpian (Domitius Ulpianus), 243

universality, 252–3, 261

Varro of Atax, 226, 229

Virgil
WORKS: *Aeneid*, 39; *Eclogues*, 214; *Georgics*, 39

voting, *181*

war, attitudes to, 6, 7, 11, 15–16, 86–7

wedding songs, 42, 43, 58, 74–5, 91, 220

wisdom, Greek notions of, 138–40, 154, 173; performance of, 39, 138–40, 141–3, 155, 169–70, (Sokrates'), 153–4, 162, 167, 172; practical (*metis*), 140, 142, 144, 154, 159–60, 162, 169–70

women: Apollonios on, 225; Christian, 262; in comedy, 206–7; dramatic characters, 111–14, 206–7; emotionality, 112; epigrammatists, 233; at festivals, 25, 26, 48, 85, 86, 109–11; in fiction, 259; literacy and reading, 258; marginalization, 59, 109, 113; and philosophy, 143, 155; Sappho's society, 57–9

Wonders of the World, Seven, 238

writing, 69; early media, 14–15; hexameter poems, 13–15, 32–3; of laws, 30–1; and lyric poetry, 42; medicine, 152; and oratory, 197–8; sophists and, 150–1, 154; Xenophon and, 137; *see also* graffiti; inscriptions; papyri; philosophy; *and under individual genres and authors*

Xanthos the Lydian, 117

xenia (guest-friendship), 136–7

Xenophanes of Kolophon, 54, 56, 64–5, 116, 140, 144–5; birthplace, 55, 230; on Homer, 9, 35, 144

Xenophon of Athens, 136–7, 152, 248, 257

Xenophon of Ephesos, 256

Zeno of Kition, 143, 171, 172–3